D1277917

About the Companion CD

The CD that comes with this book contains tools to help you study for the IntranetWare CNA test:

- The CNA Study Guide for IntranetWare Practice Test, which gives you 120 sample test questions to hone your test-taking abilities for the CNA test.

- The Micro House Technical Library Encyclopedia of I/O Cards (complete version), which allows you to explore in depth how the MTL works.

- The Micro House Technical Library (demonstration version), which allows you to access the first few layers of every section of the MTL.

- The Novell Education Certification Sampler, the graphical, Windows-based testing program distributed by Novell Education.

- The Complete 801 Self Test from Big Red Self Test. This special version contains an expanded Service and Support section, providing you with extra study material for Novell Education's most practical exam.

- The CNE Test Master demo from PC Age, Inc., which provides 30 test questions for six required IntranetWare CNE tests and for the TCP/IP elective. Use the IntranetWare demo test to assess your knowledge for the CNA test and the other demo tests for CNE preparation.

For more information regarding the CD, including installation instructions, see the Readme.txt file in the root folder on the CD.

CNA Study Guide
for IntranetWare

Second Edition

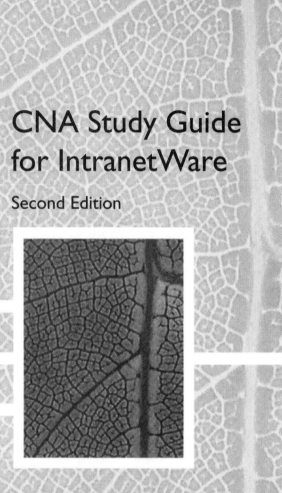

CNA^{SM} Study Guide for IntranetWare™

Second Edition

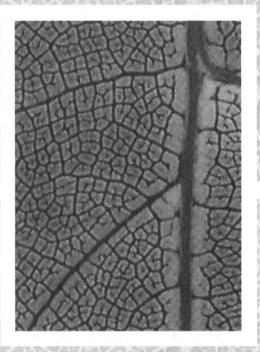

Michael Moncur
James Chellis

San Francisco • Paris • Düsseldorf • Soest

Associate Publisher: Guy Hart-Davis
Acquisitions Manager: Kristine Plachy
Acquisitions & Developmental Editor: Guy Hart-Davis
Editor: Ben Miller
Technical Editor: James Huggans
Book Designers: Patrick Dintino, Bill Gibson
Graphic Illustrator: Patrick Dintino
Electronic Publishing Specialist: Bill Gibson
CD-ROM Technical Assistant: Bill Ross
Production Coordinator: Robin Kibby
Proofreader: Theresa Gonzalez
Indexer: Matthew Spence
Cover Designer: Archer Design
Cover Illustrator/Photographer: The Image Bank

SYBEX, Network Press, and the Network Press logo are registered trademarks of SYBEX Inc.

TRADEMARKS: SYBEX has attempted throughout this book to distinguish proprietary trademarks from descriptive terms by following the capitalization style used by the manufacturer.

The author and publisher have made their best efforts to prepare this book, and the content is based upon final release software whenever possible. Portions of the manuscript may be based upon pre-release versions supplied by software manufacturer(s). The author and the publisher make no representation or warranties of any kind with regard to the completeness or accuracy of the contents herein and accept no liability of any kind including but not limited to performance, merchantability, fitness for any particular purpose, or any losses or damages of any kind caused or alleged to be caused directly or indirectly from this book.

First edition copyright ©1996 SYBEX Inc.

Copyright ©1997 SYBEX Inc., 1151 Marina Village Parkway, Alameda, CA 94501. World rights reserved. No part of this publication may be stored in a retrieval system, transmitted, or reproduced in any way, including but not limited to photocopy, photograph, magnetic or other record, without the prior agreement and written permission of the publisher.

Library of Congress Card Number: 97-67411
ISBN: 0-7821-2098-9

Manufactured in the United States of America

10 9 8 7 6 5 4

Software License Agreement: Terms and Conditions

The media and/or any online materials accompanying this book that are available now or in the future contain programs and/or text files (the "Software") to be used in connection with the book. SYBEX hereby grants to you a license to use the Software, subject to the terms that follow. Your purchase, acceptance, or use of the Software will constitute your acceptance of such terms.

The Software compilation is the property of SYBEX unless otherwise indicated and is protected by copyright to SYBEX or other copyright owner(s) as indicated in the media files (the "Owner(s)"). You are hereby granted a single-user license to use the Software for your personal, noncommercial use only. You may not reproduce, sell, distribute, publish, circulate, or commercially exploit the Software, or any portion thereof, without the written consent of SYBEX and the specific copyright owner(s) of any component software included on this media.

In the event that the Software or components include specific license requirements or end-user agreements, statements of condition, disclaimers, limitations or warranties ("End-User License"), those End-User Licenses supersede the terms and conditions herein as to that particular Software component. Your purchase, acceptance, or use of the Software will constitute your acceptance of such End-User Licenses.

By purchase, use or acceptance of the Software you further agree to comply with all export laws and regulations of the United States as such laws and regulations may exist from time to time.

Software Support

Components of the supplemental Software and any offers associated with them may be supported by the specific Owner(s) of that material but they are not supported by SYBEX. Information regarding any available support may be obtained from the Owner(s) using the information provided in the appropriate read.me files or listed elsewhere on the media.

Should the manufacturer(s) or other Owner(s) cease to offer support or decline to honor any offer, SYBEX bears no responsibility. This notice concerning support for the Software is provided for your information only. SYBEX is not the agent or principal of the Owner(s), and SYBEX is in no way responsible for providing any support for the Software, nor is it liable or responsible for any support provided, or not provided, by the Owner(s).

Warranty

SYBEX warrants the enclosed media to be free of physical defects for a period of ninety (90) days after purchase. The Software is not available from SYBEX in any other form or media than that enclosed herein or posted to *www.sybex.com*. If you discover a defect in the media during this warranty period, you may obtain a replacement of identical format at no charge by sending the defective media, postage prepaid, with proof of purchase to:

> SYBEX Inc.
> Customer Service Department
> 1151 Marina Village Parkway
> Alameda, CA 94501
> (510) 523-8233
> Fax: (510) 523-2373
> e-mail: info@sybex.com
> WEB: HTTP://WWW.SYBEX.COM

After the 90-day period, you can obtain replacement media of identical format by sending us the defective disk, proof of purchase, and a check or money order for $10, payable to SYBEX.

Disclaimer

SYBEX makes no warranty or representation, either expressed or implied, with respect to the Software or its contents, quality, performance, merchantability, or fitness for a particular purpose. In no event will SYBEX, its distributors, or dealers be liable to you or any other party for direct, indirect, special, incidental, consequential, or other damages arising out of the use of or inability to use the Software or its contents even if advised of the possibility of such damage. In the event that the Software includes an online update feature, SYBEX further disclaims any obligation to provide this feature for any specific duration other than the initial posting.

The exclusion of implied warranties is not permitted by some states. Therefore, the above exclusion may not apply to you. This warranty provides you with specific legal rights; there may be other rights that you may have that vary from state to state. The pricing of the book with the Software by SYBEX reflects the allocation of risk and limitations on liability contained in this agreement of Terms and Conditions.

Shareware Distribution

This Software may contain various programs that are distributed as shareware. Copyright laws apply to both shareware and ordinary commercial software, and the copyright Owner(s) retains all rights. If you try a shareware program and continue using it, you are expected to register it. Individual programs differ on details of trial periods, registration, and payment. Please observe the requirements stated in appropriate files.

Copy Protection

The Software in whole or in part may or may not be copy-protected or encrypted. However, in all cases, reselling or redistributing these files without authorization is expressly forbidden except as specifically provided for by the Owner(s) therein.

We dedicate this book to Laura, Sibylla, and our families and friends.

Acknowledgments

We would like to thank the following people at Network Press, whose expertise and professionalism made the development of this book proceed with the utmost efficiency: Associate Publisher Guy Hart-Davis, Editor Ben Miller, Technical Editor Jim Huggans, Electronic Publishing Specialist Bill Gibson, Production Coordinator Robin Kibby, Production Assistant Theresa Gonzalez, and Graphic Illustrator Patrick Dintino.

Michael Moncur: I would like to thank my wife, Laura, and my parents, Gary and Susan Moncur, for their support during this project. Thanks also go to the rest of my family and my friends, particularly Chuck Perkins, Cory Storm, Robert Parsons, Matthew Strebe, and Dylan Winslow.

James Chellis: Thanks to my family—Dad, Kiki, Mary Jo, Gayle, David, Paul, Aaron, Ray, and Bill—as well as my friends, especially Sibylla, Peter, Travis, John, Jairo, Bo, Heidi, Xtian, Sascha, Rune, Ishi, Oscar, Stuart, Baillee, Jim H., the Arica community, Kewei, Jin, Maia, and everyone working with EdgeTek.

Contents at a Glance

Table of Contents

Introduction

So you've decided to become an IntranetWare Certified Novell Administrator! That's a smart career move—the demand for professionals who know how to work with Novell IntranetWare is tremendous and Novell Education's CNA/CNE program is the most successful professional certification program in the computer industry today. The best news is that the CNA credential, which is widely respected in the networking industry, takes only a small fraction of the effort required for the CNE credential. With the right information (and preferably a little practice), you can quickly and easily pass the CNA exam and attain CNA certification.

In this book, we will show you the ins and outs of Novell's latest and greatest network operating system—IntranetWare. We'll show you what you need to know to manage an IntranetWare network, and we'll give you the information you need to pass the CNA exam.

Should You Buy This Book?

You're standing in the bookstore with this book in your hand. Should you buy it?

YES—if you want to attain the latest CNA certification. Whether you are seeking your first Novell credential or you simply want to upgrade your certification to the latest levels, this book is for you. This book gives you an affordable, efficient means of learning IntranetWare and preparing for the IntranetWare CNA certification exam.

YES—if you want to learn about networking and about Novell IntranetWare. This book provides an introduction to computers and computer networking, as well as an in-depth exploration of Novell's latest version of its NetWare/IntranetWare product—the most popular network operating system in the world. Whether you are a beginner trying to break into this complex but lucrative field or an accomplished network professional interested in expanding your understanding, this book will provide you with important and detailed information.

YES—if you are with a training company, since this book offers the best alternative to the expensive Novell Education IntranetWare Administration training manual.

NO—if you are really interested in Windows NT and picked up this book by accident! (We do talk about NT, though, in case you're interested.)

What Does This Book Cover?

This book covers everything you need for the IntranetWare CNA exam, and much more. To be more specific, the information presented in this book can help you in two areas:

- The world of Novell Education, with its unique perspective on how things are and what you should know about networking

- The real world, where tough demands on your time and energy require you to focus on only the most important information

This book contains not only all the information you need to sail through the IntranetWare CNA exam but also the information that will enable you to manage actual networks under real-world conditions. We know that you don't want exam-cram materials that will be of little use to you once you've taken the exam, so we've packed this book with information that will genuinely help you in your work with Intranet-Ware networks before and after you take the exam. We've presented everything you need to know in a logical and clearly accessible format, adding extra information and examples wherever they will help.

How Do You Become an IntranetWare CNA?

You need to pass only one exam to become an IntranetWare CNA. Anyone can take the exam. The exam is a combination of multiple choice and interactive questions. The interactive questions give you a simulated IntranetWare interface and require you to complete certain tasks (which we cover in this book). Novell's exams are administered by Sylvan Prometric testing centers. For more information on Sylvan Prometric testing (including where to find the center nearest to you), you can call Sylvan at 1-800-RED-EXAM.

How to Use This Book

This book is organized in four parts. If you want to make sure you have an in-depth understanding of IntranetWare management, read all four sections. Part 2 focuses on what you need to understand for the CNA exam. The best way to prepare for the exam is as follows:

- Study each chapter of the second part carefully, making sure that you fully understand the information. If possible, practice using what you've learned on a network.

- Take the practice exam related to that chapter. (The answers to the practice exam questions are located in Appendix A.)

- Note which questions of the practice exam you did not answer correctly and study those sections of the book again. Read the remaining parts of the book.

- Take and pass the real CNA exam.

Having access to an IntranetWare network on which to practice is definitely an advantage in the process of preparing for the exam. If you are practicing on a network used by others, be sure that you do not try anything that may affect their data in any way.

Consider setting up a practice network to help you prepare for the exam. You can obtain a two-user license for IntranetWare inexpensively from various sources; some networking companies and associations even include them as special offers. A server and a single workstation will function well for most exercises. You may also want to consider running your practice network using OS/2, under which one computer can serve as a client and a server simultaneously.

The following pages contain a great deal of information. To learn all of this you will need to study regularly and with discipline. Try to set aside the same time every day to study, and select a comfortable and quiet place in which to do it. If you work hard, you will be surprised at how quickly you can learn this material. Good luck!

Conventions Used in This Book

Where possible, we have tried to make the information clear and accessible by including Notes, Tips, and Warnings based on our personal experiences in the field of networking. Each has a special margin icon and is set off in special type.

Notes provide helpful asides, reminders, and bits of information that deserve special attention.

Tips provide information that will make the current task easier. Tips include shortcuts and alternative ways to perform a task.

Read any Warnings, so you can avert a possible disaster. The Warnings will help you avoid making mistakes that could require a tremendous effort to correct.

What's on the CD?

On the CD that comes with this book, you will find a Windows-based test-preparation program. It includes over 100 questions and answers to help you prepare for the IntranetWare CNA exam.

Be sure that you really understand the questions and answers. If there is anything you don't understand, go back to the book and study the relevant chapters carefully. The testing program is a great way to help make sure that you have thoroughly assimilated the material in this book.

For your further reference, we have included a demonstration copy of the Micro House Technical Library, the authoritative guide to computer hardware specifications and configurations. This copy includes the entire I/O library.

If you are planning to pursue your IntranetWare CNE certification after obtaining your CNA, you'll be happy to see that we've provided demo versions of two leading CNE testing programs; the Big Red Self Tests and PC Age's CNE TestMaster. These testing programs contain an additional 50 questions related to the IntranetWare CNA exam. Also included is Big Red Self Test's entire Service and Support practice exam. This is a very useful tool you can use as you prepare for your CNE.

How to Contact the Authors

Here's how to contact Michael Moncur and James Chellis:

- Michael Moncur

  Internet: cna4@starlingtech.com

  CompuServe: 102516,224

  World Wide Web: htttp://www.starlingtech.com/books/cna4

- James Chellis

  Internet: chellis@scruznet.com

P A R T

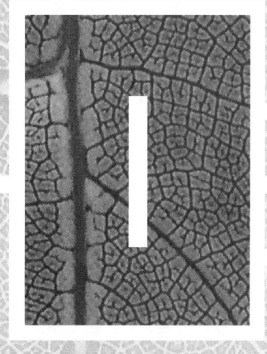

I

INTRODUCTION TO
NETWARE 4.11

CHAPTER

1

An Introduction to Networking

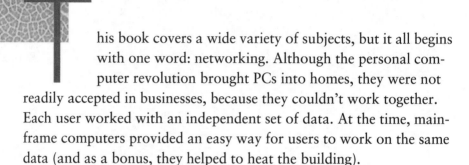

This book covers a wide variety of subjects, but it all begins with one word: networking. Although the personal computer revolution brought PCs into homes, they were not readily accepted in businesses, because they couldn't work together. Each user worked with an independent set of data. At the time, mainframe computers provided an easy way for users to work on the same data (and as a bonus, they helped to heat the building).

The advent of networking brought these advantages to the PC. Since that time, the PC networking industry has blossomed. It's hard to find a company with more than 10 employees that doesn't have a network of some sort. The use of mainframe computer systems, in the meantime, started a sharp decline, and millions of companies have had to turn back to conventional methods of heating.

What Is a Network?

In its simplest form, a network is a group of computers that are connected in some fashion. This connection allows the separate computers to communicate with one another; share files, printers, and other resources; and communicate with mainframe computers and larger networks.

As you might have guessed from the size of this book, a network is rarely in its simplest form. In order for a typical network to function, several components are necessary:

- One or more *servers*. A server is a specialized machine that acts as a host for the other computers, or workstations. In a type of network called peer-to-peer, there is no dedicated server. NetWare networks always use a server.

- One or more *workstations*. The workstations are where the work is done—at least as far as the users of the network are concerned.

- A *network board* for each workstation or server. Since a typical PC doesn't have a network connection built in, the network board acts as an interface between the PC and the network.

- *Peripherals*. These are the devices other than computers that are used in a network, such as printers, tape backup devices, and modems.

- A *communications medium* for network signals to travel across. This is a fancy term for the actual wiring between the computers—the heart of the network itself.

A typical network including all of these components is shown in Figure 1.1. Not all networks look like this one, of course. Although the components are basically the same, an infinite number of combinations are possible. The components used in a network depend on the needs of the users of the network and, frequently, the company's budget.

FIGURE 1.1

A typical network includes a server, workstations, wiring, and peripherals.

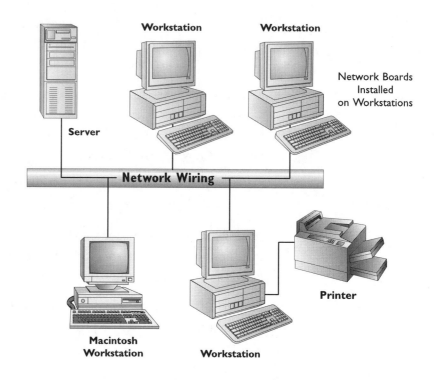

Let's take a closer look at each of the network components.

The Server

The network server acts as a host for the workstations. On the outside, the server often looks exactly like a workstation. In the case of a NetWare server, the server is an ordinary IBM-compatible PC with a 386, 486, Pentium, or better microprocessor. However, that's where the similarity ends.

While you can use standard IBM-compatible PCs as servers, several companies make computers that are intended for use as servers. These may be more suited to the task than standard PCs.

Rather than a client operating system such as DOS or Windows, the server runs a *network operating system* (NOS for short). The NOS is the software that makes a PC into a server. This software provides resources to the workstations. As you might have guessed, this book will focus on one particular NOS: NetWare 4.11. You'll learn more about the benefits of NetWare and other NOS choices, as well as the requirements for a NetWare 4.11 server, later in this chapter.

Because one of the main functions of a network server is to provide file-sharing services, the server is commonly referred to as a *file server*. The keyboard and screen of the server PC are referred to as the *server console*.

Workstations

A workstation is any computer that has a connection to the server. Workstations request resources from the server and exchange information with it. Workstations are also referred to as *clients*. Because the network revolves around the concept of clients communicating with servers, this type of network is called a *client/server* network.

The workstation is where users of the network do their work, using all types of software, including applications such as word processors, spreadsheets, and databases. In addition to this software, the workstation runs *network client software*. This is the link between the workstation and the network. This software uses the network board installed in the workstation to communicate with the network.

The types of workstations supported depend on the NOS. NetWare 4.11 can support a wide variety of clients.

Although the server requires a 386 or higher processor, a wide range of IBM-compatible PCs can work as NetWare workstations—from the most powerful Pentium or P6 to the vintage 1975 8088-based machine lurking in the corner of your basement. Of course, in order to enjoy the full benefits of NetWare 4.11, you should have a more recent machine. NetWare supports PCs running a variety of operating systems:

- DOS (Disk Operating System), including Microsoft MS-DOS, IBM's PC DOS, and Novell DOS.

- OS/2, IBM's graphical operating system. Version 3 (Warp) and older versions are supported.

- Microsoft Windows 3.11 runs under DOS, and uses the DOS client software.

- Windows 95, running NetWare Client 32.

NetWare 4.11 provides most of the same support for Apple Macintosh and Macintosh-compatible machines as it does for PCs. Client software is available for older machines, but you will need Apple's System 7.0 or newer operating system in order to take full advantage of the latest client software, included with NetWare 4.11.

UNIX machines are another type that can serve as NetWare 4.11 workstations. Although Macintosh and UNIX machines are fully supported as workstations, you will need a DOS or Windows machine to run some NetWare administration utilities.

Network Boards

The server and each workstation use a network board (also called a *network card*) to communicate with the network. In the case of a PC, this is a card that plugs into the ISA, VESA, EISA, or PCI slot. The back of the card has a connector that connects to the network cabling. Credit card–sized PC-Card versions of network cards make it possible to connect notebook and hand-held machines to the network.

Network boards are not available from Novell, and they don't come with NetWare. You purchase them from a computer dealer. A wide variety of network boards are available from hundreds of manufacturers. Common ones include Intel, 3COM, and SMC. These days, it is common to purchase PCs with network cards already installed.

In order to use the network card, you will need a *network driver* (also called a *LAN driver*) for the workstation or server. This is a specialized piece of software that works with the NetWare client or server software and knows how to communicate with that particular board. The network driver is the only program that is not guaranteed to be provided with NetWare 4.11. Although NetWare includes drivers for common network cards, such as the Novell NE2000, on the installation CD-ROM, you should use the most current driver provided by the manufacturer of the network card.

It's helpful to standardize on one type of network board for all of the computers within a company network. This makes it easy to find the right drivers, and it also simplifies troubleshooting and support.

Peripherals

Peripherals provide extra functions to the network and its workstations. These are typically attached to a workstation, but they may also be connected directly to the network cable, or to a server. Peripherals fall into several categories:

- *Output devices*, such as printers and plotters. These are used to provide printouts of network data, which you can then scatter around your office to look busy.

- *Storage devices*, including disk drives and tape drives. These are used to store information needed for network applications and backup data.

- *Communication devices*, such as modems. These are used to communicate with computers that are not connected to the network or with other systems such as mainframes.

Communications Media

All of the components described so far won't do any good until they're hooked together. That's where the communications medium comes in. Many different types of wiring are available. These are referred to as *topologies*. Different topologies use different systems and types of wiring to communicate. A few of the topologies supported by NetWare 4.11 include:

- ARCnet (using coaxial cable)

- Ethernet 10Base2 (using thin coaxial cable)

- Ethernet 10BaseT (using twisted-pair cable)

- FDDI (using high-speed, fiber-optic cable)

- Token Ring (using twisted-pair or fiber-optic cable)

Different topologies don't just use different types of wire; the overall structure of the network is also different. The two most common structures are:

- A *bus* structure, where each workstation is connected to the next workstation in the line. This is shown in Figure 1.2. In some ways, this method works like a cheap string of Christmas lights; if the cable to one workstation is disconnected, the entire network can go down. Ethernet 10Base2 networks use this system.

- A *star* structure, which connects each workstation to a central device called a network *hub*. This structure, shown in Figure 1.3, will keep the network going even if a single workstation is disconnected, and thus is much safer for your network than a bus structure.

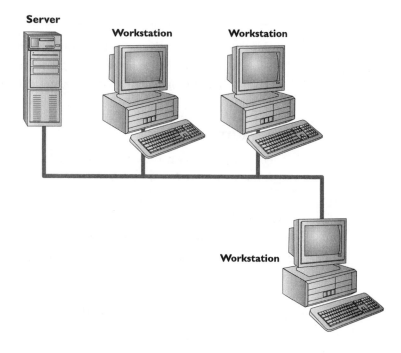

FIGURE 1.2

A bus structure connects each workstation in the network to the next one in the line.

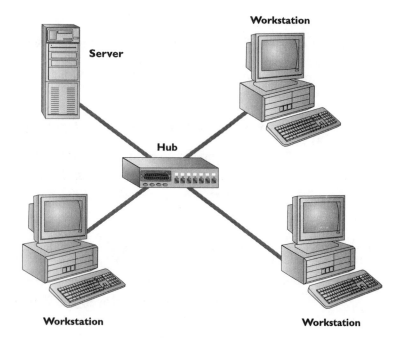

FIGURE 1.3

A star structure connects each workstation to a central hub.

We've included only the most common network topologies here. There are many other networking standards and topologies available, including wireless systems which communicate via radio.

The Network Administrator

Because of the complexity of networks, one more component is necessary: a *network administrator*. This is an expert who knows all of the details of the network—how to set it up, how to keep it running smoothly, and how to solve problems when they occur. By the time you make it to the end of this book, you'll be well prepared for the job. The responsibilities of a network administrator can include the following:

- Setting up servers, workstations, wiring, and applications

- Organizing the network's resources

- Keeping the network and data secure

- Fine-tuning the server and network to improve performance

- Managing user access, passwords, printing, and other network features

- Creating and maintaining a system for backing up data

- Keeping detailed documentation of network wiring, security, NDS, and other network features used

What Does NetWare Do for Networks?

For about 10 years, Novell NetWare has been the world's most widely used NOS. NetWare has gone through many versions in that time, starting with 1.0. By version 2.2, NetWare networks had become commonplace. NetWare 2.2 can still be found in a few companies. NetWare 3, originally introduced in 1989, was the first version to take advantage of the 386 processor. The most recent version of NetWare 3 is NetWare 3.12, released in 1993. At the time of this writing, Net-Ware 3.12 is still available (although, as you will learn in this chapter, there are many good reasons to choose NetWare 4.11 instead).

NetWare 4.0, also introduced in 1993, was originally intended as an *enterprise* networking system, which means that it was designed for large companies with multiple locations, and it had a price tag to match. This continued with the release of versions 4.01 and 4.02, which were still widely regarded as unstable compared to NetWare 3.12 and not worth the trouble unless you really needed the extra features.

With NetWare 4.1, Novell introduced a robust, easy-to-maintain NOS with many features that make it an ideal solution for a wide range of networks. In addition, the hefty price was reduced, making it as affordable as NetWare 3.12. Novell began marketing NetWare 4.1 to all companies, large and small, as a replacement for earlier versions.

The latest version, NetWare 4.11—formerly known by the code name Green River—was released in mid-1996. This version added some important new features. It is now sold as part of IntranetWare, Novell's solution for Internet servers and company-wide intranets.

The features added to NetWare in versions 4.1 and 4.11 are detailed in Chapter 2.

NetWare 4.11 includes server software—the NOS itself—which you run on the server. In addition, it provides client software for a variety of clients. NetWare also includes a myriad of utilities, which are programs that you can use to manage the network and its resources. Although the server is the heart of the network, you will run most of these utilities from a workstation. There are also a few utilities that run on the server console.

When you access the network, you use network resources and services:

- *Resources* are devices you can use through the network, such as disk drives and printers.

- *Services* are the tasks that the network server performs, such as file and printer sharing.

The following sections summarize the resources and services that NetWare 4.11 provides.

Network Resources

The network's resources are devices that you can access and use through the network. These may be inside the server itself, such as disk drives, or may be attached to a server or workstation, as a printer is. As a network administrator, your main job is to manage these resources: install them, make them accessible, control access to them, and fix them when they're broken.

Each resource provides a different function to network clients. Resources offered by NetWare 4.11 include servers, volumes (disk drives in the NetWare server), printers, backup devices, routers, modems, and any other device users can access through the network system.

NetWare 4.11 Services

Although the definition of a network is simple, a modern server is expected to do much more than just connect computers. The NetWare 4.11 server offers many different services. Because the NetWare 4.11 server wears many hats, it can be overworked. In large networks, specialized servers are sometimes used to perform just one or two of these functions, acting as a communications server or a printer server.

File Sharing and Applications

File sharing is the most basic service a network can provide, and it is the most important. File sharing simply means that users on different workstations can share files. Rather than store the files on their own disks, the users store the files on a *network drive*. This is a disk drive inside the NetWare server. Thanks to the NetWare client software, workstations can use this drive as if it were one of their own. For example, they can save files to it, copy files to and from it, and run applications from it.

With file sharing, you can access a file easily, no matter which workstation you are using, as long as you have access to the server. Users can also literally share a file—two or more users can be accessing the same file at the same time. Network database applications take advantage of this and allow many users to read, add, and change records in the same database at the same time.

Although the network server may be in another room (or another building), the network drive can be accessed quickly. In fact, you may find that it is faster than the workstation's disk drive. This speed is due to features of NetWare, such as *file caching*, which keep frequently used files in memory, where they can be accessed instantly.

One important use for file sharing is to provide access to applications. You can install an application (such as a word processor or spreadsheet) on the network server's file system, and make it available to users at any workstation on the network. NetWare's security features allow you to control access to applications.

Printer Sharing

Another main service a network provides is printer sharing. You can set up a printer as a network printer, which may be attached to the NetWare server or to a workstation. In addition, many new printer models can be attached directly to the network cable. Regardless of how a printer is hooked up to the network, any user on the network can access it. The client software fools the workstation into thinking that the printer is local, so any application that can print to a local printer can be used with a network printer.

You may be wondering what happens if two users print to the printer at the same time. Users would be upset if their documents were actually printed at the same time—paper sharing is an idea that hasn't quite caught on. Fortunately, NetWare handles these situations very well. Rather than sending your document directly to the printer, Net-Ware uses a *print queue* to store the print jobs. The jobs wait in line in the print queue until it is their turn to print. This allows even the busiest of printers to be managed efficiently.

Printing to a network, and setting up network printers, is actually much more involved than we've described here. Chapter 9 covers all the details.

Directory Services

A NetWare server on a large network can include hundreds or even thousands of users, printers, and other resources. NetWare keeps track of all of these in a database called the *Directory*. This system of organization is called *NetWare Directory Services*, or NDS. NDS is new to NetWare 4, and allows much better organization than previous versions. Each user, server, printer, or other resource is cataloged in the Directory, making it easy for users, workstations, and other servers to locate these resources.

Since NDS is the most important feature of NetWare 4.11, you will be reading a lot about it in this book. This begins with Chapter 5, which covers NetWare 4.11 fundamentals.

Security Features

Locks and alarm systems protect the resources of a company by preventing unauthorized access to them. The security features of

NetWare 4.11 offer this same benefit for network resources. NetWare 4.11 provides security for all types of network resources. As a network administrator, you can control this security. You can specify the users who can access each resource.

NetWare provides many levels of security, from the most basic features that every network should use to advanced features that may only be useful for government organizations with abbreviations for names. By taking advantage of these features, you can be sure that unauthorized users don't access the network and that authorized users access only what they should.

There are actually many different components of network security, including the following:

- **Login security:** Users must log in to the network by entering a username and password before they can access anything. As the network administrator, you will need to create usernames for each of the users. The username is also used to identify files created by the user and to send messages to the user.

- **Console security:** If someone has access to the server console, that person can do all sorts of harm, including taking the server down, or worse, erasing data on the disks. To prevent this, you can require a password for access to the console.

- **Physical security:** Even a password can't protect the server from some types of attacks (such as turning it off, stealing it, or knocking it off the table). Most often, these happen by accident. The solution is obvious, but often overlooked: Place the server in a locked room and be sure only authorized individuals can get in.

- **File system security:** You can control access to each of the directories and files on the server's disk. This allows you to give users access to the data they need to view or update and keep them from viewing data they shouldn't see.

- **NDS security:** NDS security controls the management of NDS objects, including users, printers, and so on. You can keep tight control over who can create or delete objects, and assign administrators to manage portions of the Directory.

- **Communication security:** The data in the network cables can sometimes be vulnerable to unauthorized snooping. NetWare features such as *packet signature* ensure that nobody can read your passwords or data in this manner.

- **Network auditing:** New to NetWare 4.11 is a versatile auditing system. The server can keep a log of files and NDS objects that are accessed, created, deleted, or changed. This allows you to be sure there is no unauthorized access.

You'll learn more about security in Chapter 7, which covers both file system and NDS security.

Backup and Restore Capabilities

No matter how secure your server is, there is always a chance that you will lose data due to hardware failure or software error. Keeping timely backups of the data can ensure that these failures will cause small headaches, rather than large ones.

NetWare includes built-in support for backups through the *Storage Management System*, or SMS. NetWare 4.11 also includes a backup utility called SBACKUP, which works with SMS to back up files on the network. SMS allows you to back up data on the server, and it also allows data on network workstations to be backed up.

Backups are done to a *backup device*. Most often, this is a tape drive. These drives are available at an economical cost and can hold anywhere from 80MB to 8GB (gigabytes) of data. When you plan a network server setup, always include a backup device. The first time a disk crashes on the server, you'll be glad you did. (We will describe the backup software and techniques in detail in Chapter 5.)

> NetWare's SBACKUP is a very basic backup application. Backup software is available from several third-party vendors. These programs provide additional features and may be more reliable than SBACKUP.

Communications Services

In a large network, things are a bit more complicated than a simple collection of workstations and a server. Multiple servers are often included, and there may be more than one set of network cabling, using different network topologies. You may even need to communicate with other network systems, such as Windows NT, AppleTalk, Banyan VINES, or IBM LAN Server.

NetWare 4.11 makes all of this possible through the NetWare *Multi-Protocol Router*, or MPR. The MPR is a piece of software that runs on the NetWare server and allows it to act as a router. A *router* is simply a device that connects two different types of networks.

Choosing a Network Operating System

Which NOS is right for your network? Usually, this is not an easy question. The answer depends on the needs of your users and on how much money you are willing to spend. You may also need to consider other factors, such as familiarity with a particular system, connectivity with mainframes or other systems, and the software that users will be running. We will now examine several of the alternatives, starting with the subject of this book: NetWare 4.11.

NetWare 4.11

NetWare 4.11 has many benefits compared to other NOSs. In fact, it has many benefits over NetWare 3.1*x*. These new features are the subject of Chapter 2. Areas that used to be the most difficult in NetWare 3.1*x*, such as server installation, printing configuration, and changing system parameters, have been greatly simplified in NetWare 4.11. Although many new features have been added, you should find NetWare 4.11 easy to learn.

NetWare 4.11 does have some new requirements, which are described in the following sections.

Cost Considerations

For new NetWare installations, the cost per user of NetWare 4.11 is similar to that of NetWare 3.*x*, so NetWare 4.11 is the obvious choice. When you are upgrading existing networks, however, the cost can be higher, because the user license for your earlier version of NetWare (for example, 25-user or 50-user) does not carry over to NetWare 4.11.

In NetWare 3.*x*, licenses were issued for set amounts of users. NetWare allows only that many users to access the network at any time. For example, if your company purchased a 25-user version of NetWare 3.*x* initially, and later needed to add two or three more users, you would have no choice but to jump to the next level—in this case, 50 users. It's hard to justify the cost of 25 additional users when you only need a few.

The *additive licensing* feature of NetWare 4.11 provides a solution to this problem. This system lets you upgrade your network in increments of as few as five users. The license is provided on a *license diskette*, which is included with your copy of NetWare. If you have more than one copy of NetWare, you can add the license diskettes to the same server. For example, if you have a 5-user license and a 25-user license, you can install both licenses and make room for 30 users. This is where NetWare 4.11 can really save you money.

If you have several servers on your network, you can even remove a license from one server and install it on another. This makes it easy to modify your network for changing user loads without a great deal of expense. In a large corporate network, it may be useful to have a few extra 5-user licenses handy. Then you can add licenses to whichever servers need them as the company expands.

You can't install the same license diskette on more than one server. This would be illegal, and not very nice. In addition, NetWare includes copyright protection features that make it impossible to use the same license on multiple servers in a network. Also, needless to say, you can't add the same license diskette to a server twice.

Hardware Considerations

As with most software, the latest version of NetWare 4.11 requires a slightly better computer system to run efficiently. These requirements include a bit more disk space and 12MB to 16MB more RAM (random-access memory) than an equivalent NetWare 3.1*x* server requires. These requirements are explained in the next sections.

Disk Storage Requirements   To run NetWare 4.11 on your server's disk drive, you need at least 75MB of disk storage. However, if you plan on installing all of the NetWare files (including optional files, such as client software, online documentation, and OS/2 utilities), you will need at least 100MB. An existing NetWare 3.1*x* server needs to have approximately 50MB free to perform the upgrade to NetWare 4.11.

These are minimum disk space requirements. You should always have at least 50MB more than you need, because running out of disk space can cause your network to go down, and you might lose data.

Memory Requirements   Novell recommends 20MB as the minimum amount of RAM in a NetWare 4.11 server. A NetWare 4.11 server with only 20MB will be painfully slow, unless your network is very small (five to ten users). If your network has 20 or more users, you will probably need at least 32MB.

The amount of memory your server needs will depend on the number of users, disk storage, and types of applications used.

Compatibility Issues

NetWare 4.11 is *backward-compatible* with software and clients used in previous NetWare versions, which should mean that all of your software and hardware will work fine when you upgrade to NetWare 4.11. This is only true in an ideal world, however. In the real world, there are all sorts of applications available, and it's impossible to know whether they will all work with NetWare 4.11. Some may be written to take advantage of features (or bugs) in the earlier versions.

When you are considering an upgrade, you should be sure that your hardware and software will work with the new NOS. Ideally, you should install NetWare 4.11 on an identical server as a test. Unfortunately, not everyone has a spare server handy. The best solution is to examine the documentation to determine whether each item is compatible. This should include drivers for network cards, disk and tape drives, software such as backup software, and any network-aware applications your users run. If you can't find compatibility information in the item's documentation, contact the vendor.

Network Support and Training

The advanced features of NetWare 4.11 can be a bit difficult to master, particularly if you are used to working with another version of Net-Ware. The users of the network should not notice a difference, but they still may need training to take advantage of NetWare 4.11's new features. System administrators also need training. If you make it through this book, there will be one less network administrator who needs to learn NetWare 4.11.

Users and administrators who are not already familiar with another system will certainly need training. Since NetWare 3.1*x* may not be supported in the future, it's best to learn the newer version. NetWare 4.11 features such as graphical management of users and security make it much easier than earlier versions of NetWare for the beginning network administrator to learn.

NetWare Server for OS/2

In early (2.*x*) versions of NetWare, you could run NetWare in a *nondedicated* configuration. This meant that the computer that NetWare was running on could also be used as a workstation. (You could even do this on a 286 machine.) In NetWare 3.1*x*, Novell no longer allows this setup. NetWare servers are *dedicated* machines; they can only run server software. In NetWare 4, you can once again run a nondedicated NetWare server. This is made possible by IBM's OS/2 operating system.

After you install NetWare Server for OS/2 on an OS/2 system, that server is able to function like any other NetWare 4.11 server. DOS and OS/2 clients running under OS/2 can share the network board used by the server. In this way, you can actually log in on the same machine that the server is running on. Thus, you can have a network inside your computer—what a way to impress your friends.

Although it sounds impressive, NetWare Server for OS/2 is not always practical. It may work for small networks in "mom-and-pop" companies (with up to five users), but this is probably not a good idea for anything larger. The disadvantages of this setup include:

- **Memory**: OS/2 requires 8MB of RAM to run, and NetWare 4.11 requires at least 8MB of RAM to run. This means that you'll need at least 16MB just to get NetWare Server for OS/2 to start. You may have a 16MB Pentium machine, which is a great workstation or NetWare server. But if you install NetWare Server for OS/2, you'll realize just how slow your machine can be. For practical use, you should have at least 20MB, and even more than that won't hurt.

■ **Reliability and security:** Because NetWare Server for OS/2 runs on the same machine as a workstation, your entire network is at the mercy of the workstation's user. The user can access the console. If the user's software causes the machine to crash, the server can crash as well. And if that user is one of those who just can't bear to leave their desk without turning their computer off, the network will go down whenever the user takes off.

■ **Compatibility:** Because it tries to run NetWare and OS/2 at the same time, NetWare Server for OS/2 may not be compatible with all NetWare applications, device drivers, and utilities. Considering all of this, it is remarkably compatible. Most server software included with NetWare will run on an OS/2 server without a problem.

Although NetWare Server for OS/2 sounds like something of a novelty, it can be useful in many situations. For example, many of the screenshots and much of the testing for this book were done on a machine running a server under OS/2 and logging in to a client window on the same machine. If you have a machine that can run it, you might find this type of server useful for practice in your CNA studies.

The installation process for NetWare Server for OS/2 is complex, and beyond the scope of this book and the CNA curriculum. For the details of this process, consult the installation manual in the DynaText documentation included with your copy of NetWare 4.11.

NetWare 3.12

Although this is a book about NetWare 4.11, NetWare 3.12 may actually be a better networking solution for certain situations. Net-Ware 3.12 does provide many of the same benefits as NetWare 4.11, including the enhanced client software and menu system described in this book. The main feature missing from NetWare 3.12 is NDS.

You might want to stick to NetWare 3.12 for your network in the following situations:

- If you, other administrators, or the users are well-trained on NetWare 3.12, you may want to wait until NetWare 4.11 training is completed before moving on.

- If the budget is tight, NetWare 3.12 can usually handle more users on a server than NetWare 4.11 would on the same machine. Upgrading may require more disk storage or RAM.

- If you are using a third-party product, such as for accounting software or mainframe connectivity, these products may not yet support NetWare 4.11.

NetWare 4.11 includes support for full connectivity with clients and servers running older versions of NetWare, so you may want to make the move to NetWare 4.11 a gradual one, one server at a time. Servers that don't require the additional features of NetWare 4.11 may not ever need to be upgraded. If it works, why fix it?

Windows NT

A war is being waged right now between vendors of different NOSs, and the two biggest competitors are NetWare 4.11 and Microsoft's Windows NT 4.0. NT (an acronym for *New Technology*) was originally intended as an upgrade to the Microsoft Windows operating system, and is becoming popular as an alternative to Windows 95. Windows NT also includes powerful networking features, and some companies have chosen Windows NT as an alternative to NetWare.

Versions of Windows NT

The latest release of Windows NT, version 4.0, is available in two versions:

- Windows NT Workstation is a client workstation operating system similar to Microsoft Windows. It uses the same user interface as Windows and can run most Windows applications.

Windows NT 4.0 uses the Windows 95 user interface and can run most Windows 95 and Windows 3.1 applications. Unlike Windows (or even Windows 95), Windows NT Workstation is a 32-bit, preemptive multitasking operating system.

■ Windows NT Server is a more expensive version optimized to work as a server, similar to NetWare 4.11. It also includes all of the features of Windows NT Workstation. Clients on a Windows NT network can include Windows NT, Windows, DOS, and OS/2.

You can manage Windows NT through utilities on the server or on a workstation. A system of *trusted domains* allows central management of the network, similar to what NDS provides for NetWare 4.11.

Why Choose Windows NT?

Windows NT has several advantages over NetWare 4.11:

■ NT's pricing is lower than NetWare 4.11's for small networks. Server licenses allow an unlimited number of users; however, client software must be licensed for each workstation. The latest version, 4.0, includes a "concurrent connection" licensing option, similar to that of NetWare 4.11.

■ Windows NT provides greater integration with Microsoft Windows clients, because some common components are shared between Windows and Windows NT. Since the server and clients can run the same operating system, there is less to learn. The Windows NT user interface is nearly identical to that of Windows 95.

■ Windows NT 4.0 supports PowerPC, DEC Alpha, and other high-powered RISC-based processors. It also supports Symmetric Multi-Processing (SMP), a feature that was added to NetWare with the release of version 4.11.

On the other hand, Windows NT has a few disadvantages compared with NetWare 4.11:

- Although NT includes a domain system that is similar to NDS, it is not as versatile or as expandable. Microsoft intends to remedy this with a future version of NT, code-named Cairo, which is scheduled to ship sometime in 1997.

- Novell has a large number of training programs, including the CNA and CNE certification programs, so there are plenty of people around who know NetWare. Support for Windows NT is not quite as easy to find, although the MCSE (Microsoft Certified Systems Engineer) certification for Windows NT is gaining in popularity.

- Windows NT's security, although adequate for most companies, isn't as sophisticated as that of NetWare 4.11. If your network is in a top-secret organization that requires high security, NetWare is currently a better choice. Microsoft is planning many security improvements for the Cairo release.

- Some of the features of NetWare 4.11, such as the MultiProtocol Router, are not included in Windows NT. Once again, Microsoft expects the release of Cairo to remedy this.

If you choose Windows NT, the decision doesn't need to apply to the whole network. NT has the capability to integrate with NetWare 4.11 and other network systems. Windows NT is gaining in popularity as an *application server*, which is a server that works in conjunction with the NetWare server and processes data for applications, reducing the workload of the workstations.

IBM LAN Server

IBM's LAN Server is a relatively low-cost system that provides basic networking services. It is based on IBM's OS/2 operating system. This allows the server to be run on the same machine as a workstation, similar to NetWare 4.1's NetWare Server for OS/2.

IBM also offers an Advanced Server option, which provides high-speed file and network access, as well as enhanced security. LAN Server's principal advantage is that it allows easy integration with other IBM systems, including older mainframe and minicomputer systems, such as AIX and AS/400.

Although LAN Server has become less popular due to the explosive growth of NetWare and Windows NT, it is still used in many companies, particularly those that need strong connectivity with AS/400 systems.

Banyan VINES

VINES was introduced when NetWare 3.1 was still young. Although it has a catchier name than NetWare (it's actually an acronym for VIrtual NEtworking System), Banyan's product has always had a smaller market. It is most often used in larger networks that span multiple locations.

One benefit of VINES is that it provides a directory service similar to NetWare 4's NDS. For this and other reasons, VINES was the preferred enterprise network system for many companies. This was, after all, before NetWare 4 became available.

The directory service provided by VINES is called StreetTalk. Now that NetWare 4.11 is becoming prevalent in large networks, Banyan has introduced methods of integrating StreetTalk with NetWare and other popular NOS software. Banyan's recent focus has been on integrating VINES and StreetTalk with the largest network of them all, the Internet.

Peer-to-Peer Networking

Some networks don't use a server at all. These *peer-to-peer* networks allow each workstation to share its own files or printers. In a sense, each workstation acts as a server to provide access to its own disk drives and printers. Peer-to-peer networks are easy to set up and usually easier to maintain than a dedicated server. In addition, there's no server to buy, so the price is lower.

Peer-to-peer networking isn't the answer for all networks, however. Because the file and printer sharing are done in the background on workstations, the system can't be as fast as a dedicated server and can't handle nearly as many users. In addition, peer-to-peer systems usually lack the more advanced network services, such as messaging and directory services. Thus, peer-to-peer networks are best suited for smaller networks (up to 20 users) or systems that require a minimum of resource sharing.

There are many peer-to-peer systems available from different companies. Here are a few:

- Microsoft Windows for Workgroups

- Microsoft Windows 95 and Windows NT

- Artisoft LANtastic

- AppleTalk

- IBM OS/2 Warp Connect

Peer-to-peer systems can usually be used in combination with server-based networks such as NetWare. This allows the best of both worlds: users can access files and printers on other users' workstations when needed, and they can enjoy the benefits of a full-scale network server.

Review

The concept of *networking* has revolutionized the use of PCs in businesses. A network is a system that connects multiple computers, allowing them to communicate with each other, share resources (files, printers, and so on), and communicate with mainframes and large networks.

Network Components

A typical network consists of several components:

- The *server* runs software called the *network operating system* (NOS), which allows it to act as a server.

- *Workstations* are where the users of the network run applications. Workstations use the resources of the server.

- Each workstation or server has a *network board* (or card), which interfaces that computer to the network.

- *Peripherals*, such as tape backup drives, modems, and printers, can be made available through the network and accessed by all users at workstations.

- A *communications medium* connects the machines. This is the actual network wiring.

NetWare 4.11 includes *server software* (the NOS) that you run on the server. In addition, *client software* is provided for a variety of clients. NetWare also includes utilities that you can use to manage the network and its resources. You will run most of these utilities from a workstation, but some run on the server console.

Network Services

NetWare 4.11 is a NOS that provides the following services:

- *File sharing* allows users to access the same files, even at the same time. Users can also access applications on the network.

- *Printer sharing* allows users to print to a network printer from anywhere on the network.

- *NetWare Directory Services* (NDS) provides an organization for network resources and keeps the information about each resource in a database.

- *Security* allows the administrator to control access to each network resource. There are several types of security: console, physical, file system, NDS, communication, and network auditing.

- *Backup and restore capabilities* let you keep a copy of network data on a tape or other media for safekeeping and restore it to the server if needed.

- *Communications features* allow multiple networks, using different cable and different operating systems, to be connected together.

Network Operating Systems

Which NOS your network should use depends on the needs of your users, your company's budget, the users' familiarity with a particular system, connectivity with mainframes or other systems, and the software that will be running. The alternatives include the following:

- NetWare 4.11

- NetWare Server for OS/2

- NetWare 3.12

- Microsoft Windows NT

- IBM LAN Server

- Banyan VINES

- Peer-to-peer networks (such as Novell Personal NetWare or Microsoft Windows for Workgroups)

CHAPTER

2

What's New in NetWare 4.11?

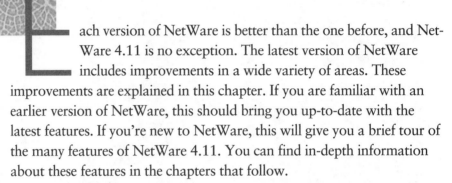

ach version of NetWare is better than the one before, and NetWare 4.11 is no exception. The latest version of NetWare includes improvements in a wide variety of areas. These improvements are explained in this chapter. If you are familiar with an earlier version of NetWare, this should bring you up-to-date with the latest features. If you're new to NetWare, this will give you a brief tour of the many features of NetWare 4.11. You can find in-depth information about these features in the chapters that follow.

We will begin this chapter with a description of the basic differences between NetWare 3.1*x* and NetWare 4. The final section summarizes the additions in the latest versions, NetWare 4.11 and IntranetWare.

NetWare Directory Services for Managing Network Objects

In order to manage all of the users, groups, printers, and other network objects, NetWare uses a database. In NetWare 3.1*x* this database is called the *bindery*. The bindery is a simple, flat database, similar to a phone book, but not even in alphabetical order. This arrangement is inefficient for networks with many objects. Imagine trying to find a particular name in a randomly ordered phone book, and you'll get the idea.

In NetWare 4, the bindery has been replaced by *NetWare Directory Services* (NDS). Rather than just list the objects in the network, NDS allows you to organize them. The NDS database uses a tree structure—an upside-down tree, to be exact. A typical NDS tree is shown in Figure 2.1. Even if you have more than one server, you can manage them all through the same NDS tree.

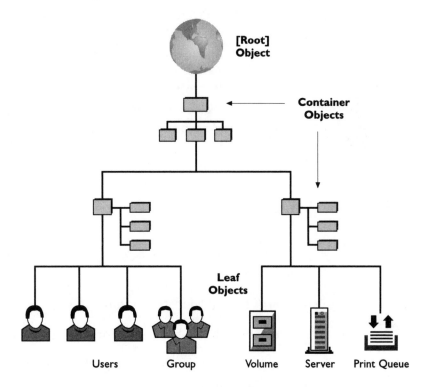

FIGURE 2.1

NDS uses a tree-like structure to organize network resources.

The NDS database is called the *Directory*. This is written with a capital *D* to avoid confusion with disk directories.

In NDS, every resource on the network is an *object*. You can organize objects in NDS by placing them inside *container objects*, which are special objects used to contain, or hold, other objects. The objects that represent actual resources—printers, users, and other objects—are called *leaf objects.* These form the leaves of the Directory tree, and they can't contain other objects.

To manage NDS objects, you use a utility called NetWare Administrator, or NWADMIN. NWADMIN runs from Microsoft Windows and provides a graphical look at the Directory tree. From this utility, you can manage every type of object and control security. A DOS utility, NETADMIN, allows you to perform most of the same functions, although it isn't nearly as good-looking.

NDS is explained in detail in Chapter 5. Managing NDS objects with NetWare Administrator is explained in Chapter 6.

Server Features

NetWare 4 includes several improvements to the server software itself. These include:

- A simplified installation process

- The SERVMAN utility, for managing server settings

- Time synchronization, which allows multiple servers to keep the same time

- Support for new hardware, including the Pentium and Pentium Pro processors

- NetWare Server for OS/2, which allows you to run a server and workstation on a single computer

The Installation Process

Back in NetWare 2.2, installing a NetWare server was a complicated process. NetWare 3.11 was easier to install, but still required you to perform many of the steps manually. NetWare 3.12 includes an INSTALL program that does most of the work for you, making it easy to install, even for people who are not network experts. NetWare 4's installation is even easier. In addition, it includes options that allow you to set up the new NetWare 4 features.

NetWare 3.12 has only one kind of installation. The installation program asks you questions about each phase of the installation. NetWare 4 has even more features and options, so it has a lot more questions to ask. To keep it easy for the nonexpert, Novell wisely chose to include a Simple installation option.

Even if you use the Custom installation, the NetWare 4 installation process is quite simple once you understand it. A typical installation takes about 20 minutes.

If you choose the Simple installation, NetWare answers many of the questions for you. If you are installing an "average" network, these answers are probably correct. If not, you should use the other choice, Custom installation. This is the old-fashioned method, which asks every possible question.

One more improvement: If you are upgrading the server from a previous version of NetWare, NetWare 4 is much more careful about replacing your files than previous versions were. NetWare checks before installing any file to make sure that the version to be installed is newer than the original version. If it is not, NetWare will prompt you to decide whether to overwrite the file or leave the original version intact.

We'll look at a simple installation of NetWare 4 in Chapter 10. The NetWare 4 installation options are explained in detail in Part IV of this book.

Manage the Server with SERVMAN

NetWare 3.1*x* has many parameters that you can adjust. You can change these using the SET console command. This allows you to fine-tune the network, improve compatibility with software and hardware, and to mess things up horribly if you don't know what you're doing. Typically, SET commands are placed in the AUTOEXEC.NCF file, which is a special file that contains commands to be executed when the server starts, similar to the AUTOEXEC.BAT file on a DOS workstation.

NetWare 4 includes a new server console utility, SERVMAN, which allows you to change these same parameters. However, SERVMAN is much more polite about it. It is a menu-based utility. You can choose the type of parameter to adjust from a list of categories and adjust settings without needing to remember the SET command syntax. Almost any change that you can make with the SET command can be made from within SERVMAN. An example of a SERVMAN screen for changing Directory Services settings is shown in Figure 2.2. The SERVMAN functions are also available as a submenu from the MONITOR utility.

When you exit SERVMAN, you are given the choice of saving the changes in the AUTOEXEC.NCF or STARTUP.NCF files.

Synchronized Time

Workstation PCs have a built-in clock. NetWare uses this clock to mark the time that events occur, such as the creation of a file. This

makes it easier to determine which version of a file is the newest. In
addition, events such as backups can be scheduled at a certain time.

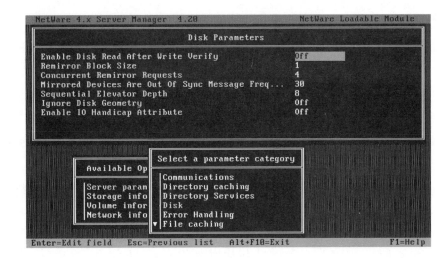

FIGURE 2.2

SERVMAN allows you to
change network settings
without remembering
complicated SET
commands.

As the saying goes, a man with one watch knows what time it is; a
man with two watches is never sure. A network with 30 workstations
has 30 different clocks. How's that for unsure? Fortunately, NetWare
manages the clocks so that they keep the same time.

In NetWare 3.1*x*, your workstation's time is set according to the
server's time when you log in. This keeps the workstations on the same
time. If you have multiple servers, each will keep its own time. As long
as the times on the servers are reasonably close to each other, this
doesn't cause a problem.

In NetWare 4, accurate time is even more important. NDS is used to
manage multiple servers at once, and time stamps are used to keep track
of changes to NDS objects. In order to work together, all of the servers
must keep the same time. Fortunately, you don't need to monitor the
times yourself. NetWare 4 handles this with *time synchronization*.

Time synchronization uses one or more *time servers* to maintain the time on the network. Each NetWare 4 server is a time server of one type or another.

You'll find more information about how time synchronization works and configuring time servers in Part III of this book.

Hardware Support

NetWare 4 supports a wider variety of hardware than previous versions. Here are the new features:

- NetWare 4 supports Intel's Pentium series processors and takes advantage of their advanced features. These include a *paging* feature that allows memory to be moved in entire blocks, rather than one byte at a time.

- The PCI (*Peripheral Component Interconnect*) bus is the latest innovation in hardware interfaces for PCs. It is often seen in systems that include the Pentium processor. NetWare 4 now supports PCI communication as well as the older standards: ISA, EISA, and VESA local bus.

- PC Card (formerly PCMCIA) is a standard for tiny, credit card-sized peripherals, usually used with notebook computers. Network cards, modems, sound cards, and even hard disk drives are available. If you're wondering how you'll ever remember the abbreviation, you're in luck. The standard has recently been renamed and is now called PC Card. NetWare 4 supports network cards and disk drives that use this type of interface.

NetWare Server for OS/2

NetWare Server for OS/2 is included with NetWare 4. It allows you to run NetWare 4 as a nondedicated server, so that a single machine can serve as both a workstation and server.

NetWare Server for OS/2 requires a great deal of memory in order to run efficiently, and is only practical for smaller networks. The specifics are covered in Chapter 1, in the discussion of NOS choices.

File System Improvements

The NetWare *file system* provides access to hard disks, organizes data on them into files, and manages their storage. NetWare 4 introduced some impressive improvements to the file system.

These include the following:

- File compression

- Block suballocation

- NetWare Peripheral Architecture (NPA)

- Data migration

Although these features affect different areas of the file system, they serve a single purpose: to make access to disks more efficient. Files take less space and can be accessed faster. Let's take a closer look at each of these features.

File Compression

It seems that no matter how much disk storage your network has, it's never enough. NetWare 4 helps you save space with the *file compression* feature. File compression finds the files that you haven't used for a while and compresses them into a smaller amount of disk space. The compressed file is typically about 63 percent smaller than the original file.

How Does Compression Work?

You might expect that the only way to make a file smaller is to remove some of the data; fortunately, this is not how NetWare does it. It uses several systems that allow a small amount of bytes to represent a larger amount. You may be familiar with compression software such as PKZIP and LHARC, which use similar techniques.

Let's consider a simple example. Imagine a file that contains the character *A* 400 times in a row. The normal file would store all 400 *A*s, each in its own byte, for a total of 400 bytes. The compressed file would simply store a code that means "Insert 400 *A*s here." Thus, our 400-byte file would be reduced to 3 or 4 bytes, yet still retain all of its content.

In practice, few files compress quite that well. Different types of files will undergo different amounts of compression:

- Simple text files will compress to about one-quarter of their original size. (Of course, files containing only a single character will compress even better, but you probably don't have any of those.)

- Binary files (such as executable files or some word processor documents) will compress a bit, but the benefit is not great.

- Some graphic files (such as uncompressed TIFF and Microsoft PowerPoint) will compress well—often to as little as one-tenth of their original size.

- Many graphic formats (including GIF and JPEG) include built-in compression, so they won't compress any further.

When Does Compression Happen?

You may have experience with on-the-fly file compression systems, such as Stac Electronics' Stacker and the DriveSpace program provided with DOS and Windows. These compression programs usually have one thing in common: They slow down your system. As a file is written to the disk, it must be compressed, and compression takes a heavy toll on the CPU.

NetWare file compression works a little differently. Rather than compressing every file as it is written, NetWare periodically scans the disk and looks for files that nobody has accessed for a while. By default, this time period is seven days, but you can change it to anything from 1 to 10,000. The server compresses the files that have been unused during the specified time period. This will still slow down the server, but NetWare is smart enough to wait until everyone has gone home to do its compression work. The time defaults to 6:00 a.m., but you can set it to a more convenient time for your company.

When a user tries to access one of these compressed files, the server uncompresses it, then allows it to be accessed as usual. The file remains uncompressed until it has not been touched again for seven days.

Why Not Use Compression?

File compression is enabled on NetWare 4 servers by default. It usually works efficiently even with the default settings, and most users won't even know it's there. However, you may want to turn it off in certain situations. Here are some possible disadvantages of compression:

- When a user requests a file that has been compressed, there will be a delay as the server uncompresses the file. In most networks, this won't happen very often. But if your users often need to access files that no one has used for more than seven days, the server may slow to a creeping halt. Depending on the file size and the server speed, decompression can take from 30 seconds to as long as 10 minutes.

- If you have a backup that was made from a compressed volume, you will need to restore it onto a volume that also has compression enabled, to ensure that space is available. In addition, unless the backup system supports compression, files will be restored in an uncompressed state, and NetWare will not compress them again until seven days later. Thus, if an entire volume is restored, this could require a much greater amount of disk space than the original (compressed) volume.

- Once you enable compression on a volume, you cannot turn it off and uncompress the files without re-creating the volume (which will erase all data on the volume!). You can, however, disable compression for individual files and directories.

As a network administrator, you have full control over the compression feature. You can choose which files and directories will be compressed and which should never be compressed. You can also set some directories or files to be instantly compressed when written.

Block Suballocation

When NetWare writes data to a disk, it uses increments called *blocks*. The disk drive is divided into blocks. These blocks are all the same size. NetWare 3.1*x* usually uses 4KB as the block size. NetWare 4 chooses an optimum block size based on the size of the drive and the server's RAM.

NetWare 3.1*x* and other operating systems use only entire blocks at a time. This means that a lot of space is wasted. For example, if the block size is 4KB, a 400-byte file will use an entire 4KB block. Similarly, a file 9KB in length will use three blocks, a total of 12KB. This use of blocks is illustrated in Figure 2.3.

NetWare 4's *block suballocation* feature allows the blocks to be used more efficiently. Instead of using entire blocks at a time, each block can be subdivided into 512-byte sections. A 400-byte file will use only one 512-byte section, or *suballocation unit*. This can save you a lot of disk space, especially if the block size is larger than 4KB. Block suballocation is illustrated in Figure 2.4.

Data Migration

Many companies need extremely large amounts of disk storage. One area where much space is needed is in *imaging* applications. Imaging tries to replace filing cabinets full of paper by scanning documents and storing them as graphic files. These files are typically stored on an optical storage device, or *jukebox*. A jukebox has a very high storage

F I G U R E 2.3

Using entire disk blocks can waste space.

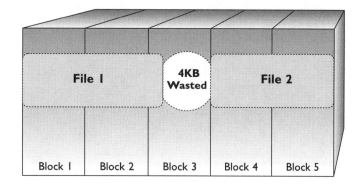

F I G U R E 2.4

With block suballocation, files take less space.

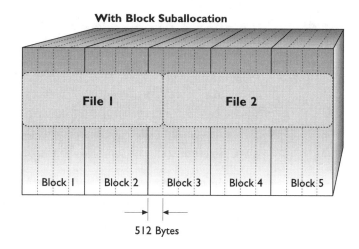

capacity and stores data in a permanent form, which is less likely to be lost in the event of a device failure or system crash. These systems require time-consuming procedures to move old data onto the jukebox.

The name *jukebox* isn't a coincidence; these systems often work in the same way as the kind that plays music. A bank of optical disks is set up so that a mechanical arm can move the appropriate disk into the drive. A jukebox system is expensive, but at least you won't need to insert a quarter each time you want to use it.

NetWare 4's *data migration* features give you the best of both worlds: you can migrate data to the jukebox, yet still keep it accessible to your users. Files that are not in use can be moved to the jukebox automatically. These files still appear to be on the NetWare volume. When a user chooses to access one of these files, it is *demigrated*, or copied back to the NetWare volume. The only effect a user might notice when accessing a migrated file is a slight delay (typically less than a minute) while the file is retrieved from the jukebox.

Data migration is performed by a NetWare service called the *High-Capacity Storage System* (HCSS). You can enable or disable migration for each of the disk volumes on your server.

NetWare Peripheral Architecture (NPA)

NetWare uses software *device drivers* to access storage devices on the Net-Ware server. The device driver provides an interface between the NetWare operating system and file storage devices, such as disk drives and tape drives. *NetWare Peripheral Architecture* (NPA) is a new standard for device drivers. In NPA, the disk driver is separated into two modules that work together to provide access to the disk or other device:

■ The *Host Adapter Module (HAM)* provides the interface between NetWare and the *host adapter*, or drive controller card. This could be a SCSI, an IDE, or another type of controller.

■ The *Custom Device Module (CDM)* provides the interface to the hardware devices (disk drives) attached to the host adapter. If several different types of disk drives are attached to the same host adapter, you can use a separate CDM for each one.

NPA provides two advantages to the traditional disk driver architecture: scalability and modularity. *Scalability* means that you can load only the particular modules that you need, saving memory and CPU resources. *Modularity* makes it easy to make hardware changes in the system. If you change the hardware configuration of the server, you will only need to replace one driver (either the HAM or CDM).

Novell is making NPA the standard for disk drivers in all future versions of NetWare. At the moment, very few NPA drivers are available. Fortunately, the old style of disk drivers can still be used with NetWare 4.

New, Improved, and Combined Utilities

To manage the NetWare server, you use NetWare *utilities*. These usually run from a workstation and serve a variety of functions to help you control the network and its resources. NetWare 3.12 includes lots of utilities—so many, in fact, that it's often difficult to remember which is which.

Novell must have realized this, because NetWare 4 actually includes *fewer* utilities. Fewer utilities doesn't mean fewer capabilities, however. You can still control everything that you could in NetWare 3.12 and much more. Many of the older utilities were simply combined into single, comprehensive NetWare 4 utilities. In addition, just about every utility has been improved in some way, and a few have been removed entirely and replaced by new utilities.

Printing Made Easy

Ask any NetWare administrator what causes the most problems in a network, and you will usually get the same answer: printing. The process of setting up network printers is a difficult one, and there are many links in the chain that a print job must go through to reach the printer. When a problem occurs, it can be difficult to tell which link has failed.

NetWare 4 doesn't solve all of these problems, but it takes a step in the right direction. For setting up network printing, the NetWare

Administrator utility (NWADMIN) and the PCONSOLE printer utility include a Quick Setup option. By using this option, you can create all the objects required to make printing work in a single step.

Like other NetWare 4 resources, printing is managed through NDS. This means that you can use the graphical NWADMIN utility to manage all aspects of printing. Using NWADMIN is much easier than working with the DOS-based utilities of NetWare 3.1x. A particularly handy feature in NWADMIN is the Print Layout Page. This option displays a diagram of all of the objects involved in the printing process, complete with lines between them to show how they relate to each other. This makes it easy to spot a problem and determine its cause.

Setting up and managing printing are explained in detail in Chapter 7.

Online Documentation

As with previous versions of NetWare, NetWare 4 includes online documentation on CD-ROM. You can view the documentation directly from the CD-ROM on a workstation or install it on the server for viewing from any workstation attached to the server.

The online documentation in NetWare 3.1x was called *ElectroText*. In NetWare 4, this has been replaced by the DynaText viewer. Although it has a different name and some new features, DynaText works in much the same way as ElectroText did.

The DynaText viewer is produced by a third party and licensed to Novell. The manufacturer is actually Electronic Book Technologies, based in Providence, RI.

NetWare 4 includes DynaText viewer programs for several operating systems, including Microsoft Windows, Macintosh, OS/2, and

Novell UnixWare. A sample screen from the Windows version is shown in Figure 2.5.

All of the NetWare 4 manuals are included in the online version. DynaText uses a *hypertext* system, which means that you can click highlighted words and instantly skip to the section they refer to. You are probably familiar with similar hypertext systems, such as the Help system in Microsoft Windows. You can view graphics, tables, and screenshots by clicking their icons.

Novell's manuals are not known for their organization; it can be difficult to find a particular item in a book, or even figure out which book to look in. If you have access to the DynaText documentation, you can easily search for a word or phrase in all the books, and skip directly to that section.

FIGURE 2.5

The DynaText viewer allows you to view NetWare online documentation.

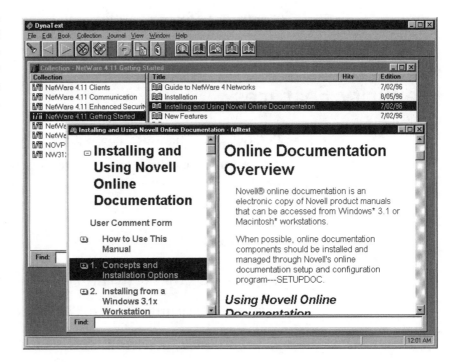

The DynaText documentation is included with the NetWare 4.11 and IntranetWare packages. This is usually the second CD-ROM in the package, labeled NetWare 4.11 Documentation. To install the documentation from within Windows 3.1 or Windows 95, follow these instructions:

1. Insert the CD-ROM.

2. Select Run from the Start menu or the Program Manager File menu.

3. Type **D:SETUPDOC.EXE**. Replace **D:** with the letter of your CD-ROM drive.

4. An icon will be created for the online documentation; you will need to insert the CD-ROM when you wish to use the online documentation.

For instructions for other platforms and more details, see Chapter 16.

Security Features

NetWare has always provided strong security features. Most companies don't need all of these features, but they can be useful for high-security situations. NetWare 4 adds even more security features—enough to make even the most paranoid network administrator happy.

Types of Security

There are two main types of security in NetWare 4:

- *NDS security* controls access to NDS objects.

- *File system security* controls access to disk files and directories.

For those companies that need high security, NetWare 4 provides extensive *auditing* features. An *auditor* is a special user who can monitor other users' actions on the network, including the actions of the network administrator. Even if you aren't interested in playing Big Brother, you may still find auditing useful to track usage of network resources and determine if adequate resources are available.

Memory Protection

The *memory protection* feature protects the server's memory from corruption. An NLM, or NetWare Loadable Module, is a program that is loaded on the file server. NetWare uses an *unprotected* memory management system to run NLMs. This means that every NLM has access to the server's entire memory. Because of this, a badly written or faulty NLM can write to memory belonging to other NLMs. Worse, it can write over the NetWare operating system itself. This causes corruption in the server's memory, usually resulting in a server crash or *abend* (abnormal end, NetWare's word for "crash and burn").

To pass Novell's NetWare Tested and Approved certification program, NLMs must be shown not to cause these memory conflicts. Unfortunately, many NLMs are not Novell-certified, and even certified ones may not be perfect.

NetWare 4 allows you to play it safe with these suspect NLMs by using the *memory protection* feature. NetWare sets aside a *domain* (an area of memory) called the *protected domain* for unstable NLMs to run in. NLMs in this domain can only access memory in this domain, which keeps them away from the memory used by the operating system and other modules. This allows you to run otherwise unsafe NLMs (if you must) or to test new versions before allowing them full access to the server's memory.

Better Client Support

The client software used with NetWare 4 is also an improvement over older versions. The actual client software is called the *NetWare DOS Requester*. This provides an improved way of accessing the network and its resources.

The DOS Requester was introduced with NetWare 3.12, and an updated version is included with NetWare 4. The DOS Requester handles the connection between the network and the workstation. Previous versions of NetWare used the *DOS shell*. The DOS Requester provides more features, tighter integration with DOS, and support for NDS.

Novell recently released newer client software called Client 32. This client software is included with NetWare 4.11, and it will also work with previous versions. Client 32 makes further improvements, although there are some situations where you will still want to use the DOS Requester.

Clients running the DOS shell can still use the NetWare 4 network. However, you will need to use the DOS Requester to take full advantage of the features of NDS.

NetWare 4 supports a wider variety of clients, including PCs running DOS, Microsoft Windows, and OS/2; Apple Macintosh computers; and UNIX workstations. Non-PC workstations were not fully supported in older versions of NetWare. With NetWare 4, these machines get the respect they deserve: full support for NDS and most of the same features as DOS and Windows clients.

NetWare 4 also includes support for SNMP (Simple Network Management Protocol), which is an industry-standard network management protocol. Support for SNMP is now provided directly by the NetWare client software. Taking advantage of SNMP allows you to manage large networks efficiently.

Communication Improvements

Another set of improvements in NetWare 4 involves the way that data is sent over the network. NetWare 4 supports more protocols, or communication methods, than the previous versions. In addition, it includes two features that streamline communication and improve speed: Packet Burst Protocol and Large Internet Packets.

More Protocol Support

Protocols are the languages that the server uses to communicate across the network. The most common network protocol is IPX, or *Internetwork Packet Exchange*. In NetWare 3.1*x*, IPX was the only protocol installed with a new server setup. If you required support for alternate protocols, such as AppleTalk, you needed to install them manually.

NetWare 4's installation program allows you to choose whether to install two protocols in addition to IPX support:

- The AppleTalk protocol allows easy integration of NetWare with Apple Macintosh networks and peripherals.

- TCP/IP (*Transport Control Protocol/Internet Protocol)* is used to integrate NetWare with UNIX systems. In addition, TCP/IP is the standard protocol for communication over the Internet.

Packet Burst Protocol

The IPX protocol sends data across the network, divided into *packets*. Packets are a specific size and contain a certain amount of information. The packets are sent using a *handshaking* process. In this process, after each packet is sent successfully, the other machine sends back an acknowledgment. The sender waits until it receives this acknowledgment before sending the next packet.

Although the term *packet burst* sounds slightly violent, it doesn't describe literally what happens when a packet grows too large and explodes. The Packet Burst Protocol simply lets the server send groups of packets, or *bursts*, all at once. The burst is sent without handshaking, and the recipient sends an acknowledgment for the entire burst. If an error occurs, the sender needs to resend only the packet containing the error. Packet Burst Protocol is enabled by default in NetWare 4, and supported by both the server and workstation software. Figure 2.6 shows a comparison between Packet Burst Protocol and regular IPX communication.

Large Internet Packets

The packets transmitted over the network are usually a specific size, depending on the network protocol. When these packets are passed through a router to another network, however, they are reduced to 512 bytes.

NetWare 4's *Large Internet Packet*, or LIP, feature lets packets be passed through a router without changing their size. This allows for faster communication between networks. LIP can be combined with Packet Burst Protocol for efficient communication. NetWare 4 enables LIP by default.

International Features

NetWare 4 greatly improves the international capabilities of NetWare with full support for multiple languages. Users can use NetWare utilities in their choice of language (English, French, Italian, German, or Spanish—the acronym FIGS might help you remember the

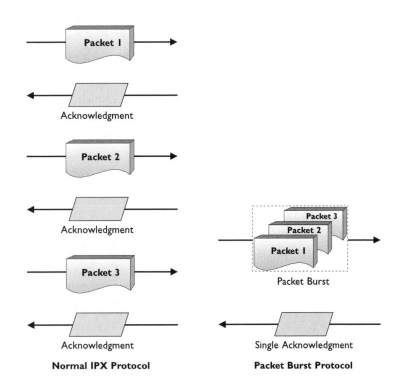

F I G U R E 2.6
Packet Burst Protocol
allows large amounts of
data to be sent across the
network at once.

non-English languages supported). You can choose a language for
server and workstation utilities. Users at different workstations can
even use the same utility in different languages. Future releases of Net-
Ware 4 may include support for additional languages.

Other international features allow the server to use language-specific
keyboards and to change the format of dates and numbers displayed
by the system. NetWare 4 is sold in an English-only version and an
international version. If you need support for another language, make
sure you purchase the international version.

New Features in NetWare 4.11

The improvements we've looked at so far are all available in Net-Ware 4.1, and to some extent in the earlier versions of NetWare 4. In this section we will examine the key new features in the latest release: Net-Ware 4.11. NetWare 4.11 is currently sold as part of the IntranetWare package, which includes additional features; we will also present those features here.

NDS Improvements

With NetWare 4.11, a few improvements have been made to the NDS database and the utilities you use to manage it:

- A new type of object, the Application object, allows you to create custom Windows-based menus for users. This replaces the DOS-based NMENU package included with versions 3.12 and 4.1.

- NWADMIN, the NetWare Administrator utility, has been updated with a toolbar and a few new features; additionally, it is now available in a native Windows 95 version.

- You can now manage multiple Directory trees from within NWADMIN.

- The Partition Manager utility for NDS partitioning and replication has been replaced by the NDS Manager utility, which also includes several new troubleshooting features.

File System Improvements

The most important change to the file system in NetWare 4.11 is the addition of the LONG.NAM module, which you can load at the server to support long file names. This can be used to support Windows 95, Windows NT, and OS/2 file names.

Additionally, NetWare 4.11 supports more files per disk volume. Previous versions were limited to 2 million directory entries (individual file or directory names) per volume; NetWare 4.11 supports up to 16 million entries per volume.

The SMS (Storage Management Services) backup system included with NetWare 4.11 has also been improved. It can now back up the NDS Directory more effectively, includes additional logging features, and allows backups of Windows 95 and Macintosh workstations.

Server Improvements

The server software itself has been improved in NetWare 4.11 in several ways:

- NetWare now handles abends (crashes) much more effectively. Memory management has been improved to prevent badly written server utilities from causing a crash.

- SMP (Symmetric MultiProcessing) allows a NetWare server to take advantage of multiple-processor machines with up to 32 processors. (Currently, machines are available with 2 to 4 processors.)

- Memory management features of Intel's latest microprocessor, the Pentium Pro, are supported.

Printing Improvements

NetWare 4.11 includes a few significant improvements related to printers and printing:

- The Quick Setup option, added to PCONSOLE in NetWare 4.1, is now also available in the NetWare Administrator utility.

- A new utility, NPRINTER Manager, allows you to configure a printer attached to a Windows 95 workstation as a network printer.

- NDPS (NetWare Distributed Print Services) is an entirely new system that can be used as an alternative to traditional queue-based printing. We'll look at NDPS and other printing features in detail in Chapter 9.

Client Software Improvements

Although NetWare 4.11 supports the client software supplied with Net-Ware 4.1 (the NetWare DOS Requester), it also includes Novell's new 32-bit client software, Client 32. Versions of Client 32 are available for DOS, Windows 3.1, and Windows 95. Client 32 supports several important new features, such as the ability to run login scripts within Windows 95. We will look at client software in detail in Chapter 5.

Security Improvements

NetWare 4.11 implements a new set of security features called NetWare Enhanced Security. These features increase the security of NetWare to match the DOD (U.S. Department of Defense) C2 security specification. In addition, several security-related utilities have been updated.

Miscellaneous Changes

Here are some other items that changed with the release of NetWare 4.11:

- NLS (NetWare Licensing Services) was added. This enables Net-Ware to control licensing for third-party products as well as for NetWare itself.

- Message Handling Services (MHS) was included in NetWare 4.1. These services provided a basic e-mail capability for clients on the NetWare network. MHS is not included with NetWare 4.11, but it can be downloaded from Novell's online services.

- Net2000 is a new set of application programming interfaces (APIs) which allows third-party programmers to take advantage of Net-Ware 4.11's features, such as NDS.

- The installation process can now detect hardware, such as disk drives and network cards, and configure it automatically. This makes it much easier for a nonexpert to install a new NetWare 4.11 server.

Internet/Intranet Features

Currently, NetWare 4.11 is available only as part of Novell's new IntranetWare package. This package includes the NetWare operating system along with several components that make it easy to use the server to communicate with the Internet or a company-wide intranet. The other components of IntranetWare are as follows:

- NetWare Web Server is a World Wide Web server which runs under NetWare 4.11.

- Novell Internet Access Server (NIAS) includes a new version of the Multiprotocol Router (MPR); a gateway to communicate between Novell's standard IPX protocol and the TCP/IP protocol, used with UNIX machines and the Internet; and a set of extensions that improve support for WANs (wide-area networks.)

- Novell FTP Services allows you to run an FTP (file transfer protocol) server on the NetWare 4.11 server, as well as running other UNIX-like services.

Review

NetWare 4.11 provides many new features that were not present in NetWare 3.1*x*. These include features that increase the speed of the network, improve communication, and provide additional services and resources.

The most important new feature of NetWare 4.11 is NDS, or NetWare Directory Services. NDS stores information about all of the users, printers, and other resources on the network in a database called the Directory. The Directory is organized into a tree-like structure and consists of container and leaf objects.

Server Improvements

NetWare 4.11 includes several improvements to the server software itself. These include:

- A simplified installation process that lets you use default settings.

- The SERVMAN utility that makes it easy to manage server settings.

- Time synchronization that allows multiple servers to keep the same time.

- NetWare now supports new hardware, including the Pentium Pro processors.

- NetWare Server for OS/2 allows you to run a server and workstation on a single computer.

File System Improvements

The NetWare file system has also been improved, including the following features:

- *File compression* compresses data that is not in use, allowing more information to fit on the network disks.

- *Block suballocation* divides the disk into smaller units, to allow more efficient storage.

- *NetWare Peripheral Architecture (NPA)* provides a new method for vendors to write disk drivers.

- *Data migration* is provided by the *High-Capacity Storage System* (HCSS) and allows files that are not in use to be migrated to an optical storage device, or *jukebox*.

Utility Improvements

Improvements to NetWare utilities include the following:

- Many of the utilities in NetWare 3.1*x* have been combined into single utilities for convenience.

- The PCONSOLE utility includes a Quick Setup option, which creates objects needed for printing in a single step.

- NetWare Administrator provides additional features for managing network objects.

As with previous versions of NetWare, NetWare 4.11 includes online documentation on CD-ROM. You can view the documentation directly from the CD-ROM on a workstation or install it on the server for viewing from any workstation attached to the server. The software used for this purpose is the DynaText viewer.

Security Improvements

NetWare has always provided strong security features. Improvements to security in NetWare 4.11 include:

- Two types of security are used: file system security and NDS security.

- Auditing features allow you to monitor use of the network and its resources.

- The memory protection feature protects the server's memory from corruption.

Other Improvements

Some of the other improvements in NetWare 4.11 are:

- Improvements to the client software include the NetWare DOS Requester, support for additional clients (Macintosh, OS/2, and UNIX), and support for the Simple Network Management Protocol (SNMP).

- Communications improvements include support for additional protocols, Packet Burst Protocol, and Large Internet Packets (LIP).

- International features of NetWare 4.11 allow the server and utilities to be used in multiple languages, including English, French, Italian, German, and Spanish.

The Latest Version: 4.11

The latest release of NetWare, version 4.11, includes improvements in NDS, the file system, the server operating system, printing, security, and client software. NetWare 4.11 is included as part of Novell's IntranetWare package, which also includes NetWare Web Server, Novell Internet Access Server (NIAS), and Novell FTP Services.

CHAPTER

3

PC Hardware

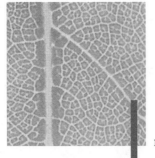

I n this chapter, we are going to take a look at the fundamental components of PC hardware. As a network administrator, having a good understanding of the nuts and bolts of the computers that make up your network will serve you well.

Networks these days typically contain a variety of old and new technologies. Workstations may range from 12-year-old systems that boot from floppies (honestly!) to top-of-the-line Pentium Pro multimedia workstations. As you might have guessed, not all companies have moved to the latest and greatest equipment. The next sections should give you an idea of what to expect.

This chapter and the next chapter are basic reviews of PC hardware, DOS, and Windows. If you are an experienced computer professional, you may wish to skip these chapters; they are very basic and geared toward ensuring that everyone reading this book has an understanding of some fundamental concepts.

PCs (personal computers) are normally the most visible feature on a NetWare network. So let's begin with an examination of what is under the cover of a PC. A PC has the following basic components:

- A **motherboard,** which includes

  - The CPU (Central Processing Unit), also called the processor, the heart of the PC

  - The memory (RAM, or Random Access Memory)

  - The BIOS (Basic Input/Output Services)

- A **Data Bus** and **Controller cards**, which may include the following:

    - A disk controller, which allows the PC to communicate with disk drives

    - An I/O (Input/Output) controller, which provides one or more serial ports, used for communications, and parallel ports, usually used for printers

    - A NIC (Network Interface Card), which allows the PC to communicate with servers on the network

- **Storage devices,** including hard disk drives, floppy disk drives, and tape backup drives

- A **Case** and **power supply** to hold the PC securely together and power the components

- A **monitor** to send output to the user

- A **keyboard** to receive input from the user

Let's take a look at these components in detail.

The Motherboard and Microprocessor (CPU)

The motherboard is the foundation upon which many of the most critical components of a PC rest. The large, printed circuit board, known as the motherboard, also serves as the backbone into which peripheral hardware is connected. Figure 3.1 shows a typical motherboard.

The most important pieces on the motherboard are the memory; the interrupts, addresses, and ports; the data bus; and the microprocessor, or CPU. The CPU is commonly called the "brains" of a computer.

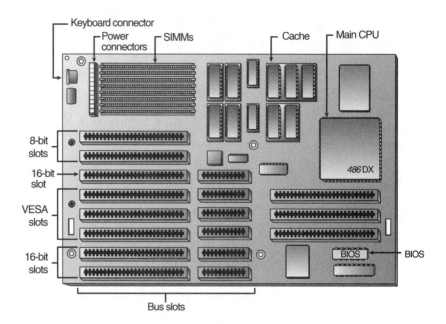

Without the CPU, your computer would not be able to execute programs; it would be declared "dead."

In order to effectively execute programs, a CPU must be able to read
and write information into the computer's memory, it must be able to
recognize and carry out the series of commands or instructions supplied by the programs, and it must be able to direct the operation of
the other parts of the computer. Furthermore, to survive in today's
world, it must do all of this very quickly.

Intel is the manufacturer of the leading type of CPU. These processors range from the early 8086 and 8088 to the latest Pentium and
Pentium Pro. Intel introduced its first CPU in June 1978, and since that
time Intel chips have been the standard for PC processors.

Intel has built upon a successful design to create a series of CPUs,
called the X86 family. Each new design has maintained 100 percent
compatibility with previous versions, allowing every new design to
execute software written for previous designs.

Although it is called the X86 family, the first Intel CPU to be widely accepted was called the 8088.

The speed of the CPU is measured in terms of megahertz (MHz). Because 1 MHz is equal to 1,000,000 cycles per second, we're talking about a lot of processing in the CPU. Typical speeds range from 16 MHz for the older 386 computers to 200 MHz and beyond for the latest Pentiums.

These speeds are called *clock speeds* and are controlled by an internal timing source, or clock, on the CPU. However, some instructions—basic actions the CPU performs—can take more than one clock cycle to complete. Therefore, we measure the actual work that a processor can perform in MIPS—millions of instructions per second.

To the end user, the most noticeable difference between Intel CPUs is the speed. The chronological order of Intel CPUs, along with their processing speeds (measured in MIPS), follows:

8086	0.33 MIPS
8088	0.33 MIPS
80286	3 MIPS
80386	11 MIPS
80486	41 MIPS
Pentium (80586)	over 100 MIPS
Pentium Pro (80686)	over 300 MIPS

Other manufacturers, including AMD and Cyrix, sell Intel clone processors. They typically offer similar performance and a better price, but they may not be 100 percent compatible with all software and devices.

NOTE The 8088 was implemented with 29,000 transistors. Pentium-class processors have transistors numbering in the millions!

What Do You Really Need?

Although Pentium processors and their successor, the new Pentium Pro or P6, are the most powerful processors, not everyone uses them—or needs them. Practically speaking, a low-end Pentium can be used for just about any application, and even a 386 is still usable for DOS-based applications. Nevertheless, you'll find that many companies still try to do the nearly impossible—run Windows applications from the network using a 386, or even a 286. Even if the system does work, it will be very slow.

Statistically, 486 and Pentium machines are the most popular work-stations, but a great many 386 (and lower) machines are still out there. Some applications don't need anything better, and some companies aren't willing to spend the money to upgrade. Keep in mind, however, that the latest NetWare client software requires a 386 or better processor—so, although a 286 can access the network, you won't be able to access NDS from that workstation.

Bits and Bytes

All of the information traveling across the motherboard of a computer is represented digitally as either the digit 1 or the digit 0. For example, the instruction that tells an Intel X86-family CPU to subtract is 0010110. This method of using 1s and 0s to represent information is called the *binary system*. The 1s and 0s are called binary digits, or, more easily, *bits*. When a computer processes 1s and 0s, however, it does so in groups of 8, known as *bytes*.

Computer circuitry is capable of reacting to two states in the flow of the electric current that runs through it: high current and low current. These states of high and low current are what is represented by the 1s and 0s. One of the primary factors contributing to the development of computers as we know them is that it is relatively easy and inexpensive to create a circuit that can recognize the difference between high and low current (with an extremely low error ratio.)

Because today's typical machine has over 8 million bytes of memory, we have adopted several metric terms to describe quantities of memory storage. Here are the most common terms:

- A byte is 8 bits.

- A kilobyte (K or KB) equals 1,024 bytes.

- A megabyte (M or MB) equals 1,048,576 bytes.

- A gigabyte (G or GB) equals 1,073,741,824 bytes.

Note that these terms aren't the nice round numbers that the metric system is famous for. This happens because of the binary system that computers use to address memory. Although 1,000 is a round number to you or me, it's not round to a computer—in binary, 1,000 is expressed as 1111101000. Therefore, we measure memory in amounts convenient to the computer. Thus, a kilobyte is 1024 bytes—in binary, a nice, round 10000000000. A megabyte is 1024 kilobytes, or 1024 × 1024 bytes, and so on.

Memory

Memory is crucial to the CPU's operation. It provides a quickly accessible storage place for all of the instructions that the CPU processes. Memory resides on the motherboard in close contact with the CPU.

The are two main types of memory:

- RAM (Random-Access Memory)
- ROM (Read-Only Memory)

RAM

Because PC CPUs operate at such a high speed, they need quick access to the raw data that needs to be processed, and they must be able to store the results of what has been processed quickly. The CPU itself can hold only a few bytes at a time, so memory must be able to hold enough bytes to support complex programs. Disks and tapes can store large quantities of information, but they are simply too slow for the CPU. The solution is RAM.

Random-access memory (RAM) has several characteristics that make it appropriate for working with the CPU. One of these characteristics is that the CPU can access programs and data that are stored in RAM directly, or "randomly." This access method is similar to the way you use a dictionary: You can open it directly to the entry you're looking for.

The terms memory and RAM are often used interchangeably.

The type of RAM most frequently used is *volatile*, which means that it requires a constant supply of electricity to maintain the data. If electricity is shut off, this RAM will lose its data. *Volatility* means that you can lose data that has not been saved to a disk or tape if the power to your PC goes down accidentally. Disks and tapes are examples of *non-volatile* storage.

Newer PC motherboards often have two kinds of RAM:

- Dynamic RAM (DRAM)
- Static RAM (SRAM)

DRAM is typically found in the main memory. For example, a typical Pentium PC will have 8 or 16 megabytes of this type of RAM. DRAM is relatively inexpensive (single megabytes currently sell for about $40.00). It is, however, much slower than SRAM.

Although SRAM and DRAM are both volatile, SRAM is able to maintain the data as long as the power is on. DRAM, on the other hand, requires that each byte of memory be accessed several times per second in order to keep it. This constant cycle, called memory *refresh*, is the reason DRAM is slower.

SRAM often appears on a motherboard in small banks of chips that are used as data caches. Because SRAM is much faster than DRAM, it can help boost system performance.

Most PCs have another type of RAM called *complementary metal oxide semiconductor (CMOS)*. CMOS is used to store system information about such things as the floppy and hard disk, the amount of installed memory, and the type of display. The CMOS memory is also volatile but is powered by a small battery to hold this information after you shut off your PC. Your system uses this information when it boots up again.

ROM

Read-only memory (ROM) is a type of permanent memory. It does not disappear when you shut off the PC and does not require a battery to keep it running. The data stored on ROM is usually stored on the chips by the manufacturer and cannot be changed. An important piece of ROM on a PC is called the *Basic Input/Output System* or BIOS.

The information stored in ROM is frequently called *firmware*.

The BIOS is responsible for some very fundamental functions in a PC, such as displaying text on a monitor and allowing keyboard input.

When a PC boots up, the BIOS programs perform an elemental system test and use information supplied by the CMOS to identify the disk drives attached to the system, which are then searched for the operating system.

Interrupts, Addresses, and Ports

Hardware devices installed in the PC, such as modems and network cards, use several methods to communicate with the computer. These are explained in the sections below.

Interrupts (IRQs)

The CPU in a PC has several inputs that allow devices to get its attention—to interrupt it—if it is performing another task. These are called *interrupts*, or IRQs (for Interrupt Requests). Interrupts are numbered from 0 to 15. Some are used for specific purposes, while others are available for new devices you may install. The table below summarizes the IRQs and their typical uses.

Interrupt Number	Standard Use	Notes
0	System timer	Reserved by system
1	Keyboard	Standard for all machines
2	System I/O	Reserved by system
3	COM2/4 (serial port)	Standard for most machines
4	COM1/3 (serial port)	Standard for most machines
5	LPT2 (printer)	Available on most machines

Interrupt Number	Standard Use	Notes
6	Floppy disk	Standard for all machines
7	LPT1 (printer)	May be shared with some devices
8	Real-time clock	Reserved by system
9	Redirected IRQ2	Available in some cases
10	Unused	Available on most machines
11	Unused	Available on most machines
12	Unused	Available on some machines
13	Math coprocessor	Reserved by system if math coprocessor is installed
14	Hard Disk	Standard for most machines
15	Unused	Available on some machines; sometimes used for hard disks

An interrupt can typically be used by one device. When you install a new device, such as a network card, in the computer, you must choose an unused interrupt. You usually specify an interrupt by setting a jumper, or switch, on the device, or by running a special configuration program.

The interrupts listed here are for 386 and newer CPUs. Although the list is similar for older systems, they did not allow the use of interrupt numbers above 9.

When two devices use the same interrupt, a conflict occurs. This conflict may cause the computer to *crash,* or refuse to function at all; or it may allow things to work normally and then crash when one or both of the devices are used. In any case, you should resolve the conflict quickly, since it can seriously affect the operation of your computer, and you may lose valuable data.

Ports (I/O Addresses)

Along with an interrupt, most devices use a small part of the upper memory area to send data back and forth to the CPU. This area is called a *port address*, or sometimes an *I/O address*. These addresses are used in small blocks—usually 16 bytes or less. Addresses are specified using a hexadecimal number and typically range from 300 to 360.

Like interrupts, multiple devices using the same address can cause a conflict. The use of addresses is not as standardized as interrupts, so you will often need to consult a device's manual to see which port address it is using.

Memory Addresses

Some devices, particularly video cards and high-speed network cards, use another area of memory as a larger buffer. These areas are specified with a hexadecimal number and usually range from C000 to E000.

DMA Channels

A final resource that a device may use is a DMA (direct memory access) channel. These are high-speed interfaces to the bus that allow a device to access memory directly. DMA channels are numbered from zero to two and are typically used only by time-critical devices, such as sound cards and high-speed disk controllers.

How a PC Uses Memory

Today's PC typically includes 8, 16, or 32MB of memory, well over ten times the original 640 KB. However, because of the limitations of the 8086 architecture—still present in today's Intel processors—memory must be accessed in several different ways. Here are the types of memory that can be accessed in a PC:

- **Conventional memory:** The 640 KB area has been a standard for too long now. It is the same 640 KB that the original IBM PC used when it first shipped. This area is used to store programs; many programs can still use only this area of memory.

- **Upper memory:** The memory just above the 640KB area, which includes a total of 384KB. Your video card, NIC, and other hardware components use a sizable amount of this space. Conventional 640KB and the upper 384KB add up to the first 1024KB—the first megabyte of RAM.

- **Expanded memory (XMS):** This memory uses a 64KB block of memory to access the higher areas of memory, swapping memory in and out of the block or *page frame*. This system is rarely used in today's PCs, but remains as a standard.

- **Extended memory:** The memory above 1MB. A computer that has 16MB of RAM has only 15MB of extended memory. Today's PCs can access this memory without swapping, but use of extended memory still requires a different method of access.

- **High memory:** This is a 64KB area that begins at the 1MB boundary. It is addressed by HIMEM.SYS, which is shipped with later versions of DOS or Windows. The most common use of high memory is for part of the COMMAND.COM file in DOS 5 and 6.*x* products from Microsoft. This allocation scheme allows DOS to take a much smaller portion of the precious 640KB area.

The IBM XT's 8086 could address a maximum of 1MB of RAM. The 286 addressed 16MB RAM. The 80386 and later processors can address as much as 4GB of RAM. However, a computer that has an 80386 processor will not always address more than 16MB of RAM. The computer's motherboard must also support the addressing. For example, the IBM PS/2 Model 80 is an 80386 machine that was commonly used as a file server. System administrators who installed more RAM were disappointed to find that the IBM PS/2 Model 80 supported a maximum of 16MB of RAM, even though the Intel 80386 processor in the IBM is capable of addressing up to 4GB.

A PC operates in two modes when accessing memory: *real mode* and *protected mode*. Real mode is a backward-compatible technology developed for x86 processors. When a 286, 386, 486, or 586 is running in real mode, it is running like an 8086 processor. This feature means that programs created for the original IBM XT will still run on your Pentium Pro chip (although just a bit faster).

Protected mode was developed for 286 chips or later. Programs written for the original 8086 chip could access the same area of memory, causing conflicts and instability. Protected mode helps solve this conflict by making programs request memory from the operating system.

The theory is that memory used by a program is protected by the operating system. Another program running on the PC is required to request memory from the operating system. The operating system will give access only to memory that is not used.

Optimizing Memory

When Intel designed the 8088 CPU for IBM to use in the original IBM PC, it could address only 1MB of memory, and programs were able to use only the 640KB base memory. Later, Intel CPUs kept this memory design to maintain backward-compatibility and to ensure programmers that new Intel hardware would not make their programs obsolete. This guarantee eventually created an enormous base of prospective software buyers, because all existing computers could run the software. Consequently, Intel-based computers have the largest commercial software selection in the world.

Lotus, Intel, and Microsoft joined forces at the 286 introduction to create the LIM (Lotus/Intel/Microsoft) memory standard, which was a method for programs to access more than 640KB of memory. The LIM standard has given way to *extended memory,* now widely implemented through Microsoft's HIMEM.SYS files and EMM386.EXE drivers for Windows and DOS.

Although the use of extended memory has overcome the 640KB barrier, the limit still applies to many programs, which use only conventional memory. Thus, you may even get out-of-memory errors when you have 8 or 16MB of RAM. Most likely, it's the 640KB conventional memory that is running out.

In its DOS 6.*x* versions, Microsoft ships two handy utilities to optimize memory: MEM.EXE and MEMMAKER.EXE. MEM.EXE shows current memory usage file by file, and MEMMAKER.EXE optimizes the memory settings. You can also purchase third-party memory optimization programs, such as Quarter Deck's QEMM Optimize program. IBM DOS and Novell DOS also sell memory optimization utilities.

Although MEMMAKER will almost always give you an automated configuration that is superior to manual optimization, you can sometimes outdo it. If MEMMAKER doesn't give you the results you need, try loading programs in a different order as a last resort. Because memory is filled on a first-come first-served basis, this may allow for a more efficient arrangement.

The Data Bus

By itself, a CPU is useless. It can process data, but it can't read data from a disk or display it on your screen. In order for the CPU to communicate with the memory and output devices, there must be a medium through which data is transmitted. On a PC motherboard, this medium is known as the *bus*. The bus serves as a channel through which data is transmitted.The bus that connects the CPU to the memory on a motherboard is known as the *data bus*. It is made of printed-circuit wiring on the motherboard. This bus also connects to the *expansion bus*, which carries data to and from the bus slots. The slots accept the adapters that allow you to add capabilities to your computer—video cards and network cards, for example.

A PC motherboard normally has several *bus slots*. These slots are attached to the expansion bus, and are used to connect *adapter cards* to the motherboard. Adapter cards give a computer the ability to have serial, parallel, and game ports; to communicate across modems; to produce video output on a monitor and audio output to external speakers; and to connect to a network. Typical adapter cards include network interface cards, video cards, disk controller cards, input/ output (I/O) cards, sound cards, and modems.

The standard bus, developed with the advent of the PC, is the ISA (Industry Standard Architecture) bus. Newer standards that allow faster communication include the following:

- EISA is an enhanced version of ISA and is often used for network servers.

- VESA local bus is a popular high-performance bus standard. It became very popular as the first high-speed bus available at a reasonable price. Inexplicably, it is not well supported by NetWare or by network cards. It is now being rapidly replaced by PCI in most new PCs.

- PCI is the latest bus innovation and is well supported by NetWare and by network cards. The PCI bus is much faster than VESA and allows full 32-bit communication between I/O cards and the motherboard. Because the PCI specification is still in a state of flux, be sure you purchase cards that are guaranteed to be compatible with your system.

- PCMCIA, or PC Card, is a standard for credit-card size adapters. These are traditionally used to connect network cards and other peripherals to portable notebook computers. In addition, some new models of desktop PCs include slots for PC cards.

Within the circuitry of the CPU there is another bus called the *internal data bus*. This bus is used to carry data between the different parts of the CPU itself. A bus is measured in terms of how many bits it can carry at one time. Internal data buses of the first popular Intel CPU, the 8088, carried 8 bits at a time. Pentium 586s have 64-bit internal data buses. Apple Macintosh machines are also popular in many companies, particularly those involved with graphic design or art. The Macintosh architecture uses a 68000-series CPU developed by Motorola and an operating system created by Apple. The latest Mac operating system is System 7.5, although System 8 is in the works. New Macintosh machines called Power Macs use the PowerPC processor, a new processor line from Motorola and IBM. The PowerPC is as fast as a Pentium, and in some cases it is faster. The PowerPC can also run Windows NT, and a version of NetWare for the PowerPC is in the works.

Review

In this chapter we have examined the fundamental components of network hardware. Networks typically contain a variety of old and new technologies. We have explored the components of a PC; the most common network client and server; and how the CPU, memory, and external devices interact.

PC Components

The basic components of a PC include the following:

- A **motherboard**, which includes
  - The CPU (Central Processing Unit), also called the processor
  - The memory (RAM, or Random Access Memory)
  - The BIOS (Basic Input/Output Services)
- A **Data Bus** and **Controller cards**, which may include the following:
  - A disk controller, which allows the PC to communicate with disk drives
  - An I/O (Input/Output) controller, which provides one or more serial ports, used for communications, and parallel ports, usually used for printers
  - A NIC (Network Interface Card), which allows the PC to communicate with servers on the network
- **Storage devices**, including hard disk drives, floppy disk drives, and tape backup drives
- A **Case** and **power supply** to hold the PC securely together and power the components
- A **monitor** to send output to the user
- A **keyboard** to receive input from the user

PCs and Memory

All of the information traveling across the motherboard of a computer is represented digitally as either the digit 1 or the digit 0. This is called the *binary system*. The 1s and 0s are called binary digits, or, more easily, *bits*. The following other measures are used:

- A byte is 8 bits.

- A kilobyte (K or KB) equals 1,024 bytes.

- A megabyte (M or MB) equals 1,048,576 bytes.

- A gigabyte (G or GB) equals 1,073,741,824 bytes.

The are two main types of memory:

- RAM (Random-Access Memory)

- ROM (Read-Only Memory)

Hardware Communication

Hardware devices installed in the PC, such as modems and network cards, use several methods to communicate with the computer:

- Interrupts (IRQs)

- Ports (I/O Addresses)

- Memory Addresses

- DMA Channels

PC Memory

Five types of memory can be accessed in a PC:

- Conventional memory is the 640KB area that the original IBM PC used.

- Upper memory is just above the 640KB area and includes a total of 384KB. Your video card, NIC, and other hardware components use this area.

- Expanded memory (XMS) uses the top 256KB of upper memory as a swap area for system programs.

- Extended memory is the memory above 1MB.

- High memory is a 64KB area located at the 1MB boundary. It is addressed by HIMEM.SYS, which ships with later versions of DOS or Windows.

CHAPTER

4

DOS and Windows

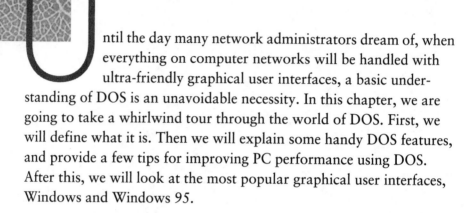

ntil the day many network administrators dream of, when everything on computer networks will be handled with ultra-friendly graphical user interfaces, a basic understanding of DOS is an unavoidable necessity. In this chapter, we are going to take a whirlwind tour through the world of DOS. First, we will define what it is. Then we will explain some handy DOS features, and provide a few tips for improving PC performance using DOS. After this, we will look at the most popular graphical user interfaces, Windows and Windows 95.

The Basics of DOS

DOS stands for Disk Operating System. DOS is a type of software that resides on a computer and provides very fundamental functionality. It has two main roles:

- DOS manages computer resources, such as memory and hard drives, acting as an intermediary between applications and system hardware. When an application requires access to the hardware on a system, it uses DOS.

- DOS provides an interface with which you can manage system resources.

Because DOS is able to communicate directly with a computer's Basic Input/Output System (BIOS), it is able to manage hardware for an application. An application can simply make a request for hardware access to DOS, which in turn communicates the request to the BIOS, which directly accesses the hardware. DOS is helpful because it speaks BIOS's language.

Many of the functions DOS provides are so basic that it is easy to take them for granted. DOS handles input with a keyboard and output to a monitor as well as communication between computer components. DOS also provides the files in which you can store information and the directories that you can use to organize files.

Microsoft's MS-DOS, the most popular type of DOS, can be found on about 90 percent of all of the microcomputers on NetWare networks.

DOS includes commands that allow you to do things like copy disks, read and write to files, and check your disk for errors—very basic stuff. These commands are the part of DOS that network administrators use daily. Because these commands are of great practical use, we'll look carefully at them later in this chapter, but first you need to understand how DOS actually gets started on your computer.

In this chapter, when you see the word *DOS,* we mean MS-DOS. IBM and Novell both have versions of DOS, PC-DOS and DR-DOS, respectively. They are actually very similar to MS-DOS. Because MS-DOS is so prevalent, however, we will focus on it.

How DOS Gets Started on a Computer

As we saw in the last chapter, the BIOS performs some very basic checks when a computer is first turned on (or warm booted). After the start-up checks, the BIOS searches the A drive (normally a floppy disk drive), the B drive, and the C drive (normally a hard drive) for an operating system. DOS may reside on either a floppy disk or a hard drive, depending on whether you have it loaded on the hard drive or boot it from a floppy.

When the BIOS finds DOS, it loads the most important DOS files into memory. Among these files are two of special concern to a network administrator: AUTOEXEC.BAT and CONFIG.SYS. Network administrators often edit these two files for workstation-specific purposes. We'll look at these files a bit further along in this chapter.

After the important files have been loaded into memory and the necessary program lines have been executed, the *DOS prompt* appears on the screen. The DOS prompt often appears as the letter A or C, representing one of the drives on your computer. It is typically followed by a colon, a greater than sign, and a blinking line, called a *cursor*, and looks like this:

C:>_

The DOS prompt can be customized using the PROMPT command. You can enhance the drive designation with your own text and information supplied by your computer, such as the time, date, or current directory.

The DOS prompt is your doorway into the inner workings of DOS. After DOS has been loaded into memory on your machine, it is in control, except for the input that you enter through the DOS prompt. By typing a recognized command, you can set DOS into motion—creating directories, copying files, or doing whatever it is that you have instructed it to do.

In order to convince DOS to carry out a command, you must be very careful to follow the correct syntax. You must type each command precisely, with no extra spaces or spelling errors. (You can, however, use either upper or lower case.) For example, to find out what version of DOS you are using, type the command **VER** at the DOS prompt and press enter. DOS will show you what version you are running on your machine. If, however, you try to spell the command phonetically and type "VURRR," DOS will quickly alert you to the error of your ways by displaying this message:

```
Bad command or file name
```

Even seasoned DOS users don't always remember the correct syntax for DOS commands. Fortunately, DOS provides online help. If, in the midst of your trials and tribulations, you can remember how to spell *help* correctly, simply type it at the DOS prompt and you will have access to DOS Help and detailed descriptions of correct DOS usage.

DOS Help contains a selection of commands on which you can get help, as shown in Figure 4.1. If you select a command, you will see the correct syntax for that command. You will see that some commands permit more than one way to spell their names. For example, to change the current directory, you can type either **CD** or **CHDIR.**

FIGURE 4.1

The main screen of DOS Help.

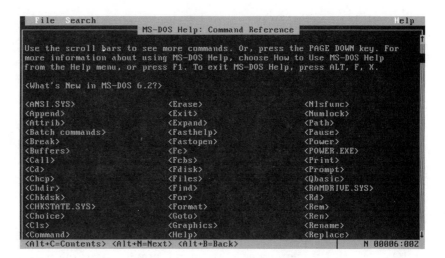

In DOS Help, you may also see references to something called a *switch*. A switch is an extension to the command that you can use to override the normal execution of many commands. For example, the command ERASE can be switched so that it prompts you for approval before erasing a file. The switch for this is /P. To have a prompt appear before erasing, you would use the ERASE command as usual, but type **/P** at the end of your command.

A switch is always indicated by a forward slash (/), not to be confused with a backslash (\), which is used to designate a directory or to separate file and directory names.

You can also get immediate help on any DOS command by typing its name followed by the /? switch. This command displays that command's available options. For example, the command below returns the list of options for the FORMAT command:

FORMAT /?

DOS versions 4 and higher offer a type of graphical interface that is one step up from the command line approach. Rather than requiring you to type in each command, you can simply make selections using a mouse or arrow keys. The interface, called the DOS Shell, is nothing to get too excited about. It is about as rudimentary as graphical interfaces get, but it does offer an alternative way of using DOS. Most professional DOS users, however, find it easier to simply memorize the commands and type them at the prompt.

DOS Files and Directories

The basic building blocks of DOS are files and directories. Anytime you enter a command, you are working with programs that are stored in files, which are organized under directories. Anything you (or an application you use) add to DOS is stored in a file that resides in a directory. So it's pretty safe to say that files and directories form the basis for DOS.

Files are simply organizational structures in which data is stored. A file can contain a letter, a spreadsheet, a program, or other types of data. Each file has a name that is unique in its directory. A directory is like a folder that you use to organize paper files in a filing cabinet, providing larger units of order.

When you view a directory, such as in Figure 4.2, you see that file entries include the following information about each file:

- File name

- Extension

- File size

- Date last modified

- Time last modified

FIGURE 4.2

A typical DOS directory

```
D:\>dir

 Volume in drive D is BS
 Volume Serial Number is 195D-08FA
 Directory of D:\

NWSERVER    <DIR>          01-01-96   12:55p
WINDOWS     <DIR>          01-16-96   11:01p
WP61        <DIR>          01-16-96   11:01p
PARADOX     <DIR>          01-16-96   11:02p
OEADM       <DIR>          01-16-96   11:02p
HTILLMAN    <DIR>          01-16-96   11:02p
FNORD       <DIR>          01-16-96   11:02p
NEWAUTO  BAT          553  06-10-95   10:04p
AUTOEXEC BAT          311  01-13-96    5:53p
SCANDISK LOG        1,915  12-13-95   11:06p
CONFIG   SYS          403  01-13-96    5:53p
COPYOFLO SYS      129,078  07-14-95   12:00a
        12 file(s)         132,260 bytes
                        17,950,720 bytes free

D:\>
```

There is one special directory that has a unique role in DOS. This is known as the *root directory*. This directory is installed by DOS when the disk is prepared. Other directories are organized under the one and only root directory. For this reason, some people call other directories *subdirectories,* since they are really branches of the root directory.

Each directory is organized under the root directory and referenced using its *path name*. Anytime you want to find a directory other than the current directory, you must use its path name. The following is an example of a path name for a directory called EDGETEK:

```
c:\COMPANY\TRAINING\EDGETEK
```

In this example, EDGETEK is a directory appearing under the directory TRAINING, which is under a directory called COMPANY, which is under the ROOT directory (C:\). A path is the route from the root directory to a particular directory or file.

To access a directory or file from a drive other than the one on which the directory or file resides, you must use the full path name, as in the example above. If you are on the same drive, you can start the path at the current directory. For example, to get to EDGETEK from the COMPANY directory, you could simply use the following path:

```
TRAINING\EDGETEK
```

File Names

DOS has rigid rules about how you can name files. Some of them, such as the eight-character limit on file names, are pretty unpopular. Nevertheless, we're stuck with them. The rules you'll want to keep in mind when creating file names are as follows:

- File names consist of a name that is no longer than eight characters, a period (.), and an extension of up to three letters.

- File names cannot have any spaces.

- File names can include any letter, number or symbol on the keyboard except the following:

  *

  ?

```
[

]

<

>

,

"

;

:

/

\

+

=
```

- DOS reserves the following file names: AUX, CLOCK$, COM1 through COM4, CON, LPT1 through LPT3, NUL, and PRN.

Extensions are often used to identify file types. For example, Microsoft Word uses the extension DOC to identify the files it creates. DOS reserves several types of file name extensions for special functions. They are as follows:

- EXE—Executable files containing programs.

- COM—Another type of executable program file, called a command file.

- BIN—Another type of executable program file.

- BAT—A batch file containing programs composed of DOS commands. Batch files allow you to execute multiple commands automatically or by entering a single command.

- SYS—System driver files that allow DOS and computer hardware to interface.

Some examples of valid DOS file names are the following:

- AUTOEXEC.BAT

- COMMAND.COM

- CONFIG.SYS

- SALES.DOC

- MISC.XXX

- 123.ABC

- MGM@XM.9_9

When you create a file with a valid file name, DOS registers it in the File Allocation Table (FAT). The FAT is where DOS keeps track of file statistics, such as name and extension, size, and location on the disk.

File Attributes

Another feature of the file system is file attributes. These are characteristics that a file can have. Attributes are often called flags, because they indicate a certain characteristic of a file. DOS includes the following file attributes:

- H (Hidden)

- S (System)

- R (Read Only)

- A (Archive)

To change attributes, you use the ATTRIB command, described later in this chapter.

CONFIG.SYS and AUTOEXEC.BAT

As we mentioned earlier, AUTOEXEC.BAT and CONFIG.SYS are two DOS files of special importance. Let's go ahead and look at these.

CONFIG.SYS

During the boot process, DOS automatically reads and processes a file called CONFIG.SYS. The contents of this file help determine how your PC is configured; it includes options for how your PC runs and commands that load programs that allow DOS to communicate with computer hardware. These programs, called *device drivers*, support devices that the BIOS does not support directly. Here is an example of a CONFIG.SYS file:

```
DEVICE=C:\DOS\HIMEM.SYS

DEVICE=C:\DOS\EMM386.EXE NOEMS

DOS=HIGH,UMB

LASTDRIVE=Z

FILES=40

BUFFERS=25
```

Let's take a closer look at each command:

- HIMEM.SYS is a driver that allows the high memory area to be used.

- EMM386.EXE is the expanded memory manager. In this case, the NOEMS switch is used. This means that no expanded memory will be allocated, but the upper-memory area is made available.

- DOS=HIGH,UMB specifies that DOS will be loaded into high memory. This is a feature of MS-DOS 5.0 and higher. The UMB switch provides upper-memory blocks for application use.

- LASTDRIVE=Z specifies the last drive letter used for DOS drives. If the DOS Requester is being used for network connectivity, this line also includes network drives.

- FILES=40 specifies the number of DOS file handles that are available. Effectively, this controls how many files DOS can have open at one time.

- BUFFERS=25 specifies the number of buffers available for file reads and writes. A low number can cause a decrease in speed.

CONFIG.SYS commands are completely separate from DOS commands. One good way to recognize them is that the CONFIG.SYS commands always include an equals sign (=).

AUTOEXEC.BAT

Next in the boot process, DOS executes commands from another file: AUTOEXEC.BAT. These commands are actual DOS commands, as described in the next section. These are the same type of command you can type at the DOS prompt.

Commands in AUTOEXEC.BAT are typically used to load TSR (terminate and stay resident) programs. These are programs that run in the background and provide an extra function. The network drivers that allow access to NetWare 4.1 are examples of TSR programs. Here is an example of an AUTOEXEC.BAT file, including the network drivers. Detailed explanations of each of these commands are given under the appropriate command name in the next section.

```
C:\DOS\SMARTDRV.EXE

PROMPT $P$G
```

```
PATH C:\DOS;C:\WINDOWS;C:\

CD\NWCLIENT

LH LSL

LH 3C5X9

LH IPXODI

VLM

F:

LOGIN MAIN\BOB
```

Understanding DOS Commands

DOS commands are easy to use—after you've played with them a few times. All you need is to understand the syntax and spelling and to press enter after you type the full command. As you go through this section, you may wish to practice and experiment with the commands.

After you've used these basic commands for a while in your work on computers, spend some time looking through DOS Help to discover the subtleties of the DOS commands you use most. Sometimes adding one little switch to your repertoire can really speed up your routine work.

You can place most of these commands in the AUTOEXEC.BAT file to execute when the computer boots, to avoid having to type them routinely. Of course, some are more useful than others.

CD (CHDIR)

If you type **CD** at the prompt, you will see the name of the current directory. This may seem odd, since CD stands for Change Directory. But if you type **CD** followed by the name of a directory, DOS will move you to that directory. Hence, the name CD.

There are a few different ways you can use CD:

- CD\ takes you to the root.

- CD\ followed by the name of a directory takes you to that directory if it is under the root. For example, CD\DOS will take you to the DOS directory. Note that there is no space between CD\ and DOS.

- CD followed by the name of a directory takes you to that directory if it is under the current directory. For example, if you type **CD TEMP** while in the DOS directory, you will be taken to the C:\DOS\TEMP directory.

- CD .. moves you to the parent directory of the current directory. Note that there *is* a space between CD and "..". For example, if you are in the C:\DOS\TEMP directory, typing **CD ..** will take you to the DOS directory.

CHKDSK

DOS version 6.2 introduced a command called SCANDISK, which you should use instead of CHKDSK, if you have it. Otherwise, you may want to use CHKDSK on occasion to recover lost disk space. DOS loses disk space when it fails to keep its file tracking system in order. The CHKDSK command produces a hard disk status report that can alert you to errors in DOS's filing system. It also has a limited ability to fix disk errors.

To check a hard disk and attempt to resolve disk errors, type **CHKDSK** followed by the drive letter and the switch /F, as in the following example:

```
CHKDSK C: /F
```

CLS

Anytime you have too much useless stuff printed on your screen, type the clear screen command, CLS, to wipe it away. This command clears the screen and returns you to a DOS prompt at the top of the screen.

COPY

This command makes a duplicate of one or more files. For example, if you want to make a backup of your CONFIG.SYS file, you can go to the directory in which it is stored and make a copy using the copy command as follows:

```
COPY CONFIG.SYS CONFIG.BAK
```

You can also make copies to save in other locations. For example, if you want to copy your CONFIG.SYS file to a floppy on the A: drive, type the following:

```
COPY C:\CONFIG.SYS A:
```

COPY also allows you to duplicate a file to other directories on the same drive. For example, the following command makes a duplicate of the CONFIG.SYS file in a directory called BACKUP under the OTHERS directory:

```
COPY C:\CONFIG.SYS C:\OTHERS\BACKUP
```

If you want to copy multiple files at the same time, you may find that a wildcard is helpful. For example, to copy all of the files on a floppy in the A: drive that end with EXE to a directory on the C: drive called MISC, you could type the following:

```
COPY A:*.EXE C:\MISC
```

Two of the most useful DOS tools are the wildcard characters: the question mark (?) and the asterisk (*). These can be used in place of any group of characters when you want to work with groups of files, or when you're just not sure what exactly you named a file. The wildcard characters can be used in the file name and/or the extension. The question mark can match any single character except a blank. The asterisk can match any number of characters, blanks included.

If you COPY a file to a destination directory with a file that has the same name, the new file will overwrite the existing file in the destination directory. Even worse, you cannot undelete the file using UNDELETE!

The syntax for the COPY command is as follows:

```
COPY [source drive and file name][target drive and
file name]
```

If you are copying to and from the same directory, you do not need to specify the drive.

DEL

When you want to delete one or more files, you can use DEL (or ERASE.) The following, for example, deletes the document NONEED:

```
DEL NONEED.DOC
```

DEL can also be used with wildcards. To delete all files ending with DOC in a directory, for example, you could type the following:

```
DEL *.DOC
```

Using wildcards can be dangerous. When using them, be sure that you won't accidentally erase a needed file. DOS versions 4 and later allow you to add the /P switch at the end of a DEL command. This switch instructs DOS to prompt you before deleting a file.

DELTREE

This command was introduced with DOS 6. It allows you to delete a directory and all the file and subdirectories contained within it (i.e., a "tree") in one fell swoop. Normally, you will be prompted to confirm the deletion, but if you are feeling especially bold, you can add the switch /Y to skip the prompt. To delete a directory called EXTRA, along with all subdirectories and files, the following would suffice:

```
DELTREE C:\EXTRA
```

If you delete a file's directory, you cannot undelete it.

DIR

When you want to know what files and directories are in the current directory, type **DIR.** This command produces a listing that includes the file names, extensions, size, and the times and dates of the last updates.

If you are ever bored, go to a Windows directory and type **DIR.** Try to read the files as they fly by. Once you are thoroughly frustrated, type **DIR /P.** This switch allows you to move down the list one screen at a time. The command DIR /W lists files in five columns across the screen, but the only information listed will be file names and extensions.

DISKCOPY

You use this command to copy diskettes. The diskettes must be the same size and density (e.g., 3.5" high-density floppies). To make a copy using this command, type **DISKCOPY** followed by the location of the original diskette and the location of the target diskette. For example, the following command copies a floppy in drive A: to a similar floppy in drive B:

```
DISKCOPY A: B:
```

If you have only one floppy drive, you will be prompted to do the floppy swap to get the job done.

DISKCOPY will automatically format and unformat disks for you.

DOSSHELL

Although, on first glance, this command may look like a terrible place to go, DOSSHELL really takes you to a relatively pleasant graphical interface called the DOS Shell. The DOS Shell allows you to use DOS by selecting elemental graphics, rather than typing commands. The shell is fairly useful for beginners, but you'll probably find that typing command lines is actually much quicker. The DOS Shell is not included with DOS 6.2.

EDIT

To make changes to your AUTOEXEC.BAT or CONFIG.SYS files, you can use the EDIT command. For example, the following command opens the editor using the CONFIG.SYS file:

```
EDIT C:\CONFIG.SYS
```

The editor is a full-screen interface that allows you to save, load, and search and replace within the file. You can type in the editor window directly to change the file. Use ALT+F to access the file menu and save your file. You can also press F1 while in EDIT for a useful help system.

Edit first appears in DOS 5. If you have an earlier version, you can use the command EDLIN.

FORMAT

The FORMAT command prepares a disk for its first use. (Your hard disk was probably formatted when it was installed.) The formatting process creates the FAT and divides the disk so that it is ready to store files.

The most common use for FORMAT is for formatting floppy disks (although many of these now come preformatted). Here is the command to format a disk in the A: drive:

```
FORMAT A:
```

Note that formatting permanently erases all data on the disk. There is one exception to this rule: In DOS 5.0 and later, the UNFORMAT command can recover a disk you just formatted. However, if you've used the disk after the format, there's nothing you can do to recover lost files.

If you *want* to erase a disk and ensure that it cannot be unformatted, add the /U switch. This command prevents any data from being saved on the disk in the A: drive:

```
FORMAT A: /U
```

WARNING FORMAT is one of the few commands that can really damage something if you're not careful with it. Do not format a disk unless it's blank or unless you are certain there is no useful data on it. FORMAT can be used on hard drives, such as C:, so be especially careful.

MD (MKDIR)

MD stands for Make Directory. To create a subdirectory called Sales in your current directory, simply type

```
MD SALES
```

If you want to create a directory somewhere other than in the current directory, specify the path. For example, if you are in another directory but want to make a Sales subdirectory under a directory called BIZNIZ, you could type the following

```
MD C:\BIZNIZ\SALES
```

MEM

DOS versions 5 and later have this memory status command. By typing **MEM** at the DOS prompt, you can see what portion of the total RAM on your computer is available. If you add the switch /C, you can see how much memory is being used by the programs that are currently loaded. If a long list is whizzing by, you can use the /p switch to view single pages at a time.

MOVE

DOS 6 and later include the MOVE command. It is used to move files from one location to another. For example, to move the file MAACK from the directory C:\WORK\ALLDAY to a new directory called C:\PLAY\BOY, you could type the following

```
MOVE C:\WORK\ALLDAY\MAACK C:\PLAY\BOY
```

You can also use the MOVE command to rename a directory. The following command renames a directory called ANCIENT:

```
MOVE C:\ANCIENT C:\MODERN
```

PATH

If you want DOS to be able to find a DOS program file that is not in your current directory, you can use the PATH command to expand the DOS search range.

By default, DOS searches only the current directory. DOS will then proclaim "Bad Command or Filename" if you attempt to execute a program file (such as a file ending with .COM, .EXE, or .BAT) that is not in your current directory.

When you put a PATH command in your AUTOEXEC.BAT, for example, you can set DOS to search in additional directories. To have DOS search your DOS directory, your LOTUS directory, and your root directory, in that particular order, use the following command:

```
PATH C:\DOS;C:\LOTUS;C:\;
```

Notice that directories are separated by semicolons.

PRINT

If you type **PRINT**, followed by the name of a text file, DOS will print that file to the default printer. If you want to print multiple files, simply list them. For example, use the following command to print the text files DOG and BARK:

```
PRINT DOG.TXT BARK.TXT
```

RD (RMDIR)

If you have an empty directory just hanging around, you can delete it using the remove directory command, RD. Simply type **RD** followed by the name of the directory.

REN

The rename command, REN, allows you to rename files. Type **REN** followed by the name of the file and the desired new name, and REN changes the file's name. The file will no longer exist under the original name.

SCANDISK

As we mentioned earlier, SCANDISK is the preferred method of analyzing and repairing hard disks. After you type SCANDISK, the program checks the current drive for errors. If SCANDISK finds an error, a dialog that explains the problem will appear, as shown in Figure 4.3.

SCANDISK is very easy to understand and use; it works on both compressed and uncompressed drives.

F I G U R E 4.3

A Problem Found dialog in
SCANDISK.

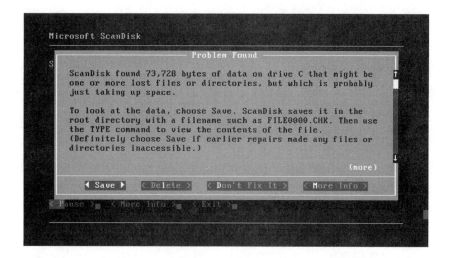

TYPE

If you want to view the contents of a text or batch file, use the TYPE
command. In order to prevent the contents of the file from whizzing
by as you try to view them on your screen, type |**MORE** at the end of
the command. The contents will appear one screen at a time. The following command displays your CONFIG.SYS file.

```
TYPE C:\|CONFIG.SYS |MORE
```

If you use this command on a program file (such as one that ends
with an .exe or .com) you will see a jumble of binary characters that
won't make any sense—even if you are a programmer.

UNDELETE

Suppose that you have somehow accidentally deleted a very important
file. What do you do? If you have DOS 5 or later, try UNDELETE! It's
surprising more children have not been named Undelete out of grati-
tude for the files this little command has saved.

To attempt to undelete a file, type **UNDELETE** followed by the name of the file ASAP. Do it before the file is written over! Here is an example:

```
UNDELETE C:\WORD\YURJOB
```

Note that UNDELETE can't work if the file has already been over-written. Any data that is written to the disk will overwrite the deleted file. For this reason, the safest time to run UNDELETE—and the only time you can be absolutely sure it will work—is immediately after you have deleted the file.

XCOPY

XCOPY is COPY on steroids. If you have a large group of files and DOS 5 or higher, XCOPY is probably the way to go. This command allows you to copy files and subdirectories all in one shot. The following switches give XCOPY its extra power:

- /S extends the copying to include an entire directory, subdirectories included.

- /E copies empty subdirectories when it is typed after /S.

- /V verifies data integrity by employing read-after-write verification.

- /P means XCOPY will prompt you for permission before copying.

WARNING If you XCOPY a file to a destination directory with a file that has the same name, the new file will overwrite the destination directory file! Even worse, you cannot undelete the file using UNDELETE!

Using DOS Batch Files

A *batch file* is a special type of file that contains a list of DOS commands. These files can be very useful to simplify the operation of your PC. If you execute any commands frequently, you can simply place them in a batch file.

Batch files have the extension .BAT and are considered executable files by DOS. We've already introduced one batch file: AUTOEXEC.BAT. DOS executes this file's commands automatically when the machine boots. Although other batch files aren't executed automatically, they can be very useful.

For example, let's look at the following commands, which are required to attach and log in to a NetWare 4.1 network:

```
SET NWLANGUAGE=ENGLISH

CD\NWCLIENT

LSL

3C5X9

IPXODI

VLM

F:

LOGIN FRED
```

Each time this user logs in to the network after rebooting, all of these commands must be executed. This can be a lot of typing! The solution is to place all of the commands above in a batch file. You can create a batch file with any text editor; EDIT, provided with DOS 5.0 and above, is a good choice.

Once these commands are in a batch file, say STARTNET.BAT, all the user would need to do is type one command to load all of the network drivers and log in:

```
STARTNET
```

As a matter of fact, the NetWare client installation program does create a STARTNET.BAT file with the required commands. This file is called from the AUTOEXEC.BAT file by default.

Versions of DOS

MS-DOS (Microsoft Disk Operating System) was the first operating system for IBM PCs. At the time of this writing, the current version is 6.22. This is the last official version, as Microsoft has focused development on Windows 95 and Windows NT. (Technically, a version of DOS that identifies itself as DOS 7.0 is hidden inside Windows 95. However, this version of DOS is not currently available by itself.)

Because DOS has had many upgrades and at least three different manufacturers in the past five years, it's rare to find a network where all the DOS machines are running the same DOS version. Each manufacturer's versions operate a little differently than the others, and not all software will run on all DOS versions.

You will still see DOS 5.0 on many network workstations, and DOS 3.3 is not uncommon. There are even a few machines still running DOS 1.0. Most of these machines could benefit from a DOS upgrade. The latest versions are more versatile, include more commands, and can support higher levels of hardware. DOS versions below 4.0, for example, can't access more than 32MB per disk partition.

Other DOS Versions

Other companies have also produced disk operating systems:

- IBM has maintained PC-DOS as long as MS-DOS. PC-DOS was originally a licensed version of MS-DOS, so there are many similarities. The latest version, PC-DOS 7, is newer than any version of MS-DOS and includes a variety of new features, including better memory management and a sophisticated text editor.

- Digital Research produced DR-DOS. Novell bought DR-DOS 6.0 from Digital and later upgraded it and marketed it as Novell DOS 7.0. Novell has recently announced that it is no longer in the DOS market. Because Novell DOS is often discussed in NetWare courses and tests, we've included a further description of it in the next section.

DR DOS and Novell DOS

DR DOS was originally developed by Digital Research Corporation. Novell purchased DR DOS when it was at version 6.0 and continued to develop it. The final version was called Novell DOS 7.0. Novell left the DOS market recently, and Novell DOS is no longer available. However, you will still run into Novell DOS and DR DOS in the real world (as well as on the current version of Novell's Service and Support CNE test).

Novell went to great lengths to maintain compatibility with Microsoft DOS and to surpass it in features and ease of use. Two of this operating system's alluring features are its excellent memory management and disk compression programs. Novell DOS 7.0 was the first operating system to ship with its own disk defragmenting utilities, disk caching, and task switching so you could run more than one DOS program simultaneously without Microsoft Windows.

One downfall of DR DOS and Novell DOS was that administrators who were familiar with MS-DOS could not switch over to this version of DOS painlessly. Its memory management programs and commands, although good, are quite different in their use and settings. Switching from Microsoft DOS to Novell DOS required a considerable amount of time to come up to speed—a luxury that most network administrators cannot afford.

These are a few of the enhancements you'll find on Novell DOS:

- **DiskMax:** A disk management utility with considerable power. Disk compression, optimization, caching, and undelete capabilities are a few of its features.

- **DOSBook:** An online documentation program for this version of DOS.

- **TaskMax:** The task-switching utility. It allows multiple DOS programs to run simultaneously in expanded, extended, and conventional memory; the user can switch between them with a keystroke. It also supports cut-and-paste operations between applications.

- **Lock:** Allows users to lock their keyboards. Unlocking requires a password.

- **Setup:** A comprehensive, full-screen setup utility for many of the DOS features, including Memo, DiskMax, TaskMax, and security.

- **HIDOS.SYS:** A memory configuration driver for this DOS.

The command

```
HIDOS=ON, HIBUFFERS=xx
```

is the equivalent to Microsoft's DOS=HIGH command, which allows high memory and upper memory use. It also supports the transfer of COMMAND.COM out of conventional memory to the high memory area.

Novell DOS, in the most recent version (7.0), also includes a peer-to-peer networking system, based on Personal NetWare. This enhancement made version 7.0 an excellent value, but the networking system is very difficult to configure and use.

Just like MS-DOS 6.*x*, Novell DOS and DR DOS will display help information for any DOS command if you execute the command with a /? switch.

Novell DOS and DR DOS also included improved versions of the following DOS commands:

- CHKDSK
- HELP
- MEM
- REPLACE
- TREE
- XCOPY
- UNDELETE
- TREE
- DISKCOPY

The Graphical Alternative: Windows

The last great computer revolution came when Microsoft introduced Windows 3.0 and the world became interested in GUI (Graphical User Interface) computing. (Of course, the Macintosh had been available with a powerful GUI—comparable to Windows 95—for years, but Apple simply didn't have the marketing budget that Microsoft had.) Microsoft quickly followed Windows 3.0 with Windows 3.1, which fixed the bugs in 3.0 and became a fixture in most workplaces. At least half of the computers in use in businesses today are running Windows.

The screen you typically see when Windows 3.1 starts is the Program Manager, shown in Figure 4.4. This is an arrangement of windows and icons that allows you to run applications or utilities.

FIGURE 4.4

The Windows 3.1 Program Manager allows you to run applications or utilities.

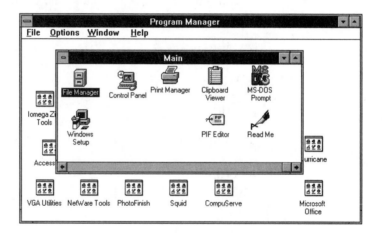

Alternate versions of Windows include Windows for Workgroups, which includes peer-to-peer networking features, and Windows 3.11, a minor upgrade to 3.1 that fixed a few bugs.

Technically, Windows isn't an operating system. It actually runs on top of DOS. The latest version of Windows, known as Windows 95, is an entirely self-contained OS (although it does include a DOS command-line interpreter, which identifies itself as DOS 7.0).

The Latest: Windows 95

At this writing, Windows 95 is Microsoft's latest operating system release. Windows 95 is a true 32-bit, multitasking OS that includes many features not found in Windows 3.1. (Although DOS is still hidden inside it, DOS and Windows are now integrated into a single system.) To take full advantage of Windows 95, you'll need to run 32-bit applications whenever possible.

Windows 95 includes most of the functions of Windows 3.1 and many enhancements and additions. It includes a better user interface, many more networking features, and improved multitasking (the ability to run multiple programs at once). A simple Windows 95 desktop is shown in Figure 4.5.

FIGURE 4.5

A typical Windows 95 desktop

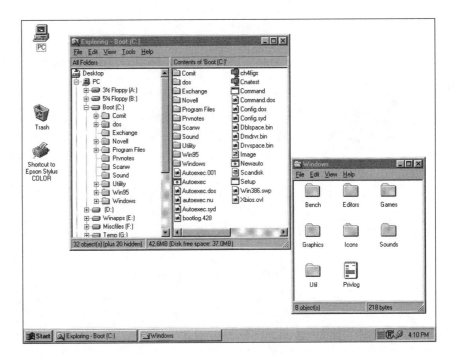

All of the power of Windows 95 doesn't come without a price, however. It requires a much more powerful system to run. Windows 95 requires a minimum of 12MB of RAM to run efficiently; in addition, the system takes about 60MB of hard disk space—not to mention the space you'll need for 32-bit applications. Windows 95 can be slower than Windows 3.1, unless you have a fast machine; we recommend at least a 486/66.

Windows 95 will run most of your Windows 3.1 applications, and at about the same speed. To really benefit from Windows 95, you need 32-bit applications. Most software vendors have released 32-bit versions of their products.

If you're rich, you may be tempted to purchase a machine that uses Intel's latest processor: the Pentium Pro (P6). However, because Windows 95 still contains quite a bit of 16-bit code, it may actually run *slower* on a P6 than on a Pentium. The P6 is optimized for 32-bit software. A future release of Windows (Windows 97, perhaps?) should remedy this situation. If you really can't wait, you may want to look into an OS that does run faster on the P6: Windows NT or OS/2.

At this writing, Microsoft is preparing to release its next operating system: Windows 97. This will be an updated version of Windows 95, and is expected to be released in the first quarter of 1998.

Other Operating System Choices

While DOS and Windows are running on 90 percent of the computers in most businesses today, there are a few alternatives. These may be useful in specialized situations or even as an alternative to Windows. We'll describe each of them below to give you a basic introduction.

Windows NT Workstation

Microsoft's Windows NT Workstation is a client workstation operating system similar to Microsoft Windows. It uses the same user interface as Windows 95 and can run most Windows and Windows 95 applications. Unlike Windows (or even Windows 95), Windows NT Workstation is a fully 32-bit, preemptive multitasking operating system. Thus, it can run quickly and communicate with hardware at optimum speeds over high-speed buses, such as PCI, and can run just about any application in the background.

Windows NT doesn't offer much of an advantage as a NetWare client. However, Microsoft is working on NetWare support for future versions, which would allow a tight integration between Windows NT (workstation or server) and NetWare 4.1. Novell has already released a Windows NT requester, which allows full client access to NDS.

OS/2 Warp and Warp Connect

IBM's OS/2 was originally Microsoft's attempt to create a new, 32-bit OS in the late 1980s. Microsoft decided to abandon the project, and IBM took over. OS/2 is a very robust system. The latest version, OS/2 Warp 3.0, runs Windows applications almost as quickly as Windows itself and performs extremely well with OS/2 applications. It includes many of the features found in Windows 95 and was available a full year earlier than the Microsoft product. Unfortunately, because of the stranglehold Microsoft has on the market, OS/2 applications are scarce. Nevertheless, it's worth a try.

OS/2 does have some advantages over Windows—and even over Windows 95. It is a more solid OS with many years of development. It multitasks better, particularly when you are running several DOS applications at once. It is also fully 32 bit, so it can take advantage of the speed of the P6 processor.

OS/2 Warp Connect is the latest package from IBM. Although it is more expensive, it includes a full array of network support. It can easily connect with NetWare, Windows NT, and even Windows 95 and also includes tools for Internet support. Unfortunately, OS/2 is not well supported by software.

Macintosh System 7

One company, Apple, produced an OS with many of the features of Windows 95 way back in 1984. This OS, built into Apple's Macintosh line of computers, introduced the world to graphical user interfaces. The latest version of the Mac OS, System 7.5, provides many improvements, and many users (notably Macintosh users) believe it to be better than Windows 95.

The Macintosh is a non-PC-compatible system. It runs on the Motorola 68000 series of processors (68040 being the most recent). The new Macintosh machines, called PowerMacs, use the PowerPC processor, a fast RISC processor that rivals the speed of the Pentium Pro.

Probably the main reason that Macintosh and its OS don't do as well in the market as PCs, DOS, and Windows is that the Macintosh was a proprietary system. While thousands of companies entered the PC-clone market and provided cheap alternatives to the original IBM PC, Apple kept strict control over its architecture, and the only Macintosh machines were made by Apple.

Apple has finally realized the error of its ways, and several companies are now producing lower-priced Macintosh-compatible machines. Although it will probably never overtake Windows, the Macintosh is still popular in specialized markets, such as scientific research and graphics production.

At this writing, Apple is preparing to release its newest operating system, based on NextStep, a UNIX-like operating system. This system may also be made available for Intel-based machines.

Review

In this chapter we've looked at DOS—the most commonly used operating system for clients on NetWare networks. We've looked at the commands and features that DOS provides. In addition, we've taken a look at the new trend in operating systems: graphical interfaces such as Windows and Windows 95. Finally, we've introduced a few OS alternatives.

DOS

DOS stands for Disk Operating System. DOS is a type of software that resides on a computer, providing very fundamental functionality. It has two main roles:

- It manages computer resources, such as memory and hard drives, acting as an intermediary between applications and system hardware.

- It provides an interface with which you can manage system resources.

After the important files have been loaded into memory and the necessary program lines have been executed, the *DOS prompt* appears on the screen. The DOS prompt often appears as a letter A or C, representing one of the drives on your computer.

The basic building blocks of DOS are files and directories. Anytime you enter a command, you are working with programs that are stored in files, which are organized under directories. Anything you (or an application you use) add to DOS is stored in a file that resides in a directory.

DOS provides a wide variety of commands, which allow you to manage files, directories, and disks on your system.

DOS Batch Files

A *batch file* is a special type of file that contains a list of DOS commands. These files can simplify the operation of your PC. If you execute certain commands frequently, you can simply place them in a batch file.

Batch files have the extension .BAT and are considered executable files by DOS. One example is AUTOEXEC.BAT, which executes automatically when the machine starts.

DOS Versions

MS-DOS (Microsoft Disk Operating System) was the first operating system for IBM PCs. At the time of this writing, the current version is 6.22. Other companies have also produced disk operating systems:

- IBM has maintained PC-DOS as long as MS-DOS. PC-DOS was originally a licensed version of MS-DOS, so there are many similarities. The latest version, PC-DOS 7, is newer than any version of MS-DOS and includes a variety of new features.

- Digital Research produced DR-DOS. Novell bought DR-DOS 6.0 from Digital and later upgraded it and marketed it as Novell DOS 7.0. Novell has recently announced that it is no longer in the DOS market.

Windows and Windows 95

The last great computer revolution began when Microsoft introduced Windows 3.0. Microsoft quickly followed up with Windows 3.1, which fixed the bugs in 3.0 and became a fixture in most workplaces. At least half of the computers in use in businesses today are running Windows.

Technically, Windows isn't an operating system. It actually runs on top of DOS. The latest version of Windows, known as Windows 95, is an entirely self-contained OS (although it does include a DOS command-line interpreter, which identifies itself as DOS 7.0).

Windows 95 includes most of the functions of Windows and many additional capabilities. It includes a better user interface, many more networking features, and much improved multitasking (the ability to run multiple programs at once); however, it requires more powerful (and expensive) hardware than Windows and may require a fast processor to achieve the same speeds.

Other Operating Systems

Although DOS and Windows are running on 90 percent of the computers in most businesses today, there are a few alternatives.

Microsoft's Windows NT Workstation is a client workstation operating system similar to Microsoft Windows—it uses the same user interface as Windows 95 and can run most Windows and Windows 95 applications. Windows NT Workstation is a fully 32-bit, preemptive multitasking operating system. Thus, it can run quickly and communicate with hardware at optimum speeds over high-speed buses such as PCI. It can run just about any application in the background.

OS/2 is IBM's alternative to Windows. It has some advantages over Windows—and even over Windows 95. It is a more solid OS with many years of development. It multitasks better, particularly when you are running several DOS applications at once. It is also fully 32 bit, so it can take advantage of the speed of the P6 processor.

The Macintosh is a non-PC-compatible system. It runs on the Motorola 68000 series of processors (68040 being the most recent). The new Macintosh machines, called PowerMacs, use the PowerPC processor, a fast RISC processor that rivals the speed of the Pentium Pro. The Macintosh OS provides most of the same benefits as Windows 95.

P A R T

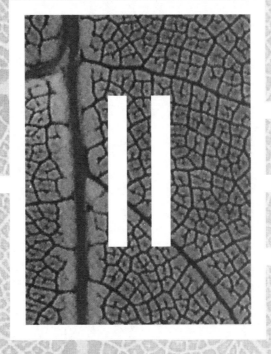

II

NETWARE 4.11
ADMINISTRATION

CHAPTER

5

NetWare 4.11
Networking Fundamentals

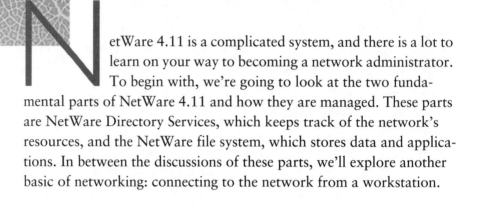

etWare 4.11 is a complicated system, and there is a lot to learn on your way to becoming a network administrator. To begin with, we're going to look at the two fundamental parts of NetWare 4.11 and how they are managed. These parts are NetWare Directory Services, which keeps track of the network's resources, and the NetWare file system, which stores data and applications. In between the discussions of these parts, we'll explore another basic of networking: connecting to the network from a workstation.

How NDS Organizes the Network

NetWare 4.11 manages the network's resources through Net-Ware Directory Services, or NDS. Information about each of these resources—users, groups, printers, servers, and other items—is organized into a single database: the NetWare *Directory*. This database works for the entire network, rather than for just one particular server.

We will spend a lot of time talking about NDS in this chapter, because NDS is at the heart of the NetWare 4.11 network. Once you understand NDS, you will have no trouble understanding most other aspects of the network and servers.

To distinguish it from a disk directory, the NetWare Directory is written with a capital *D*.

What Does NDS Do for the Network?

NDS provides many benefits to your network. They include the following:

- **Ease of administration:** Users and other NDS objects can be managed from NetWare Administrator, a friendly Microsoft Windows program.

- **Organization:** You can bring order to the chaos of network administration by dividing the objects in the Directory into manageable groups.

- **Increased security:** Security can be applied to any NDS object.

- **Scalability and interoperability:** These are fancy words meaning that NDS can work with networks of any size and can interface with other types of networks.

- **Fault tolerance:** The Directory is stored on multiple servers. Thus, if an accident should befall one of the servers, the data is intact on the others.

Let's take a closer look at each of these benefits.

Ease of Administration

NetWare 3.1*x* uses the *bindery* to keep track of the network's resources. The bindery is a simple, flat database—a simple list of resources, similar to a phone book. When you attempt to access a resource, the server must read entries from the bindery until it stumbles upon the one you need.

Each server keeps its own bindery, and there is no connection between the binderies on the servers. If you want to access a resource, you need to log in to the server where it's located. If you need resources on two servers, you need to log in to each one. Worse, you must have an account on each server, with the appropriate rights to each resource you want to access. (The need to set up and manage all these user accounts may explain the sour mood exhibited by many NetWare 3.1*x* network administrators.)

Because NetWare 3.1*x* and earlier versions keep a separate list of resources for each server, they have what is called a *server-centric organization*. This means that each server is the center of its own little world. It may be connected to other servers, but it doesn't cooperate with them very well. This server-centric organization is illustrated in Figure 5.1.

FIGURE 5.1

A server-centric organization keeps a separate list of resources at each server.

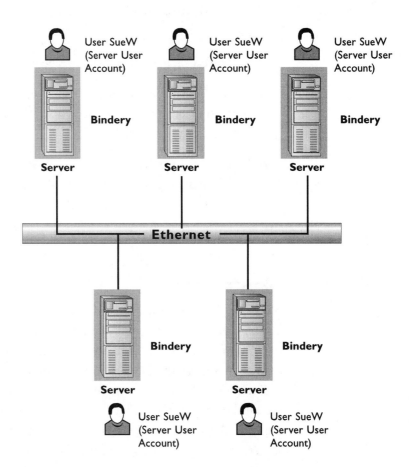

NetWare 4.11, on the other hand, uses a *network-centric* system. Each server on the network is part of a single, unified network. The network has only one list of resources. These resources may be on different servers, but the Directory lists them all, and you can access them all. This network-centric organization is shown in Figure 5.2.

FIGURE 5.2

A network-centric organization provides a global list of resources.

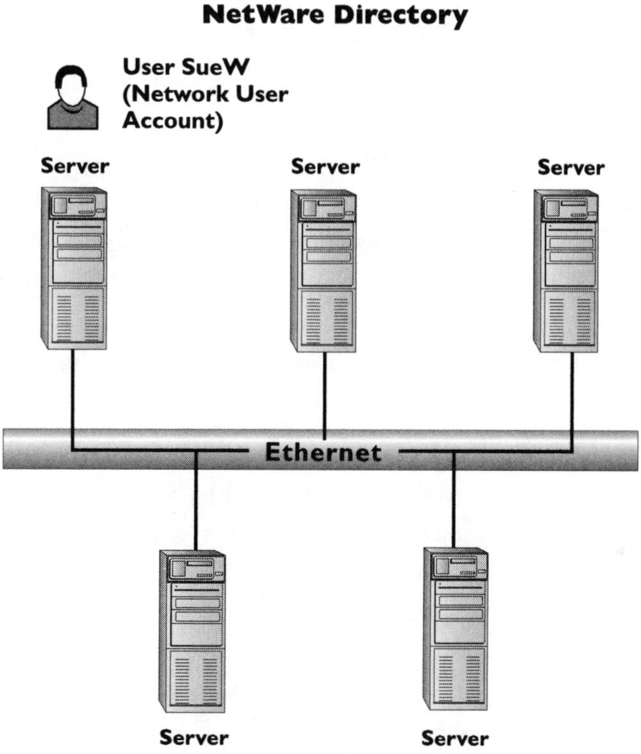

NetWare Directory

User SueW
(Network User Account)

In a network-centric system, you can access any resource just by knowing its name and where it fits into the Directory tree. If someone moves it to a different server, you shouldn't even notice the difference.

Best of all, you only need to create one account for each user. You can then give the user access to whichever resources he or she needs, no matter where that user is in the network.

NDS allows very versatile methods of administration. You can give a single, all-powerful administrator access to manage all of the objects in the network, or you can divide the Directory tree and assign an administrator for each branch. You can even create very specific administrators, who might have exciting titles such as "Phone number correctness verifier" or "Terminated employee account remover."

Organization

NDS stores information about each object in the Directory tree. The Directory tree is organized like an inverted tree. You can create separate limbs of the tree for each department, location, or workgroup within the company. This makes it easy to organize users and other objects into logical groups, rather than one big messy bindery.

Increased Security

NDS offers improved security by providing encrypted, single-login authentication. All this means is that the user logs in once for the entire network. The authentication, or password-checking, process uses *encrypted* versions of passwords, so it is impossible to "snoop" on people's passwords by detecting the data on the network cable.

The tree-like structure of NDS allows you to manage sophisticated security features using a simple graphical interface. Because you can control the entire network from a single workstation, you can easily monitor the network and make sure everything is secure, without flying to other locations or taking someone else's word for it.

Scalability and Interoperability

Although they're buzzwords in the computer industry and are thrown around constantly by computer magazines, *scalability* and *interoperability* do have meanings, and they do benefit your network.

Scalability means that NDS is constructed in a *modular* fashion (another buzzword). You can easily expand the network to include more resources and services. You can add users more easily with additive licensing (discussed in Chapter 2). Novell's Application Program Interface (API) allows programmers to make their own improvements and to add specialized objects to NDS.

Interoperability means that NDS is backward-compatible with previous Novell products, such as the bindery of NetWare 2 and NetWare 3. You can even manage these objects from within NDS. The NetWare Directory is also compatible with other Directory Services, particularly the X.500 standard, an international specification for network directories. NDS borrows much of its structure from the X.500 specification.

Fault Tolerance

NDS is a *distributed database*. This means that copies of the database, or portions of it, are stored on several servers throughout the network. Thus, the safety of your data doesn't depend on one particular server. If a server goes down, a replica (another copy) of the database on another server can take over. When the server is restored, the Directory information can once again be copied to that server.

WARNING
Fault tolerance applies to NDS data; it doesn't protect the data on your servers. Be sure to make regular backups. Many backup packages allow you to back up NDS data, which is also a good idea. You can never be too safe.

How the Directory Is Organized

In NDS, every resource on a network is represented by a record in the Directory database. This record is called an *object*. Objects exist for each type of resource, such as User objects, Printer objects, Server objects, and so on.

There are three basic types of objects in the Directory database:

- The [Root] object

- Container objects

- Leaf objects

A sampling of these objects is illustrated in Figure 5.3, and they are explained in the following sections.

FIGURE 5.3

NDS is organized into a [Root] object, container objects, and leaf objects.

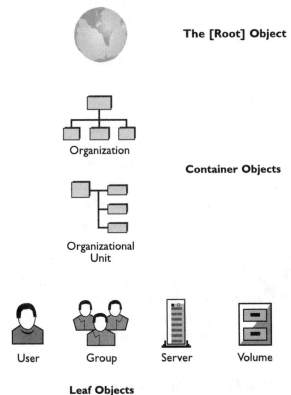

The [Root] Object

Organization

Container Objects

Organizational
Unit

User   Group   Server   Volume

Leaf Objects

The [Root] Object

As you might guess from its name, the *[Root] object* is at the top of the Directory's upside-down tree structure. There is only one [Root] object in the Directory. It is created when NDS is installed on the first server. You can't delete, rename, or move this object. The [Root] object is always referred to with brackets around its name.

Container Objects

A container object doesn't represent a network resource directly. Instead, it's used to organize other objects. Container objects can hold leaf objects (users and printers, for example). In addition, they can hold other container objects. This allows you to create resources in a very organized fashion.

The [Root] object is the ultimate container object; it contains every single object in the Directory tree. The other kinds of container objects are Country, Organization, and Organizational Unit objects.

Country   If you use them, Country objects go directly under the [Root] object. Country objects let you divide a multinational corporation into sections for each country. The name of the Country object must be a valid two-character abbreviation for a country.

The Country object is included as part of the X.500 standard, and that's where the two-letter abbreviations come from. For example, US represents the United States, FR is France, DE is Germany, and CH is Switzerland. Some of these abbreviations may seem odd, but they should be obvious if you happen to speak every language. (If you do, you could probably find a more profitable job than network administrator.)

Although the Country object is available in NDS, Novell doesn't recommend its use in most situations. It was included just because the X.500 standard needed it. X.500 actually includes another container object, the Locality object. NDS doesn't support this one at all, although it is included in the NetWare manuals. Locality objects may show up in a future version of NetWare.

Organization   The *Organization* object is used to divide the network into big pieces, such as a company, a university, or a department. The Directory tree must have at least one Organization object. Since most networks do not need to use Country objects, the Organization object is usually the first object beneath the [Root] object.

Some large corporations and governments might require multiple Organization objects, but the vast majority of companies use a single Organization object to hold the entire Directory tree. You can subdivide the Organization object with Organizational Units, or create leaf objects directly under the Organization if you wish.

Organizational Unit   The Organizational Unit object is where the network really gets organized. You can use several levels of Organizational Units to further divide the tree into categories. For example, one company could have different Organizational units to represent Accounting, Marketing, and Customer Service departments, as illustrated in Figure 5.4.

Leaf Objects

Leaf objects are the leaves of the Directory tree. They can't contain other objects. Leaf objects represent the network resources. They must be placed within either Organization or Organizational Unit objects. About 20 leaf objects are available. Here are the common ones:

- **User:** The User object represents a user on the network.

- **Group:** You can organize users into logical groups, called Group objects, so that they share the same rights.

- **Organizational Role:** This is an assignment that is given to a user. For example, an Organizational Role called "backup administrator" might be used for the person who runs a tape backup. You would assign the user who currently does the job to the Organizational Role. This would give that user whatever rights are needed to back up the server. If a different user was assigned to the task, you would simply switch that user to the Organizational Role. Organizational Roles are explained in Chapter 6.

FIGURE 5.4

Organizational Unit objects can be used to further divide the network's resources.

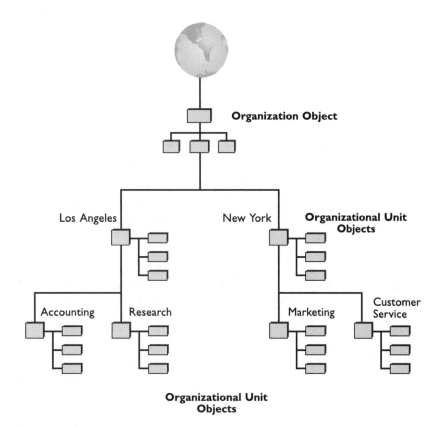

- **NetWare Server:** This object represents a NetWare 4.11 server.

- **Volume:** A Volume object represents a disk volume on a server. By browsing objects under a Volume object, you can look at the files and directories on the volume.

- **Profile:** You can use a Profile object to group users who require a similar login script. Login scripts are explained in Chapter 8.

- **Printer, Print Queue, Print Server**: These are used for network printing. Network printing is explained in Chapter 9.

- **DOS Application, Windows Application, Windows 95 Application**: These are used for NAM (NetWare Application Manager), the Windows-based menu system included with NetWare 4.11. This system is explained in Chapter 8.

Properties and Values

Each type of object in NDS has a list of *properties*. These are pieces of information about that type of object that can be stored. For example, a User object has properties such as Login Name, Full Name, Title, and Telephone Number. The information stored in a property is called the *value* of the property. For example, the value of the Title property might be "Vice President."

Not all properties make sense for all objects. It's unlikely that a Printer object will have a telephone number, for instance. Because of this, NDS has a different list of properties for each of the types of objects. However, the same types of objects have the same properties available. For example, all User objects have the same list of properties, and all Printer objects have the same properties list.

For each type of object, certain properties are *required*. For example, the required properties for a User object are Login Name and Last Name. Other properties of the User object, such as Telephone Number and Title, are optional. Nonetheless, you may find it useful to fill these out in order to identify and catalog the objects in your network.

Some properties can hold more than one value. For example, the Telephone Number property for a User object can hold multiple numbers for each user. This type of property is called a *multivalued* property. The majority of properties are the opposite; they are *single-value* properties, which can have only one value.

NetWare 4.11 includes utilities that let you work with properties and their values. The NLIST utility, for example, allows you to search for objects with a certain property value or to list certain properties, such as all users and their phone numbers.

It will be easier to search for resources on your network if you keep property values consistent. In planning your network, you should decide which properties you will use for objects and how to format their values.

The type of objects you can create and the list of properties for each one of them are defined in the *NDS schema*. This defines the basic structure of NDS and is installed on the server with NDS. The NetWare API allows programmers to *extend* the NDS schema. This makes it possible to add specialized types of objects or new properties for existing objects.

Referring to NDS Objects

You can access any object in the Directory if you know its name and its location in the tree. The next sections describe the different types of syntax you can use to refer to NDS objects and how to determine the name for each object.

Object Names

Each object in a Directory tree has an *object name*. NetWare 4.11 has a specific terminology for object naming. The object name is usually the most obvious name for the object; a user's object name is the login name, and a server's object name is the server name. The object name is also referred to as the object's *common name*.

The common name isn't enough to identify an object uniquely. NDS allows you to create Users or other objects with identical object names, as long as they are in different container objects. To completely identify the object, you also need to know where it is in the tree.

Understanding Context

An object's *context* is a description of the object's location in the tree. The context is the name of the object's parent object, which is the container object that it resides in. A context is described with a list of container objects, beginning with the furthest one from [Root]. For example, if the Organizational Unit IDAHO is under the Organization WESTERN in the Country US, the context for any leaf object under IDAHO is:

```
.IDAHO.WESTERN.US
```

NDS keeps track of your *current context*, or default context. This is usually the context that contains your User object. When you access a resource without specifying its full location, NetWare will look for it in the current context.

Full Distinguished Names

By combining an object's common name with its context, you can determine its *full distinguished name*. Since this name includes the name and location of the object, it is a unique name for the object. Although two objects can have the same common name, each has a unique distinguished name.

Distinguished names begin with a period and also use a period between each object's name. For example, if the User object JOHN is in the Organizational Unit MARKETING, which is in the Organization ABC, John's full distinguished name is:

```
.JOHN.MARKETING.ABC
```

Relative Distinguished Names

To avoid needing to specify all of the container objects over an object, you can use a *relative distinguished name,* or RDN. The RDN relies on your current context, and starts there instead of at [Root] to look for the object.

Remember the period that begins a full distinguished name? If you leave it out, the name is considered to be an RDN. The simplest example of using an RDN is when you access an object that is in your current context. For example, if your current context is .ACCT.PHILCO (the ACCT Organizational Unit under the PHILCO Organization) and you want to access a printer called PRINTER1 in the same context, you can simply specify its name as:

```
PRINTER1.
```

When an object is outside your current context, you can still use an RDN. Enter a period at the end of the RDN to move up a level in the Directory tree. For example, if you are in the .ACCT.PHILCO context and you wish to access a printer called PRINTER2 in the MKTG.PHILCO context, the RDN is:

```
PRINTER2.MKTG.
```

Typeless Names and Typeful Names

So far, we've been using *typeless* names. They include the names of objects but not the types of objects. For instance, in the distinguished name .SUE.PR.ACCT.WNC, we know that SUE is a common name, but we don't say whether PR, ACCT, and WNC are Organizations or Organizational Units. We can make an educated guess, and NetWare can too. These typeless names can be used in almost any situation where NetWare asks for an object's name.

Nevertheless, a more formal method of naming is possible: *typeful* naming. As the name implies, this kind of name includes the type for each object. The object types can include the following:

C	Country
O	Organization
OU	Organizational Unit
CN	Common Name

To make the typeful name, add the object type and an equal sign to each object. The typeful name for the user SUE mentioned above would be:

```
.CN=SUE.OU=PR.OU=ACCT.O=WNC
```

You should understand typeful names, because you will need to use them occasionally. For the vast majority of NDS tasks, however, the typeless name works fine, and it is much easier to type.

Connecting to the Network

To access the network, you will need to establish a connection to a server. This is accomplished by running *client software* at the workstation. Because DOS and Windows workstations are the most common clients, we refer to that type in the following discussion. Similar client software is used with OS/2 and Macintosh workstations, and is discussed in Chapter 13.

A workstation normally works as a standalone machine. The operating system provides access to the workstation's own resources, such as disk drives and printers. You can install network client software on the workstation to provide these same features for network resources, such as disk drives and printers.

Once the client software is running, network drives can act just like local drives, and network printers can act just like local printers. This allows any software—even applications that were never intended to run on a network—to be used with network resources.

The current client software for DOS, Windows, and Windows 95 is called Client 32. Client 32 was introduced in 1996 to replace the client software used by previous versions of NetWare (the NetWare Shell and the NetWare DOS Requester.) Client 32 provides the following benefits:

- Support for NDS.

- Background authentication through NDS.

- Support for Packet Burst Protocol and Large Internet Packets (LIP).

- Full 32-bit support for Windows 95, including login scripts and a graphical login utility.

- In Windows 95, you can configure client parameters with a simple graphical interface, rather than modifying a configuration file.

Microsoft includes a client for Novell networks with Windows 95; however, it does not fully support NDS. For all of these features, you will need to install Client 32.

Client 32 requires the following hardware and software components:

- DOS 5.0 or later, Windows 3.1, Windows for Workgroups, or Windows 95.

- A 386 or better processor.

- RAM: 6MB free under Windows 95; 5MB free under Windows 3.1 or DOS. Client 32 also requires approximately 6KB of conventional memory (below 640K).

- For DOS and Windows 3.1, a memory manager such as EMM386 is required. This ability is built into Windows 95.

- A network card is required; you should also have the driver software that was provided with the card, although a driver may be included with NetWare. Of course, the network card should be connected to the network cable.

We'll look at the components of Client 32 in detail after a discussion of the underlying network protocols.

Network Protocols

Your workstation communicates with the NetWare server through the use of *communications protocols*. A protocol is a set of rules for moving data across the network. In a sense, the protocol is the "language" used for communication on the network, and it is important that the client and the server speak the same language. The principal protocol used for NetWare workstation connections is IPX.

The IPX Protocol

The IPX (Internetwork Packet Exchange) protocol is the standard protocol for NetWare networks. IPX divides data into *packets*. These packets contain the data that is to be transmitted, along with addressing information that determines the workstation or server that the packet should be sent to. There are three main addresses used for NetWare networks:

- The *IPX external network number* is set for all servers in a network. Multiple servers in the same network use the same number. This number is used to transmit data across multiple networks.

- The *IPX internal network number* is set at each server. This number is used to locate the server on the network, and it must be unique.

- Each workstation has a *network address*, similar to the internal network number of the server. This address is used to locate a specific workstation on the network. Network addresses are usually set in hardware in the network card and usually cannot be changed.

The ODI Specification

ODI (Open Data-link Interface) is a specification used with the IPX protocol for DOS and Windows workstations on the network. ODI allows workstations or servers to use multiple protocols on the same network.

Each workstation can use a combination of protocols on the same network card. This allows your workstation to communicate with the NetWare 4.11 network and other systems, such as a mainframe computer or Internet connection, concurrently.

In addition, the ODI specification provides a modular way of installing network drivers. When a network adapter is replaced, only one piece of client software—the LAN card driver—needs to be changed.

Components of Client 32

Like most complex software, Client 32 actually includes several different components. Data passes through each of these components as it is sent from and received by a node on the network. The software components of Client 32 are NetWare Loadable Modules, or NLMs. The most important components of Client 32 include the following:

- LAN card driver (MLID)

- LSLC32.NLM (Link Support Layer)

- IPX.NLM (IPX protocol)

- CLIENT32.NLM (Main Client Software)

All of these components are loaded automatically by the Client 32 installation program. Figure 5.5 shows the interaction between these components. We will examine each component in detail in the following sections.

Network Card Driver (MLID)

The LAN driver is the software that communicates with the network card. After the data is sent across the network and received by the network card, this program converts it into a standard format that the NetWare client software understands. The type of LAN driver used for

FIGURE 5.5

Data passes through several components between the workstation and the server.

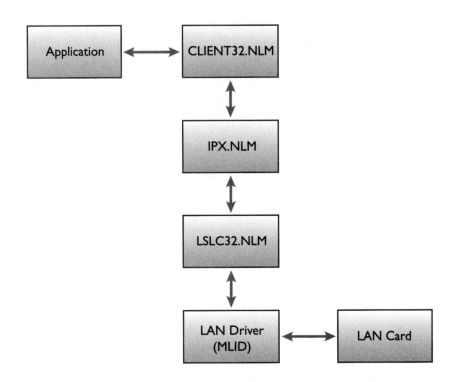

NetWare 4.11 is called an MLID, or Multiple Link Interface Driver. This is a term for any driver that supports the ODI specification.

The LAN driver is the only part of the client software that is not guaranteed to come with NetWare 4.11. Although NetWare provides drivers for common network cards, you should use the most current driver provided by the manufacturer of the network card. That driver should be included on a disk that came with the card. Client 32 LAN drivers are NLMs, but use the special extension LAN. For example, the driver for an NE-2000 card is CNE2000.LAN.

LSL (Link Support Layer)

The LSL handles the ODI protocol. This program communicates with the protocols, such as IPX, and makes the connection between these protocols and the network card. In Client 32, these functions are handled by the LSLC32.NLM module.

The IPX Protocol

The IPX.NLM program handles the IPX protocol. Packets are created and passed on to the LSL for processing by the network card. If you use other protocols, such as TCP/IP or AppleTalk, you load them along with (or instead of) IPX.

The NetWare Client

The final layer of communication is provided by the CLIENT32.NLM module. This module is responsible for communications with the operating system and application software on the workstation. Client 32 allows applications to use network resources, such as files and printers, as if they were local to the workstation.

Installing Client 32

Client 32 can be installed from diskettes, CD-ROM, or over the network. Follow these instructions to install Client 32 for Windows 95 on a workstation. For other platforms, refer to Chapter 13.

1. Insert the NetWare 4.11 Operating System CD or the first Client 32 diskette, or map a path to the installation directory on the network.

2. Run the SETUP program. For the CD installation, this will be D:\PRODUCTS\WIN95\IBM_ENU\SETUP.EXE. Replace D: with the letter of your CD-ROM drive.

3. You are now presented with a license agreement for Client 32. Click Yes to agree to the terms of the license and continue.

4. The main Client 32 installation dialog box is now displayed, as shown in Figure 5.6. Click Start to begin the installation process.

5. The installation program will now install the files for Client 32, and remove any previously installed client software. You may be required to insert your Windows 95 CD-ROM during this procedure.

FIGURE 5.6

Client 32 includes an
automated installation
program.

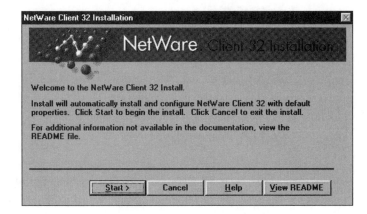

6. The final installation dialog box is displayed, as shown in Figure 5.7. Click Reboot to restart the computer with Client 32, or Customize to change the properties for Client 32.

FIGURE 5.7

This final screen is
displayed after the
Client 32 installation is
complete.

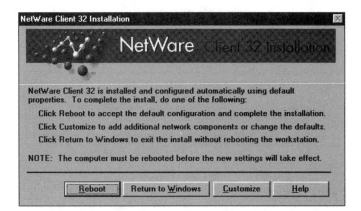

If you click Customize as the final step, you are shown the Client 32 Properties dialog box. You can also access this dialog box at any time from the Networking icon in the Control Panel. This dialog box includes several categories of properties you may need to modify.

Login and Logout

On a DOS workstation, once the client software is loaded, you can log in to the network by using the LOGIN command followed by your username. You must first switch to a network drive. For example, to switch to network drive F and log in as user SUE, use the commands:

```
F:

LOGIN SUE
```

The LOGIN program is called LOGIN.EXE, which is located in the LOGIN directory on the server. This directory is the only one you can access when you are not logged in. Once you type the LOGIN command, you will be asked to enter your password. If you type the password correctly, you will be allowed access to the network.

Before you can log in, you will need an account on the network, which means that a User object must be created in NDS. This process is explained in Chapter 6.

The opposite of LOGIN is LOGOUT. The LOGOUT command disconnects you from the network.

In Windows 3.1 or Windows 95, you can select the NetWare Login icon in the Start menu or Program Manager to log in. Depending on the installation of Client 32, this dialog box may be displayed automatically when you start the computer.

The NetWare File System

NetWare's *file system* is the system that manages disk storage on the network. NetWare uses files and directories similar to those used by DOS. In fact, the NetWare file system is specifically designed to be compatible with DOS clients.

Components of the File System

The NetWare file system organizes disk access into several components. These include volumes, directories and subdirectories, and files. The next sections describe each of the components.

Volumes

A *volume* is the major unit of storage in a NetWare server. This is similar to a disk drive under DOS. However, a NetWare volume isn't necessarily a single disk drive. There is a sophisticated relationship between disks and volumes. A single disk drive can be divided into multiple volumes. In addition, a volume can span more than one disk drive.

A volume is located on a NetWare server. Each server can have many separate volumes. NDS uses a Volume object to represent the volume. Volume objects are automatically given a name that combines the name of the server and the name of the volume. For example, the VOL1 volume on file server CENTRAL has the NDS common name of CENTRAL_VOL1. This allows several servers to have volumes with the same name, even if they reside in the same NDS container.

When you install NetWare 4.11, at least one volume must be created: the SYS volume. This volume contains the NetWare operating system files for the server's use. Each server must have a SYS volume. If you delete or rename the SYS volume, the server will become confused and refuse to start properly.

Directories and Subdirectories

A volume is divided into directories. These allow you to organize the file system in the same way that container objects organize the NDS tree. The structure of file system directories is similar to the NDS Directory. But don't let that fool you; they are two very different things.

Each file system directory can contain other directories or subdirectories. When you install a NetWare server, several directories are created automatically on the SYS volume:

- SYSTEM contains NetWare server utilities, configuration files, and NLMs. Most tasks performed on the file server use the SYSTEM directory.

- PUBLIC contains utilities that run from a workstation. By default, all users on the network have access to PUBLIC.

- MAIL is used to store configuration files for each user. This directory is used mainly for access by bindery-based clients.

- LOGIN contains the LOGIN.EXE utility and other files essential for the login process. By default, this is the one directory users can access before logging in.

- ETC contains sample files for the TCP/IP protocol. TCP/IP is an optional protocol that can be used to integrate NetWare with UNIX systems and the Internet.

A subdirectory is simply a directory inside another directory. The terms *directory* and *subdirectory* are often used interchangeably.

When you refer to a directory on a NetWare volume, the standard syntax uses a colon between the volume name and the directory, and a backslash (\) between directory and subdirectory names. For example, the SYSTEM directory on the SYS volume is referred to as SYS:SYSTEM. To refer to the DATA subdirectory under the PUBLIC directory on the VOL1 volume, use this syntax:

```
VOL1:PUBLIC\DATA
```

Because you can access multiple servers at the same time, you can specify the server name as well. Include the server name before the volume name, and use a backslash between the server name and the volume. As a final example, the CHECKS subdirectory under the AP subdirectory under the DATA directory on the VOL5 volume on the QED server (did you get all that?) is called:

```
QED\QED_VOL5:DATA\AP\CHECKS
```

Files

At last we come to the really useful item. The whole point of the file system is to store and manage files. A file can contain an application program, a word processor or spreadsheet document, a database, a graphic image—any item that can be stored on a disk.

NetWare 4.11 uses the DOS file name format to store files. Each file has an eight-character name and a three-character *extension*. The extension is usually used to specify the type of file, such as TXT for a text file or EXE for a DOS program. File names are usually written in all uppercase letters, but the file system is not case-sensitive; you can type names in either case.

Using Command-line Utilities

NetWare includes a wide variety of utilities. These are programs that you can use to manage the server and network resources.

Some of the utilities that you can use to manage the file system are *command-line* utilities. This means that they don't present you with a menu or ask you questions. You must specify all of the parameters for the command after the name of the command itself. You can run these utilities on any DOS workstation attached to the network.

Because the NetWare file system acts just like a DOS file system, you can also use any DOS or Windows utility to manage files on the server. However, most of these utilities don't support the additional features of NetWare's file system, such as security and file attributes.

You can display a list of available options for just about any NetWare utility by typing the name of the utility followed by /?. For example, type NDIR /? to see a list of the options for the NDIR utility.

The following are two command-line utilities that you might find useful for managing your network file system:

- **NDIR:** You are probably familiar with the DIR command in DOS. This is probably the most commonly used command. Its function is to list all of the files in a directory. The NDIR command is a special NetWare version. In addition to the list of files, the NDIR listing includes NetWare-specific information, such as the name of the owner of the file. Typing NDIR by itself will list all the files in the current directory. Advanced options allow you to view only certain files or to search an entire volume for a file.

- **NLIST:** When you need to see a list of items, you can use this utility. NLIST is a general-purpose utility for listing NDS objects. The NLIST VOLUME command lists Volume objects that are available in the Directory tree. You can also use the /D option to display additional information about a specific volume. PUBLIC contains utilities that run from a workstation. By default, all users on the network have access to PUBLIC.

Using Network and Search Drives

As we mentioned before, DOS doesn't really understand networks. The network client software adds networking capabilities to DOS, but it still isn't tightly integrated with NetWare. Most DOS applications don't allow you to refer to NetWare volumes by their volume names. This is where *mapped drives* come in.

DOS uses drive letters to refer to the drives on the workstation. Typically, drives A: and B: are floppy drives, and the workstation hard drive is usually the C: drive. If your workstation has several drives, they will use additional letters. The remaining letters are used for the two types of mapped drives: network drives and search drives.

Mapping Network Drives

When you map a network drive, you basically assign a drive letter, or *drive pointer*, to a certain volume and directory. Unless you change the defaults, drives A: through E: will be reserved for local drives, and the first available network drive will be F:.

You use the MAP command to map network drives. The MAP command line includes the drive letter to be used, an equal sign, and the network volume and directory to map the drive to. For example, the following command maps drive G: to the PUBLIC directory on the SYS: volume:

```
MAP G:=SYS:PUBLIC
```

By default, NetWare maps the next available drive (usually F:) to the SYS: volume. Before you log in, the LOGIN directory will be the only accessible directory on that drive.

Mapping Search Drives

NetWare uses a second kind of drive mapping called a *search drive*. Search drives point to directory paths that will be searched when you type a command name. For example, the MAP command itself is in the SYS:PUBLIC directory. A search drive that points to this directory allows MAP to be found when you type the command, no matter which directory you are in at the time.

Search drives are assigned both a number and a letter. The map command refers to them by number. You can map up to 16 search drives, numbered S1 through S16. When you type a command, NetWare looks for the command file in each of the search drives, beginning with S1. The first one that it finds is executed.

For example, the command to map the S1: search drive to the SYS:PUBLIC directory is:

```
MAP S1:=SYS:PUBLIC
```

Backing Up the File System

Of course, no matter how well you organize and manage your file system, there is always a risk of losing data due to hard drive crashes, user error, and other problems. While there's no sure way to prevent these types of problems, you can make sure that the data is safe by keeping a backup copy. Along with disk storage, your network should include a backup device—typically a tape drive. We'll start this section with a technical explanation of how NetWare 4.11 supports backups; we'll then explore the different types of backups and their advantages.

Although we're focusing on the NetWare 4.11 file system here, NetWare 4.11 provides you with the capability to back up NetWare 3.1x servers, client workstations, and the NDS database.

Understanding SMS

As we mentioned in Chapter 1, NetWare 4.11 includes built-in support for backup utilities. This system is called SMS, or Storage Management Services. SMS is not a backup program; rather, it is a system that allows backup software to work with the operating system to allow simple backups of data. SMS includes the following components:

- The *backup engine* is the actual backup application. Novell provides a simple application called SBACKUP.

- *Target Service Agents* (*TSAs*) are components that allow a particular device—or target—to be backed up.

TSAs are available for a wide variety of systems:

- TSA410.NLM supports backups of NetWare 4 server volumes.

- TSA312.NLM supports NetWare 3.12 server volume backups.

- TSA311.NLM supports NetWare 3.11 server volume backups.

- TSANDS.NLM supports backup and restore of the NDS database.

- TSADOS.NLM is a host TSA that runs on the server and supports backup of DOS workstations. You must also load the TSA executable on the workstation.

- TSAPROXY.NLM is called a host TSA that supports backup of OS/2, UNIX, Windows 95, and Macintosh workstations. Again, you must also load a workstation version of the TSA.

When you install client software for DOS, OS/2, Windows 95, or Macintosh, you have the option of installing the workstation TSA component. You can also install it at any time by running the client software installation program.

The SBACKUP Utility

NetWare 4.11 includes a simple backup application called SBACKUP. While not the best possible backup software, it is able to support all types of backups supported by SMS. SBACKUP runs on the server console; to use it, you'll need a tape drive or other backup device attached to the server. If your tape device is attached to a workstation, you can still use it with third-party backup software.

To start the SBACKUP utility, type **LOAD SBACKUP** at the server's console prompt. The main SBACKUP menu, shown in Figure 5.8, includes the following options:

- **Backup:** Backs up files or other data. Before you begin a backup, you must run the appropriate TSA on the server or workstation to be backed up.

- **Restore:** Reads data from a backup device. You can replace the data at its original location or choose a new location.

- **Verify:** Reads a backup tape to verify its integrity.

- **Log/error File Administration:** Allows you to view and delete the log files created by the SBACKUP utility.

- **Storage Device Administration:** Allows you to manage the list of backup devices available for use by SBACKUP.

- **Change Target:** Allows you to choose a volume, server, workstation, or other target to be backed up or restored to.

FIGURE 5.8

The SBACKUP utility is a simple backup application.

Choosing a Backup Strategy

Unlike many utilities, a backup program isn't very useful if you only run it occasionally. Instead, you should have a *backup strategy*. This strategy determines when you make backups, which type of backups you make, and the tapes you back up to. We will look at the types of backups and tape rotation you can include in your strategy in the following sections.

Full Backup   A full backup is the simplest type of backup, and the safest. It includes all the data on a volume or workstation. For servers with relatively small amounts of data storage, a regular full backup is the best solution. There are several advantages to this strategy:

- All files are available on each backup tape if you need to restore them.

- A minimum of configuration is required to run the backup.

There are disadvantages, however:

- The backup and restore process can be very slow with large amounts of data.

- If you have a large amount of data, a single backup tape may not be enough to hold a full backup.

Incremental Backup   An incremental backup strategy begins with a full backup at regular intervals—perhaps once a week. Backups that take place between the full backup store only the files that have changed since the previous backup.

For example, if you make a full backup on Monday, Tuesday's backup includes only the files changed since Monday, Wednesday's backup includes only the files changed since Tuesday, and so on. This system has a few advantages:

- Incremental backups are the quickest, as far as backup time is concerned.

- The latest changes are always available on the most recent tape.

However, there are some significant disadvantages to this strategy:

- Restoring a group of files can be time consuming, because they may be located on several different tapes.

- If you must restore all files, you will need all of the incremental tapes, along with the last full backup tape; if any tape is damaged or missing, you will not have an up-to-date backup of some files.

Differential Backup   The differential backup strategy is popular because it offers the best of both worlds; it is something of a compromise between the full and incremental strategies. In this system, again, you make a full backup regularly. Between full backups, you make differential backups, which include the information changed since the full backup.

For example, if you make a full backup on Monday, Tuesday's backup includes all files changed since Monday. Wednesday's backup also includes all files changed since Monday, and so on. The advantages of this strategy are clear:

- Backups are reasonably fast because a large amount of data usually remains unchanged.

- To restore a file, or even all files, you need a maximum of two tapes: the last full backup and the last incremental backup.

As you might have noticed, each successive differential backup will be larger and more time consuming than the one before. For a successful differential backup strategy, you should schedule full backups frequently enough so that the differential backups don't become inconvenient. This will depend on your users and how often data is changed on your volumes.

Tape Rotation   With any backup method, you need a number of tapes—a minimum of one for the regular full backup and one for each day of incremental or differential backups. However, you may want to add additional tapes to provide a regularly archived backup.

In deciding on a tape-rotation scheme, realize that backups have two purposes for most companies. While they are obviously useful in case of data loss or system problems, they can also be handy for accounting and auditing purposes.

For example, a company may need to run a report on the data from the end of the previous month or year. The company might have five tapes, labeled MON through FRI. MON is used for a full backup, and TUE through FRI for differential backups. To keep an archive, the company might have four MON tapes and use MON1 one week, MON2 the next week, and so on. This ensures that backups are available for the previous four weeks, along with the current backup.

Review

In this chapter, we had an overview of three fundamental areas of NetWare 4.11:

- NetWare Directory Services (NDS)

- Connecting to the Network

- The NetWare file system

NetWare Directory Services

NetWare 4.11 manages the network's resources through NetWare Directory Services, or NDS. Information about each of these resources is organized into a single database: the NetWare *Directory*. This database works for the entire network, rather than one particular server.

NDS offers many benefits, including ease of administration; a more manageable organization; increased security, scalability, and interoperability, and fault tolerance.

In NDS, every resource on a network is represented by a record in the Directory database. This record is called an *object*. Objects exist for each type of resource. There are three basic types of objects in the Directory database:

- The [Root] object

- Container objects (Country, Organization, Organizational Unit)

- Leaf objects (User, Printer, and so on)

Each type of object in NDS has a list of *properties*. These are pieces of information that can be stored about that type of object. The information stored in a property is called the *value* of the property. There is a separate list of properties for each type of NDS object.

NDS Object Naming

The following guidelines are used in naming NDS objects:

- Each object in an NDS tree has an *object name*. The object name is also referred to as the object's *common name*.

- An object's *context* is a description of the object's location in the tree.

- An object's *full distinguished name* is its common name and context.

- A *relative distinguished name* (RDN) provides a path to the object from the current context.

Client Connections

The client software runs on the workstation and establishes a connection to a server. The client software for DOS, Windows, and Windows 95 is called NetWare Client 32, which replaces the NetWare DOS Requester and the NetWare shell, used by previous versions of NetWare.

The workstation communicates with the server through the use of *communications protocols*. The principal protocol used for NetWare workstation connections is IPX (Internetwork Packet Exchange).

ODI (Open Data-link Interface) is a specification used with the IPX protocol for DOS workstations on the network. ODI allows workstations or servers to use multiple protocols on the same network. It also provides a modular way of installing network drivers.

Client 32 is composed of several key items:

- **LAN driver (MLID):** This is the software that communicates with the network card. After the data is sent across the network and received by the network card, this program converts it into a standard format that the NetWare client software understands. The type of LAN driver used for NetWare 4.11 is called an MLID (Multiple Link Interface Driver). LAN drivers have the extension LAN.

- **LSL (Link Support Layer):** This program (LSL32C.NLM) handles the ODI architecture. It communicates with the protocols, such as IPX, and makes the connection between these protocols and the network card.

- **IPX.NLM:** This program handles the IPX protocol. You can load other protocols, such as TCP/IP or AppleTalk, along with (or instead of) IPXODI.

- **CLIENT32.NLM:** This program is the actual client software, responsible for communications with the operating system and application software on the workstation.

From the workstation that has the client software loaded, you can log in to the network by using the LOGIN command followed by your username, after you switch to a network drive. The LOGIN program (LOGIN.EXE) is located in the LOGIN directory on the server. This directory is the only one you can access when you are not logged in. To disconnect from the network, use the LOGOUT command.

The File System

NetWare's *file system* manages disk storage on the network. NetWare uses files and directories, similar to those used by DOS. Components of the file system include the following:

- *Volumes* are the major unit of NetWare disk storage.

- *Directories* and *subdirectories* divide the volume.

- *Files* store data or applications within a directory.

In order to access a NetWare volume from DOS, you map a drive. Mapped drives include the following:

- *Network drives* are used to access volumes and directories.

- *Search drives* provide a list of possible locations for executable commands.

You should also choose a *backup strategy* for the file system and other data. NetWare 4.11 supports backups with the *Storage Management System*, or SMS. SMS includes two main components:

- TSAs (target service agents) allow various devices (targets) to be backed up.

- A *backup engine*, such as Novell's SBACKUP utility, performs the actual backup.

Your backup strategy should specify the types of backups used:

- A *full backup* backs up all data in each backup cycle.

- An *incremental backup* backs up data since the last full or incremental backup.

- A *differential backup* backs up data since the last full backup.

Finally, the backup strategy should include a plan for *tape rotation*, which specifies which tapes are used for which backups.

CNA Practice Test Questions

1. NetWare Directory Services (NDS):

   A. Stores information for each network resource

   B. Uses a tree-like structure

   C. Refers to each resource as an object

   D. All of the above

2. Which of the following is *not* a benefit of NDS?

   A. Better organization of resources

   B. Fault tolerance

   C. An efficient file system

   D. Increased security

3. The type of organization NDS uses is:

   A. Server-centric

   B. Network-centric

   C. Noncentralized

   D. Resource-centric

4. The three basic types of NDS objects are:

   A. Container, Leaf, [Root]

   B. Properties, Values, Objects

   C. Organization, Organizational Unit, Country

   D. Typeless, typeful, distinguished

5. The [Root] object:

A. Can be located anywhere in the Directory

B. Contains all objects in the Directory

C. Can be deleted when it is no longer needed

D. All of the above

6. Container objects include:

A. Country, Group, Organization

B. Organization, [Root], Group

C. Country, Organization, Organizational Unit

D. Organization and Group

7. Leaf objects include:

A. User, Group, Organization

B. User, Printer, Resource

C. User, Group, Printer

D. All container objects, plus User

8. NDS properties:

A. Are the same for all objects

B. Are used by container objects only

C. Are all optional

D. Can be assigned values

9. An object's name in its context is:

A. Its distinguished name

B. The relative distinguished name

C. Its common name

D. Its context name

10. An object's context is:

A. Any object in the same container

B. The container object it resides in

C. Its common name

D. The name of the Directory tree

11. A relative distinguished name (RDN)

A. Begins at the [Root] object

B. Begins at the current context

C. Begins with the first Organization object

D. Uses the default system context (DSC)

12. Which is an example of a *typeless* name?

A. CN=FRED.OU=ACCT.O=ORION

B. CN=FRED

C. FRED.ACCT.ORION

D. CN=FRED.ACCT.O=ORION

13. The protocol usually used with NetWare is:

   A. VLM

   B. IPXODI

   C. IPX

   D. TCP/IP

14. In which order does data flow through Client 32 components?

   A. CLIENT32, LSL, IPX, LAN driver

   B. LSL, IPX, LAN driver, CLIENT32

   C. IPX, LSL, CLIENT32, LAN driver

   D. LAN driver, LSL, IPX, CLIENT32

15. Which program represents the main NetWare Client?

   A. IPX.NLM

   B. CLIENT32.NLM

   C. LSLC32.NLM

   D. CNE2000.NLM

16. Until you log in, the only files you can access are:

   A. LOGIN.EXE and client software

   B. All files in the PUBLIC directory

   C. All files in the LOGIN directory

   D. All files on the SYS: volume

17. Which is the correct order of NetWare file system organization?

  A. Directory, file, volume

  B. Volume, directory, file

  C. File, volume, directory

  D. File, directory, NDS

18. The NDIR utility:

  A. Must be used in place of the DOS DIR command

  B. Lists files in the current directory

  C. Lists information about NDS objects

  D. All of the above

19. The NLIST utility:

  A. Can be used to list volumes or other NDS objects

  B. Displays a list of files in the current directory

  C. Is another name for NDIR

  D. Was used in NetWare 3.1x

20. Which is the correct syntax to map drive F: to the SYS:PUBLIC directory?

  A. MAP F: SYS\PUBLIC

  B. MAP SYS:PUBLIC /D=F

  C. MAP SYS:PUBLIC=F:

  D. MAP F:=SYS:PUBLIC

21. Which backup strategy takes the longest time to back up data?

    A. Incremental

    B. Differential

    C. Full

    D. Partial

22. Which backup strategy takes the longest time to restore data?

    A. Incremental

    B. Differential

    C. Full

    D. Partial

CHAPTER

6

How to Manage
Container and Leaf Objects

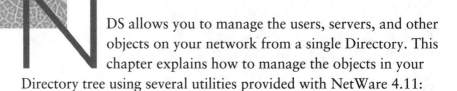

DS allows you to manage the users, servers, and other objects on your network from a single Directory. This chapter explains how to manage the objects in your Directory tree using several utilities provided with NetWare 4.11:

- NWADMIN (NetWare Administrator) is a Windows-based utility that allows you to browse through the objects in the tree and create, modify, and delete them. This utility also includes additional features to manage the file system and its security and to control partitioning and replicating.

- UIMPORT is a utility for creating multiple users automatically. We will also look at other methods of creating and managing multiple users, since you will probably use User objects more than any other NDS object.

- NETADMIN is a DOS-based alternative, similar to the SYSCON utility in NetWare 3.1*x*. You can manage the Directory and its objects with NETADMIN, but it doesn't include file system or partitioning features. For those features, you can use the FILER and PARTMGR utilities.

You should become familiar with these utilities, because you will use them in your career as a network administrator, and because you'll need a basic knowledge of them for the CNA tests. This chapter provides an overview of each utility and how to use them to create and manage NDS objects. The final section describes the NDS objects you will use most often.

Using NetWare Administrator

NetWare Administrator, also known as NWADMIN, is probably the most important utility in NetWare 4.11. You can manage all aspects of the network with NWADMIN. This includes users, security, printing, and even the file system. As a network administrator, you'll spend a lot of time using NWADMIN.

Since NWADMIN is a Windows-based utility, you need a version of Windows to run it. Here are your options:

- To run NWADMIN for Windows 3.1, 3.11, or Windows for Workgroups, use the file name NWADMN3X.EXE. In order to access NDS, you need to be running the latest version of the DOS and Windows client software.

- To run NWADMIN for Windows 95, use the file name NWADMN95.EXE. Be sure you are using Client 32 for Windows 95; other client software, such as the Microsoft client included with Windows 95, will not access NDS effectively.

- OS/2 2.1 or OS/2 Warp can run NWADMIN in a Windows session. However, the OS/2 Requester software doesn't give NDS access to Windows applications. A special option in the NetWare client software, VLMBOOT, provides a way around this.

- There is currently no version of NWADMIN for Macintosh or UNIX workstations. For this reason, you'll need at least one Windows machine on your network.

Running NetWare Administrator

Here are the steps to get started with NWADMIN:

1. Be sure you are running the correct client software and are logged into the network.

2. Choose Run from the Program Manager's File menu or the Windows 95 Start menu.

3. Type the name of the program to run, using the guidelines in the previous section. Because NWADMIN is in the PUBLIC directory, you should not need to specify a path if you have a search drive mapping for PUBLIC.

Since you will be running NWADMIN frequently, you may wish to create an icon or Start Menu entry for it in Windows. When NWADMIN starts, you will see a picture of the Directory tree and a standard Windows menu bar, as shown in the example in Figure 6.1.

FIGURE 6.1

NetWare Administrator is the most important utility in NetWare 4.11.

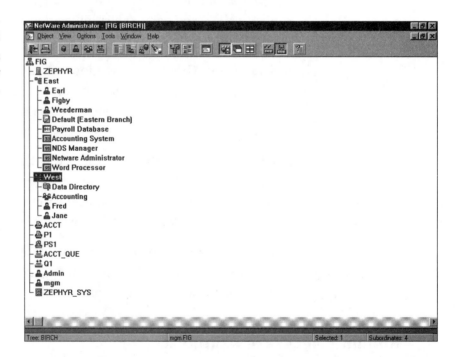

We will now take a guided tour of the options that NetWare Administrator makes available. If you have access to a NetWare 4.11 server, you might find it useful to try things out on your own Directory tree as you read.

The Object Menu

The Object menu, shown in Figure 6.2, allows you to create, rename, or delete an object; modify properties; and control object rights. Before you select an option from this menu, highlight the object you want to affect.

Instead of using the Object menu, you can click the right mouse button ("right-click") after highlighting the object. You will see a pop-up menu listing common commands that can be performed on that type of object. You can also double-click an object to go directly to the Details option.

FIGURE 6.2

The Object menu allows
you to perform functions
related to objects.

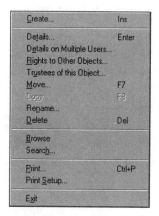

Creating an Object

The Create option allows you to create a new NDS object. Before selecting this option, highlight the container object that will hold the new object. The new object will be created in this container. After you select the Create option, NWADMIN presents a list of object types, as shown in Figure 6.3. Choose the type of object that you wish to create and click OK.

F I G U R E 6.3

Select the type of object
you wish to create.

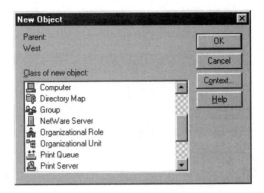

The next dialog box presents some properties of the object for you
to fill in. The properties listed will depend on the type of object. For
example, when you are creating a User object, the Create User dialog
box asks you to specify the Login Name and Last Name properties,
as shown in Figure 6.4. These are the values you are required to
specify to create the object.

F I G U R E 6.4

You are required to enter
certain properties to
create an object.

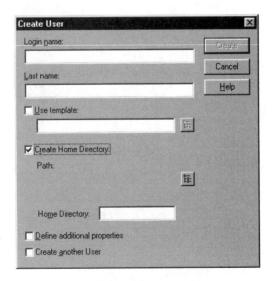

There are also four checkboxes in the Create User dialog box, which you can use to set additional options:

- **Use Template:** Copies the default settings for a new User object from a user template. User templates are explained later in this chapter.

- **Define Additional Properties:** Brings up the Details dialog box to allow you to set values for the other properties of the object.

- **Create Another User:** Returns you to the Create User dialog box after creating the user, so that you can create another user immediately.

- **Create Home Directory:** Sets up a home directory for the user and allows you to specify its location (the server, volume, and directory).

Viewing Property Values

The Details option on the Object menu allows you to view all of the properties of an object and specify or change their values. For example, when you highlight a User object and select Details, you will see the dialog box shown in Figure 6.5.

Properties are divided into categories. The categories and properties displayed depend on the type of object that is being modified. Use the buttons along the right side of the dialog box to select a category. You can then fill in the values of properties or change existing values.

Moving a Leaf Object

The Move option on the Object menu allows you to move a leaf object from one container to another. Select the leaf object that you wish to move, then select the Move option. Next, you will see the Move dialog box, shown in Figure 6.6. Browse the Directory to find the destination container object, and then select OK.

FIGURE 6.5

Choosing the Details option produces a dialog box that allows you to change properties of an object.

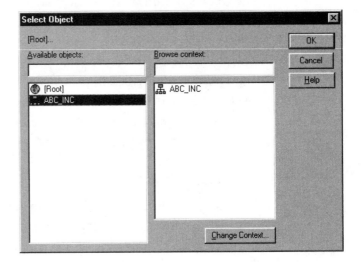

User : Fred

Identification

Login name:	Fred.West.FIG	
Given name:	Fred	
Last name:	Smith	
Full name:		
Generational qualifier:	Jr.	Middle initial:
Other name:		
Title:	Controller	
Description:		
Location:	Las Vegas	
Department:	Accounting	
Telephone:	555-5554	
Fax number:		

Identification
Environment
Login Restrictions
Password Restrictions
Login Time Restrictions
Network Address Restriction
Print Job Configuration
Login Script
Intruder Lockout
Rights to Files and Directories

OK   Cancel   Page Options...   Help

FIGURE 6.6

Select the container object to move the leaf object into.

Select Object

[Root]...

Available objects:

Browse context:

OK
Cancel
Help

[Root]
ABC_INC

ABC_INC

Change Context...

Although you can select the Move option for a container object, you won't be allowed to move the container objects using this menu option. You must use the NDS Manager utility, described in Part III of this book, to move container objects.

Deleting an Object

The Delete option of the Object menu allows you to delete an object. You can use this option to remove any leaf object or empty container object (you cannot delete a container object unless you first delete all of the objects within the container). After selecting Delete, you are prompted to confirm that you wish to delete the object.

Renaming an Object

The Rename option of the Object menu allows you to change an object's common name. After selecting Rename, type the new name for the object. The Rename dialog box also contains two options that you can control with checkboxes:

- **Save Old Name:** Adds the object's old name to the object's Other Names property. This allows you to track an object after renaming it.

- **Create Alias in Place of Renamed Container:** For container objects, check this box to create an Alias object with the old name of the container. This allows users to continue using the old name to refer to the object. Alias objects are discussed later in this chapter.

Searching for an Object

The Search command on the Object menu allows you to search the Directory tree for objects with certain property values. The options in the Search dialog box, shown in Figure 6.7, allow you to set specific parameters for the search.

FIGURE 6.7

The Search command
allows you to find objects
with certain property
values.

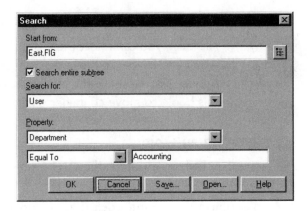

These options work as follows:

- **Start From:** Allows you to specify a container object where the search will begin. If the Search Entire Subtree box is checked, NWADMIN will search all the objects in child containers of the container; otherwise, the search will be confined to a single container. The Browse button to the right of the Start From value allows you to select a container from a graphic display of your Directory tree.

- **Search For:** Allows you to specify the type of object that will be searched for, such as User, Printer, or Server.

- **Property:** Specifies the property that you want to find. The list of properties here depends on the type of object you have selected.

Beneath the Property option are two boxes that allow you to specify a condition for the search. In the box on the left, you can choose whether to find properties that are Equal To or Not Equal To a value, or Present or Not Present. Enter the value to search for to the right of the condition. This will be used with the Equal To or Not Equal To option to match objects. For example, the options in Figure 6.7 will search for User objects with a value of Accounting in the Department property.

The Save button allows you to save the search parameters to a file. After you save the search parameters, you can later load those parameters using the Open button in the Search dialog box. In this way, you can keep a library of frequently used search criteria and quickly perform specific searches.

After the search is completed, you are presented with a list of objects that meet the criteria you selected. You can then perform any of the operations described in this chapter on those objects.

Printing the Directory Tree

The Print option on the Object menu allows you to print the listing of objects in the current context. You can use the Print Setup option on the Object menu to change options related to printing or to change the printer to be used.

The View Menu

NetWare Administrator's View menu, shown in Figure 6.8, provides several options that allow you to control the way in which NDS objects are displayed. These include setting the current context, choosing objects to include, sorting objects, and expanding or collapsing the display.

FIGURE 6.8

The View menu allows you to control the way in which NDS objects are viewed.

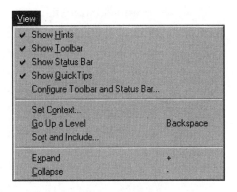

Choosing a Context

The Set Context command on the View menu allows you to change the current context. You can select any container object. This object will be the first shown in the NWADMIN window, and it will be the default context for further operations. The Set Context dialog box is shown in Figure 6.9.

FIGURE 6.9

The Set Context option allows you to view objects in a different context.

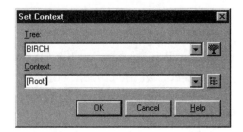

You can type the name of a container object in the New Context area, or click the button to the right of this space to browse the Directory tree and select a container object as the context.

Selectively Viewing and Sorting Objects

The Sort and Include option on the View menu allows you to specify which types of NDS objects are displayed in the NWADMIN window. The Sort and Include dialog box, shown in Figure 6.10, lists all of the possible object types. You can highlight the ones you wish to include in the display and move them to the Included Classes list. By default, all types are included.

Object types are listed in the order in which they will be displayed. To change this order, highlight an object type and use the up and down arrow buttons on the left side of the dialog box to move the object up and down in the list.

After making changes, click the OK button. The settings you have chosen will be used next time you run NWADMIN, until you change them again.

FIGURE 6.10

The Sort and Include
option allows you to
display only certain types
of objects.

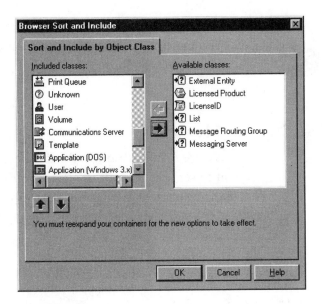

The sort options only change the order in which you view NDS
objects. They don't affect the NDS database itself.

Expanding and Collapsing Container Objects

The Expand and Collapse options on the View menu allow you to control whether objects under a container object are displayed. Highlight a
container object before selecting these commands. The Expand command displays all objects under the container. The Collapse command
displays only the container object.

If you make changes to the Include or Sort settings, you must
re-expand the containers in the display before the settings will take
effect. A quick way to do this is to highlight the object at the top of
the display (usually [Root]) and select Collapse, then select Expand.

You can also double-click a container object to expand it. Double-click again to collapse the display.

The Options Menu

NetWare Administrator's Options menu, shown in Figure 6.11, allows you to set several options related to the behavior of the program. Selecting each of the options toggles the option's status. A checkmark is displayed to the left of each activated option.

FIGURE 6.11

The Options menu allows you to control the behavior of NWADMIN.

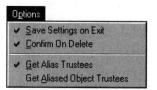

- **Save Settings on Exit:** Controls whether settings, including window sizes, current context, and view settings, are saved as the default when you exit the program.

- **Confirm on Delete:** Controls whether the confirmation dialog box is displayed when you delete an object. If this option is turned off, the object will be deleted immediately when you select Delete.

- **Get Alias Trustees** and **Get Aliased Object's Trustees:** Control how the Trustees of This Object command works with Alias objects (described later in this chapter). You can choose to see the trustee list of either the original object or the Alias object itself. Only one of these options can be selected.

The Tools Menu

NetWare Administrator's Tools menu provides options to open new NWADMIN windows and start other programs:

- **NDS Manager:** Opens the NDS Manager utility. This utility is used to control NDS partitioning and replicating (explained in Part III of this book).

- **NDS Browser:** Opens a new NWADMIN window, with the selected container object at the top. This allows you to examine objects within the container in a separate window.

- **Salvage:** Provides a method of restoring deleted files. The Salvage window, shown in Figure 6.12, lists the deleted files and allows you to salvage (restore) or purge (permanently remove) them.

FIGURE 6.12

The SALVAGE option allows you to restore deleted files.

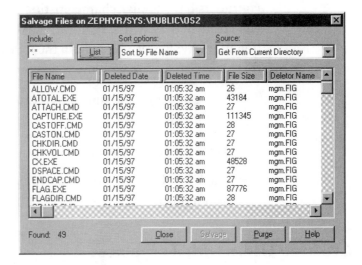

- **Remote Console:** Runs the Remote Console (RCONSOLE) utility in a window. (The first screen you see will remind you that RCONSOLE is not always reliable when it's run under Windows.)

- **Install License:** Allows you to manage application licenses using NLS (NetWare Licensing Services).

- **File Migration** and **DS Migrate:** These options are for migrating file system and NDS information to a new server. You will use these features in Chapter 17.

- **Print Services Quick Setup:** A feature to quickly set up printers and other important objects for printing. See Chapter 9 for details on this feature.

Creating and Managing Multiple Users

No matter what your organization, chances are that many of your users have similar characteristics. For example, all of the users you create in the EAST Organizational Unit might have the same Location property: Eastern Branch. In the following sections we'll introduce three ways of dealing with multiple users at once:

- You can define a template to create users with similar characteristics.

- You can modify multiple users at once using NWADMIN.

- The UIMPORT utility allows you to create users using an automated process.

Creating Users with Templates

Most of the time when you create a user, you'll use a similar set of properties. You can easily create more than one user with similar properties using a *user template.* This is a special type of object that is used to assign default properties for new User objects that you create. The users remain associated with the template, and you can later use it to modify their properties.

You can create as many Template objects as you need. To create a user template, choose Template from the list of object types after choosing the Create option. You can then specify properties for the template. The properties of the Template object are similar to those of a User object, as shown in Figure 6.13.

FIGURE 6.13

Property values entered for the user template can be copied to new User objects you create.

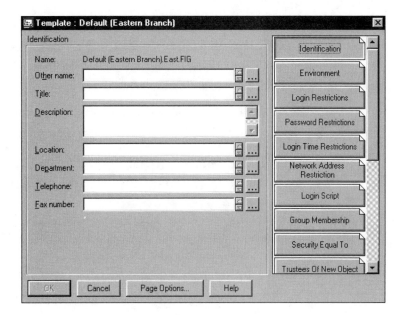

To create a user by using the template, follow the usual procedure but check the Use Template box in the Create User dialog box and specify the template to use. Any users you create become associated with the Template object, and appear in its Members of Template property. You can modify all of the member users of a template, as described in the next section.

Modifying the Template's properties does not have an effect on existing users, whether members of the template or not. This only affects new users created after the change. To modify the existing members of a template, use the Details on Multiple Users option, described below.

Managing Multiple Users

The latest version of NWADMIN includes a Details on Multiple Users option. This option allows you to modify a group of users at once. You can either specify certain users, or choose an object associated with the users:

- To select multiple users, hold down the Ctrl key and click on them, or press Shift to select a range of users.

- Highlight an Organization, Organizational Unit, Group, or Template object to modify all of the users currently associated with the object.

Once you've made your selection, choose the Details on Multiple Users option from the Object menu. A modified version of the User object properties dialog box is displayed. Any properties you change in this dialog box will affect all of the users you selected.

Changing properties for a large number of users may take some time. NWADMIN will warn you of this and allow you to abort the process.

Creating Users with UIMPORT

Suppose you need to create users automatically on a regular basis, or create users based on a database of users you already have in an application. You can use the DOS-based UIMPORT utility to create users based on a database file. We'll look at this process in detail in the sections below.

Creating the Database File

First, you'll need a database of user information. The database can include as much or as little information as you need. You can create this database using a database or spreadsheet program. You may already have a database you wish to use, such as a listing of mainframe users or a payroll database.

In order to use the database with UIMPORT, you will need to export it to an ASCII file. Follow your application's instructions to create a comma-delimited ASCII file. For example, a file that includes last names, first names, department names, and phone numbers might look like this:

```
PUBLIC, JANE Q.,ACCOUNTING,555-1234

DOE, JOHN, MARKETING,555-1235

TILLMAN, HENRY J., COMPUTER ROOM, 555-1255
```

Creating the Control File

Once you have a comma-delimited database, you need to create a *control file*. This is an ASCII file that specifies the fields used in the database file and the method of importing them. You can also specify the NDS context for the new users in this file. If you don't specify the context, users will be created in your current context.

Here's a simple example of a control file that would work with the data file example above:

```
Import control

     Name context=.acct.abc_inc

     Create home directory=n

Fields

     Last name

     Given name
```

Department

Phone

There are many other keywords you can use in control files. For details on the syntax, see the Novell documentation. Here are some highlights:

- Use the IMPORT MODE=R option in the Import control section to delete users instead of creating them.

- Use the keyword Skip to skip one of the fields in the data file.

Performing the Import

If you have a valid database file and control file, you're ready to perform the import. Copy both files to the same directory. Start a DOS session, and switch to that directory. In this example, the control file is called USERS.CTL and the data file is called USERS.DAT. Simply type UIMPORT followed by the control file name and data file name:

```
UIMPORT USERS.CTL USERS.DAT
```

You will be notified of any errors after UIMPORT has finished. Once the users have been created, you can easily define additional properties using the method described in "Managing Multiple Users" earlier in this chapter.

NETADMIN: Managing NDS Under DOS

NETADMIN is NetWare's DOS-based utility for managing network objects. This program provides most of the same features as NetWare Administrator (NWADMIN). NETADMIN can be useful on DOS-only machines or for users who prefer to use DOS utilities. It is in the SYS:PUBLIC directory on the file server.

You run NETADMIN by typing **NETADMIN** at the DOS prompt. NETADMIN's main screen is shown in Figure 6.14.

FIGURE 6.14

NETADMIN allows you to manage NDS objects in a DOS environment.

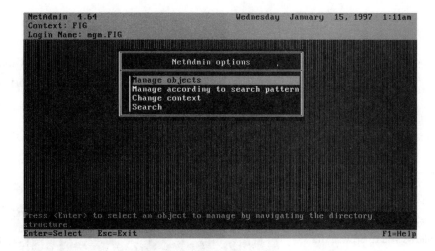

The following sections explain how to manage objects with NETADMIN. You will find that most of the options are similar to their counterparts in NetWare Administrator.

NWADMIN should run on just about any version of DOS, but you need the latest DOS client software, the DOS Requester, to provide access to NDS.

The Main Menu

The main NETADMIN menu offers the following options:

- **Manage Objects:** Lists objects in the Directory tree and allows you to modify, delete, rename, and move them.

- **Manage According to Search Pattern:** Allows you to enter a pattern to search for, and then lists only objects that match the pattern.

- **Change Context:** Changes your current context.

- **Search:** Allows you to search for a specific type of object or for objects with certain property values.

The Manage Objects option takes you to a Directory tree display, the Object, Class screen, as shown in the example in Figure 6.15. From this screen, you can browse the tree. Press ↵ on a container object to see the objects in the container. When you find the object you want to manage, select it. Then you can perform any of the actions described in the next sections.

FIGURE 6.15

The Manage Objects function of NETADMIN allows you to browse the Directory tree.

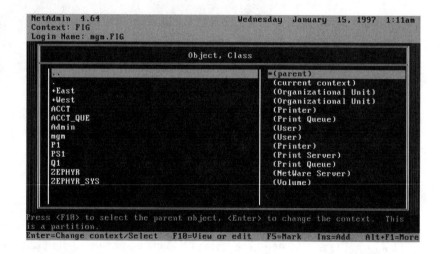

Creating an Object

You can create a new NDS object from NETADMIN's Directory tree display. Follow these steps:

1. Type **NETADMIN** at the DOS prompt.

2. Choose Manage Objects from the main menu.

3. On the Object, Class screen, highlight the container object in which you want to create the new object and press ↵ to change the context.

4. Press Insert. You are asked to choose the type of object to create, as shown in Figure 6.16.

FIGURE 6.16

The Select Object dialog box allows you to select the type of object to create.

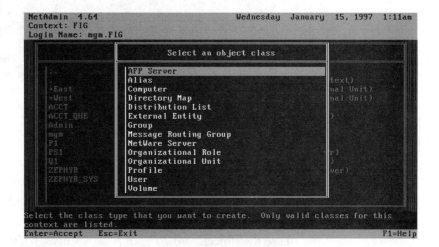

5. Select the type of object to create and press ↵. You are presented with a screen that allows you to enter the required properties for the object. The properties that are required depend on the type of object being created. For example, for a new User object, you must enter the Login Name and Last Name properties, as shown in Figure 6.17.

6. After you have entered the object's name and other information, press F10 to create the object.

FIGURE 6.17

Enter the user's login name and other information to create a User object.

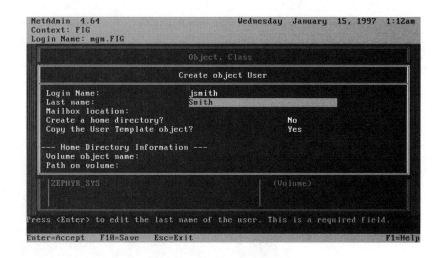

Managing an Object

You can press F10 on any object in the Directory tree display to manage the object. This brings up the Actions menu, shown in Figure 6.18. From this menu, you can change the object's properties; delete, rename or move the object; and control NDS security for the object. These actions are described in the following sections.

FIGURE 6.18

The Actions menu allows you to manage an object or its properties.

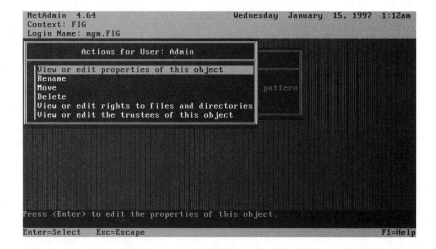

Modifying Property Values

To modify an object's properties, select View or Edit Properties of This Object from the Actions menu. The next menu lists property categories for the type of object you selected. The property categories for a User object are shown in Figure 6.19.

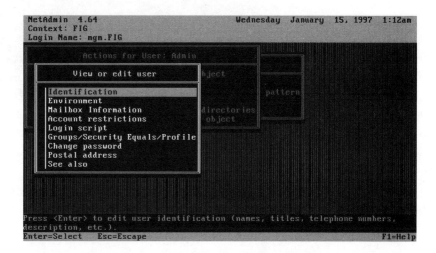

FIGURE 6.19

To change object properties, select the category of properties to manage.

Press ↵ while highlighting the category of properties you wish to modify. NETADMIN displays a list of properties in the category and their current values. You can change any of these values by typing a new value and pressing ↵. After you have made your changes, press F10 and then Esc to save the changes and exit.

Renaming an Object

Select Rename from the Actions menu to rename the object. You will see the screen shown in Figure 6.20.

Enter the new name for the object in the first blank. Answer Yes or No to save the old name. If you select Yes, NETADMIN will store the object's old name in the object's Other Names property.

FIGURE 6.20

Enter the new name for
the object.

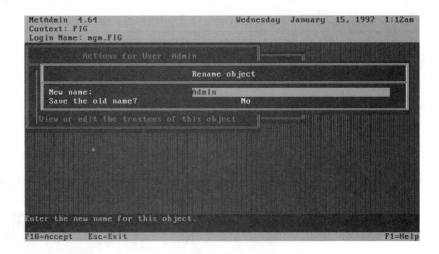

Deleting an Object

Select Delete from the Actions menu to delete the object. You will be asked to confirm the action by selecting Yes or No. After you select Yes and press ↵, the object is deleted from the Directory.

Moving a Leaf Object

You can move a leaf object to a new context by selecting Move from the Actions menu. You will see the screen shown in Figure 6.21.

FIGURE 6.21

To move an object, enter
a new context to move
the object into.

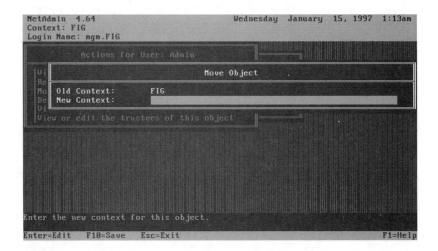

The object's current context is shown on the first line. Enter the new context for the object on the second line. This option does not work with container objects; it moves leaf objects only.

Types of Leaf Objects

Now that you know how to manage the objects in the Directory, we'll take a look at the types of leaf objects available for your Directory tree. There are actually about 25 leaf objects available in NDS. The following are the ones you'll need to understand for the Basic Administration test:

User	Represents a user on the network.
Group	Represents a set of users who share the same rights.
Organizational Role	Represents a role, or job, assigned to one or more users.
NetWare Server	Represents a NetWare 4.11 server.
Volume	Represents a volume (disk area) on a server.
Alias	Serves as a pointer to another object in the Directory.
Profile	Provides a way to group users who require a similar login script.
Directory Map	Points to a directory in the file system.
Printer	Represents a network printer.
Print Queue	Represents a network print queue.
Print Server	Represents a network print server.

You can create some of these objects with NWADMIN or NETADMIN. Others are created automatically and can't be changed, but you can examine and modify their properties.

In the next sections, we'll take a closer look at each of these objects and how to manage them. The exceptions are the Printer, Print Queue, and Print Server objects. These are used for network printing, which is the subject of Chapter 9.

The NDS container objects (Country, Organization, and Organizational Unit) are described in Chapter 5.

User Objects

Each user who needs to access the network must have a User object. When you create the User object, you specify the login name and last name for the user. After that, the user is ready to log in to the network. If necessary, you can give the user rights to files, directories, or other NDS objects.

As explained earlier in the chapter, you can create any number of Template objects, which can be used to create or manage multiple users.

Group Objects

When you create multiple users in a container object, they form a *natural group*—they are automatically given rights based on the container object. The Group object lets you do the same thing for a list of User objects, whether they're in the same container or not. This presents two possibilities:

- You can choose only some of the users in a container.

- You can choose users from multiple containers.

You can create a Group object in any container. After you create it, you can add users to it by using a special property of the Group object: the Member List. You can choose User objects in the current container or in other containers. These users are called the *members* of the group. A User object can be a member of more than one group.

The Group object is used for security and also is useful in login scripts (to assign drive mappings, printer queues, and so on). Any member of a group will receive the same rights that the Group object has. We'll talk more about security in Chapter 7.

Organizational Roles

The Organizational Role object is similar to a Group. It is usually used to assign a role, or job, to a particular user. This user is called the *occupant* of the Organizational Role. An Organizational Role can have more than one occupant.

Using Organizational Roles makes it easier to manage a network in a changing company. If you assign rights to users individually, you will need to do so any time a new person takes the job. Thanks to the Organizational Role object, the process is simple. You can just add a new occupant and remove the old one.

An important use of Organizational Roles is in assigning administrators—users who have the right to manage an area of the Directory tree or file system. The various types of administrators you can set up for your network are explained in Chapter 7.

The NetWare Server Object

The Server object is used to represent a server on the network. You cannot create this type of object; it is automatically created when a server is installed. You should not need to change the properties of the Server object.

Be careful, you *can* delete the Server object. Although this won't destroy the server or the data on it, it will make it inaccessible through NDS. You should do this only if you want to remove the server from the network.

The Volume Object

When you install the server, a Volume object is created for each disk volume on the server. You cannot create a Volume object yourself. Like the Server object, the Volume object should not be deleted unless the volume is no longer in use.

Although the Volume object is not a container object, you can "expand" it like a container object in NWADMIN. Under the Volume object you will find a list of directories on the volume. You can browse through the directories of the file system in the same way that you can view NDS objects. This is how you control security in the file system. You can also do routine file management tasks, such as creating new directories and deleting and renaming files.

Using Alias Objects

You've seen the word *alias* on wanted posters, and the Alias NDS object has basically the same purpose: it's another name for an object. However, a criminal uses an alias to avoid being found; NDS aliases are usually used to help users find the object.

You can create an Alias object yourself. The main use for this is to make a resource, such as a printer, in one container available to users in another container. For example, users in the CACTI Organizational Unit might need to access a printer in the MKTG Organizational Unit. You can create an Alias object for the printer in the ACCT container. To the users, it's just another available printer. They can access it without specifying a different container.

In addition, NWADMIN will automatically create Alias objects to help users find an object that has been moved or renamed. When you move or rename an object, you can check the Create Alias in Place checkbox. This will create a pointer from the old object to the new object.

Using Profile Objects

Each user in NDS has a login script, which is a series of commands that are executed each time the user logs in. The Profile object has its own login script. Assigning users to a Profile object provides an easy way to give them all the same login script.

Profile objects and their use with login scripts are discussed in Chapter 8.

Directory Map Objects

The Directory Map object is a special object that points to a directory in the file system. This allows you to simplify MAP commands and to make it easier to maintain the system when an application or data directory is moved.

When you create a Directory Map object, you set the Directory Path property to the path that the Directory Map object will point to. You will need to find the Volume object in the NDS tree first.

As an example, suppose you created a Directory Map called WP to point to the directory that you used for word processing files, SYS:APPS\WP. Users who wish to map a drive to that directory could simply type a MAP command like this:

```
MAP F:=WP
```

A more important benefit of using a Directory Map object is the work it can save you when you reorganize your directories. For example, suppose that you moved word processing files to a different volume to make more space available on the SYS: volume. The new location is VOL2:APPS\WP. Rather than changing all the login scripts to point to the new directory, and telling everyone about the change, you can simply point the Directory Map to the new location. Once you've done that, users could use the same MAP command to reach the new directory.

Review

NDS allows you to manage all of the users, servers, and other objects on your network from a single Directory tree. In this chapter, you learned the details of managing objects using two utilities: NWADMIN (a Microsoft Windows-based utility) and NETADMIN (a DOS-based utility). This chapter also provided descriptions of the commonly used NDS objects.

NWADMIN

With NWADMIN you can browse through the objects in the tree and manage them. You can run NWADMIN by choosing Run from the Windows Program Manager's File menu. NWADMIN's menus offer options for managing and viewing information about your network:

- The Object menu allows you to create, rename, or delete an object; modify properties; and control object rights.

- The View menu allows you to control the way in which NDS objects are displayed, including setting the current context, choosing objects to include, sorting objects, and expanding or collapsing the display.

- The Options menu allows you to set several options related to the behavior of the NWADMIN program.

- The Tools menu provides options to open new NWADMIN windows and start other programs.

NETADMIN

The NETADMIN program provides most of the same features as NetWare Administrator (NWADMIN). To run this utility, type NETADMIN at the DOS prompt.

To create a new object, choose Manage Objects from the main menu. On the Object, Class screen, highlight the container object in which you want to create the new object and press Insert. Choose the type of object to create and fill in the necessary properties.

To manage an existing object, press F10 on the object in the Object, Class screen. This brings up the Actions menu. From this menu, you can change the object's properties; delete, rename, or move the object; and control NDS security for the object.

Commonly Used Leaf Objects

The leaf objects you will use most often include the following:

- User object, which represents a user on the network. You must create a User object for anyone who needs to log in to the network.

- Group object, which allows you to organize users into logical groups that share the same rights.

- Organizational Role object, which is an assignment or "job" given to a user. You can change the occupant of the Organizational Role to give the rights to a new user.

- NetWare Server object, which represents a NetWare 4.11 server. It is created automatically when the server is installed.

- Volume object, which represents a volume (disk area) on a server. This object is created automatically when the server containing the volume is installed.

- Alias object, which is a pointer to another object in the Directory. This is used to make an object accessible to users in a different container and as a pointer from the old name or location of an object to the new one.

- Profile object, which you can use to group users who require a similar login script.

- Directory Map object, which points to a directory in the file system. This object allows MAP commands to be simplified and makes it easy to move directories without updating MAP commands in login scripts.

- Printer, Print Queue, and Print Server objects, which are used for network printing.

CNA Practice Test Questions

1. The two utilities used to manage NDS objects are:

A. NetWare Administrator and NWADMIN

B. NETADMIN and NetWare Administrator

C. SYSCON and NETADMIN

D. NDSADMIN and NWMANAGE

2. The Create function in NWADMIN is found under:

A. The File menu

B. The Function menu

C. The Actions menu

D. The Object menu

3. The required properties when creating a User object are:

A. Login name and address

B. First name and last name

C. Login name and last name

D. Network address and first name

4. A user template:

A. Is created for each user

B. Specifies defaults for new User objects

C. Lets you change all User objects at once

D. Lets you control access rights

5. The menu item used to display property values is:

A. Properties

B. Values

C. Attributes

D. Details

6. The Move option can move which types of objects?

A. User, Server, and Printer

B. Container objects only

C. Leaf objects only

D. User objects only

7. NETADMIN can be used to manage:

   A. User objects only

   B. Only the basic NDS objects

   C. All NDS objects

   D. Bindery objects

8. The Group object can group users:

   A. In the same container only

   B. In different containers only

   C. In the same or different containers

   D. In the [Root] container only

9. To assign a user to an Organizational Role, you use the:

   A. User's Role property

   B. Organizational Role's Member property

   C. User's Profile property

   D. Organizational Role's Occupant property

10. The NetWare Server object:

   A. Can be created when you wish to install a new server

   B. Is created automatically when the server is installed

   C. Is deleted automatically when the server is removed

   D. Can be used to add logins to the server

11. The Alias object:

    A. Represents, or points to, another object

    B. Is created whenever an object is deleted

    C. Can be used instead of the User object

    D. All of the above

12. Which is the correct MAP command for the Directory Map DATA?

    A. MAP F:=DATA:

    B. MAP F:=DATA.MAP

    C. MAP F:=DATA

    D. MAP F: DATA /DM

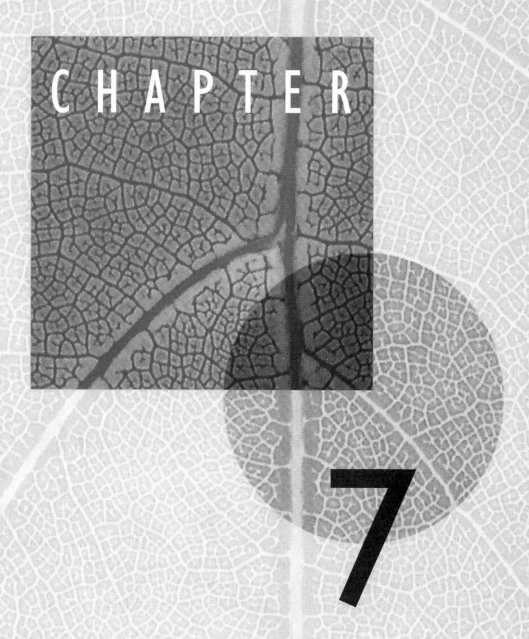

CHAPTER

7

How to Use NetWare Security

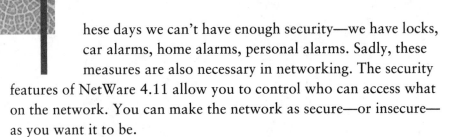

These days we can't have enough security—we have locks, car alarms, home alarms, personal alarms. Sadly, these measures are also necessary in networking. The security features of NetWare 4.11 allow you to control who can access what on the network. You can make the network as secure—or insecure—as you want it to be.

NetWare 4.11 provides several types of security:

- *Login security* allows users to connect to the network using passwords.

- *File system security* controls access to the file system.

- *NDS security* controls access to NDS objects.

- *Server security* controls access to the file server itself. We'll examine this type of security in Chapter 10.

- *Network Printing security* controls access to network printers. We'll examine printing in Chapter 9.

All of these types of security have their uses. We'll begin this chapter with a look at login security, then introduce the concept of trustees, which applies to both file system and NDS security. We'll then examine file system security and NDS security in detail.

Using Login Security

The first type of security a user encounters when accessing the network is *login security*. Although a workstation is connected to the network, the user has virtually no access to the network's resources until they successfully log in. We examined the login process and the LOGIN command in Chapter 5.

You define a user's login name and password as part of the User object. We looked at the basics of creating a User object in Chapter 6. Here we will examine the technical side of the login process and take a look at the properties of the User object that affect login security.

The Login Process

From a user's point of view, the login process is simple, but behind the scenes, it's actually more complex. While NetWare 3.1*x* and earlier versions required a separate login for each server on the network, NetWare 4.11 and NDS allow you to use a single login to access the entire Directory tree, and all servers within it. The process that NetWare uses to accomplish this is called authentication.

When you enter your username and password, NetWare does not send the password across the network for authentication; this would be a security risk. Instead, the username, password, workstation, and other vital details are encrypted to form a unique *user code*. The same process is performed at the authenticating server, and if the codes match, the user is given access.

Along with preventing password snooping, this process also ensures that accurate information is being received, and that the workstation, network address, and other data have not been tampered with. This ensures that the login process is secure—provided users choose effective passwords and don't reveal them.

Restricting User Access

Several of the property categories of a User object are labeled as *restrictions*. These are various categories of items you can control to keep the network secure. For example, you can restrict the number of times a user can log in at once, the workstations the user can log in from, or the time of day the user is allowed to log in. The following categories of restrictions are available:

- Login Restrictions allows you to disable the account entirely, make it expire on a certain date, or limit the number of concurrent logins for the user. Figure 7.1 shows this property category displayed in the NWADMIN utility.

FIGURE 7.1

Login Restrictions allow you to control account expiration and other features.

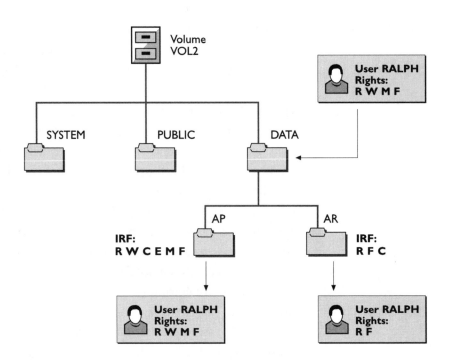

■ Password Restrictions includes a variety of options dealing with passwords. You can specify whether the user can change passwords, how often the user will be required to change the password, and how many grace logins are allowed with the old password once a change is required. This property category is shown in Figure 7.2.

FIGURE 7.2

Password Restrictions
allow you to control the
user's password features.

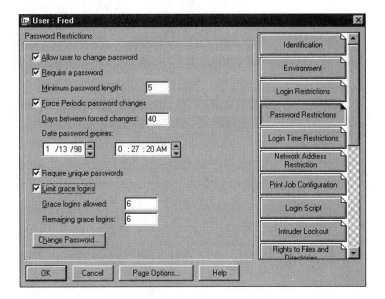

■ Login Time Restrictions controls the times and days the user is allowed access to the network. For example, in Figure 7.3, the user's access has been restricted to Monday through Friday from 8:00 a.m. to 6:00 p.m.

■ Finally, Network Address Restrictions allows you to create a list of workstation addresses the user is allowed access from. This allows you to limit the user to a single workstation or a particular group of workstations.

FIGURE 7.3

Login Time Restrictions allows you to specify the days and times the user can log in.

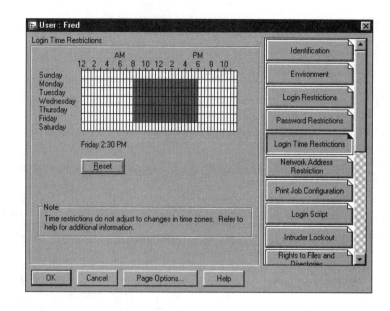

Detecting Intruders

NetWare uses the term *intruder* to refer to anyone who attempts to log in using an invalid password, and is able to quickly lock the account when such an intruder is detected. Of course, users occasionally make mistakes, so you can configure the system to be lenient. You can control this feature from the Intruder Detection property category of an Organization or Organizational Unit object. These properties are shown in Figure 7.4.

You can specify a number of login attempts that will be allowed before the account is locked. You can also specify a reset interval, which will unlock the account if a certain time elapses after the intruder detection. If a user's account is locked and is not reset automatically, you can unlock it from the Intruder Lockout property category of the User object.

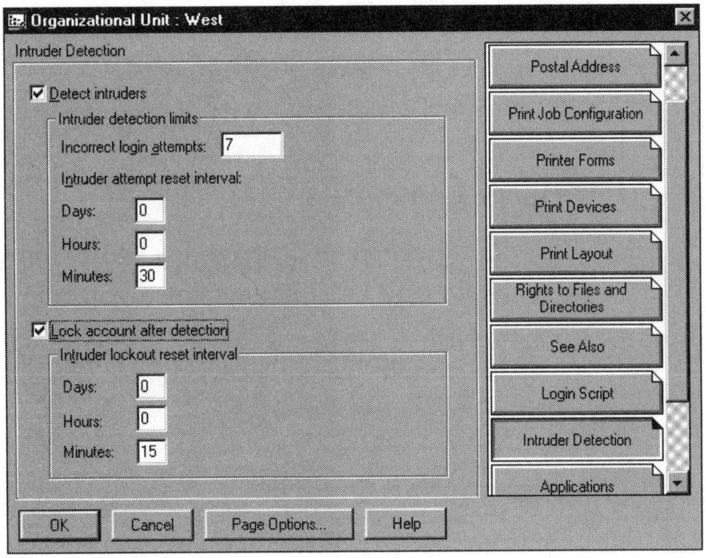

FIGURE 7.4

Intruder Detection
options allow you to
control what happens
when an invalid password
is used.

Trustees

File system security and NDS Security are similar, and both center around *trustees*. A trustee is, simply, anyone who has rights to a file, directory, or NDS object. Well, anyone or *anything*, to be precise. With NDS security, any object can be a trustee—in other words, any object can be given rights to any other object.

The following types of objects are often used as trustees in the file system or in NDS:

- The [Root] object

- Organization objects

- Organizational Unit objects

- Organizational Role and Group objects

- User objects

- The [Public] trustee

These objects are explained in the sections that follow.

The [Root] Object

Rights can be assigned to the [Root] object. This can be dangerous because all users in the Directory tree are given these rights. For small networks, assigning rights to the [Root] object can be an easy way to assign rights to publicly available files, such as those in the PUBLIC subdirectory.

Organization Objects

Since an Organization object is usually a major division of the Directory tree, the warning given about the [Root] object applies here. Rights should only be assigned to an Organization object when files need to be made available to the entire organization.

Organizational Unit Objects

The Organizational Unit object is the most common place to assign file system rights—and the most convenient. Since these containers are usually specific to a particular department or class of users, rights assigned here can be given to logical groups of users. This is where the advantages of a well-designed directory tree become obvious.

Organizational Role and Group Objects

Organizational Role objects or Group objects can be used when files are not needed by all members of a container object. This allows you to keep tight control of who can access these files. This may be useful for applications that you want to restrict to a specific set of users. When using this method, be sure to add the users to the Group or Organizational Role object.

User Objects

Finally, rights can be assigned to a User object. In a well-designed network, you should rarely have to use user rights because assigning rights to the previously discussed objects allows easy maintenance without having to assign rights to each user. Assigning rights to a User object can be useful, however, when only a certain user should have access to a file or directory.

The [Public] Trustee

The [Public] trustee object does not represent an actual object in the Directory tree. Instead, it provides a method of assigning rights to all users attached to the network—*even those who are not logged in*. Obviously, it would be dangerous to assign many rights to this trustee. You should use this method only for special cases. NetWare 4.11 assigns a minimal set of rights to this trustee to enable users to log in.

Using File System Security

First, we'll look at file system security, which is the most common kind of security used in NetWare 4.11. By controlling access to the file system, you can protect data from users who should not access it. In addition, you can give users access to the directories and files they need, while keeping those files safe.

File System Rights

A trustee can have several different types of rights to a file or directory. These rights specify which actions the trustee can perform in that file or directory.

If you are assigned rights in a directory, these rights are called *explicit rights* or *trustee rights*. You can also receive rights from a group that you belong to; these are called *group rights*.

Here are the available file system rights:

- **Read [R]**: Read data from an existing file.

- **Write [W]**: Write data to an existing file.

- **Create [C]**: Create a new file or subdirectory.

- **Erase [E]**: Delete existing files or directories.

- **Modify [M]**: Rename and change attributes of files.

- **File Scan [F]**: List the contents of a directory.

- **Access Control [A]**: Control the rights of other users to access files or directories.

- **Supervisor**: Users with the Supervisor right are automatically granted all other rights.

Inherited Rights

If a user is a trustee of a directory, the rights are *inherited* into subdirectories of that directory. The *Inherited Rights Filter (IRF)* controls which rights can be inherited. The IRF cannot be used to grant rights; it can only block or allow rights that were given in a parent directory.

The IRF is simply a list of the rights that a user or other trustee can inherit for that directory or file. If a right is included in the IRF, it can be inherited. If you leave a right out of the IRF, that means no user can inherit that right for that directory.

WARNING The IRF allows you to filter the Supervisor right, which gives administrators (such as the default user, Admin) rights to all directories. Be sure you don't filter this right unless you've given explicit access to another administrator.

Effective Rights

Your rights in a directory begin with the rights granted explicitly to you or your group or inherited from a parent directory. These rights are then filtered by the IRF. The end result is called your *effective rights* in the directory. This is what NetWare actually looks at when controlling user access.

For example, in Figure 7.5, user RALPH has been given the rights RWMF in the DATA directory. He inherits the same rights in the AP directory because the IRF allows all rights [RWCEMF]. In the AR directory, however, his rights are limited to R and F by the IRF. Although the C right is included in the IRF, user RALPH does not receive this right because he did not have it in the DATA directory.

FIGURE 7.5

Effective rights are the actions a trustee can perform in a file or directory.

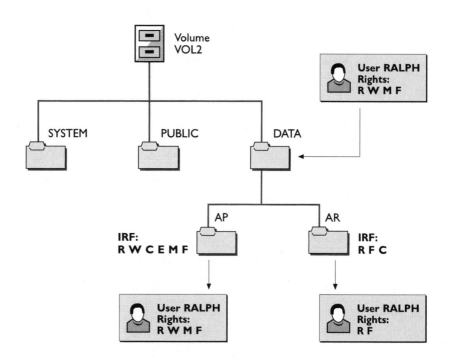

File Attributes

Another layer of file system security is *attribute security*. Attributes are options that can be applied to a file or directory to give it certain behaviors. An example is the Hidden attribute, which hides a file from the directory listing. Some attributes are set by the user or system administrator; others are set automatically by NetWare to indicate a condition. For example, the Archive Needed attribute indicates that the file has changed since the last backup.

Listed below are the possible file attributes. Many of these concern NetWare 4.11 features such as file compression and disk suballocation; these will be discussed in a later chapter.

- **A (Archive Needed):** NetWare sets this attribute automatically when a file is changed. Backup programs use this to indicate which files need to be backed up.

- **Ci (Copy Inhibit):** Stops users from copying the file (Macintosh files only).

- **Cc (Can't Compress):** This attribute is set by NetWare to indicate that no significant amount of space would be saved by compression.

- **Dc (Don't Compress):** Prevents file or directory contents from being compressed.

- **Di (Delete Inhibit):** Prevents a file or directory from being deleted.

- **Dm (Don't Migrate):** Prevents file or directory contents from being migrated to an optical jukebox, tape, or other high-capacity storage.

- **Ds (Don't Suballocate):** Causes the file to be written in whole blocks, regardless of whether block suballocation is enabled.

- **Ic (Immediate Compress):** Causes the file, or all files in the directory, to be compressed immediately when written.

- **M (Migrated):** Indicates files that have been migrated to high-capacity storage.

- **H (Hidden):** Prevents a file or directory from being shown in the directory listing. This affects DOS programs only; the NDIR utility shows hidden files if the user has the File Scan right.

- **I (Indexed):** Activates the turbo FAT indexing feature on the file.

- **N (Normal):** This is not an actual file attribute but is used by the FLAG command to assign a default set of attributes (Shareable, Read/Write).

- **P (Purge):** Causes the file to be purged (erased) immediately when deleted. The file cannot be recovered using the SALVAGE utility.

- **Ri (Rename Inhibit):** Prevents the user from renaming the file or directory.

- **Ro (Read Only):** Prevents users from writing to, renaming, or erasing the file. This automatically sets the Ri (Rename Inhibit) and Di (Delete Inhibit) attributes.

- **Rw (Read/Write):** Allows both reading and writing to the file. This attribute is set when the Ro (Read Only) attribute is cleared.

- **S (Shareable):** Allows multiple users to access the file at the same time.

- **Sy (System):** Indicates files used by the system. A combination of the Read Only and Hidden attributes.

- **T (Transactional):** Indicates that the file is a TTS file and is protected by the Transaction Tracking System. This feature can be used only with applications that support TTS.

- **X (Execute Only):** Prevents the file from being modified, erased, renamed, or copied. Once set, this attribute cannot be removed.

Managing File System Security

To run the NetWare Administrator utility, make sure you are logged in to the NetWare 4.11 network, start Windows, and choose Run from the Program Manager menu. In the dialog box, type **NWADMIN,** and press ⏎. NetWare Administrator should start.

Note that you cannot make changes to security unless you have the correct rights. If possible, log in as the user ADMIN or an equivalent to follow along with the examples in this chapter.

Browsing the File System

In order to control file system security, you can browse the hierarchy of files and directories from within the NWADMIN utility. You can browse a volume in two ways:

- Double-click the name of a volume. This expands the listing with the names of files and directories under the root directory of the volume, as shown in Figure 7.6.

- Click the volume name once to highlight it. Select Tools from the menu bar, then Browse. This opens a new window that shows only the volume and its contents.

After you open the volume for display, you can navigate through the directories. Double-clicking a directory opens that directory. If you select a file or directory, the Object menu includes options that allow you to perform file operations, such as copy, move, rename, and delete. In addition, the Details option on the Object menu allows you to view the attributes and trustees of the file or directory and to make changes.

You can also manage files using the Windows *drag-and-drop* feature. If you drag a file into a directory, you can move or copy the file. This feature is similar to dragging and dropping in the Windows File Manager.

FIGURE 7.6

Double-click a volume name to view the contents of the volume in the main NDS window.

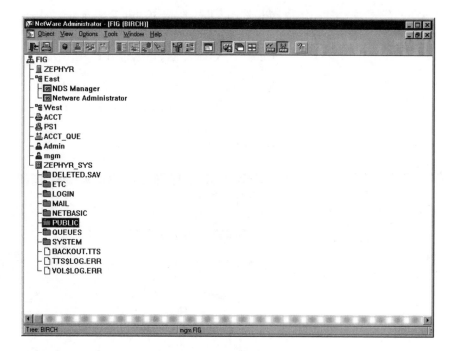

Assigning Trustee Rights

You can assign trustees in several ways:

- Add users as trustees to a file using NETADMIN, the NetWare Administrator utility (NWADMIN), or the FILER utility.

- Add file and directory trustee rights to a user using the NetWare Administrator or NETADMIN utility.

Assigning Trustees to a File or Directory

In the NetWare Administrator utility, you can assign trustees to a file or directory by following these steps:

1. Click the file or directory to highlight it.

2. Select the Object menu, then Details. The Details screen for the file appears.

3. Click the Trustees of this Directory button, located along the right side of the Details screen, to display the trustees information for a directory, as shown in Figure 7.7.

4. If trustees are already assigned to the directory, they will be listed. If you select one of these, the rights for that user in the directory will be shown.

FIGURE 7.7

Click the Trustees of this Directory button to display the current trustees of the directory.

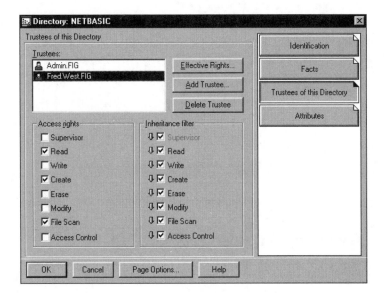

5. You can add or remove rights by clicking the checkboxes next to their names.

6. To add a new trustee, click the Add Trustee button. This presents the Select Object dialog box that allows you to select a user, group, or another object, as shown in Figure 7.8.

7. After you have added a trustee, you can assign rights by clicking the checkboxes. The Read and File Scan rights are granted by default.

8. Click the OK button to save your changes.

NetWare Administrator provides a shortcut to accessing the Details option. After selecting the file or directory, click the right button on your mouse to display a pop-up menu. The Details option is listed first. Which other options can be accessed from this menu depends on the type of object selected.

FIGURE 7.8

After choosing the Add Trustee button, use the Select Object dialog box to find the user or other object to be added.

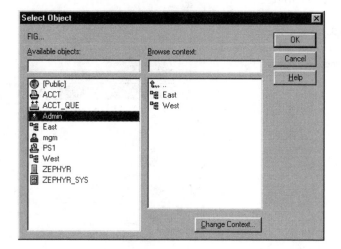

Assigning File Rights to a User

An alternate method of adding trustee rights is to start with the user. This method also works with other objects, such as groups or containers. Follow these steps:

1. Navigate through the NDS tree, and highlight the user (or other object) you want to add as a trustee.

2. Select the Object menu, then Details. The Details screen for the user (or other object) appears.

3. Select the Rights to Files and Directories button.

4. Select which volumes are to be displayed. The simplest way is to use the Find button. This allows you to quickly find all volumes in the current directory. All directories and files that the user has rights to are displayed, as shown in Figure 7.9.

F I G U R E 7.9

The current trustee rights given to a user are displayed when you choose the Rights to Files and Directories button.

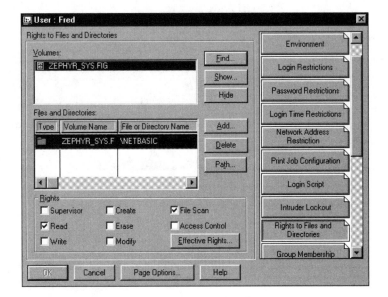

5. To add the user as a trustee to another directory or file, click the Add button. You'll see the Select Object dialog box, which allows you to select files. (The Select Object dialog box was shown in Figure 7.8.)

6. After a file or directory has been added to the list, highlight it. NetWare Administrator displays the rights that the trustee has. By default, these are Read and File Scan.

7. Click the checkboxes to add or remove rights.

8. Select the OK button to save your changes.

Modifying the Inherited Rights Filter (IRF)

You can view and modify an IRF for a directory by using the Details screen, which is the same screen that displays the trustees for that directory. To display this screen, select the directory, choose the Details option (from the Object menu or the pop-up menu that appears when you click with the right mouse button), and then click the Trustees button.

In the Inheritance Filter list, you can change the inheritance status for each right by clicking its checkbox. An arrow icon to the left of the checkbox indicates whether the right is allowed or blocked.

Displaying Effective Rights

An Effective Rights button appears in both the User object's Rights to Files and Directories screen and on the directory's Trustees screen. Click this button to view the current effective rights for the user in that directory. Rights that the user has been granted are displayed in black. Those that the user does not have are grayed. Figure 7.10 shows the Effective Rights dialog box.

The effective rights in this dialog box are updated whenever you view them; the user doesn't have to log in or out to display the current effective rights. However, when you make a change to a user's rights, you must save the changes with the OK button before the Effective Rights dialog box can reflect those changes.

By viewing the Effective Rights dialog box, you can easily determine whether you have assigned rights correctly. It is a good idea to check the effective rights whenever you have made changes, because of the interaction between explicit, inherited, and group rights.

FIGURE 7.10

A user's effective rights can be displayed for the file or directory.

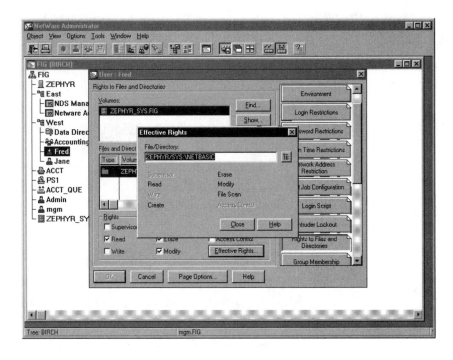

Modifying File Attributes

You can also modify file attributes using the NetWare Administrator program. Follow these steps:

1. Click the file or directory to highlight it.

2. Select the Object menu, then Details.

3. Click the Attributes button on the right side of the screen to see the current attributes for the file, as shown in Figure 7.11.

4. You can add or remove attributes by clicking the checkboxes next to the attribute names.

5. Select the OK button to save your changes.

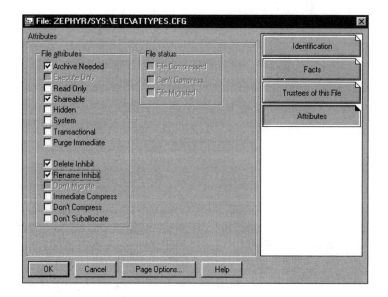

FIGURE 7.11

File and directory attributes can be modified in the NetWare Administrator utility.

The list of attributes is dynamic. If an option is not available for the current file or directory, the item is grayed on the menu, and you cannot select it. Also, some selections are made automatically. For example, selecting the Read Only attribute automatically selects the Delete Inhibit and Rename Inhibit attributes.

Using NDS Security

While file system security allows you to control access to volumes, files, and directories on a server, NDS security is used to control access to objects in the Directory—users, groups, printers, and entire organizations. You can control users' ability to modify and add objects and to view or modify their properties. With an understanding of NDS security, you can assign users the rights they need in the Directory, while maintaining a secure network.

Login Security

NDS provides *login security* for the network. This security was also provided by the bindery in NetWare 3.1*x*. Login security is handled by a password for each user object. The workstation software sends this password to NDS in an encrypted form, so there is no way of reading these passwords from elsewhere in the network.

Although NDS provides incredibly sophisticated levels of security, none of them will be effective if your users use simple passwords or no passwords at all. You should require passwords on the network and advise users not to use common words or names. (You would be amazed how many users on the average network use their children's names for passwords.) This policy ensures that there are no weaknesses in network security.

Trustee Rights

Like the file system, NDS security assigns rights through the use of trustees. The trustees of an object are called *object trustees*. An object trustee is any user (or other object) that has been given rights to the object. The list of trustees for an object is called the *Access Control List*, or *ACL*. Each object has a property containing the ACL.

While the file system has a set list of rights that a trustee can receive, NDS security provides two categories of rights: object rights and property rights.

Object Rights

Object rights are the tasks that a trustee can perform on an object. There are five types of object rights:

- **Supervisor:** The trustee is granted all of the rights listed below. Unlike the Supervisor right in the file system, the NDS Supervisor right can be blocked by the Inherited Rights Filter (IRF).

- **Browse:** The trustee can see the object in the Directory tree. If the Browse right is not granted, the object is not shown in the list.

- **Create:** The trustee can create child objects under the object. This right is available only for container objects.

- **Delete:** The trustee can delete the object from the Directory. In order to delete an object, you must also have the Write right for All Properties of the object.

- **Rename:** The trustee can change the name of the object.

Property Rights

Property rights allow a trustee to perform certain tasks on the object's properties. This allows the trustee to read or modify the property values. There are five types of property rights, which are not the same as the types of object rights:

- **Supervisor:** The trustee is given all of the property rights listed below. Once again, this right can be blocked by the IRF. Trustees with the Supervisor object right are automatically given supervisory rights to all properties of the object.

- **Compare:** The trustee is allowed to compare the property's values to a given value. This allows the trustee to search for a certain value but not to look at the value itself.

- **Read:** The trustee can read the values of the property. The Compare right is automatically granted.

- **Write:** The trustee can modify, add, or remove values of the property.

- **Add Self:** The trustee is allowed to add or remove itself as a value of the property. For example, a user that is granted the Add Self right for a group can add himself or herself to the group. The Write right automatically grants the Add Self property.

Property rights can be granted in two ways: All Properties or Selected Properties. If All Properties is selected, the same list of rights is granted to each of the properties of the object.

You should think twice before assigning rights to All Properties of an object. This can be a security risk. It is usually better to assign rights to only the properties that the trustee needs to access.

When granting Selected Properties, you are allowed to activate or deactivate each of the property rights for each property of the object. This allows you to fine-tune security and allow access only to what is needed. Because of the security risks involved in using the All Properties option, you should use Selected Properties for all users except administrators.

An object trustee can have both All Properties rights and Selected Properties rights for the same object, if the All Properties rights were inherited from a parent object. In this case, selected Properties rights override the All Properties rights for that property. For example, you could give a trustee the Supervisor right to All Properties for a parent object and then use Selected Properties to limit rights to certain properties of its child objects. Rights without a Selected Properties assignment follow the All Properties assignment.

One of the object properties that can be selected is the Object Trustees property. This property contains the trustee list, the ACL (Access Control List), itself. If a user is given Supervisor or Write rights to this property, the user can add and delete trustees from the object. To avoid this security risk, don't assign the Write or Supervisor rights to this property or to All Properties.

Inherited Rights in NDS

Like the file system, NDS uses a system of *inherited rights*. When an object trustee is given rights to a container object, the trustee also receives the same rights for all children of the object. Inheritance affects both object rights and property rights.

Object Rights Inheritance

Object rights are inherited in the same fashion as file system rights. When a trustee is given object rights for an object, the rights are inherited by the child object—the trustee receives rights for these objects also, unless the rights are blocked.

Property Rights Inheritance

Property rights can be inherited in the same manner as object rights, with one exception—only rights given with the All Properties option can be inherited. If a trustee is given rights to Selected Properties of an object, those rights cannot be inherited by child objects. This is because each of the different types of objects, such as users and organizational units, has a different list of properties.

Blocking Inherited Rights

When a trustee is given rights to a container object, the rights flow down the Directory tree until they are blocked. You can block inherited rights in two ways: with a new trustee assignment or with the IRF.

Explicit Assignments   You can block the rights a trustee can inherit for a particular object by giving the trustee a new explicit assignment to the object. For example, in Figure 7.12, user RON is given full rights [SBCDR] to the entire NHA_CO Organization. However, RON has been given a new explicit assignment of Browse and Rename only [BR] for the ORLANDO Organizational Unit. While RON receives full rights in the TAMPA Organizational Unit, his rights in ORLANDO are limited to [BR] by the new trustee assignment.

FIGURE 7.12

Inherited rights can be
blocked with a new
explicit assignment.

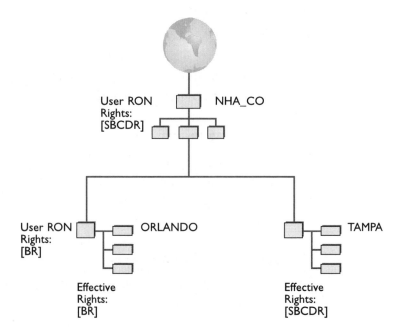

A new trustee assignment can be used to block rights, as in the
example, or to add additional rights. The new trustee assignment
replaces the rights that would have been inherited. The trustee assignment is also called an explicit assignment. Because an explicit assignment
blocks inherited rights, you do not need to consider inherited rights if an
explicit assignment has been granted.

The Inherited Rights Filter (IRF)

Each NDS object has an IRF for object rights. The IRF is a list of the
rights that a user can inherit for the object. For example, in Figure 7.13,
user JANS has been given the [BCDR] rights to the ACCTG Organizational Unit. She inherits these same rights in the AP Organizational Unit,
which has the default IRF. The IRF for the PR Organizational Unit has
been set to [SBR], so JANS' rights in PR are limited to [BR].

FIGURE 7.13

The Inherited Rights
Filter can be used to block
inherited rights.

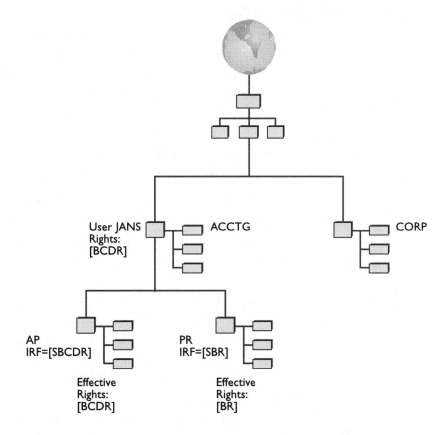

Each object also has an IRF for property rights. Like the rights themselves, the IRF can be set for All Properties or Selected Properties. You can also set an IRF for All Properties and set different IRFs for certain Selected Properties. Remember, the rights are inherited only if they were assigned to All Properties for the parent object.

Remember, the IRF cannot give a user additional rights; it can be used only to filter (block) rights that a user would otherwise inherit. Also, the IRF affects only inherited rights—it doesn't block security equivalence, which is described in the next section.

Security Equivalence

In several situations in NDS, a trustee automatically receives all of the rights given to another trustee. This is referred to as security equivalence. By understanding these equivalences, you can easily grant rights to users and make sure that unnecessary rights are not granted. There are two types of security equivalence: implied and explicit.

Implied Security Equivalence

When rights are given to a container object, all objects within the container receive the same rights through security equivalence. If one of these objects is a container object, the objects underneath it also receive the rights. This is referred to as implied security equivalence or container security equivalence.

For example, in Figure 7.14, giving a trustee assignment to the ACCTG Organization would give the same rights to the PAYABLES and BILLING Organizational Units and all leaf objects under them. Giving a trustee assignment to the [Root] object would give the same rights to all objects in the entire tree.

Because rights flow from container objects to their children, you may be tempted to describe this process as "inheritance." However, this is not inheritance in the NetWare definition. Inheritance means that rights given to a trustee for a container object are given to the same trustee for the object's children.

It is important to understand the difference between inheritance and implied security equivalence because the IRF does not affect security equivalences. This distinction can be one of the most difficult concepts to master in NDS security. You can avoid confusion by remembering the following statements:

- An object inherits the trustees assigned to its parent objects. These rights can be blocked by the IRF.

- A trustee is security equivalent to its parent objects. These rights cannot be blocked by the IRF.

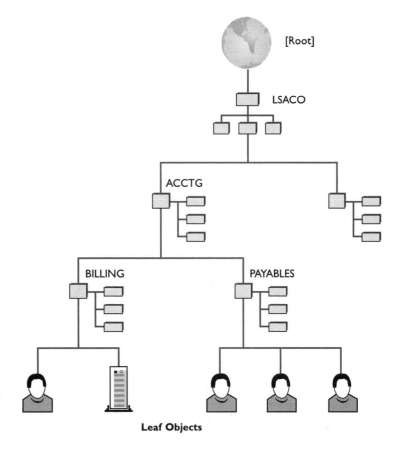

FIGURE 7.14

In implied security equivalence, rights given to a container are passed on to objects within the container.

Leaf Objects

These concepts are further illustrated in Figure 7.15. Look at this Directory tree carefully, and read the following statements about the objects in the Directory.

- The CORP Organizational Unit has been given full rights to the ACCTG Organizational Unit. (CORP is a trustee of ACCTG.)

- The ADMIN and PAYROLL Organizational Units both have an IRF of [BR] (Browse and Rename only).

- Jane receives full rights [SBCDR] to objects in the ACCTG Organizational Unit. This is because Jane has an implied security equivalence to the CORP container object. The IRF given to the ADMIN Organizational Unit does not affect Jane's rights.

FIGURE 7.15

This Directory tree shows examples of both *inherited rights* and *implied security equivalence*.

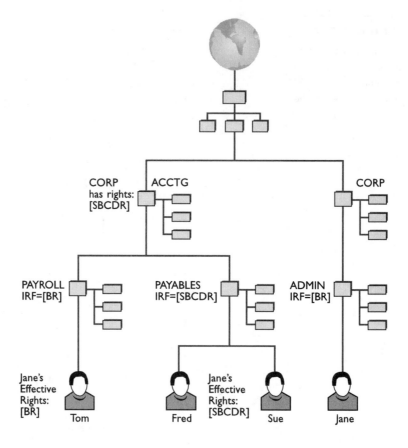

- Jane inherits full rights to all objects in the PAYABLES organizational unit, including the User objects Fred and Sue.

- Jane's rights to the User object Tom are limited to Browse and Rename only [BR] by the IRF of the PAYROLL Organizational Unit.

Explicit Security Equivalence

A second, much simpler type of security equivalence is also available: *explicit security equivalence*. This is a security equivalence that is specifically given to a user. You can assign explicit security equivalences in three ways:

- Each user has a Security Equal To property. You can add users or other objects to this list, and the user receives the rights given to those objects.

- If a user is assigned to the membership list of a Group object, the user becomes security equivalent to the Group object.

- If a user is an occupant of an Organizational Role object, the user becomes security equivalent to the Organizational Unit object.

All explicit security equivalences are listed in the user's Security Equal To property. Security equivalences that the user receives through an organizational role or group membership are automatically added to this list.

 Security equivalences cannot be combined or "nested." For example, if the user John is made security equivalent to another user, Wendy, and Wendy is made security equivalent to the ADMIN user, John does not become security equivalent to ADMIN and does not receive administrative rights. He receives only those rights given to (or inherited by) Wendy's User object.

Calculating Effective Rights

A user's effective rights are the tasks the user can actually perform on the object. As you have learned, there are many factors that affect a user's rights to an object in the Directory:

- Rights given directly to the user (explicit trustee assignments).

- Inherited rights from rights the user has been given to objects higher in the Directory tree.

- The Inherited Rights Filter or an explicit assignment can block inherited rights.

- Rights received from containers the user resides in through implied security equivalence.

- Security equivalences to Group or Organizational Role objects.

Luckily, the NetWare Administrator utility provides a simple method of displaying a user's effective rights to an object. If you find it necessary to calculate effective rights manually, you can do so by following these steps:

1. Start with any explicit rights given to the user for the object.

2. If there are no explicit rights, calculate the inherited rights—any rights given to the user for parent objects minus those blocked by the IRF.

3. Add any rights given to the user's security equivalents for the object. These include group memberships, organizational roles, or members of the user's Security Equivalent To property.

Using NetWare Administrator to Control NDS Security

You can use the NetWare Administrator utility to manage the following aspects of NDS security:

- Viewing trustee rights

- Adding a trustee

- Changing object and property rights

- Modifying the IRF

- Displaying effective rights

These topics will be discussed in the following sections.

Viewing a Trustee's Rights

NetWare Administrator provides two ways to view trustee rights. Both of these options are accessed from the Object menu:

- The Trustees of This Object option allows you to view a list of trustees for the object you have selected, as shown in Figure 7.16. You can then select a trustee to view detailed information.

- The Rights to Other Objects option allows you to view a list of objects that the selected object is a trustee of. First, enter a context to search in. You can then select an object from the list to view the trustee's rights to the object, as shown in Figure 7.17.

FIGURE 7.16

The Trustees of This Object option allows you to view an object's trustee list.

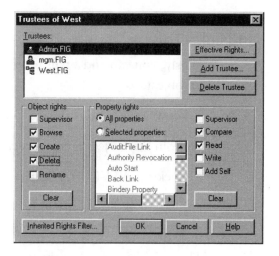

Each of these screens includes all of the possible rights for the object. A checkbox next to the option displays whether the right is granted and allows you to grant or revoke the right.

These techniques allow you to view and change explicit rights only. To view a user's effective rights, see the *Displaying Effective Rights* section later in this chapter.

F I G U R E   7.17

The Rights to Other
Objects option allows
you to list a trustee's
rights.

Adding a Trustee

Similarly, you can add a trustee in two ways. The first is to add trustees to an object:

1. Browse the Directory tree to find the object, and highlight it.

2. From the Object menu, select Trustees of This Object.

3. Click the Add Trustee button to access the Select Object dialog box.

4. Find the object that will become a trustee in the Select Object dialog box, and click the OK button.

The trustee is added to the list. You can change the trustee's rights, as described in the next section, *Changing Object and Property Rights*. A second way to add a trustee is to add objects to a trustee:

1. Browse the Directory tree to find the object that will become a trustee, and highlight it.

2. From the Object menu, select Rights to Other Objects.

3. Click the Add Assignment button to access the Select Object dialog box.

4. Select the object that the trustee will have rights to, and click OK.

The object is added to the list of objects the trustee has rights to. You can change these rights, as described in the next section.

Changing Object and Property Rights

While either the Rights to Other Objects or Trustees of This Object dialog box is displayed, you can change the object rights given to the trustee. Simply highlight the trustee or object, and click the checkbox next to each type of right to grant (check) or revoke (uncheck) it.

You can also change property rights from either of these dialog boxes. You can assign rights for All Properties by selecting All Properties, and then checking or unchecking the box next to each property right.

To assign rights to selected rights, click the Selected Properties button. You are presented with a list of properties that depends on the type of object. Select the property to change rights for, and check or uncheck the boxes as appropriate.

A checkmark is displayed to the left of each property that you have changed the rights for. Properties without a checkmark have not been changed in Selected Properties and will default to the setting for All Properties.

Modifying the IRF

The IRF can be changed from the Trustees of This Object dialog box. Follow these steps to change the IRF for an object:

1. Browse the Directory tree to find the object, and highlight it.

2. From the Object menu, select Trustees of This Object.

3. Click the Inherited Rights Filter button. The dialog box shown in Figure 7.18 is displayed.

4. To change the IRF for object rights, use the checkboxes on the left. A checked box means the right is allowed for inheritance; an unchecked box means the right is blocked. An arrow or blocked arrow to the left of the checkbox indicates this visually.

5. To change the IRF for All Properties, click the All Properties button, and then check or uncheck the box by each possible property right.

FIGURE 7.18

You change an object's IRF by clicking the checkbox for each type of right.

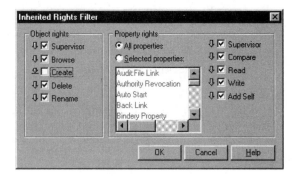

6. To change the IRF for Selected Properties, click the Selected Properties button, and then select the property to be changed. Check or uncheck the appropriate boxes. A checkmark to the left of the property name indicates that the All Properties IRF is overridden for this property.

Displaying Effective Rights

An Effective Rights button appears in both the Trustees of This Object and the Rights to Other Objects dialog boxes. Click on this button to view the current effective rights for the user for the object. Rights that the user has been granted are displayed in black. Those that the user does not have are grayed. Figure 7.19 shows an example of the Effective Rights display.

FIGURE 7.19

You can display a trustee's effective rights for an object.

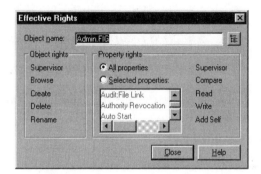

If you have made changes to a trustee's rights, you must save the changes with the OK button before the Effective Rights display can reflect those changes.

By viewing the Effective Rights display, you can easily check to determine whether you have assigned rights correctly. It is a good idea to check the effective rights whenever you have made changes because of the interaction between explicit, inherited, and group rights.

Review

The security features of NetWare 4.11 are used to control which users and other NDS objects have access to files, directories, and objects.

Several types of security can be controlled by NetWare 4.11:

- *Login security* allows users to connect to the network using passwords.

- *File system security* controls access to the file system.

- *NDS security* controls access to NDS objects.

- *Server security* controls access to the file server itself.

- *Network Printing security* controls access to network printers.

Login Security

Login security is the first type of security a user encounters when accessing the network. A User object must be created for each user, and the properties of this object can control and restrict logins to that account:

- Authentication is the basic process that controls logins, and allows a single login to access multiple servers.

- User account restrictions allow you to restrict when and where the user can log in.

- Intruder Detection counts incorrect login attempts, and locks out accounts that may have been compromised.

Trustees

Much of NetWare 4.11 security centers around *trustees*. A trustee is a User object, or another NDS object, that has been assigned rights to a file, directory, or NDS object. With NDS security, any object can be a trustee—in other words, any object can be given rights to any other object.

The following types of objects are commonly used as trustees in the file system or in NDS.

- The [Root] object

- Organization objects

- Organizational Unit objects

- Organizational Role and Group objects

- User objects

- The [Public] trustee

File System Security

The available file system rights are as follows:

- **Read [R]:** Read data from an existing file.

- **Write [W]:** Write data to an existing file.

- **Create [C]:** Create a new file or subdirectory.

- **Erase [E]:** Delete existing files or directories.

- **Modify [M]:** Rename and change attributes of files.

- **File Scan [F]:** List the contents of a directory.

- **Access Control [A]:** Control the rights of other users to access files or directories.

- **Supervisor:** Users with the Supervisor right are automatically granted all other rights.

NDS Security

While file system security allows you to control access to volumes, files, and directories on a server, NDS security is used to control access to objects in the Directory—users, groups, printers, and entire organizations. You can control users' ability to modify and add objects and to view or modify their properties. With an understanding of NDS security, you can assign users the rights they need in the Directory, while maintaining a secure network.

Like the file system, NDS security assigns rights through the use of trustees. The trustees of an object are called *object trustees*. An object trustee is any user (or other object) that has been given rights to the object. The list of trustees for an object is called the *Access Control List*, or *ACL*. Each object has a property containing the ACL.

While the file system has a set list of rights that a trustee can receive, NDS security provides two categories of rights: object rights and property rights.

Object rights are the abilities of a trustee to perform certain operations on an object. Here are the five types of object rights:

- **Supervisor:** The trustee is granted all of the rights listed below. Unlike the Supervisor right in the file system, the NDS Supervisor right can be blocked by the Inherited Rights Filter (IRF).

- **Browse:** The trustee can see the object in the Directory tree. If the Browse right is not granted, the object is not shown in the list.

- **Create:** The trustee can create child objects under the object. This right is available only for container objects.

- **Delete:** The trustee can delete the object from the Directory. In order to delete an object, you must also have the Write right for All Properties of the object.

- **Rename:** The trustee can change the name of the object.

Property rights allow a trustee to manipulate the object's properties. This allows the trustee to read or modify the property values. There are five types of property rights, which are not the same as the types of object rights:

- **Supervisor:** The trustee is given all of the property rights listed below. Once again, this right can be blocked by the IRF. Trustees with the Supervisor object right are automatically given supervisory rights to all properties of the object.

- **Compare:** The trustee is allowed to compare the property's values to a given value. This allows the trustee to search for a certain value but not to look at the value itself.

- **Read:** The trustee can read the values of the property. The Compare right is automatically granted.

- **Write:** The trustee can modify, add, or remove values of the property.

- **Add Self:** The trustee is allowed to add or remove itself as a value of the property. For example, a user that is granted the Add Self right for a group can add himself and herself to the group. The Write right automatically grants the Add Self property.

Property rights can be granted in two ways: All Properties or Selected Properties. If All Properties is selected, the same list of rights is granted to each of the properties of the object.

NDS Inheritance

Like the file system, NDS uses a system of *inherited rights*. When an object trustee is given rights to a container object, the trustee also receives the same rights for all children of the object. Inheritance affects both object rights and property rights.

Object rights are inherited in the same fashion as file system rights. When a trustee is given object rights for an object, the rights are inherited by child objects—the trustee receives rights for these objects also, unless the rights are blocked.

Property rights can be inherited in the same manner as object rights, with one exception—only rights given with the All Properties option can be inherited. If a trustee is given rights to Selected Properties of an object, those rights cannot be inherited by child objects. This is because each of the different types of objects, such as users and organizational units, has a different list of properties.

When a trustee is given rights to a container object, the rights flow down the Directory tree until they are blocked. You can block inherited rights in two ways: with a new trustee assignment or with the Inherited Rights Filter (IRF).

Security Equivalence in NDS

There are several situations in NDS in which a trustee automatically receives all of the rights given to another trustee, which is referred to as *security equivalence*. There are two types of security equivalence:

- *Implied security equivalence* means that an object receives rights given to its parent containers.

- *Explicit security equivalence* is given with the Security Equal To property, group membership, or Organizational Role occupancy.

Effective Rights in NDS

A user's *effective rights* are the tasks the user can actually perform on the object. If you find it necessary to calculate effective rights manually, you can do so by following these steps:

1. Start with any explicit rights given to the user for the object.

2. If there are no explicit rights, calculate the inherited rights—any rights given to the user for parent objects minus those blocked by the IRF.

3. Add any rights given to the user's security equivalents for the object. These include group memberships, organizational roles, or members of the user's Security Equivalent To property.

CNA Practice Test Questions

1. The two types of NetWare 4.11 trustee rights are:

A. File system security and NDS security

B. File system security and object rights

C. Trustee rights and object rights

D. All properties and selected properties

2. Which of the following *cannot* be a trustee:

A. Organization

B. User

C. Organizational Role

D. File

3. The File Scan right:

A. Allows you to copy files

B. Allows you to list files in a directory

C. Allows you to read the contents of files

D. Allows you to search for a file

4. The IRF affects:

    A. Security equivalence

    B. Inherited rights

    C. Explicit assignments

    D. All of the above

5. File attributes:

    A. Are always set by NetWare itself

    B. Are always set by the user

    C. Cannot be changed

    D. Give a file certain behaviors

6. You can manage file system security with:

    A. NetWare Administrator

    B. NETADMIN

    C. SYSCON

    D. SECURE

7. The IRF lists:

    A. Rights to be blocked

    B. Rights to be granted

    C. Rights allowed to be inherited

    D. Rights that cannot be inherited

8. The list of trustees for an object is stored in:

   A. The Trustees property

   B. The ACL

   C. The Trustee database

   D. The Trustee file

9. The two types of rights in NDS are:

   A. Object rights and file rights

   B. Object rights and property rights

   C. All Properties and Selected Properties

   D. Object rights and the IRF

10. Inherited rights can be blocked with:

   A. The IRF

   B. An explicit assignment

   C. Both A and B

   D. None of the above

11. Explicit security equivalences can be granted with:

   A. Container occupancy

   B. Group, Organizational Role, Security Equal

   C. Group, container occupancy

   D. All of the above

12. Which of the following does NOT affect effective NDS rights:

  A. Explicit rights

  B. Inherited rights

  C. Rights given to child objects

  D. Rights given to parent objects

13. The [Public] Trustee:

  A. Assigns rights to all users when logged in

  B. Assigns rights to anyone attached to the network

  C. Assigns rights to ADMIN only

  D. Assigns rights to the file system only

CHAPTER

8

Managing Login Scripts and Applications

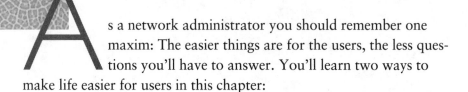

As a network administrator you should remember one maxim: The easier things are for the users, the less questions you'll have to answer. You'll learn two ways to make life easier for users in this chapter:

- *Login scripts* can set up drive mappings and other defaults for the user, so that he or she doesn't have to type DOS commands to set up drives or printers.

- *NetWare Application Manager (NAM)* lets you define lists of applications a user can run and gives the user a simple way of accessing them.

If you're careful about setting up these options, you can make the network friendly and accessible to users—even those who fear computers. In addition, even the most computer-literate user appreciates not having to type the same complicated commands each time he or she logs in or accesses an application.

Using Login Scripts

A *login script* is a list of commands that NetWare executes each time the user logs in. You can use login scripts to set defaults for the user, such as drive mappings, search drive mappings, printer configurations, and variable settings; and to execute commands, such as starting a menu.

You can create and edit login scripts using the NetWare Administrator or NWADMIN utility. Each of the objects we'll talk about below—User, Container, and Profile—has a Login Script property, which you use to enter login script commands.

Login Script Types

There are four types of login scripts: user, container, profile, and default login scripts. When a user logs in, NetWare checks for each of these and executes them. Login scripts are always executed in the same order:

1. **Container login script** for the user's parent container (if found)

2. **Profile login script** (if assigned)

3. **User login script** (if defined)

4. **Default login script** (If NetWare doesn't find a user login script, it executes the commands in the default login script instead.)

Each of the types of login script has its own purpose. You can provide a complete configuration for your users with a minimum of maintenance by taking advantage of each of these types of scripts. The sections below explain each of the login script types.

A NetWare 3.1x has a *system login script,* which is executed for any user who logs in to the server. There is no system login script in NetWare 4.11. You can use container login scripts for the same purpose, but if users are in several different containers you will need to provide a container login script for each one.

Container Login Scripts

You can create a *container login script* for any Organization or Organizational Unit object. This script is the first script executed for users in the container. You can use this login script for drive mappings, printer settings, and other options that are needed by all users in the container.

NetWare executes only one container login script—for the user's parent container. For example, in Figure 8.1, user JOHNM has the distinguished name JOHNM.AP.ACCT.AQP_CO. Although JOHNM is in the containers AP, ACCT, and AQP_CO, only the login script for AP is executed because AP is JOHNM's parent container. If the AP Organizational Unit has no login script, no container login script is executed.

FIGURE 8.1

Only one container login script is executed for each user.

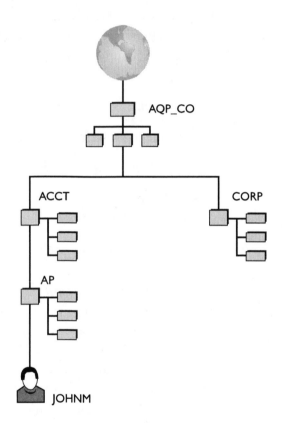

To edit the container login script, you can use NetWare Administrator or NETADMIN. The login script is stored in the container object's Login Script property. The container script must be edited by a user with rights to this property, usually the ADMIN user or container administrator.

Profile Login Scripts

The Profile object is a special NDS object that you can use to assign the same login script to several users. You can use a *profile login script* to execute a certain set of drive mappings or other commands for certain users in the directory, even if they are in different containers.

Follow the steps below to set up a profile login script. This can be done from NetWare Administrator or NETADMIN:

1. Create a Profile object. You can place this object in any container, but the logical place for it is in the same container as the users who need it.

2. Edit the Profile object's Login Script property, and insert the desired commands.

3. For each user who will execute the profile login script, make his or her User object a trustee of the Profile object. As a minimum, the User object must have the Read [R] right for the Profile object's Login Script property.

4. Each User object has a Profile property. Edit each User object's Profile property, and select the Profile object you have created. You can select only one Profile object per user.

User Login Scripts

The final login script to execute is the *user login script.* You can use a user login script to execute specific commands for a particular user. One important use for the user login script is to override certain commands in the container login script.

Each user has a Login Script property. You can edit this property using NetWare Administrator or NETADMIN to create or modify the user's login script.

The Default Login Script

The *default login script* is built into the LOGIN utility. You cannot edit it. The default script is executed when a user has no user login script. The default login script provides a basic set of search and drive mappings—for example, a search mapping for the PUBLIC directory.

The default login script allows users to log in to a new system without having to create a login script. If you are using container or profile login scripts, the default login script may cause conflicts. You can prevent conflicts with a special login script command: NO_DEFAULT. If you include this command in the container or profile login script, it prevents the execution of the default login script, even if the user has no user login script.

The following are the commands executed by the default login script. You will learn what each command means later in this chapter.

```
MAP DISPLAY OFF

MAP ERRORS OFF

MAP *1=SYS:

MAP *1=SYS:%LOGIN_NAME

IF "%1"="ADMIN" THEN MAP *1:=SYS:SYSTEM

MAP INS S1:=SYS:PUBLIC

MAP INS S2:=SYS:PUBLIC\%MACHINE\%OS\%OS_VERSION
```

Login Script Variables

Login script variables let you include changing information in a login script. You can use login script variables anywhere in the login script; NetWare substitutes the current value of that item. Use the percent (%) sign at the beginning of each variable name to indicate that it is a variable. Variables may be uppercase or lowercase, but since some commands require them to be uppercase, it's best to use uppercase all of the time.

Listed below are the most common login script variables. The full list of variables can be found in the NetWare manuals.

- **MACHINE:** Specifies the type of computer being used; typically IBM_PC.

- **OS:** Specifies the type of DOS. Usually MS_DOS.

- **OS_VERSION:** Specifies the DOS version, such as 6.22.

- **STATION:** Represents the connection number (network address) of the workstation.

- **LOGIN_NAME:** Gives the login name of the user.

- **GREETING_TIME:** Specifies a time of day—MORNING, AFTERNOON, or EVENING.

Login Script Commands

Each login script is a sequence of *login script commands*. Each type of login script uses the same set of commands. Although some of these commands are the same as NetWare commands, most are specific to login scripts. The most important login script commands, including those that are new to NetWare 4.11, are explained in the sections below. For a complete list of commands, refer to the NetWare manuals or the online documentation.

MAP

MAP is probably the most commonly used login script command. You can use this command to assign drive letters as network drives and search drives, just like the MAP command-line utility, with one exception: The MAP NEXT command, which is used to map the next available drive letter to a directory, cannot be used in login scripts.

In addition to the usual MAP commands, you can use two additional commands in login scripts: MAP DISPLAY and MAP ERRORS. Both of these have a single parameter, ON or OFF.

- **MAP DISPLAY** controls whether NetWare displays a list of drive mappings when the user logs in.

- **MAP ERRORS** controls whether NetWare displays map error messages as it executes the login script. These errors are usually caused by an invalid path or by a MAP command for a path the user does not have rights to.

IF, THEN, and ELSE

You can use the IF command to execute a command or set of commands *conditionally*. The IF command is followed by a condition, then by the keyword THEN, and a command or list of commands to be executed. Here is a simple IF command:

```
IF MEMBER OF "PAYABLES" THEN MAP F:=SYS:DATA\AP
```

In this example, the MAP command for drive F will be executed only if the user is a member of the PAYABLES group.

You can use two keywords for more sophisticated conditions:

- The ELSE keyword specifies commands to be executed when the condition is not met.

- The END keyword ends a complex IF statement. It must be used if the IF statement uses more than one line.

Here is a more complicated example of an IF command:

```
IF %LOGIN_NAME = "ADMIN" THEN
MAP F:=SYS:SYSTEM
MAP J:=VOL1:TOOLS\ADMIN
ELSE
```

```
MAP F:=SYS:HOME\%LOGIN_NAME
MAP J:=VOL1:TOOLS\PUBLIC
END
```

In this example, drives F and J are mapped to certain directories for the ADMIN user and to different directories for all other users.

The condition in the IF statement uses login script variables. NetWare sets these variables when running the login script. You can use them to test individual information for the user or workstation. You can also use these variables with the WRITE command, described below.

You can use another keyword, IF MEMBER OF, to perform actions based on group membership. The first example uses this method. You can use IF NOT MEMBER OF to perform actions if the user is not a member of the specified group.

INCLUDE

The INCLUDE command allows you to include another login script within the current script. The other script can be the script belonging to another container or profile or a DOS text file containing login script commands. Here are some examples:

- **INCLUDE .OU=VIP** runs the login script for the VIP Organizational Unit.

- **INCLUDE SYS:PUBLIC\LOGIN1.TXT** executes commands from a text file.

NetWare executes the commands in the other login script or file as if they were included in the current login script. If the login script or file ends with the EXIT command, the current login script ends; otherwise, the current script continues with the commands after the INCLUDE command.

CONTEXT

You can use the CONTEXT command to set the current Directory context for the user. For example, the following command sets the context to the AP Organizational Unit under the main ZYX_CO Organization:

```
CONTEXT .AP.ZYX_CO
```

WRITE

You can use the WRITE command to display a message to the user. You can use login script variables to display specific information for the user. For example, the following WRITE command is typically used to greet users:

```
WRITE "Good %GREETING_TIME, %FULL_NAME."
```

This displays a message such as "Good Morning, Bob Smith." Another example displays the current time:

```
WRITE "The time is %HOUR:%MINUTE:%SECOND %AM_PM."
```

This displays a message such as "The time is 11:30:23 AM." By taking advantage of the WRITE command, you can advise users of conditions that may affect their use of the network.

DISPLAY and FDISPLAY

You can use these commands to display the contents of a text file when the user logs in. FDISPLAY uses a *filtered* format to display the file, removing printer codes and unprintable characters; DISPLAY writes the file to the screen in raw format. Here is an example of the FDISPLAY command:

```
FDISPLAY SYS:PUBLIC\NEWS.TXT
```

This command simply displays the NEWS.TXT file to the user during the login process.

You can use the display commands to display information, such as system news or warnings about system problems. You can also combine them with the IF command to display detailed error messages. For example, you might use the FDISPLAY command below to explain a printer error to the user:

```
#CAPTURE L=1 Q=LASER1_QUEUE

IF ERROR_LEVEL  0 THEN FDISPLAY
SYS:PUBLIC\PRTERROR.TXT
```

In this example, if the CAPTURE command fails, the PRTERROR .TXT file is displayed. This file could give instructions on correcting the problem or tell users who to call for help.

REM or REMARK

These commands allow you to insert a comment in the login script. A semicolon (;) or asterisk (*) can also be used to indicate a comment. The following are all comments:

```
REM The following commands set up drive mappings

***Be sure to include the user's mappings here***

;Don't try this at home

Remarkably enough, this line won't execute.
```

COMSPEC

You can use the COMSPEC command to specify the location of the COMMAND.COM file. DOS uses this file to run the command interpreter. Some DOS programs unload COMMAND.COM and reload it when they finish. If this is not specified correctly, the workstation reports the error message "Unable to Load COM-MAND" and requires rebooting.

You must use COMSPEC if your users are using a version of DOS loaded on a network volume/drive. If they run DOS from their individual workstations only, this command is not needed.

PAUSE

The PAUSE command simply stops the login script until you press a key. This command can be useful in debugging login scripts; by including PAUSE in strategic places, you can view messages that would normally have scrolled off the screen.

DOS Commands

You can also use any DOS command in your login scripts. Precede each DOS command with the number sign (#). DOS commands are most commonly used with the CAPTURE command to control network printing. You can use any DOS command, with the following restrictions:

- You should execute only DOS commands that return immediately, such as CAPTURE. If you wish to execute a menu or other program and end the login script, you should use the EXIT command.

- Don't use the number sign with the MAP command. There is a login script version of MAP.

- You can't use the SET command to set DOS variables in a login script. You should use the DOS SET login script command instead.

- The DOS commands here are *external* commands, meaning that they are contained in a separate program. *Internal* DOS commands, such as DIR, cannot be used unless you execute a copy of COMMAND.COM.

Using Client 32 as the network client, Windows 3.1 and Windows 95 can also run login scripts. However, using DOS commands in this fashion may not work the way you expect on these platforms.

Using EXIT with Login Scripts

You can use the EXIT command to end the current login script. You can also include a command that executes at the DOS prompt after the user logs in. One use for EXIT is to run a menu, as described in the previous section.

Because the EXIT command ends the login script, it should be the last command in the script. In addition, the EXIT command prevents any further scripts from executing. Thus, if the EXIT command is included in the container login script, it prevents the profile and user login scripts from executing. If you include EXIT in the profile login script, it prevents the user login script from executing.

You can use the EXIT command by itself or follow it with a command in quotation marks, such as in this example, which would automatically exit a menu at the end of the login script:

```
EXIT "NMENU ACCT"
```

DOS executes the command after the login script has finished. NetWare actually places the command in the keyboard buffer, so DOS believes the user typed it. The size of the keyboard buffer limits the command to 14 characters. This trick works only under DOS; you can't use EXIT to execute a command in other operating systems.

If you are executing a DOS program that will stay running, such as NMENU, you should run it with the EXIT command. Although you can execute DOS commands anywhere in the script with the # prefix, the LOGIN.EXE program remains in memory while they execute. By passing commands to DOS using the keyboard buffer, EXIT executes the command after the LOGIN program has finished.

By default, users have the rights to edit their own user login scripts. You can add the EXIT command at the end of the container or profile login script if you wish to prevent user login scripts from executing.

Using NetWare Application Manager

NetWare Application Manager, or NAM for short, is a system added to NetWare in version 4.11. This system allows you to define applications as NDS objects and to give users access to these applications. Users can run NAL (NetWare Application Launcher) under Windows 3.1 or Windows 95 to access the applications.

The NAL window displays icons and allows the user to double-click an icon to start an application. If this sounds familiar, that's because it's very similar to what you can do with a folder on the Desktop (Windows 95) or in a Program Manager group (Windows 3.1.) So why use NAM? There are some definite advantages:

- You can define an application's icon once to make the application available to a large group of users.

- Users can use a nearly identical interface to launch applications, whether they are using Windows 3.1 or Windows 95.

- You can assign the same list of applications to multiple users easily.

- You can use NAL as the Windows shell; this allows you much more control over the features a user can access.

- Most importantly, once you've set things up, you can add an icon to a user's menu without walking to their workstation, and users can't inadvertently delete icons.

NAM consists of two components: NetWare Application Launcher (NAL) and Application Objects, which you can create from NWADMIN. We'll look at these components in the following sections.

NAM is useful only for Windows workstations. NetWare 4 also includes a DOS-based menu system called NMENU; see the NetWare manuals or Dynatext documentation for details.

Creating and Managing Application Objects

There are several types of Application Objects, each for a different operating system:

- Application (DOS): This is for DOS applications, which can run under DOS, Windows 3.1, or Windows 95.

- Application (Windows 3.*x*): This is for Windows 3.1 applications, which can run under Windows 3.1 or Windows 95.

- Application (Windows 95): This is a Windows 95-specific application that can run only under Windows 95.

- Application (Windows NT): This is a Windows NT-specific application, and will run only under Windows NT.

We will describe the process of creating applications, setting their properties, and configuring them for users in the following sections.

Creating an Application Object

You only need to create an Application Object once for each application. Follow these steps to create and configure an Application object:

1. Choose an NDS container (context) for the Application Object to reside in. The most convenient approach is to use the same container as the users who need access to the application.

2. In NWADMIN, highlight the container object and choose Create from the Object menu.

3. You are now shown a list of objects, including four types of Application objects. (See Figure 8.2.) Choose the correct application type and click OK.

FIGURE 8.2

Choose one of the Application object types depending on the platform.

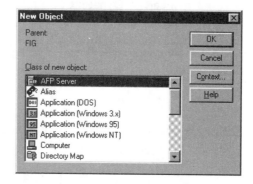

4. You are now prompted for the application's name and location, as shown in Figure 8.3. You can press the small button to the right of the Path field to browse through NDS and the file system to find the application.

FIGURE 8.3

Enter the application's name and location.

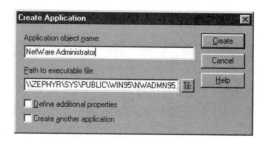

5. Optionally, check the Define Additional Properties box if you wish to further configure the Application object, or check the Create another application box if you wish to create a second Application object. You can choose only one of these options.

Managing Application Properties

You have now successfully created an Application object. However, before users can access the application, you need to define some of its properties. Select the object and choose Details from the Object menu to display the Details dialog box shown in Figure 8.4. If you chose the Define Additional Properties option in step 5, this dialog box will be displayed automatically.

FIGURE 8.4

The Details dialog box includes various properties of the Application object.

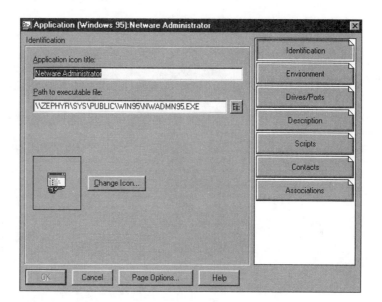

The properties of the Application object include the following categories:

- **Identification:** Includes the application's name and path, which you entered in step 4. You can also change the icon used for the application here.

- **Environment:** Allows you to specify command-line parameters for the application. You can also specify a working directory; this directory will be set as the current directory before the application starts. The Run Minimized option specifies to run the program as an icon, and the Clean Up Network Resources option specifies whether drives and printers (see below) are disconnected after the user exits the application.

- **Drives/Ports:** (Shown in Figure 8.5.) Allows you to specify drive mappings and printer port captures for the application. These will be set up before the application starts, and disconnected when it exits if you enabled the Clean Up Network Resources option above.

F I G U R E 8.5

The Drives/Ports property category allows you to specify drive mappings and printer capture settings for the application.

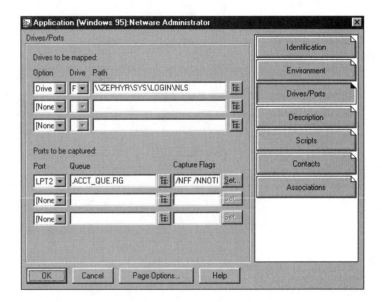

- **Description:** A text field you can use to describe the application. Users running NAL can view the description.

- **Scripts:** Allows you to define two lists of commands. The first is executed before starting the application, and the second is executed after the user exits the application. You can use these scripts to set up any special configuration needed for the application.

These use the same commands as login scripts, described earlier in this chapter.

- **Contacts:** A list of users who are responsible for the application. These users will be notified when there is a problem with the application.

- **Associations:** (Shown in Figure 8.6) is a list of users or groups of users that will be given access to the application. You can add individual users, Organizational Units, Organizations, and Groups to this list.

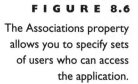

FIGURE 8.6

The Associations property allows you to specify sets of users who can access the application.

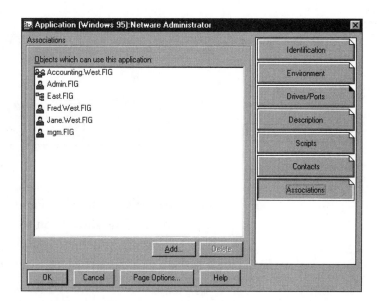

User and Container Properties for Applications

There are also two properties of User, Organization, Organizational Unit, and Group objects that are used to configure applications and settings for that user or set of users:

- **Applications:** (Shown in Figure 8.7) is a list of applications the user (or users in the container or group) has access to. You can add applications here as an alternative to adding users to the application's Associations property. This is also an easy way to view the list of applications a user has access to.

FIGURE 8.7

The Applications property allows you to configure access to applications.

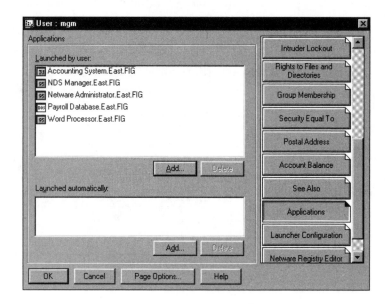

- **Launcher Properties:** (Shown in Figure 8.8) includes a variety of settings for NAL. This allows you to specify whether the user can exit NAL or log out, whether window positions are saved, and whether the user inherits applications the context container has been given access to. This property is available for User objects and Container objects only, not for Group objects.

At this point you should also assign whatever file system rights are necessary for the user to run the application; NAM does not do this for you. See Chapter 7 for details about security.

FIGURE 8.8

The Launcher Properties
dialog box allows you to
configure NAL settings for
a user or container.

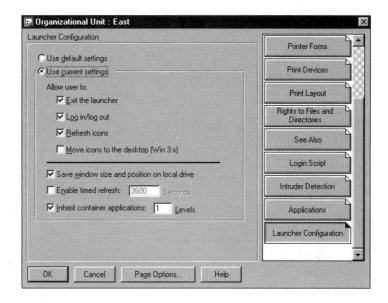

Installing and Using NAL

Once you've created Application objects, you still need to configure the
workstations to run NAL. You can do this in a few different ways:

- Allow the user to run NAL from an Icon

- Configure NAL to start automatically along with the standard
  Explorer or Program Manager shell

- Configure NAL to act as the shell in place of Explorer or Program
  Manager

We'll look at each of these approaches in the sections below. For a
description of how NAL works from the user's point of view, see the
Launching Applications with NAL section later in this chapter.

Setting Up an Icon for NAL

The simplest, and least secure, approach is to allow the user to run NAL
from an icon. The user will still have access to other items in the Start
Menu or Program Manager, and can choose to run NAL only when

needed. This is useful if you are not using NAL for all applications, or if users run some applications from their local disk drives. The disadvantage of this approach is that you have little control over the user's abilities; the user can even delete the NAL icon.

To add an icon for NAL in Windows 3.1, follow these steps:

1. Choose a Program Manager group to contain the icon and highlight it.

2. From the Program Manager, select New from the File menu.

3. Select Program Item as the type to create.

4. Enter a description of the program and the location of the NAL application. In most cases, this is F:\PUBLIC\NAL.EXE. Be sure to use a drive letter mapped to the SYS: volume. You do *not* need to specify a working directory.

To add a Start menu entry for NAL in Windows 95, follow these steps:

1. From the Start menu, choose Settings, then Taskbar.

2. Choose the Start Menu Programs tab.

3. Press the Add button, and enter the location of NAL, usually F:\PUBLIC\NAL.EXE. Click Next.

4. Select a menu folder to place the new entry in and click Next.

5. Enter a name for the program and click Next.

Starting NAL Automatically

You can also configure NAL to start automatically. The user will still be able to access the Start Menu or Program Manager, but the NAL window will be displayed immediately. This approach has the same disadvantages as the approach described above, but it is useful when security is not an issue.

To do this, you must first create an icon as in the previous section. Then move the icon to the Startup folder (in Windows 95) or the Startup Program Manager group (in Windows 3.1). NAL will be launched when Windows starts.

Using NAL as the Windows Shell

A more severe approach is to use NAL as the Windows shell, replacing Program Manager or the Start Menu. This allows you total control over what the user can access, and prevents the user from adding or deleting icons; however, it has the disadvantage of forcing the user to use NAL. Users will be unable to access applications on local hard drives, and may not be familiar with NAL's interface.

Before you can set up NAL as the shell, you will need to copy several files to the workstation's hard drive. You will find these files in the SYS:PUBLIC directory on the server. We suggest copying them to the C:\WINDOWS directory on the workstation. The list is different depending on the version of Windows used:

Windows 3.1:

NALW31.EXE

NALRES.DLL

NALBMP.DLL

NAL.HLP

Windows 95:

NALW95.EXE

NALRES32.DLL

NALBMP32.DLL

NAL.HLP

Once you've copied the required files, you'll need to edit the SYSTEM.INI file in the C:\WINDOWS directory. An easy way to do this is to run the SYSEDIT utility, included with Windows 3.1 or Windows 95. You should find a line in the [boot] section that looks like one of the following:

```
SHELL=EXPLORER.EXE
```

```
SHELL=PROGMAN.EXE
```

Delete the original SHELL entry or add a semicolon at the beginning of the line to comment it out. If the SHELL entry is not present, you can add it. The new shell entry for Windows 95 should read:

```
SHELL=C:\WINDOWS\NALW95.EXE
```

And for Windows 3.1:

```
SHELL=C:\WINDOWS\NALW31.EXE
```

The next time you restart the workstation, NAL will be launched instead of the usual shell. If you need to change it back, simply replace the SHELL entry in the SYSTEM.INI file with the previous value.

WARNING If NAL is configured as the shell, the workstation will become completely useless when the network is down or disconnected. If this is an issue, you should run NAL automatically, as described in the previous section.

Launching Applications with NAL

Now that you're familiar with the process of configuring Application Objects and installing NAL, here's a look at how NAL works from the user's point of view. To run NAL from a workstation, use the icon you created above or simply run the program, usually F:\PUBLIC\NAL.EXE.

The main NAL screen is shown in Figure 8.9. As you can see, icons are displayed for each of the applications available to the user. The most important function, of course, is that the user can double-click an icon to run it. There are a few other options available from the NAL menu.

FIGURE 8.9

NAL displays icons for each Application Object the user has access to.

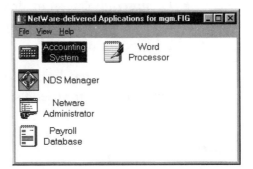

- File ➤ Open starts the currently selected application.

- File ➤ Properties displays some of the application's properties, such as the user to contact and the description. You cannot modify the properties from within NAL.

- File ➤ Exit exits NAL, if the user is allowed to do so.

- The View menu allows you to choose between formats for the display, and to refresh the display. The refresh option is useful if an application has recently been added or modified.

- The Help menu provides access to a simple online help system that describes the functions of NAL.

Review

This chapter has discussed two systems that affect the user's environment:

- *Login scripts* can set up drive mappings and other defaults for the user, so that he or she doesn't have to type DOS commands to set up drives or printers.

- The *menu system* lets you define lists of applications a user can run, and gives the user a simple way of accessing them.

Login Scripts

There are four types of login scripts: user, container, profile, and default. Login scripts are always executed in the same order:

1. Container login script for the user's parent container (if found)

2. Profile login script (if assigned)

3. User login script (if found)

4. Default login script (if no user script is found)

Each of these can be used for a specific purpose:

- You can create a *container login script* for any Organization or Organizational Unit object. This script is the first script executed for users in the container.

- You can use a *profile login script* to execute a certain set of drive mappings or other commands for certain users in the directory.

- You can use *user login scripts* to execute specific commands for a particular user.

- The *default login script* is built into the LOGIN utility. You cannot edit it. The default script is executed when a user has no user login script.

The login script is composed of login script commands:

- MAP for mapping network drives and search drives.

- IF, THEN, and ELSE for conditional actions.

- INCLUDE to include other files or scripts.

- CONTEXT to set the current context.

- WRITE to display a message to the user.

- DISPLAY and FDISPLAY to display an entire file.

- EXIT to end a script.

- Any external DOS command or program preceded with the # sign.

NetWare Application Manager (NAM)

NAM is a system that allows users convenient access to applications, and allows you to manage these applications through NDS. NAM consists of two components:

- Application Objects

- NetWare Application Launcher (NAL)

Application Objects

You can create an application object from NWADMIN, similar to other types of objects. Four types of application objects are available:

- Application (DOS): DOS applications run under DOS, Windows, or Windows 95.

- Application (Windows 3.*x*): Windows 3.*x* applications run under Windows or Windows 95.

- Application (Windows 95): Windows 95 applications run under Windows 95 only.

NetWare Application Launcher (NAL)

NAL is the program a user runs to gain access to applications defined as Application Objects. The file name for NAL is NAL.EXE. You can run NAL from an icon, automatically from the Startup group, or as the Windows shell. Once NAL is started, you can double-click an icon to launch the application.

CNA Practice Test Questions

1. Which is the correct order for login script execution:

A. User, container, default, profile

B. Container, user, profile, or default

C. Container, profile, user, or default

D. Container, default, user, or profile

2. The container login script is executed:

A. For each container the user is in

B. For the user's parent container

C. For the profile container only

D. For the [Root] container only

3. Which is a correct MAP command in a login script?

   A. MAP F:=SYS:APPS

   B. #MAP F:=SYS:APPS

   C. MAP NEXT SYS:APPS

   D. MAP F:=SYS

4. The INCLUDE command:

   A. Exits the login script and starts another

   B. Executes another script, then returns

   C. Adds commands to a login script

   D. Adds a login script to the Profile object

5. Which of the following is *not* a valid comment:

   A. REM Do not change this script

   B. ***Do not change this script***

   C. # Do not change this script

   D. ;Do not change this script

6. To use a DOS program in a login script:

   A. Include the name of the program only

   B. Include # and the name of the program

   C. Include ; and the name of the program

   D. Place the program in an INCLUDE file

7. The two components of NAM are:

A. NAL and NAM

B. NAL and NMENU

C. NAL and Application Objects

D. NAL and Windows 95

8. NAL runs under which operating systems?

A. Windows 95 only

B. Windows 3.1 or Windows 95

C. DOS or Windows 3.1

D. DOS, Windows 3.1, or Windows 95

9. Application objects are created using:

A. NAM

B. NWADMIN

C. APCONFIG

D. NAL

10. To configure NAL as the Windows shell, which of these files is modified?

A. SYSTEM.INI

B. WIN.INI

C. SHELL.INI

D. SHELL.INF

11. Which operating system does not have a corresponding Application object?

A. Windows 95

B. Windows 3.*x*

C. OS/2

D. Windows NT

12. To give a user access to an application, modify the:

A. User Object's Application property

B. Application Object's Association property

C. Both A and B

D. None of the above

CHAPTER

9

How Printing Works

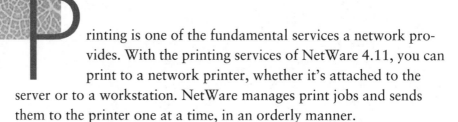

P rinting is one of the fundamental services a network provides. With the printing services of NetWare 4.11, you can
print to a network printer, whether it's attached to the
server or to a workstation. NetWare manages print jobs and sends
them to the printer one at a time, in an orderly manner.

There's more to printing than just you and a printer. The next section introduces the components of the NetWare 4.11 printing services.

Components of NetWare 4.11 Printing

S everal components interact to provide NetWare 4.11 printing services: print servers, print queues, and printers. You can create these objects
under NDS and maintain them from within the NetWare Administrator
(NWADMIN) utility. Additional components include the CAPTURE
utility and the port driver (NPRINTER.EXE or NPRINTER.NLM),
which complete the interface between the workstation and the printer.
The components of NetWare 4.11 printing are shown in Figure 9.1 and
are described in the next sections.

FIGURE 9.1

Several components
interact to provide net-
work printing services.

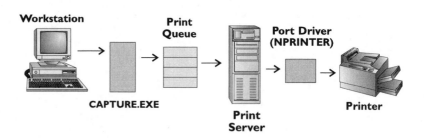

Print Queues

In order to print to a printer on the network, you must first send the data to a *print queue*. The print queue stores each set of data, or *print job*, that it receives. The jobs are then sent, one at a time, to the print server (described next). Print queues serve two main purposes:

- To allow you to continue working while the printer prints. Your workstation quickly sends the job to the print queue, and printing is performed by NetWare, without using your workstation.

- To allow multiuser printing. Many users can add jobs to the queue, and they are printed in the order received. A complete job is always printed before another job starts.

NetWare 4.11 stores all print queue information in properties of the Print Queue object. This includes identification information for the print queue and information for each of the print jobs. The print jobs themselves are stored on a file server volume. The process of selecting a volume is described later in this chapter.

Print Servers

The *print server* accepts print jobs from print queues and sends them to the appropriate printer. In NetWare 3.1*x*, print servers were limited to 16 printers; in NetWare 4.11 this limit has been increased to 256. This allows you to easily use a single print server for the entire network.

You create the Print Server object in NDS. The properties of the Print Server object provide identification information and define the list of printers the server can send jobs to.

Along with the NDS object, you must run the print server software (PSERVER.NLM) on a server. This is the program that actually controls the printing process.

Printers

You must create a Printer object to represent each network printer. The properties of the printer object identify the printer and list the print queues that the printer accepts jobs from. Other properties define the type of printer, and how it is accessed. Printers can be attached to a server, to a workstation, or directly to the network. Printer types are described in the following sections.

Printers Attached to the Server

Printers can be connected directly to a printer port on a server. This is the simplest method and is easy to configure and use. Before you configure a printer in this way, note the following:

- You must have an available port (serial or parallel) on the server for each printer. A typical machine has 1 to 3 parallel ports and 2 serial ports.

- The printer usually needs to be located near the server. The limit for a parallel printer cable is 15 feet. Serial devices have a longer range.

- Unlike NetWare 3.1x, in NetWare 4.11 you do not need to load PSERVER.NLM on the same server the printer is attached to. However, you must run NPRINTER.NLM to drive the printer. NPRINTER.NLM is described later in this section.

Remote (Workstation) Printers

Printers can also be attached to workstations. These printers are referred to as workstation printers or *remote printers*. The print server sends each job to the workstation, and the workstation sends it to the printer. Workstation printers can run under DOS and Windows 3.1 or Windows 95. We'll look at the specifics for each operating system below.

Configuring DOS Workstation Printers In order to use a work-station printer on a DOS or Windows 3.1 workstation, you run the NPRINTER.EXE program on the workstation. This replaces the RPRINTER program used in NetWare 3.1x. NPRINTER is faster and much more reliable than RPRINTER. You can run up to seven copies of NPRINTER on your workstation to drive multiple printers. A workstation can have a maximum of three parallel and four serial printers.

Because NPRINTER is a TSR (terminate and stay resident) pro-gram, you can continue to use the workstation while the network printers are being used. You must leave the workstation turned on in order to make the printer available to network users. Remote printing has the following disadvantages:

- The workstation can be slowed down if a printer is used heavily or if multiple printers are supported.

- If the workstation crashes or is turned off, the printer is unavail-able to network users.

- A small amount of memory (approximately 10KB) is used for each remote printer on the workstation.

You can run Windows 3.1 on a workstation that supports remote printers. In order to do this, you must run NPRINTER for each printer before starting Windows. NPRINTER is more reliable under Windows than RPRINTER, but some Windows applications can cause instability even with NPRINTER.

To use NPRINTER, specify the printer name on the command line. For example, the following command might be used to remotely attach the Check_Printer Printer object:

```
NPRINTER .Check_Printer.ABC_INC
```

WARNING If you use a workstation printer as a network printer, be sure to use the CAPTURE command on the workstation to send jobs to the queue. If the user prints to the printer locally, network print jobs can be interrupted, and the workstation may crash.

Configuring Windows 95 Workstation Printers   Windows 95 includes a utility called NPRINTER Manager that makes it convenient to set up a workstation printer. Follow these steps to start a remote printer:

1. Run NPRINTER Manager. The file to run is NPTWIN95, in the SYS:PUBLIC\WIN95 directory.

2. Select an NDS Printer object for the printer. You can also select a bindery-based printer.

3. Select the Activate When NPrinter Manager Loads option to automatically start the printer each time you load NPRINTER Manager; otherwise, you will have to specify the printer each time.

The printer is now active. You must leave NPRINTER Manager running to drive the printer. In order to configure the printer automatically, you may wish to add NPTWIN95.EXE to the Startup folder in the Start Menu.

Directly Connected Network Printers

A final type of printer is attached directly to the network. This capability is built into many high-end printers, and many others can be attached to the network with an add-on card. Hardware devices are also available to interface the network to one or more printers. Directly connected printers are a very efficient way to manage printing.

Directly connected printers can be configured in one of two modes:

- In **remote mode,** the printer acts as a remote (workstation) printer. Instead of running NPRINTER.EXE on a workstation, the hardware device handles these functions. This configuration is better than a workstation printer because no workstation is slowed by printing.

- In **queue server mode**, the printer acts as a separate print server. Jobs are sent directly from the print queue to the printer. This can be the best arrangement because the load on the server is insignificant.

Many printers are not yet NDS aware; however, network printers developed for NetWare 3.1*x* can be used on NetWare 4.11 networks with no problems. You need to enable Bindery Services (discussed in Chapter 5) to use printers or hardware print servers without NDS support.

To determine which mode to use, consult the documentation for your printer or network interface. Most network printers also include an installation program that can create the needed bindery or NDS objects and configure the printer.

Redirecting Printers with CAPTURE

Some applications (such as WordPerfect) support network printing directly. You can select a network queue to print to rather than a local printer. However, many applications do not provide this support. You can use the CAPTURE command-line utility to print to network printers from these applications.

CAPTURE is a TSR (terminate and stay resident) program that allows you to *redirect* printing to a network printer. You specify a local printer port (usually LPT1, LPT2, or LPT3) with the CAPTURE command. After the CAPTURE command is executed, any printing that your workstation sends to this port is redirected to the network queue you specified.

A basic CAPTURE command specifies the local port to redirect and the network queue to redirect to. The following command redirects the workstation's LPT1 port to a print queue called WEST41_Q:

```
CAPTURE /L=1 /Q=WEST41_Q
```

A new feature of NetWare 4 allows you to specify a printer name, without knowing which queue it is attached to. This command captures the LPT2 port to a printer called PRINTER5:

```
CAPTURE /L=2 /P=PRINTER5
```

> Even if you specify a printer to capture to, a print queue is used. Net-Ware finds the first available print queue serviced by the printer you specify. Since NetWare must search for a queue, you can improve performance by specifying the queue name rather than the printer name.

You can use other CAPTURE options to control the printing process. Use forward slashes (/) or spaces to separate the parameters. CAPTURE options are summarized below.

- **AU (Autoendcap) or NA (No Autoendcap)** allows jobs to be sent as soon as the application exits or signals that it is finished sending the job to the printer. Not all applications support this option. Autoendcap is enabled by default. You can use the NA option to deactivate it.

- **B=*text* (Banner) or NB (No Banner)** specifies whether a *banner* is printed before the job. The banner is a page that describes the job and the user that sent it and can be used to send printouts to the appropriate person. If you specify the B option, follow it with text to be included at the bottom of the banner, such as **B=ACCOUNTING**.

- **C=*number*** (**Copies**) specifies the number of copies to be printed.

- **CR=*filename*** (**Create file**) allows you to redirect printing to a file instead of a printer. The file can later be sent to a printer.

- **D** (**Details**) displays details about a captured port. Use the L option (described below) to specify the port.

- **EC** (**End Capture**) ends capturing to the port. This option replaces the ENDCAP command in NetWare 3.1*x*. Any job that is currently being sent is completed. There are three options for EC:

  - **EC L=*port*** ends capturing for the specified port. If no port is specified, LPT1 is assumed.

  - **EC ALL** ends capturing for all ports.

  - **ECCA** ends capturing and cancels the current job. Nothing is sent to the print queue.

- **F=*number or name*** (**Form**) allows you to specify a form to be used with print jobs. Forms are defined with the PRINTDEF utility or in NetWare Administrator and are described later in this chapter.

- **FF** (**Form Feed**) or **NFF** (**No Form Feed**) specifies whether a *form feed* character is sent to the printer after the print job is completed. This option ensures that printing for the next job starts at the top of a page. Most applications send a form feed by default. Using the FF option unnecessarily results in blank pages being printed between jobs.

- **/?** or **/H** (**Help**) displays a list of options for the CAPTURE command.

- **HOLD** (**Hold job**) specifies that print jobs are to be *held* in the print queue and not printed. You can later release the jobs using PCONSOLE or NWADMIN.

- **J=*name*** (**Specify job**) selects a *print job configuration* to be used. A print job configuration contains options similar to CAPTURE options, and its name can be used with no other options. You can create print job configurations using the NWADMIN or PRINTCON utilities.

- **K** (**Keep**) tells CAPTURE to keep your print job even if the capture is not ended correctly. A capture may not end correctly if your workstation is disconnected or turned off while a job is being printed. Without this option, the job is discarded when this happens. With the Keep option, the job is sent to the queue.

- **L=*number*** or **LPT*n*** (**Local port**) specifies the logical port number to redirect to the queue. You can use numbers from 1 to 9, as described below. The options **L=2** and **LPT2** both select the LPT2 port for redirection.

- **NAM=*name*** (**Banner name**) specifies a name to be included at the top of the banner. This defaults to your login name. This option also activates the Banner option.

- **NOTI** (**Notify**) or **NNOTI** (**No Notify**) specifies whether you are notified when the print job has finished printing. If notify is enabled, you receive a message on your screen or in a pop-up window (under Windows) when the job has completed.

- **P=*name*** (**Printer**) or **Q=*name*** (**Queue**) specifies a printer or queue for the port to be redirected to. Only one of these options can be used.

- **S=*name*** (**Server**) specifies a server name for the queue. This is used for bindery-based queues only.

- **SH** (**Show**) displays the current CAPTURE parameters for each port.

- **T=***number* (**Tab spacing**) or **NT** (**No tab conversion**) specifies the number of spaces to use in place of tab characters in the document. Use the NT option if your print job does not require conversion.

- **TI=***number* (**Timeout**) specifies a timeout in seconds to be used to end a print job. If the specified number of seconds elapses with no data having been sent to the printer, the job is considered finished and sent to the print queue.

When you use CAPTURE, data is sent to a print job in the specified queue. The following three events can end the job and send it to the printer:

- You can end capture with the EC option. This sends the job to the printer and discontinues CAPTURE.

- You can set a timeout with the TI option. If the specified number of seconds elapses with no printing having occurred, NetWare assumes that the job is finished and sends it. The port remains captured for future jobs.

- You can set the AU (Autoendcap) option. This allows NetWare to detect when an application exits or is finished with the printer. If the application supports it, this option is the fastest method. If you set both the AU and timeout options, the timeout covers the applications that don't support the AU option.

In NetWare 4, redirection is no longer limited to LPT1, LPT2, and LPT3. You can use port numbers up to 9. In order to do so, you must add a line to the workstation's NET.CFG file in the NetWare DOS Requester section to specify the number of allowed ports:

```
NETWORK PRINTERS = 9
```

Note that the port numbers used in the CAPTURE command are *logical ports*. These have no relation to *physical ports*, the actual ports used to connect printers. Your workstation does not need to have a physical port available in order to capture a logical port.

If your workstation has a physical port with the specified number, the CAPTURE command overrides the printer and sends data to a print queue instead. In order to print to a local printer (a printer hooked to a physical port on your workstation), you must either use the EC option to end capturing to that port or not capture the port. You can also define your workstation's printer as a network printer, which was described earlier in this chapter.

When you define a Printer object, you specify the LPT port it is hooked to. This is a physical port number and has no relation to the port numbers used in the CAPTURE command.

The Port Driver (NPRINTER)

Before data is sent to the printer, it is sent to the *port driver*. The port driver receives data from the print server and transmits it to the printer. NPRINTER can be run in one of three ways:

- For a printer connected to a server, load NPRINTER.NLM on the server. If the printer is attached to the same server that the print server (PSERVER.NLM) is running on, NPRINTER is loaded automatically for the printer. You can also attach the printer to a different server and load NPRINTER.NLM manually on that server.

- For remote (workstation) printers, run the NPRINTER.EXE program, described in the Remote Workstation Printers section earlier in this chapter.

- You do not need to run NPRINTER for directly connected network printers. The NPRINTER software is built into the printer or interface.

Managing Printing with NetWare Administrator

Because printing services have been integrated into NDS, you can use the NetWare Administrator utility to manage all aspects of printing. This includes creating the objects required for printing, configuring them, and managing print jobs in print queues.

Creating Objects

You can use NetWare Administrator to create the objects required for printing. The properties of these objects control how they interact and define the devices used for printing. In order to enable printing with NDS, you must create a Print Server object and at least one Printer and Print Queue object.

These objects can be created anywhere in the Directory tree. However, in order to provide easy access, it is best to create all of the objects in the context where the users who use the printers are located, or as close to it as possible. You can create the objects in any order.

Creating the Print Server

You must create a Print Server object for each server that runs PSERVER.NLM and for directly connected network printers that use queue server mode. Since each print server can provide access to up to 256 printers, you typically need only one Print Server object for the entire network.

To create the Print Server object, follow these steps:

1. Highlight the context to create the Print Server object in.

2. Select Create from the Object menu.

3. Select Print Server as the type of object.

4. Enter the Print Server name in the Create Print Server dialog box, which is shown in Figure 9.2.

F I G U R E 9.2

Enter the print server
name to create a new
print server.

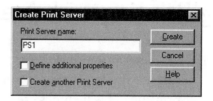

The Print Server object is now ready for use. You can change its properties by selecting Details from the Object menu.

The properties of the Print Server object are used to identify the print server and to specify parameters. Several pages (categories) of properties are available. These are described in the sections below.

Identification   This page specifies information about the Print Server object. The Identification information includes the name, network address, status, and other information. You enter this information in the Identification properties page, which is shown in Figure 9.3. Most of these properties are optional. You can use the Change Password button to choose a password for the print server; this password will be required when PSERVER.NLM is loaded at the server. The status of the print server is also shown in the Identification properties page. If the print server is running, you can disable it with the Unload button.

Assignments   This page lists the printers that have been assigned to the server. After you create the Printer object, you can use the Add button to add the printer to the list. Only printers in this list can receive jobs from the print server. The Assignments properties page is shown in Figure 9.4.

Users   You can use this page to specify which users can send jobs to printers in the print server. You can add specific users to this list or use groups or container objects to provide access to multiple users.

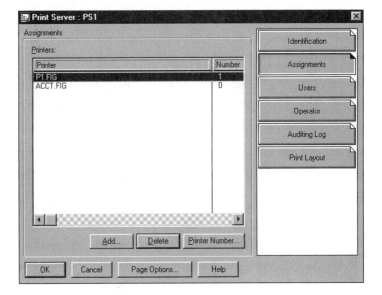

Operator   You can use this page to specify one or more users who have Operator privileges on the print server. These users can unload the print server and perform other control functions. This list can include individual users; you can also use an Organizational Role object here to assign a print server operator.

Auditing Log   This page, shown in Figure 9.5, provides a powerful *auditing* feature for printing. If this is enabled, a log of the print server's activities is maintained. Each print job is added to the log, and the information in the log specifies whether printing was successful, which printer the print job went to, and how long it took to print the job. To activate the auditing feature, use the Enable Auditing button. The text on this button then changes to read Disable Auditing and can be used to stop the auditing process.

Print Layout   The Print Layout page allows you to view the configuration of the print server graphically. This is a powerful feature that you can use to determine how printing has been configured and to troubleshoot printing problems. The Print Layout properties page is shown in Figure 9.6.

The print server, print queues, and printers are shown with lines between them to define their relationship. You can watch for two indicators of printer problems:

- An icon with a red exclamation mark is displayed to the left of objects that are not functioning. This means that the print server is not running, the printer is not connected, or the print queue is not accepting jobs.

- A dashed line is displayed instead of a solid line if the connection is a temporary one and will not be re-established the next time the print server is loaded.

FIGURE 9.5

The Auditing Log page allows you to audit printing.

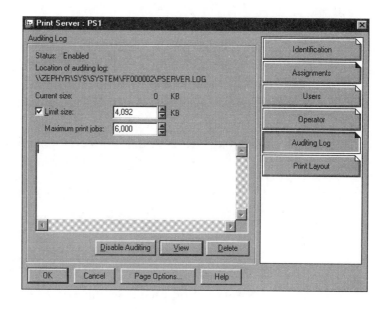

FIGURE 9.6

The Print Layout properties page provides an illustration of how the components of printing interact.

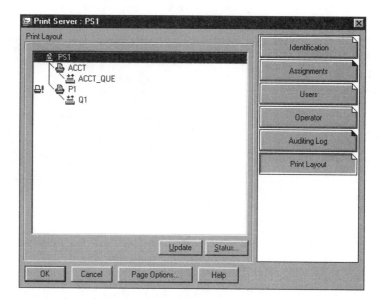

Creating Print Queues

You must create at least one print queue for each printer on the network. Print queues can also be serviced by multiple printers, and multiple queues can be routed to a single printer. In addition to NetWare 4.11 print queues, you can define a Print Queue object that sends print jobs to a queue on a bindery-based server. This makes it easy to integrate bindery and NDS printing.

To create the Print Queue object, follow these steps:

1. Highlight the context in which to create the print queue. For easiest access, it should be located in the same context as users who use this queue.

2. Select Create from the Object menu.

3. Select Print Queue as the type of object to create. You will be presented with the Create Print Queue dialog box, shown in Figure 9.7.

FIGURE 9.7

Enter the required information to create a new Print Queue object.

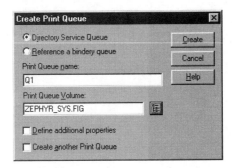

4. Select whether this print queue is an NDS queue or will reference a bindery queue.

5. Select a name for the print queue. For bindery queues, enter the name as it appears on the bindery server.

6. Select a volume to store print queue entries on. For NDS queues, this can be any volume; for bindery queues, this should be the SYS volume on the bindery server.

7. Click the Create button to create the Print Queue object.

After the Print Queue object is created, highlight it, and select Details from the Object menu to define its properties. The properties are discussed in the sections below.

Identifying the Print Queue   The Identification properties page, shown in Figure 9.8, allows you to view and change identifying information for the print queue. In addition, three checkboxes in the Operator Flags section of the page allow you to control the print queue's behavior:

- **Allow Users to Submit Print Jobs** controls whether users can add jobs to the print queue. If this option is turned off, users receive an error message when they attempt to print to a port that has been redirected to the queue.

- **Allow Service by Current Print Servers** controls whether entries in the queue are printed by the print servers. If you turn off this option, entries are added to the queue but are not printed until it is turned back on.

- **Allow New Print Servers to Attach** controls whether new print servers can be attached to the print queue. If you turn this option off, all current print servers continue to print, but new ones are not able to attach.

Viewing Queue Assignments   The Assignments properties page allows you to view the objects that have been assigned to this print queue. These include print servers that are authorized to obtain entries from the queue, and printers that are set up to print jobs from the queue.

FIGURE 9.8

The Identification properties page shows information about the print queue and allows you to control it.

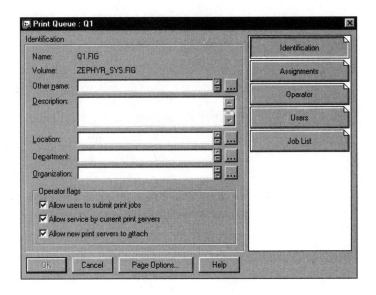

The properties on the Print Queue object's Assignments page are for your information only and cannot be changed. Changes are made from the Assignments properties of the Print Server and Printer object dialog boxes.

Queue Users and Operators The Users properties page allows you to specify a list of users who can submit jobs to the print queue. Use the Add button to add to this list. You can add individual users, but it is more common to add multiple users by using Group objects or container objects.

The Operator properties page allows you to specify users who can control print jobs in the queue, as described in the next section. You can include individual users in the list or use an Organizational Role object to assign a print queue operator.

Managing Print Jobs The final page of properties for the Print Queue object is the Job List properties page. This lists each of the print jobs that have been submitted to the queue and describes their status. This screen is shown in Figure 9.9.

F I G U R E 9.9

The Job List properties page lists print jobs waiting in the print queue.

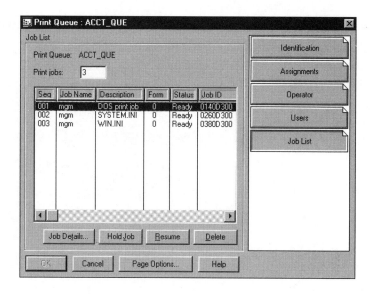

F I G U R E   9.9

The Job List properties page lists print jobs waiting in the print queue.

You can use the Job List properties page to view the jobs that have been sent to the printer. In addition, you can manage the jobs with the following functions:

- **Job Details** displays complete information about the highlighted job. This screen is shown in Figure 9.10. You can modify certain information, such as the job description, and place the job on hold if desired.

- **Hold Job** allows you to place a job on hold; the job is not printed until released.

- **Resume** allows a held job to be printed.

- **Delete** removes an entry from the queue.

Creating Printer Objects

The Printer object is the final object required for network printing. You must create a Printer object to represent each printer on the network.

FIGURE 9.10

You can view details for
an individual print job in
the Print Job Detail
screen.

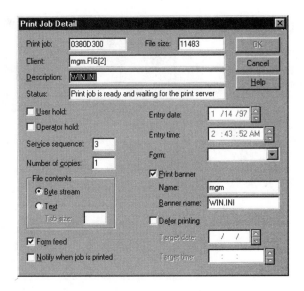

You can create a Printer object by following these steps:

1. Highlight the context to place the Printer object in.

2. Select Create from the Object menu.

3. Select Printer as the type of object to create.

4. Enter a name for the printer, and click the Create button to create
the object.

After the Printer object is created, you can modify its properties by
using the Details option from the Object menu. The properties of the
Printer object allow you to identify the printer, specify how it is connected to the network, and specify print queues to print from. These
properties are described in the sections below.

Selecting Printer Assignments   The Assignments properties page,
shown in Figure 9.11, allows you to assign Print Queue objects to be
serviced by the printer. You can use the Add button to add additional
queues. The Priority arrows allow you to change a queue's priority,
and the Delete button allows you to remove a print queue from the list.

FIGURE 9.11

The Printer object's Assignments properties page lists queues serviced by the printer.

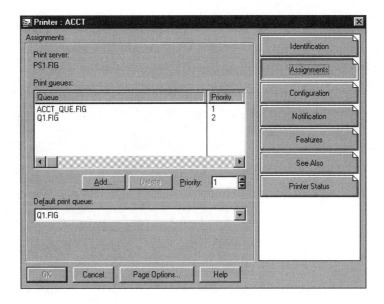

The Default Print Queue option allows you to specify a print queue to be used when a user uses the P option in the CAPTURE command to specify the printer's name rather than specifying a print queue.

Configuring Printers The Configuration properties page, shown in Figure 9.12, allows you to configure the printer. This controls the type of port the printer is connected to, the communication parameters, and other settings. Available options on this screen include:

- **Printer Type** allows you to specify the type of printer. This specifies the type of port, parallel or serial, the printer is attached to. You can also specify UNIX or AppleTalk printers.

- **The Communication button** allows you to view parameters specific to the type of port used. The Parallel Communication screen for a parallel printer is shown in Figure 9.13. You use this screen to specify the physical port the printer is attached to, speed of communication, and other settings.

FIGURE 9.12

The Printer object's Configuration properties define the type of printer and its connection.

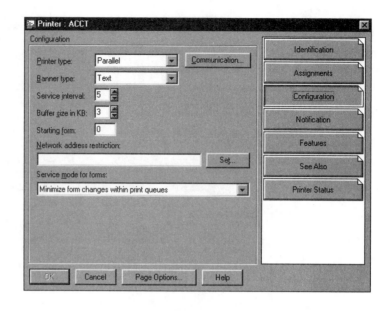

FIGURE 9.13

The Parallel Communication screen allows you to define specific communication parameters for the printer.

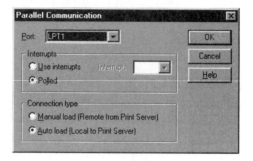

- **Banner Type** specifies whether the banner used for the printer is in text (ASCII) or PostScript format. The PostScript format can be used on compatible printers only.

- **Service Interval** controls how often the printer checks for new jobs in the print queue. The default is 5 seconds.

- **Buffer Size in KB** controls the size of the buffer used to store data before it is sent to the printer. This can range from 3KB to 20KB. The buffer is stored in the RAM of the server or workstation that runs NPRINTER.

- **Starting Form** selects the default type of form for the printer.

- **Network Address Restriction** allows you to select a certain list of network addresses that the printer can use.

- **Service Mode for Forms** specifies how form changes are managed.

Other Printer Properties   The remaining pages of printer properties allow you to identify the printer, provide notification for printer errors, and display printer status:

- **Identification** allows you to define a name and other information for the printer. Most of this information is optional.

- **Notification** allows you to list users who are notified when an error occurs at the printer.

- **See Also** allows you to reference other objects that are related to the Printer object. This is for your information only and is not used by NetWare.

- **Printer Status** displays the current printer status and information about the job that is currently printing.

Using Quick Setup

New in NetWare 4.11 is a Quick Setup option in NWADMIN. Previously, this option was available only from the PCONSOLE utility. Quick Setup allows you to easily create the necessary objects for printing—Print Server, Print Queue, and Printer—all at the same time.

To access the Quick Setup option, select a container to hold the new objects, then choose Print Services Quick Setup from NWADMIN's Tools menu. You are presented with a selection of options for the new objects, as shown in Figure 9.14.

FIGURE 9.14

Specify printer, queue, and print server information for the Quick Setup option.

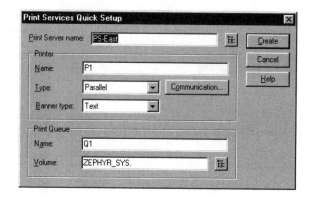

Specify the basic information for the printer, print queue, and print server. If you already have a print server running, you can select it; otherwise, a new server will be created. When finished, click the Create button. All of the needed objects will be created. This process may take a few moments.

Managing Printing with PCONSOLE

You may be familiar with the PCONSOLE menu utility, used to manage most aspects of printing in NetWare 3.1*x*. This DOS-based utility has been improved in NetWare 4.11.

If you prefer PCONSOLE to NetWare Administrator, you can use PCONSOLE to perform most of the same printing management tasks described in this chapter. In addition, PCONSOLE offers a Quick Setup feature that allows you to create all of the objects needed for printing in one step. The main PCONSOLE menu is shown in Figure 9.15.

The following sections describe how to use PCONSOLE to set up and manage network printing. See the previous section "Managing Printing with NetWare Administrator" for details on the properties of the print objects.

FIGURE 9.15

PCONSOLE is a DOS menu utility that allows you to control network printing.

Using Quick Setup

As with NWADMIN, the Quick Setup option on PCONSOLE's main menu provides the easiest way to set up network printing, without requiring you to know about the interaction between the print objects. Quick Setup creates each of the required print objects and assigns the correct properties for them to work together. You can use this option to create a working setup quickly and then examine and modify the objects if necessary.

After you select Quick Setup, you see the screen in Figure 9.16. You can specify a printer name, queue name, and print server name. Default names are provided. If the print server you specify does not exist, it is created automatically.

FIGURE 9.16

Print Services Quick Setup creates all the objects required for network printing.

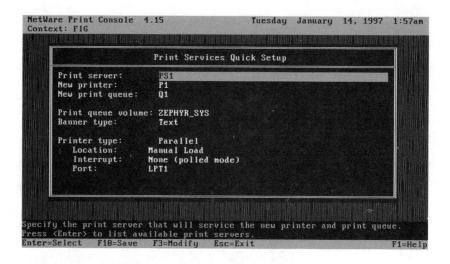

```
NetWare Print Console  4.15                    Tuesday  January  14, 1997  1:57am
Context: FIG

                        Print Services Quick Setup
            Print server:      PS1
            New printer:       P1
            New print queue:   Q1

            Print queue volume: ZEPHYR_SYS
            Banner type:        Text

            Printer type:       Parallel
              Location:         Manual Load
              Interrupt:        None (polled mode)
              Port:             LPT1




Specify the print server that will service the new printer and print queue.
Press <Enter> to list available print servers.
Enter=Select   F10=Save   F3=Modify   Esc=Exit                           F1=Help
```

Managing Printer Objects

PCONSOLE also allows you to control the three types of objects required for printing: print queues, printers, and print servers. You can create new objects and specify all of their properties from within this utility. Most of the options are similar to the ones in the PCONSOLE utility in NetWare 3.1*x*.

> You can perform many tasks in more than one way from PCONSOLE, which makes it easy to find the option you need. For example, you can create Printer objects from the Print Server option.

Print Queues

PCONSOLE's Print Queues option allows you to create and modify Print Queue objects and their settings. When you select this option, you will see a list of currently defined print queues. Press Insert to create a new print queue, or press ↵ to view information for a print queue. From the Print Queue Information menu, shown in Figure 9.17, you can control the properties of the print queue and manage print jobs.

FIGURE 9.17

The Print Queue
Information menu allows
you to monitor and
control the print queue.

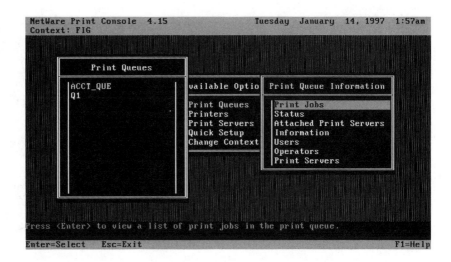

Printers

PCONSOLE's Printers option displays a list of currently defined printers.
You can create a new Printer object by pressing the Insert key from this
screen. Press ↵ when the name of a printer is highlighted to display the
Printer Configuration screen, shown in Figure 9.18. This screen allows
you to set options for the printer type, configuration options, and other
properties of the Printer object.

Print Servers

Press ↵ on PCONSOLE's Print Servers option to view a list of currently defined print servers. You can press Insert to create a new Print
Server object or press Delete to delete a server. Press ↵ when the name
of a print server is highlighted to view the Print Server Information
menu, shown in Figure 9.19. This menu allows you to define the properties of the print server.

FIGURE 9.18

The Printer Configuration
screen allows you to
control the Printer
object's properties.

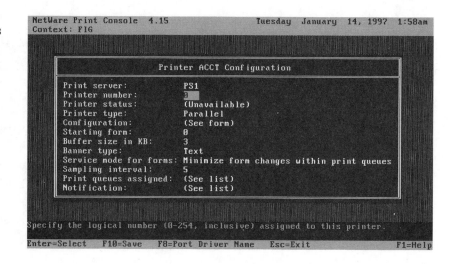

FIGURE 9.18

The Printer Configuration
screen allows you to
control the Printer
object's properties.

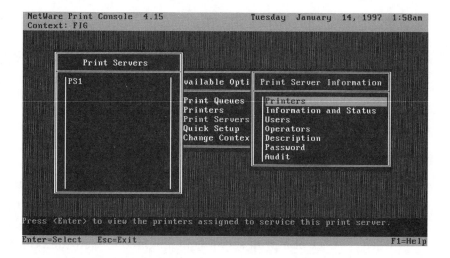

FIGURE 9.19

The Print Server
Information menu allows
you to define the print
server's properties.

Creating Custom Print Configurations and Forms with NetWare Utilities

The PRINTCON and PRINTDEF utilities, also available with NetWare 3.1*x*, have been improved in NetWare 4.11. You can use these utilities, or the NetWare Administrator utility, to create custom print configurations and to print forms.

In NetWare 3.1*x*, the print configuration and form definition databases are stored as files on the server. In NetWare 4.11, they are properties of User or Container objects in NDS.

Using **PRINTDEF** to Create Printer Forms

The PRINTDEF utility allows you to create printer *forms*. These forms can be used to specify commands to be sent to the printer at the beginning of a print job. You can also use different form types for different types of paper loaded into the printer. In this way, forms allow you to tightly control printer output, even when using software that doesn't support your printer specifically. If you specify a certain form type when you submit a job, NetWare does not allow it to be printed until that form is mounted. Figure 9.20 shows the main menu of the PRINTDEF utility.

By defining forms, you can control the printer's formatting functions for applications that do not support the printer directly. Most applications, and all Microsoft Windows applications, provide printer support that makes PRINTDEF configurations unnecessary. Nevertheless, it is very useful for older software and for many custom-written business applications.

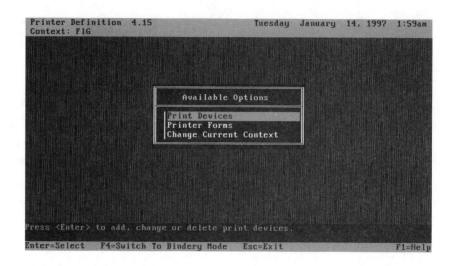

Using PRINTCON to Configure Print Jobs

The PRINTCON utility allows you to create custom print job configurations. The configurations consist of a list of options, similar to the options for the CAPTURE command. Figure 9.21 shows the main menu of the PRINTCON utility.

F I G U R E 9.21

The PRINTCON utility allows you to create custom print job configurations.

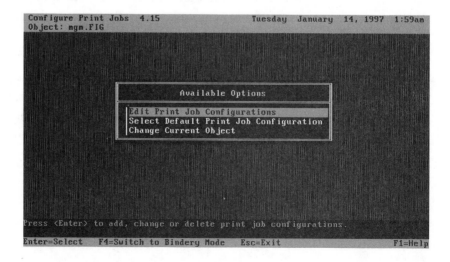

If you specify a print job configuration, you can omit all other CAPTURE options. For example, the following CAPTURE command specifies a print job configuration called TEST:

```
CAPTURE /j=TEST
```

Creating Forms and Configuring Print Jobs with NetWare Administrator

You can also control form definitions and print job configurations using the NetWare Administrator utility. The printer form information is stored as an attribute of each container object, and that information affects leaf objects in that container.

You can create print job configurations using the NetWare Administrator utility as follows:

- Each user has a Print Job Configurations property that can be used to define configurations specific to the user.

- Each Organization or Organizational Unit object also has a Print Job Configurations property. This allows you to define job configurations that can be used by any user in the container.

Review

Printing is a fundamental service of NetWare 4.11. Printing is handled by several components:

- In order to print to a printer on the network, you must first send the data to a *print queue*. The print queue stores each set of data, or *print job*, that it receives. The jobs are then sent, one at a time, to the print server.

- The *print server* accepts print jobs from print queues and sends them to the appropriate printer. In NetWare 3.1*x*, print servers were limited to 16 printers; in NetWare 4.11 this limit has been increased to 256. This allows you to easily use a single print server for the entire network. You create the Print Server object in NDS. The properties of the Print Server object provide identification information and define the list of printers the server can send jobs to.

- You must create a Printer object to represent each network printer. The properties of the printer object identify the printer and list the print queues that the printer can accept jobs from. Other properties define the type of printer and how it is accessed. Printers can be attached to a server, to a workstation, or directly to the network.

- CAPTURE is a TSR (terminate and stay resident) program that allows you to *redirect* printing to a network printer. You specify a local printer port (usually LPT1, LPT2, or LPT3) with the CAPTURE command. After the CAPTURE command is executed, any printing that your workstation sends to this port is redirected to the network queue you specified.

- Before data is sent to the printer, it is sent to the *port driver*. The port driver receives data from the print server and transmits it to the printer. The port driver is also called NPRINTER and is run by NPRINTER.EXE or NPRINTER.NLM.

To manage printing, use NetWare Administrator. The print server, print queue, and Printer objects can be controlled from within this utility.

CNA Practice Test Questions

1. The NDS objects used for printing are:

A. Print server, print queue, port driver

B. Print server, print queue, printer

C. Printer, print server, port driver

D. CAPTURE, printer, print server

2. The number of printers controlled by a NetWare 4.11 print server:

A. Is limited only by the server's memory

B. Is limited to 16 printers

C. Is limited to 256 printers

D. Is limited to 3 parallel printers and 2 serial printers

3. There are three basic types of network printer:

A. Workstation, server, queue

B. Workstation, server, directly connected

C. NDS, bindery, workstation

D. Dot matrix, laser, daisy wheel

4. Which is the correct CAPTURE command to capture the LPT2 port to the CHECKS queue?

A. CAPTURE J=2 P=CHECKS

B. CAPTURE L=1 B=2 Q=CHECKS

C. CAPTURE LPT2 P=CHECK_PRINTER

D. CAPTURE LPT2 Q=CHECKS

5. The Print Server object:

A. Is not used in NetWare 4.11

B. Moves jobs from the print queue to the printer

C. Moves jobs from the print queue to the port driver

D. Stores a list of jobs to be printed

6. To start a workstation printer, you use the _____ program.

A. RPRINTER

B. REMOTE

C. WPRINTER

D. NPRINTER

7. Which is the correct order of components when a print job is processed?

A. CAPTURE, print queue, printer

B. CAPTURE, print queue, print server, port driver, printer

C. CAPTURE, port driver, print server, print queue, printer

D. Port driver, CAPTURE, print queue, print server, printer

8. CAPTURE can use which LPT ports?

   A. LPT1-3

   B. LPT1-5

   C. Only those you have the hardware for

   D. LPT1-9

9. The Print Server object:

   A. Is created automatically when the printer is installed

   B. Needs to be created for each printer

   C. Can handle up to 256 printers

   D. Is not needed for most printers

10. You can stop and continue a print job with which NWADMIN functions?

   A. Pause and play

   B. Pause and resume

   C. Hold and resume

   D. Hold and unhold

11. The number of printers on the network is limited by:

   A. The print server

   B. The number of ports on the server

   C. The number of queues

   D. Disk storage available

12. You can CAPTURE to:

   A. A printer or a print server

   B. A printer only

   C. A printer or a queue

   D. A printer or NPRINTER

CHAPTER

10

Administering the File Server

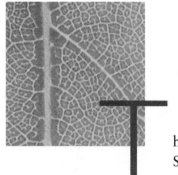

he NetWare 4.11 server doesn't work like a regular PC. Since it runs NetWare 4.11, it's a completely different system. None of the DOS commands you might be familiar with work on the server. There are special commands that do, however.

In this chapter we'll take a look at the components of a NetWare 4.11 server and the types of commands and utilities that you can use at the server. In addition, you will learn how to edit the server's configuration files, access the server from a workstation on the network, and prevent unauthorized access to the server.

What's in a NetWare 4.11 Server?

A NetWare server is any computer that runs the NetWare operating system. NetWare can run on any PC-compatible computer with a 386 or better processor. You should also have sufficient RAM and disk storage space—those requirements were discussed in Chapter 2, "What's New in NetWare 4.11."

The software that runs on the NetWare 4.11 server includes the operating system—NetWare itself—and loadable modules. Let's take a look at each of these in detail.

Operating System

The NetWare operating system provides the basic services of a network. The basic part of the operating system is called the *core* operating system. The services provided by the core OS include:

- File sharing

- Printer sharing

- Security

- Routing

- NDS

All of the other services that NetWare 4.11 provides are actually provided by additional programs called NetWare Loadable Modules (NLMs), which are described next.

NetWare Loadable Modules (NLMs)

Along with the core OS, the server can run NetWare Loadable Modules, or NLMs. NLMs are programs that run on the NetWare server. The NetWare operating system allows NLMs to integrate fully with the system; what this means is that NLMs and the OS share the same memory and can perform some of the same functions.

Because NLMs provide some of the services of NetWare, it is called a *modular* network operating system. This has some advantages over a fixed system:

- Because NLMs can be loaded and unloaded, you can load only the ones you need. This allows you to save memory for needed services.

- Third parties can also develop NLMs. You can find NLM virus software, backup software, and many other applications.

Many NLMs are provided with NetWare 4.11 itself; these fit into four categories, described in the following sections.

Disk Drivers

Disk drivers provide an interface to the disk hardware on the server. In order to access the disk, the NetWare core operating system sends messages to the disk driver. Disk drivers usually have a .DSK file extension. The new disk driver standard is called NPA (NetWare Peripheral Architecture). Drivers that use this standard actually consist of two files, with two different extensions:

- A Common Device Module, or CDM

- A Hardware Access Module, or HAM

LAN Drivers

Just as disk drivers interface NetWare with the disk drives in the server, LAN drivers provide an interface to LAN cards in the server. You can load a module for each card in the server and unload them when they are not needed. LAN driver modules have a .LAN extension.

Name Space Modules

NetWare 4.11 provides a full set of features that allow access to non-DOS computers, including the Macintosh and OS/2. Both of these operating systems allow long file names instead of the typical DOS eight-character name. In order to fully support long file names, NetWare uses a *name space module*. These modules have the extension .NAM.

If you are using an OS that requires extended file names, you should always load the name space module for that OS when you start the server.

Utility NLMs

The final category of NLMs includes utilities that perform a wide variety of functions. These have the extension .NLM. NLMs that come with NetWare or are available separately provide the following functions:

- Network printing (PSERVER)

- Backup and restore

- Remote console access

- Server monitoring

- Power supply monitoring

- Network management

- Communications

- Media management

- Data migration

NetWare 4.11 Console Commands

You're probably familiar with the DOS prompt—the prompt where you enter a command on a DOS workstation. The NetWare file server console has a similar prompt where you can enter NetWare *console commands*. These can be used to perform a wide variety of functions, maintain the server, and load and unload NLMs.

The file server prompt is referred to as the *colon prompt* because it always ends with a colon. The prompt is usually the name of the file server. For example, if you accessed the console of a server called TRIFFID, the prompt would appear as:

```
TRIFFID:
```

If you're looking at a screen that doesn't display the colon prompt, you can use the Alt+Esc key to switch screens until you see the colon prompt. The next sections list the available console commands and explain each one. You'll need to understand these in order to manage the server.

BROADCAST

The BROADCAST command allows you to send a message to users on the network. To use this command, specify a message to be sent, and a user to send it to. The keyword ALL can be used to send the message to all users who are currently attached to the network.

The main purpose of BROADCAST is to let users know about conditions that might affect their use of the network. Here's a command that would send a message to all users:

```
BROADCAST "The system will be going down at 9:00" TO
EVERYONE
```

The NetWare 4.11 console command SEND is identical to BROADCAST.

CLEAR STATION

This command allows you to force a user off the network. It's not really useful because the powerful MONITOR utility allows you to do the same. This command can be used to free a workstation that is hung; however, it does not close files correctly, and data may be lost. Use it as a last resort.

CLS

This command simply clears the screen on the file server—useful if you wish to hide the commands you've typed from prying eyes or if you just like to be tidy.

CONFIG

CONFIG displays a summary of how the server is connected to the network. This command can be useful in determining what network cards are installed and how long the server has been running. The output of the CONFIG command is shown in Figure 10.1.

FIGURE 10.1

The CONFIG command displays a summary of the server's configuration.

```
IPX internal network number: 2FB6CE6C
      Node address: 000000000001
      Frame type: VIRTUAL_LAN
      LAN protocol: IPX network 2FB6CE6C
Server Up Time:  55 Minutes 21 Seconds

Novell NE2000
      Version 3.29    November 1, 1994
      Hardware setting: I/O ports 300h to 31Fh, Interrupt Ah
      Node address: 080000292329
      Frame type: ETHERNET_802.3
      Board name: NE2000_1_E83
      LAN protocol: IPX network 6231CA67

Novell NE2000
      Version 3.29    November 1, 1994
      Hardware setting: I/O ports 300h to 31Fh, Interrupt Ah
      Node address: 080000292329
      Frame type: ETHERNET_802.2
      Board name: NE2000_1_E82
      LAN protocol: IPX network CC662033

Tree Name: MGM
Bindery Context(s):
<Press ESC to terminate or any other key to continue>
```

DISABLE LOGIN

The DISABLE LOGIN command prevents users from logging in. It does not affect users who are already logged in, only those who try to log in after you type the command. If you're feeling mischievous, you might enjoy doing this every now and then just to cause a stir; otherwise, the best use for this command is when the server is having a problem and you need to take it down. You can use the DISABLE LOGIN command to stop users from logging in and use CLEAR STATION or the MONITOR utility to take care of those who are already logged in.

DISMOUNT

This command dismounts a volume, making it inaccessible to users. This is the opposite of the MOUNT command. A volume must be mounted before it can be accessed.

DISPLAY NETWORKS

This command displays a list of internal network numbers that NetWare can detect on the server and other servers it is communicating with. This can be useful for configuring communication between servers.

DISPLAY SERVERS

This command displays a list of servers that can be seen across the network from the current server. If you are on a multiserver network, this is a way to verify that the network connection is still intact and communication is working. An example of the list of servers is shown in Figure 10.2.

DOWN

This is probably the most drastic server command—but you'll use it more often than most others. The DOWN command is used to take the server down. If any users are on the network, they are sent a message saying that the server is going down. NetWare then checks for open files; if any files are open, it asks you to type **Y** before bringing the server down. It then closes all files and dismounts all volumes.

F I G U R E 10.2

The DISPLAY SERVERS
command lists accessible
servers.

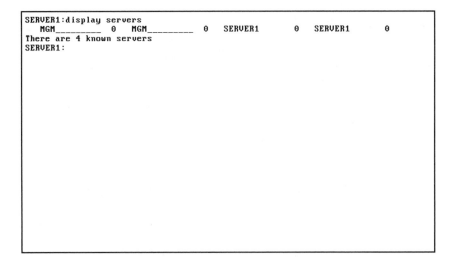
```
SERVER1:display servers
  MGM_____   0   MGM_____   0   SERVER1       0   SERVER1       0
There are 4 known servers
SERVER1:
```

After the DOWN command finishes taking the server down, you are
returned to the colon prompt. At this point only two commands can
work: EXIT or RESTART SERVER.

EXIT

The EXIT command is the second half of the server-down process. If
you wish to return to DOS after taking the server down, you can use
this command. An alternative is the RESTART SERVER command,
which brings the server back up.

HELP

HELP may be the most useful command of all. It allows you to display
instructions for any server command. For example, the following command displays a list of options for the BROADCAST command:

HELP BROADCAST

The output of this HELP command is shown in Figure 10.3.

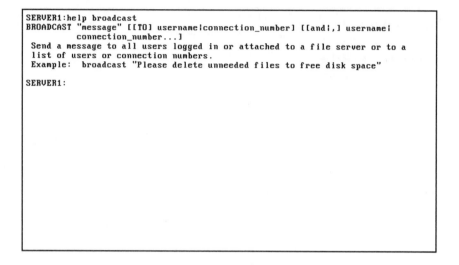

FIGURE 10.3

The HELP command displays instructions for a console command.

```
SERVER1:help broadcast
BROADCAST "message" [[TO] username:connection_number] [[and:,] username:
            connection_number...]
 Send a message to all users logged in or attached to a file server or to a
 list of users or connection numbers.
 Example:  broadcast "Please delete unneeded files to free disk space"

SERVER1:
```

LOAD

LOAD is a commonly used command. It allows you to load an NLM. After the NLM loads you may see a screen provided by that utility. NLMs are discussed later in this chapter.

A complimentary command, UNLOAD, allows you to remove an NLM from memory.

MOUNT

The MOUNT command is used to mount a disk volume. MOUNT is not really necessary in most circumstances—NetWare automatically mounts all available volumes when the server starts. You may need to use this command, or its complement DISMOUNT, if you wish to mount or remove a disk volume while the server is up.

MODULES

MODULES is another command that applies to NLMs. This command lists all of the NLMs that are currently in the server's memory. This is a way to diagnose a problem with software. An example of the output of this command is shown in Figure 10.4.

FIGURE 10.4

The MODULES command displays a list of NLMs that are currently in memory.

```
SERVER1:modules
IDE.DSK
   NetWare 4.01/4.02/4.10 IDE Device Driver
   Version 5.00    September 30, 1994
   Copyright 1994 Novell, Inc.  All rights reserved.
UNICODE.NLM
   NetWare Unicode Library NLM
   Version 4.10    November 8, 1994
   Copyright 1994 Novell, Inc.  All rights reserved.
DSLOADER.NLM
   NetWare 4.1 Directory Services Loader
   Version 1.25    October 22, 1994
   Copyright 1993-1994 Novell, Inc.  All rights reserved.
TIMESYNC.NLM
   Netware Time Synchronization Services
   Version 4.13    October 14, 1994
   (C) Copyright 1991-94, Novell, Inc.  All rights reserved.
MSM.NLM
   Novell Generic Media Support Module
   Version 2.32    August 23, 1994
   Copyright 1994 Novell, Inc.  All rights reserved.
<Press ESC to terminate or any other key to continue>
```

RESTART SERVER

When you've typed **DOWN** to bring the server down, you can use the RESTART server command instead of EXIT. This brings the server back up. This command is useful when you need to bring the server down and back up quickly; this can happen if you have installed new software or made a change to the server configuration files.

SET

SET allows you to modify parameters that affect the server's performance. For example, the following command controls whether file compression will be performed:

```
SET File Compression = OFF
```

There are literally hundreds of SET commands for different purposes—worse, you have to spell them correctly. Luckily, NetWare 4.11 comes with SERVMAN. SERVMAN is an NLM that lets you change just about every SET parameter by selecting from a convenient menu. SERVMAN will be discussed later in this chapter.

TIME

The TIME command gives you the time; in addition, it tells you the time synchronization status of the server. The output of the TIME command is shown in Figure 10.5.

FIGURE 10.5

The TIME command displays the server's time and synchronization information.

```
SERVER1:time
   Time zone string: "MST7MDT"
   DST status:  ON
   DST start:    Sunday, April 7, 1996   2:00:00 am MST
   DST end:      Sunday, October 29, 1995   2:00:00 am MDT
   Time synchronization is active.
   Time is synchronized to the network.
Monday, September 11, 1995   2:17:02 pm UTC
Monday, September 11, 1995   8:17:02 am MDT
SERVER1:
```

UNLOAD

UNLOAD lets you remove an NLM from memory; execution of the NLM stops immediately. Since a poorly written NLM may crash when you unload it, be careful using this command.

NetWare 4.11 NLM Utilities

Next we'll take a look at some of the most important NLMs included with NetWare 4.11. These provide a variety of services for managing the server, installing software, and setting parameters.

EDIT

This NLM is useful for editing files on the server, and is similar to a workstation-based editor. To use this utility, type **EDIT** followed by the name of the file, including the path. If you don't specify a path, the SYS:SYSTEM directory on the server will be the assumed path. For example, this command edits the AUTOEXEC.NCF file in the SYSTEM directory:

```
LOAD EDIT AUTOEXEC.NCF
```

INSTALL

The INSTALL loadable module is used to install NetWare 4.11, to change installation parameters, and to upgrade or install additional software. You can access this module at any time by typing **LOAD INSTALL** at the server console. The main INSTALL menu is shown in Figure 10.6.

INSTALL includes the following options:

- **Driver options** allow you to load and unload network and disk drivers.

- **Disk options** allow you to set up partitions on a disk and use the mirroring features.

- **Volume options** allow you to set up volumes on a disk partition and mount and dismount them.

- **License option** is used to add or change server licenses. The licenses are kept on a license diskette provided with NetWare. You can add additional licenses in any combination or delete installed licenses.

- **Copy files option** is used to copy files into the SYSTEM and PUBLIC directories on a new server.

■ **Directory options** allow you to install or remove NDS.

■ **NCF files options** allow you to create or edit the AUTOEXEC.NCF and STARTUP.NCF files.

■ **Multi CPU options** allow you to install and configure SMP (Symmetric Multiprocessing) for support of multiple-processor computers.

■ **Product options** is used to add or remove optional products.

FIGURE 10.6

The INSTALL NLM allows you to install and configure the server and other products.

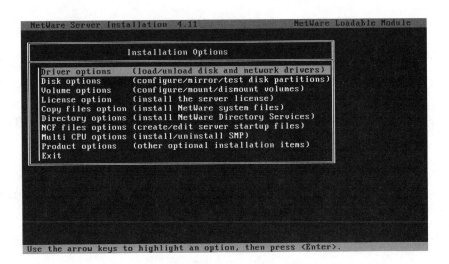

MONITOR

The MONITOR NLM is probably the most widely used NetWare utility. It is loaded on the server, usually in the AUTOEXEC.NCF file. The MONITOR screen, shown in Figure 10.7, provides a dynamic display of information about the server. If you watch these numbers carefully, you can be sure your server is running smoothly.

Along with the information displayed at the top of the screen, MONITOR has a menu that you can use to display specific categories of information. Most of these include running statistics that are updated as server conditions change. MONITOR offers these options:

- **Connection information** lets you see who is logged into the server. You can view specific information about a user in the list. Pressing the Delete key when a user's name is highlighted logs the user out by force.

- **Disk information** displays information about disks on the server and the volumes on them.

FIGURE 10.7
MONITOR provides statistics that let you know how the server is running.

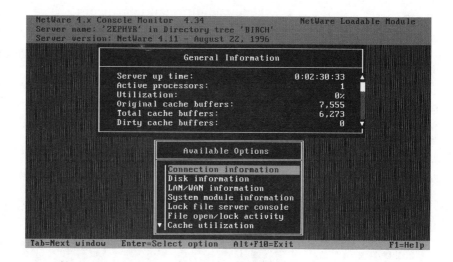

- **LAN/WAN information** displays network numbers, LAN driver information, and statistics for each LAN or WAN network.

- **System module information** lists the NLMs loaded on the server.

- **Lock file server console** allows you to enter a password to lock the console. Users won't be able to access the console without this password (or the ADMIN password).

- **File open/lock activity** displays information about open files on a volume.

- **Cache utilization** displays statistics about cache buffers and lets you determine which applications are using them.

- **Processor utilization** displays statistics about processor cycles used by each module.

- **Resource utilization** displays statistics about resources used by each module.

- **Memory utilization** displays the types and quantities of memory used by each module.

- **Scheduling information** provides a display showing what percentage of the server's time is spent with each module. You can easily determine if a particular module is slowing down the server. (See Figure 10.8.)

- **Multiprocessor information** displays information about SMP (Symmetric Multiprocessing), if installed.

- **Server parameters** allows you to view and change SET parameters. This is identical to the SERVMAN utility, described in the next section.

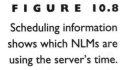

FIGURE 10.8

Scheduling information shows which NLMs are using the server's time.

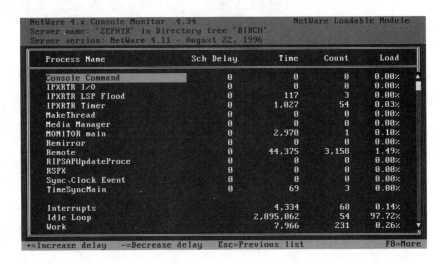

SERVMAN

SERVMAN (Server Manager) is an NLM that allows you to view server information and control server settings. Rather than use the SET command to set parameters, you can browse through available parameters with SERVMAN, select one to change, and assign a new value. Changes you make with SERVMAN take effect immediately. You are also offered the option of saving changes to the AUTOEXEC.NCF or TIMESYNC.CFG files.

To change settings, select Server Parameters from the main SERVMAN screen. The next screen, shown in Figure 10.9, lists several categories of options that you can set. After selecting a category, you are shown a list of possible settings for the category and their current values. For example, Figure 10.10 shows Directory Services Parameters. You can select a setting and press ↵ to change its value.

After you change one or more settings with SERVMAN, you are asked whether to save the changes in AUTOEXEC.NCF or TIME-SYNC.CFG, whichever is appropriate. If you answer Yes, NetWare sets that option each time the server starts. If you do not wish to save the changes, select No. Although changes are not written to the file, the setting is in effect until the server is restarted or until you change it again.

FIGURE 10.9

The SERVMAN utility allows you to browse server settings by category.

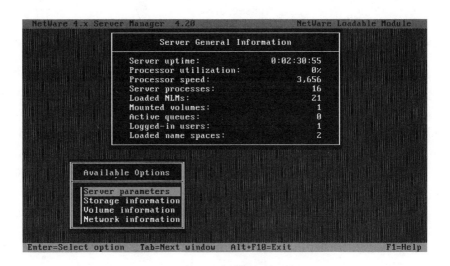

FIGURE 10.10

SERVMAN lists specific settings in each category, such as these for Directory Services.

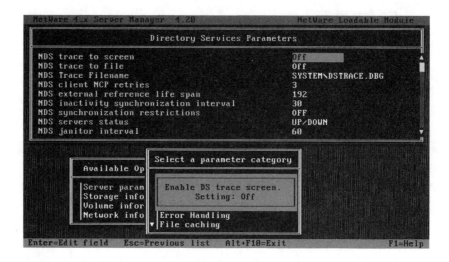

Managing Server Configuration Files

The NetWare 4.11 server uses configuration files to determine how it operates. These include the following:

- **STARTUP.NCF:** This file loads device drivers needed to bring up the server.

- **AUTOEXEC.NCF:** This file executes commands after the server starts.

Both of these are NCF files, short for NetWare Command File. These are lists of server commands. Most of the commands described in this chapter can be used in these files. You can edit either of these files using the EDIT or INSTALL utilities described earlier in this chapter. We'll take a closer look at each of these files in the following sections.

The STARTUP.NCF File

The STARTUP.NCF file contains commands that the server processes immediately after it starts. Only certain types of commands can be placed in this file; it is usually used for disk drivers and memory allocation settings. If you need to execute other commands, you should use the AUTOEXEC.NCF file, described in the next section.

NetWare can't access the NetWare partition until a disk driver is loaded, so the STARTUP.NCF file is located on the DOS partition, in the same directory as the SERVER.EXE program. STARTUP.NCF usually contains just one command, which loads a disk driver. Here's an example command for loading the IDE disk driver:

```
LOAD IDE PORT=2f8 INT=A
```

After the disk driver is successfully loaded, NetWare can access the NetWare partition. The SYS volume is automatically mounted after the disk driver loads. The next file, AUTOEXEC.NCF, is located on this volume.

The AUTOEXEC.NCF File

The AUTOEXEC.NCF file is read when the server starts and after the SYS volume has been mounted. This file is located in the SYS:SYSTEM directory. The commands in this file are executed after those in STARTUP .NCF. You can add just about any of the commands described earlier in this chapter to this file.

The most important uses for this file are to specify the file server's name and internal network number and to load and bind the network drivers. You can also use it to specify the server's time zone and time synchronization information. Here's an example of a simple AUTOEXEC.NCF file:

```
SET TIME ZONE = MST7MDT

SET DAYLIGHT SAVINGS TIME OFFSET = 1:00:00

SET START OF DAYLIGHT SAVINGS TIME = (APRIL SUNDAY
FIRST 2:00 AM)
```

```
SET END OF DAYLIGHT SAVINGS TIME = (OCTOBER SUNDAY
LAST 2:00 AM)

SET DEFAULT TIME SERVER TYPE = SINGLE

SET BINDERY CONTEXT = .OU=GROUP1.O=WEST

FILE SERVER NAME WEST_23

IPX INTERNAL NET 44998

LOAD NE2000 PORT=300 INT=5 FRAME=ETHERNET_802.2

BIND IPX TO NE2000 NET=99
```

The file in this example was created automatically when a server was installed; it includes the basics needed to run the server. You may need to add commands to this file when you install additional software on the server or if you wish to modify settings.

The SERVMAN utility, described earlier in this chapter, can automatically add SET commands to the AUTOEXEC.NCF file.

Remote Access to the Server

Most of the utilities you use to manage NetWare 4.11 are run from the workstation, but the utilities introduced in this chapter have to be run at the server. Since it's possible that your server is in another room, another office, or another country, NetWare provides another way to access the console. The *remote console* utility—RCONSOLE—runs at a workstation and allows you to "take over" the server's keyboard and screen, as if you were there. When you're online with RCONSOLE, you can do anything you would do at the actual console.

Before you can use RCONSOLE, you need to load two NLMs at the server. These handle the server's end of the communication. The following commands load the needed NLMs:

```
LOAD REMOTE password

LOAD RSPX
```

The password specified in the command line above is a password that is required for users to access the remote console. If you do not specify this password, the ADMIN password is used.

To start the remote console, type **RCONSOLE** at the workstation. You are asked to choose the connection type:

- **SPX** is used for typical connections across a network.

- **Asynchronous** is used for modem connections.

After that, you'll see a list of servers that are available—those that are running RSPX and REMOTE. Select a server, and press ⏎. You are asked for the remote console password described above. After you enter the correct password, you hear a beep, and the server's screen is displayed on your screen.

You can also start RCONSOLE within Windows by choosing Remote Console from the Tools menu in the NWADMIN utility.

You can now perform regular server functions. However, the Alt+Esc key can't be used to navigate screens from RCONSOLE. Instead, use Alt+F3 and Alt+F4 to move back and forth through the different screens.

Securing the Server Console

If you read the previous description of the DOWN command, you probably realize that you shouldn't let anyone access the server console unless authorized. You can take several precautions to be sure that the server console is safe and secure:

- To ensure *physical security*, place the server in a locked room, if at all possible. If the computer has a keyboard lock switch that uses a key, keep it locked.

- The Lock Server Console option in the MONITOR utility lets you lock the server console. You are asked for a password; after you enter it, the server is not accessible to anyone who does not know that password.

- Be sure that you use a password for RCONSOLE. As with all passwords, be careful who you tell the password to.

- The SECURE CONSOLE command can be used at the colon prompt. This removes the remains of DOS from memory, which means that the EXIT command can't be used. This prevents users from reaching the DOS prompt.

Physical security is, by far, the most important. If someone is allowed to walk up and access your file server without being watched, he or she can do damage no matter how secure your network is.

Review

The NetWare 4.11 server doesn't work like a regular PC. Since it runs NetWare 4.11, it's a completely different system. A NetWare server is any computer that runs the NetWare operating system. NetWare can run on any PC-compatible computer with a 386 or better processor. You should also have sufficient RAM and disk storage space.

The software that runs on the NetWare 4.11 server includes the operating system—NetWare itself—and loadable modules. The following services are provided by the operating system itself, the *core* operating system:

- File sharing

- Printer sharing

- Security

- Routing

- NDS

Along with the core OS, the server can run NetWare Loadable Modules, or NLMs. NLMs are programs that run on the NetWare server. The NetWare operating system allows NLMs to integrate fully with the system; what this means is that NLMs and the OS share the same memory and can perform some of the same functions.

NLMs include:

- **Disk drivers** to interface with disk drives.

- **LAN drivers** to interface with LAN cards.

- **Name space modules** to provide extended file naming services.

- **Utilities** to perform server management functions.

The NetWare file server console has a prompt where you can enter NetWare *console commands*. These can be used to perform a wide variety of functions, maintain the server, and load and unload NLMs. The file server prompt is referred to as the *colon prompt*, because it always ends with a colon. If a screen that doesn't display the colon prompt is visible, you can use the Alt+Esc keys to switch screens until you see the colon prompt.

Console commands include:

- BROADCAST for sending messages to users

- CLEAR STATION for disconnecting a user

- CLS to clear the server's screen

- CONFIG to display configuration information

- DISABLE LOGIN to prevent user logins

- MOUNT and DISMOUNT to control disk volumes

- DISPLAY NETWORKS to display available networks

- DISPLAY SERVERS to display available servers

- DOWN and EXIT to bring the server down

- HELP to display instructions

- LOAD and UNLOAD to control NLMs

- MODULES to display module information

- RESTART SERVER to bring the server back up

- SET to change server parameters

- TIME to display time and synchronization information

The final category of server utilities are NLMs. The following NLMs were introduced in this chapter:

- INSTALL for installing NetWare and other services

- MONITOR for watching file system statistics

- SERVMAN for changing SET parameters easily

CNA Practice Test Questions

1. Commands that you can use at the server console include:

A. DOS commands

B. NLMs and console commands

C. NLMs only

D. DOS or NLM commands

2. The NetWare core operating system does *not* include:

A. File sharing

B. NDS

C. Network Management

D. Printer sharing

3. NLMs come from:

A. Novell

B. Third parties

C. Both of the above

D. None of the above

4. The two parts of a NPA disk driver are:

A. NPA and CDA

B. HAM and CAM

C. HAM and CDM

D. NPA and HDM

5. LAN Driver modules have the extension:

   A. NLM

   B. DRV

   C. LAN

   D. MOD

6. The command to display configuration information is:

   A. DISPLAY CONFIG

   B. MODULES

   C. CONFIG

   D. VERSION

7. The command used to prevent logins is:

   A. SET LOGIN = NO

   B. DISABLE LOGIN

   C. LOGIN OFF

   D. SECURE CONSOLE

8. The two commands needed to bring down the server are:

   A. DOWN and QUIT

   B. DOWN and RESET

   C. DOWN and CLS

   D. DOWN and EXIT

9. The key used to switch screens in RCONSOLE is:

A. F3 or F4

B. Alt+Esc

C. Ctrl+Esc

D. Alt+F3 and Alt+F4

10. The two modules you must load to enable remote access are:

A. REMOTE and MONITOR

B. REMOTE and ACCESS

C. RSPX and REMOTE

D. RSPX and RCONSOLE

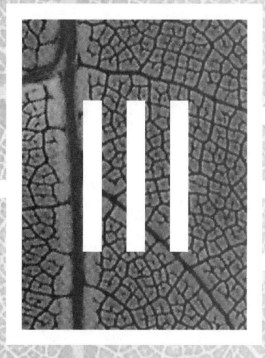

PART

III

NETWARE 4.11 ADVANCED ADMINISTRATION

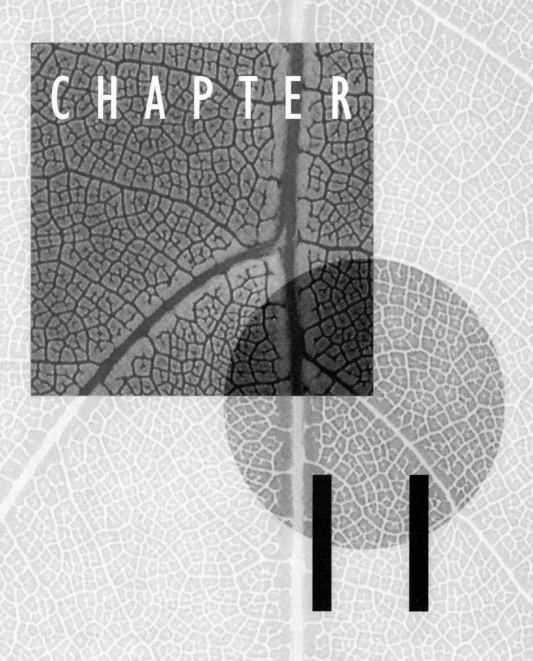

CHAPTER

11

Advanced NetWare Directory Services

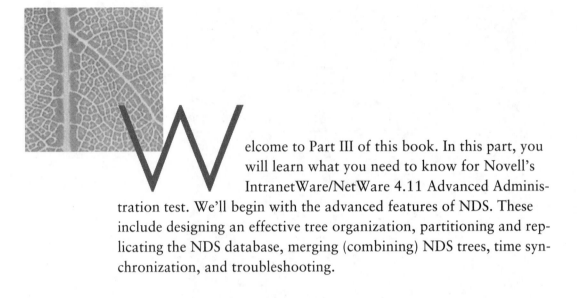

elcome to Part III of this book. In this part, you will learn what you need to know for Novell's IntranetWare/NetWare 4.11 Advanced Administration test. We'll begin with the advanced features of NDS. These include designing an effective tree organization, partitioning and replicating the NDS database, merging (combining) NDS trees, time synchronization, and troubleshooting.

Designing the NDS Tree

As you've learned in the previous chapters, NDS provides you with the ability to manage your network and its resources in simpler ways than were possible in previous versions of NetWare. However, to take advantage of these features, you must plan the structure of your Directory tree so that it suits the needs of your network.

A carefully planned and organized Directory tree will give you the following benefits:

- **Simplified administration:** By organizing users and resources into containers and groups, you simplify the job of the administrator.

- **Ease of access:** Users can quickly find the network resources that they need to access.

- **Improved security:** If your Directory tree is organized properly, you can take advantage of NetWare 4.11's many security features for your network, whether it will be managed by one administrator or several.

- **Fault tolerance:** By placing replicas and partitions strategically, you can eliminate the risk of data loss in the event of a server crash.

- **Optimized network traffic:** By using partitions and replicas and by managing time synchronization, you can minimize the traffic over wide-area network (WAN) links.

- **Transparent upgrade:** A well-planned NDS upgrade strategy can allow you to perform the upgrade piece by piece, with minimal impact on the users.

Tree Design Considerations

In order to receive the benefits listed above, you'll need to consider several items in your design:

- **Administration:** If the company has separate administrators for each location, it may be best to organize by location. This makes it easy to give each administrator the correct rights.

- **Network topology:** If WAN links are used, it may be wise to separate the locations as much as possible to minimize traffic. You can still use an integrated organization if you place partitions and replicas appropriately, as discussed later in this chapter.

- **Bindery Services:** If you use NetWare 4.11's Bindery Services feature, you must consider where to place the bindery contexts. Up to 16 of these can be assigned.

- **Tree depth:** Although the NDS tree can be as complicated as you need it to be, effective trees usually have between three and eight layers. Trees with too many layers can be difficult to work with.

Although there is no limit to the depth of the NDS tree, there is a limit to the length of an object's distinguished name. Object names are limited to 256 characters. To avoid running into this limit, make sure you do not use too many layers, and that your Organization and Organizational Unit objects have short, concise names.

Choosing a Tree Structure

The most visible aspect of your NDS plan will be the structure, or organization, of the Directory tree itself. There are several possible strategies for organizing your NDS tree. Most networks are based on one of these strategies or a combination of them. The following sections discuss each of the tree-structure strategies.

The Default Organization

When you install NetWare 4.11 and accept the defaults, a simple Directory tree structure is created for you. This tree consists of a single Organization object under the [Root]. All leaf objects (resources) on the network are created within this container. An example of this organization is shown in Figure 11.1.

With the default organization, all objects are effectively in a single, flat database, similar to the bindery used in previous versions of NetWare. This structure may be adequate for small networks (with 10 to 20 users), but it offers few of the benefits of NDS. For most networks, you will want to find a more appropriate way to organize the Directory tree.

If you've already installed NetWare 4.11 and used the default organization, don't worry—it's not too late. Read on to determine a more appropriate organization, and then modify your organization using the NDS utilities.

FIGURE 11.1

The default Directory tree structure places all objects under a single Organization object.

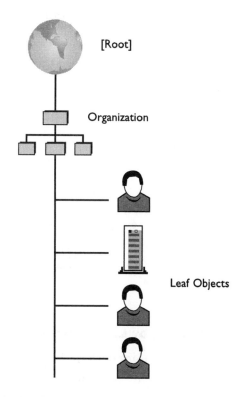

Organizing by Division

A common Directory tree organization uses the *divisional* approach. This divides the tree into Organizational Unit objects based on divisions or departments of the company, such as Sales, Accounting, Research, Production, and so on. The structure of NDS will resemble the company's organization chart. Figure 11.2 illustrates a simple divisional organization.

This is a good strategy to use when there are clear divisions within the company, as with most medium-size or large companies. Since users within a division often require access to the same data and applications, administration is simplified.

FIGURE 11.2

The divisional Directory tree organization divides the company according to functional divisions.

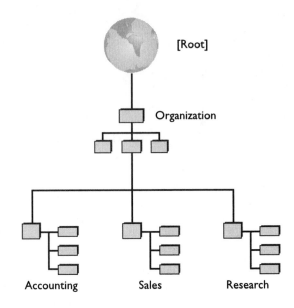

Organizing by Location

In companies with multiple locations, the *locational* strategy is often used. In this approach, you create Organizational Unit objects for each of the physical locations of the company, as shown in Figure 11.3.

FIGURE 11.3

The location organization includes separate Organizational Unit objects for each physical location.

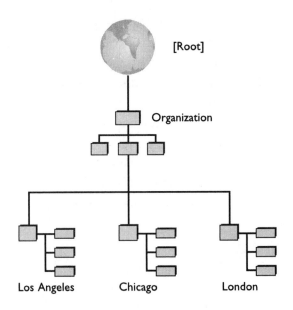

This strategy provides a simple organization and makes it easy to create partitions. A large company might choose to have a different LAN administrator at each of the locations. This type of network management is easy to implement if the locational strategy is used.

You can also organize locations using the Country object, which is placed directly under the [Root], above the Organization objects. Country objects should only be used in large, multinational corporations, or for compatibility with larger directories, such as the Internet's DNS (Domain Name Service). If you use a Country object, its name must be a valid two-character country abbreviation (determined by the ITU/TSS X.500 standard), as explained in Chapter 5.

The locational structure works well when the locations of a company are managed separately. However, if employees in various locations work closely together on projects, a workgroup or hybrid organization, described in the next sections, may be more practical.

Organizing by Workgroup

The organization of modern companies often includes *workgroups*, which are groups of users who perform similar tasks, usually on the same project. You could organize your Directory tree according to these workgroups, as shown in the example in Figure 11.4.

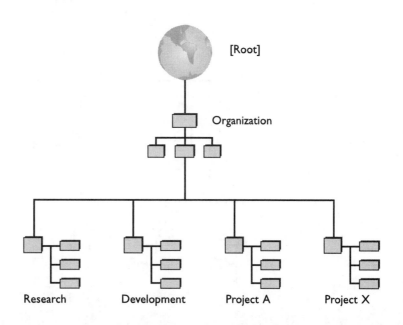

FIGURE 11.4

The workgroup organization creates Organizational Unit objects for users who perform similar functions.

[Root]

Organization

Research   Development   Project A   Project X

Usually, the workgroup organization is combined with other strategies, as described in the next section.

Using a Hybrid Organization

For many companies, particularly large ones, you will find that none of the above strategies is ideal. A *hybrid*, or combination, approach, based on the organization of your company, may be the solution. This combines the strengths of two or more types of NDS organization.

Figure 11.5 shows one example of a hybrid organization. In this example, the company's Directory tree is organized at the top level by location, with locations in Los Angeles, Chicago, and London. Each location is then divided into departments. Each location has its own Sales department to handle local sales. The Research department for the corporation is located in Los Angeles, and the Accounting department is based in London.

FIGURE 11.5

An example of a hybrid organization. This tree is divided by location, then by department.

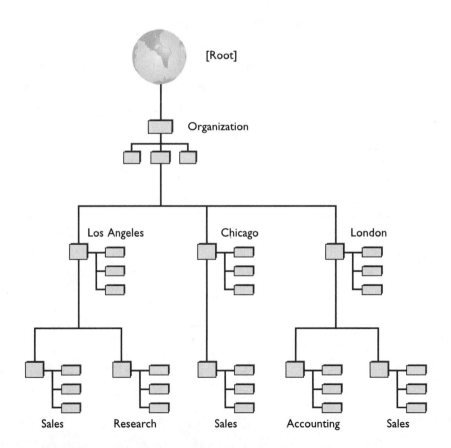

The example in Figure 11.6 takes another combination approach. This company is administered from a central location. The tree is organized by divisions of Accounting, Marketing, and Sales. The Marketing department works strictly from the Denver office. The other departments have an office in each location.

FIGURE 11.6

Another example of hybrid organization. This tree is organized by department, then by location.

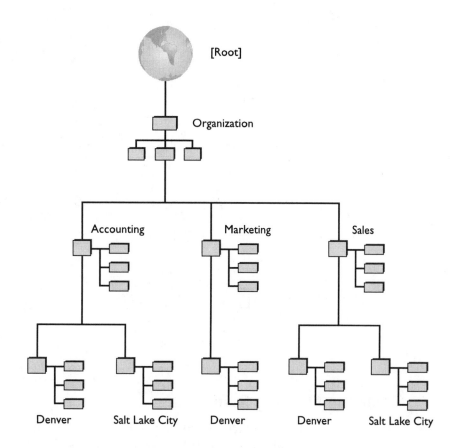

A more elaborate hybrid organization is shown in Figure 11.7. The first level is divided by departments: Marketing, Technical, and Accounting. The Accounting department has an office in each of two locations. The Technical department is further subdivided into Research, Service, and Support. Finally, the Research department is organized into workgroups.

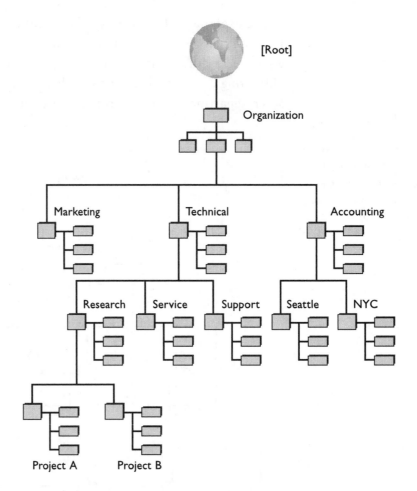

FIGURE 11.7

An example of a more complex hybrid Directory tree. This tree is organized by departments, locations, and workgroups.

Defining Naming Standards

The next step in planning your network's Directory tree is to create the standards that will be used in choosing object names and properties. Choosing standards when the network is designed is a good way to ensure that consistent names, properties, and values will be used.

Naming Objects

By using consistent naming procedures, you make network administration more efficient. For example, it will be easy to locate users, printers, servers, and other network objects that you need to maintain. Users will also benefit from consistent object names. For example, when sending e-mail, a user will have no trouble determining another user's name.

The following sections offer some guidelines for naming objects on your network.

User Login Names   Typical standards for user login names include some combination of names and initials:

- **First Name, Last Initial,** as in JOHNS. For small companies, this user naming standard might be the best solution, since employees know each other by first name. However, this can result in duplicate names and may cause confusion when employees are also known by nicknames.

- **First initial, last name,** as in JSMITH. This is another common method. There is slightly less chance of duplicate names, and it's easier to determine who the name refers to.

- **First initial, middle initial, last name,** as in JDSMITH. More complicated schemes such as this are often needed in larger companies. There is very little chance of duplication.

It is also important to determine what you will do if two users have names that would produce the same username. For example, you might decide to add a middle initial or, as a last resort, a number. You should avoid these inconsistencies whenever possible.

It is a good practice to limit user login names to 8 characters. Although NDS allows 64-character names, many e-mail systems require 8-character names.

In some companies, it may be perfectly acceptable to have two users called JOHNS, as long as they are in different containers. However, if usernames are used for e-mail, this can cause problems. In addition, no two users in bindery context containers can share the same username.

Groups, Organizations, and Organizational Units   Since Organizations and Organizational Units usually identify divisions, locations, or workgroups in the company, you should name them after the entity they represent. Use short and concise names, since the name might need to be typed in a distinguished name for a user. For example, you might use MGMT for Management, ACCT for Accounting, AP for Accounts Payable, and NYC for New York City.

Give Group objects names that represent their function, such as DATAENTRY for the data-entry group or PROJECT1 for users working on a particular project. If the group was created to give users access to an application directory, it might be named for that application, such as WORDPROCESSING or BACKUP.

Other NDS Objects   You should also have a standard procedure for naming other types of objects in the Directory tree. Here are some examples:

- Servers are often named based on their location, such as EAST1, NYC, or BLDG3. Since a user may need to type the name of a server to log in to, keep server names short. Server names must be unique, even if they are in different containers.

- Volumes are given NDS names automatically when you create them. The name combines the server name and volume name, such as EAST1_SYS.

- Printers are typically named according to the printer type and location, such as LJ4_BLDG3 or DMP_WEST.

- Print queues should be named according to their purpose or to refer to the department that uses them, as in ACCTG_QUEUE or CHECK_QUEUE.

Choosing Standard Properties

You should also determine which properties should be used for each object and how to format the property values. Look carefully at the lists of properties for all of the objects—users, printers, servers, and so on—and decide which properties will be useful. Then establish a consistent format for each property value.

For example, you may decide to use the Location property to specify the building number on a college campus. Then you should choose how to format the location: Building #17 or B17 or BLDG17. When you follow a consistent format, it will be easy to perform searches, such as to find users in a certain building.

Creating a Standards Document

In addition to planning the naming standards you will use on your network, it is important to create a *standards document*. This document should describe your company's standards for naming objects and formatting property values. If there are multiple administrators on the network, they should be given a copy of the standards document.

Here is what the users portion of the standards document might look like for a typical small company:

> **Usernames:** First initial plus name (i.e., JSMITH). Up to 8 characters.
>
> **Properties to be defined:**
>
> Given Name (first name)
>
> Last Name (full last name)
>
> Telephone (include area code)
>
> Title (full title)
>
> Location (building number in this format: BLDG XX)

Implementing NDS

In a new company, it is possible to plan and create an NDS tree structure and allow it to grow with the company. For existing networks, however, it is important to plan the implementation of NDS on the network.

By choosing and planning an *implementation strategy*, you can minimize the impact on users and the network and take advantage of the features of NDS as quickly as possible. The Directory tree structure that you have chosen will determine the best implementation strategy.

Implementing NDS by Department or Division

The *departmental*, or *divisional*, implementation is the most common strategy used. This allows each department or division (location, workgroup, and so on) to implement NDS separately, and you can later merge these into a global organization.

In this strategy, you use a separate Directory tree for each division or department. These trees should eventually be merged together so that you can have the global benefits of NDS. (The actual merging process is described later in this chapter.)

Directory trees should be designed so that merging at a later date will be simple. Three location Directory trees created with merging in mind are shown in Figure 11.8.

FIGURE 11.8

These Directory trees have been created with the intention of merging them into a single tree later.

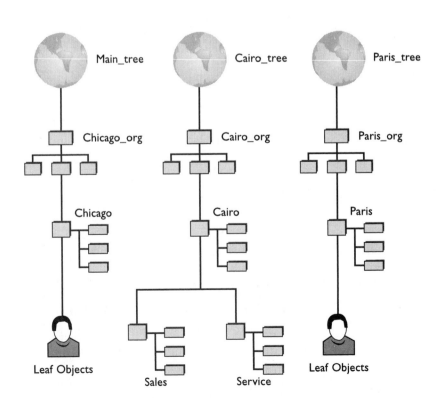

You should follow these guidelines when creating Directory trees for departments or divisions:

- Each tree should include an extra Organizational Unit object at the top. This makes it easy to move the division when it becomes part of a larger tree.

- Each tree must use a unique tree name (assigned during installation).

- Each tree must include a uniquely named Organization object at the top of the tree, because these objects will become part of the same tree when they are merged.

Figure 11.9 shows what the Directory trees in Figure 11.8 might look like after merging. Because we used the extra Organizational Unit object, it becomes easy to reorganize the merged tree and eliminate the unneeded Organization objects, as shown in Figure 11.10.

FIGURE 11.9

After merging, the Directory trees become part of a single tree.

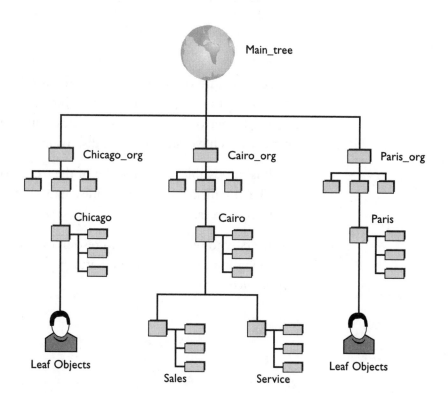

FIGURE 11.10

The merged tree can be reorganized into a better structure.

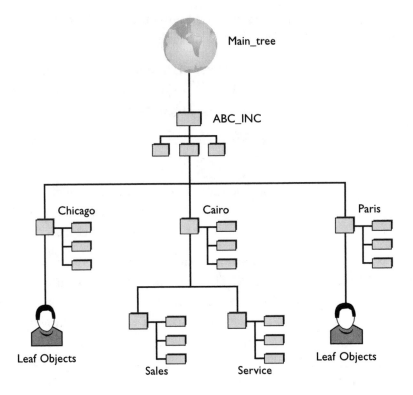

When separate trees have been created for divisions, you do not necessarily need to merge them. It is possible to keep separate Directory trees on the network, as long as they have different names. However, separate trees have the following disadvantages:

- It is impossible to manage all of the trees from a central location. The administrator must log in separately to each tree to manage its resources.

- Users who require access to resources in different trees will need to log in to a single tree and attach to the rest through Bindery Services.

Both of these disadvantages stem from the fact that the NetWare client allows only one NDS attachment at a time. Although you lose the global advantages of NDS, multiple trees may be a practical solution for companies that have separate administrators for each location and require little communication between locations.

Implementing NDS for the Entire Organization

The *organizational* approach is the other method for implementing NDS. This method is a bit drastic—you create a tree structure for the entire organization at once. This is also referred to as the *top-down* or *all-at-once* strategy.

In an ideal world, this would be the best way to implement NDS. It immediately gives you the full benefits of a global Directory structure. However, it is rarely practical. In order to implement NDS across the entire organization, the following circumstances are required:

- There must be full connectivity between locations, via a LAN or WAN.

- All network administrators must be available to plan and implement the changes.

- The Directory tree structure for the entire organization must be planned at the same time.

Combining Implementation Strategies

When the organizational approach is not practical, a combination of the two strategies may be the best solution. A central tree structure can be created for the entire organization, and individual departments or divisions can be created with their own tree. You can then merge these trees with the central tree when they are ready. See Figure 11.11 for an example of this type of implementation strategy.

Partitioning and Replicating Your Directory Tree

Because the directory can grow to include a large amount of information, Novell lets you divide it into smaller units. These units, called *partitions*, can then be *replicated* onto other servers. Because of this ability to be divided and distributed across multiple servers, NDS is referred to as a *distributed database*.

FIGURE 11.11

A department can be given a separate tree, which can be merged with the central tree later.

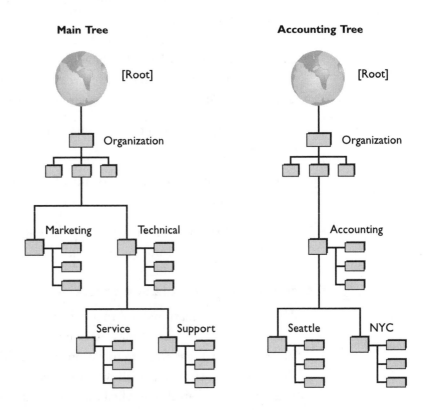

Novell's choices of terminology can be confusing. Not only are there disk directories and an NDS Directory, but also disk partitions and NDS partitions, which are two different things. The word *partition* is used exclusively for NDS partitions in this chapter.

NDS, when distributed, appears to network users as a completely unified structure without separations. The partitions may break limbs off the Directory tree and spread them about, but to the network user, the tree still appears and functions as a single cohesive Directory.

Partitioning the Directory

In NDS, a *partition* is a branch of the Directory tree. When you install NetWare 4.11, there is a single partition, which includes the [Root] object and all other objects, as shown in Figure 11.12.

FIGURE 11.12

The [Root] partition is created in the installation process.

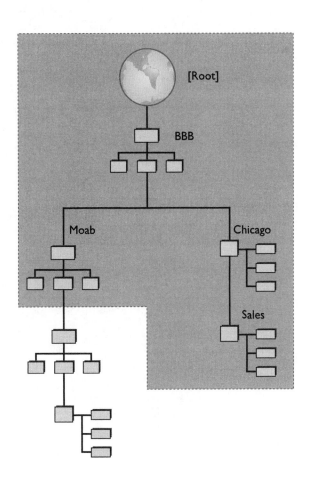

Partitions are made up of container objects, under which leaf objects are kept together as a group. Leaf objects are always kept in the same partition as the container object that holds them. The partition is named after the parent object.

Partitions are referred to as *parent* or *child* partitions, depending on their relationship to other partitions. A partition that resides above another is called the parent partition; the one below it is called the child. This relationship is illustrated in Figure 11.13.

FIGURE 11.13

Partitions are called parent or child partitions, depending on their location.

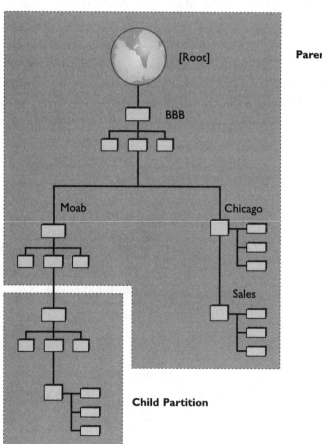

Parent Partition

Child Partition

Replicating the Directory

Each partition can be copied and stored on any NetWare 4 server on your network. This is called *replication*. Replication is useful for two main reasons:

- It establishes greater fault tolerance. By storing copies of partitions on multiple servers, you can help ensure that access to your Directory will remain intact, even if a disk crashes or servers go down. Also, you will give users greater freedom to log in without being dependent on one particular server's availability to provide authentication, since a replica can fulfill this role in place of the original partition.

- It can improve network performance. If users need to use a WAN link to access Directory information, you can decrease response time and network traffic by providing a replica that they can access locally.

Types of Replicas

There are four different types of NDS replicas. Each is used for a particular purpose, as described in the following sections.

Master Replicas   NetWare 4.11 creates a *master replica* when a partition is defined. This replica controls all partition operations, including creating, merging, and moving partitions. The master replica also controls replica creation, deletion, and repair.

NOTE

The term *replica* can be a bit confusing. Even if there is only one copy of a partition, it is still called a replica. If there is only one replica, it must be a master replica.

There can be only one master replica for each partition. When objects are changed in a master replica, the same change will be made automatically on all replicas of that partition. The server that stores the master replica of a partition must be accessible before you can split the partition (create a new partition) or join it with another partition.

Read/Write Replicas   Read/write replicas contain the same information as the master replica, but each partition may have multiple read/write replicas. Changes made to these replicas will also be reproduced automatically on all other replicas of the same partition. Read/write replicas, however, cannot be used when splitting or joining a partition.

If your network loses a master replica, you can change one of the read/write replicas to master replica status. Read/write replicas support the login process by providing authentication.

Read-Only Replicas   Read-only replicas are used on servers where reads of the partition are necessary but writes are to be prevented. Because read-only replicas do not support the authentication process, they have limited usefulness.

These replicas contain the same information as the master and read/write replicas but do not allow for alteration of objects. You can use them for searching and viewing objects.

TIP

Use a master or read/write replica on servers on which users will be using Bindery Services. A read-only replica will not work because Bindery Services requires a writable replica. What's Bindery Services? Turn to Chapter 13 for the answer.

Subordinate Reference Replicas   You do not create subordinate reference replicas. NDS creates these replicas automatically. Subordinate references do not contain object data; they point to a replica that does. They do not support user authentication, object management, or even object viewing.

NDS creates subordinate references on a server when a replica of a partition appears on that server without a replica of that partition's child. A subordinate reference is simply a "pointer" describing the location of the child partition or its replica.

Subordinate references ensure that there is efficient access to relevant portions of the NDS database on each server. NDS will automatically remove the subordinate reference if the child partition's replica is added to the server.

Guidelines for Placing Replicas

There are many factors that you should consider when deciding where to place the replicas on your network. These are discussed in the following sections.

Placing Replicas Strategically   To maximize fault tolerance and access to replicas without compromising network efficiency, place replicas on servers located near the users who will be using them regularly. This will allow access to replicas without unnecessary traffic across WAN links.

Novell recommends creating three or more replicas for each partition to ensure fault tolerance. Each server used for Bindery Services must contain a master or read/write replica that contains the bindery context.

Avoid Unnecessary Partitioning   To minimize problems with subordinate references, create as few partitions as possible. Avoid too many replicas of the [Root] partition, because this partition tends to have many child partitions. Since a child partition or a subordinate reference must accompany its replica wherever it appears, the [Root] partition can create a lot of subordinate references, which can increase network traffic unnecessarily.

WARNING   While you should avoid making too many replicas of the [Root] partition, you *do* need to replicate it at least once. If you fail to replicate it at all, you are taking a dangerous risk. You need the [Root] partition to access the Directory tree.

Replicas Increase Network Traffic The NDS database remains consistent by transmitting any change made to an object in a partition to all replicas of that partition. This is known as *Directory synchronization*.

Directory synchronization takes place across *replica rings*. A replica ring can be technically described as the list of all the replica property values of a partition. Each partition has a Replica property. The values for any one partition's Replica property form the replica ring. These values include the list of locations of the various replicas.

Because Directory synchronization requires that every replica be updated to reflect any changes to any object, a considerable amount of communication is required between NetWare 4.11 servers. On LANs, this communication does not usually become a major consideration, because most LANs have plenty of bandwidth available. The extra bandwidth needed for this communication does become a concern on WAN links where bottlenecks can occur.

Potential Problems with Subordinate References When you change a partition that has a subordinate reference, make sure the subordinate reference is accessible before making the change. If the subordinate reference is located on the other side of an unstable connection, such as some types of WAN links, you could be creating a potential problem: the data in the subordinate reference cannot be updated to match the master.

Default Partitions and Replicas

When the first server is installed, NDS creates and stores a single partition on that server's SYS volume. The next server installed into the existing NDS tree simply expands the partition. The third and fourth servers receive a read/write replica of the partition. All servers installed after that do not receive any replicas by default.

Replicas in Merged NDS Trees

When two or more Directory trees are merged, the *source* tree servers (servers of trees that are being merged into the [Root] of another tree) that hold replicas of their [Root] partition are given a read/write replica of the new [Root] partition. They also receive subordinate references to the child partitions of the new [Root] partition.

The servers of the *target* tree (the tree whose [Root] remains as the [Root]) are given subordinate references to the uppermost level partitions in the source trees if the target tree servers currently hold replicas of the [Root] partition. Figures 11.14 and 11.15 show an example of merged directories.

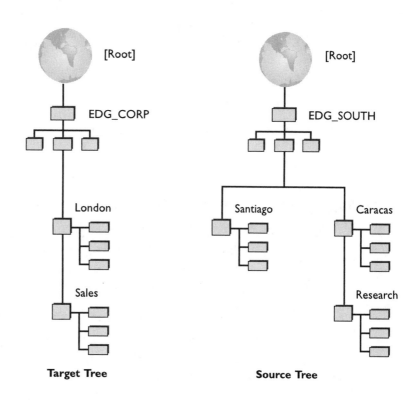

FIGURE 11.14

Two separate Directory trees before merging

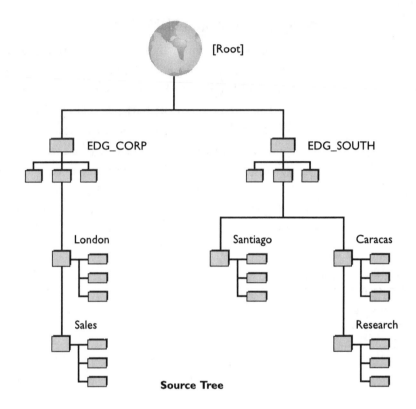

FIGURE 11.15

When directories are merged, the organizations are combined under one [Root] object.

Managing Partitions and Replicas

Now that you understand the basics of NDS partitioning and replication, we'll take a look at the actual process of creating, deleting, and managing partitions and replicas. Two utilities are provided with NetWare 4.11 for these purposes:

- NDS Manager (NDSMGR16.EXE or NDSMGR32.EXE) is a Windows-based application for managing partitions and replicas. Previous versions of NetWare 4 included a similar utility called Partition Manager.

- PARTMGR is a DOS-based program that you can use for most of the same functions.

We will examine the use of NDS Manager in the following sections. For information about the PARTMGR utility, refer to the Novell documentation.

Viewing Partitions and Replicas

When you start NDS Manager a split window is displayed, as shown in Figure 11.16. The main NDS Manager window includes two main sections:

FIGURE 11.16

NDS Manager displays information about partitions and replicas.

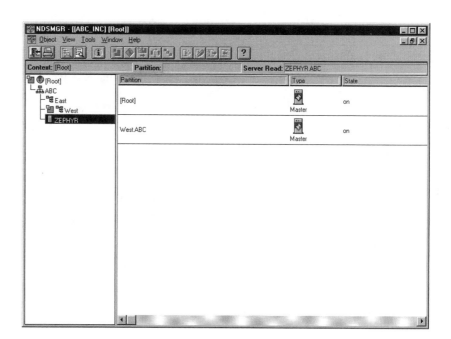

- The left section displays the Directory Tree. Only container objects and Server objects are displayed. A container that is the root of a partition appears with an icon to the left of the container object's icon.

- The right section displays a list of replicas. If you have highlighted a partition's container, the replicas for that partition are listed. If you have highlighted a Server object, the replicas stored on the server are listed.

Creating (Splitting) a Partition

The process of creating a new partition is also called *splitting* a partition, because a child container object is split from its parent container's partition. Follow these steps to create a new partition:

1. Highlight the container object that will be the root of the new partition.

2. From the NDS Manager menu, select Object ➢ Create Partition.

3. The Create Partition dialog box will appear, as shown in Figure 11.17. If you are certain you have chosen the correct object, click Yes to continue.

FIGURE 11.17

The Create Partition dialog box allows you to confirm that a new partition should be created.

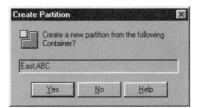

4. The new partition will now be created. Depending on the complexity of your network and the number of replicas of the parent partition, this may take several minutes.

5. Create replicas of the new partition as needed.

Deleting (Merging) a Partition

The process of deleting a partition is called *merging* partitions. When you merge a partition, it is combined with its parent partition. All objects that were contained in the partition become child objects of the parent partition. Follow these steps to merge a partition:

1. Highlight the container object at the root of the partition.

2. From the NDS Manager menu, select Object ➤ Partition ➤ Merge.

3. The Merge Partition dialog box will appear, as shown in Figure 11.18. This displays, for verification, the name of the child partition and parent partition that will be merged.

FIGURE 11.18

The Merge Partition dialog box displays information about the partitions to be merged.

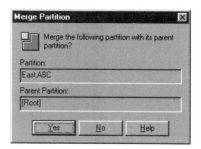

4. Click Yes to continue the merge process.

5. The partitions will now be merged. Depending on the complexity of the network and the number of replicas, this may take several minutes.

Adding a Replica

NDS Manager allows you to easily manage the replicas for a partition. Follow these steps to add a new replica:

1. Highlight the partition's root container in the left portion of the screen.

2. From the NDS Manager menu, choose Object ➤ Add Replica.

3. The Add Replica dialog box, shown in Figure 11.19, is now displayed.

FIGURE 11.19

Specify a server and
replica type to create a
new replica.

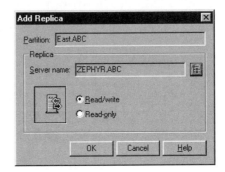

4. Choose a server to hold the new replica, and indicate whether the new replica will be Read/Write or Read only.

5. Click OK to add the new replica. This may take several minutes.

Removing a Replica

Removing a replica is also simple. Follow these steps:

1. Highlight the partition's container object on the left side of the screen.

2. Highlight the replica to be removed on the right side of the screen.

3. Right-click the replica and select Remove.

4. Click Yes to confirm that the replica should be deleted.

5. Be sure to create a new replica on a different server, if needed, to keep the partition safe.

Moving a Container Object

As we mentioned in Chapter 5, you can't move a container object using the NWADMIN utility's Move Object option. This is because moving a container object is considered a partitioning operation. You can easily accomplish this using the NDS Manager utility. Follow these steps:

1. Following the instructions in the *Creating (Splitting) a Partition* section above, split the container object you wish to move into its own partition.

2. From the NDS Manager menu, choose Object ➤ Partition ➤ Move.

3. Choose the new context for the container object.

4. Click Yes to begin the process of moving the container object. This may take several minutes.

Merging NDS Trees

If you have created multiple Directory trees for different departments or divisions within your network, you may want to merge them into a single tree. This allows all of the objects to be managed from a single Directory.

When you merge two Directory trees, objects in the [Root] of one tree (the *source* tree) are moved to the [Root] of the second (*target*) tree. The merge process must be performed at the server that contains the master replica of the source tree.

You use the DSMERGE utility to merge Directory trees. This is an NLM that you can load at the server console.

Merging Considerations

There are several conditions that must exist before you can begin the merge process. Check all of the following items before you merge the trees.

- All servers that contain a replica of the [Root] partition for either tree must be up and running, and they must be accessible over the network.

- The schema for the trees must be the same. If you have used a product that extends the Directory schema on one tree, you must make the same changes on the other tree.

- The [Root] object of the source tree cannot contain any leaf or Alias objects.

- The trees must have different tree names.

- The servers containing the [Root] partitions of the trees must be running the same version of NetWare.

- You must have the password for an administrator with access to all objects in each Directory tree.

To protect your data, back up the Directory of both trees before you begin. Most NetWare backup programs include an option to back up NDS information.

Starting the Merge Process

Follow these steps to merge Directory trees:

1. Start the DSMERGE utility by typing **LOAD DSMERGE** at the server console. You must do this on the server containing the master replica of the source tree. The main DSMERGE screen is shown in Figure 11.20.

FIGURE 11.20

The DSMERGE utility allows you to merge Directory trees.

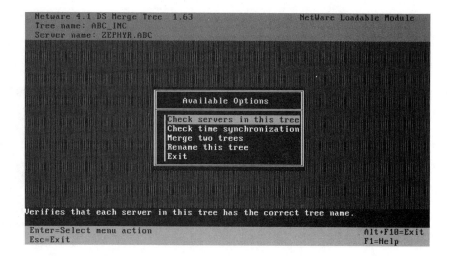

2. Select the Check Time Synchronization option. You will see a list of servers and their time synchronization status. The difference in times (Time Delta) must be under two seconds for all servers in both trees. You may need to change each server to use the same time source.

3. Select the Merge Two Trees option. The source tree is set to the server's tree automatically. Fill in the destination tree, and provide an administrator name and password for each tree, as shown in Figure 11.21.

4. Press F10 to perform the merge. The merge process may take quite a while, depending on the existing replicas and the speed of your network.

If you wish to merge several trees into a single destination tree, you must merge them one at a time. Allow the merge process to finish before merging the next tree.

FIGURE 11.21

Enter the information to merge two trees.

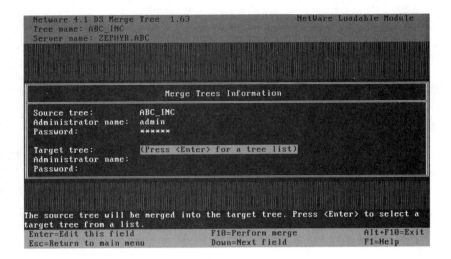

Troubleshooting NDS

NDS is the most important new feature of NetWare 4. Not surprisingly, it is also the most common source of problems with NetWare 4.11 servers. In the following sections, you will learn how to avoid some of the most common NDS problems and how to correct them when they do happen.

In a large organization where time is critical, you may want to avoid doing the troubleshooting yourself and go straight to Novell technical support, or try your local NetWare reseller or consulting company. It may be worth the expense.

Avoiding NDS Problems

There is no way to avoid all NDS problems. In fact, if you deal with a NetWare 4.11 server for any length of time, you will undoubtedly need to handle several problems. However, most common NDS problems can be avoided with a bit of planning. Here are some tips to keep NDS running smoothly:

- Always keep at least three replicas for each partition. We've mentioned this before, but it can't be stressed enough. If a replica is lost, even if it's the master replica, it can be restored if another replica is available.

- Use your backup software to make frequent backups of the NDS database. This frequency depends on how often changes are made in your network, but it should be at least once a week. Many backup programs will back up NDS data automatically while other data is being backed up.

- Use a single workstation to manage NDS partitions—when you are splitting partitions, merging partitions, or moving container objects. This will make it easy to keep track of the changes you have made and to avoid inconsistencies. Otherwise, conflicting messages can be received from different locations in the network, causing NDS corruption.

- Never let any server's SYS volume run out of space. The NDS database is kept in a hidden directory on the SYS volume. If the volume runs out of space, no changes can be made to NDS, and the server loses synchronization with other replicas. To be safe, keep at least 50MB free at all times. If possible, keep space-consuming data, such as print queues, on a volume other than SYS.

- Use DSREPAIR (described later in this chapter) to check synchronization before performing any complicated NDS operations. This includes merging partitions, splitting partitions, and moving a container object. (It is also a good idea to make a backup copy of NDS immediately before performing any of these operations.)

Managing NDS Inconsistencies

NDS is a distributed database; each change you make to NDS begins at the replica where you make the change and is passed to each of the other servers that contains a replica. Depending on communication delays, network use, and the complexity of the change, it can take anywhere from 10 seconds to an hour or two for all replicas to receive the change.

Fortunately, NDS was designed with this in mind. The NDS database is *loosely consistent*, which means that it remains functional even if replicas do not have exactly the same information. You may notice these inconsistencies, but they do not necessarily represent a problem with NDS.

The process that NDS uses to send information between replicas is called *synchronization*. Two replicas are synchronized if they contain exactly the same information. In a busy network, the synchronization process is happening constantly to update the latest changes. The process is different depending on the type of change.

Simple changes, such as adding a User object or changing a property, are synchronized quickly. All that is required is to send updates to each server that has a replica of the partition where the object is located. Creating a partition is also a relatively simple task.

Complex changes include joining partitions, moving partitions, and merging Directory trees. These changes require updates to multiple partitions, and each server with a replica of any one of the partitions must be contacted to send updates. These changes can take a long time.

Symptoms of NDS Problems

Although some inconsistencies between NDS replicas are a normal occurrence, severe inconsistencies may be an indication of a corrupt NDS database or another problem. Here are the symptoms you should watch for:

- Changes made to an NDS object or its rights seem to disappear.

- An object or its properties change unexpectedly. For example, a user can no longer log in because the password is incorrect, but the user has not changed the password.

- Errors may be inconsistent. For example, a user may be able to log in after several attempts.

■ Unknown objects, shown with a question mark, appear in the Directory tree. It is normal for these objects to show up when a server has been removed or when a partitioning operation is in progress. However, if they appear without an apparent cause, there may be a problem.

If you notice any of these symptoms, or if any part of NDS seems to behave inconsistently, follow the instructions in the following sections to narrow down and correct the problem. If a corrupt Directory is left alone, it will probably become worse. Be sure to diagnose and correct the problem as soon as you notice any symptoms.

Checking NDS Synchronization

If the problems you are having with NDS are not severe, you should let the servers run for a few hours before attempting any repairs. NDS double-checks itself, and it may repair the problem automatically. Do not take any servers down, because this would prevent NDS from synchronizing and correcting errors.

If the problem still occurs, you should check the synchronization of the server. You can use the DSREPAIR and DSTRACE utilities to accomplish this, as described in the following sections.

Checking Synchronization with DSREPAIR DSREPAIR is a versatile utility that can be used to solve many NDS problems. You can use one of the functions of DSREPAIR to check the synchronization of replicas on the network. You should do this if you suspect a problem in NDS. In addition, you should check the synchronization before performing a major operation, such as merging trees, splitting partitions, joining partitions, or moving a container object.

To use this function of DSREPAIR, follow these steps:

1. Start the DSREPAIR utility by typing **LOAD DSREPAIR** at the server console.

2. Select Replica Synchronization.

3. Enter a full distinguished name for the administrator and password. These will be used by DSREPAIR to log in to NDS.

4. DSREPAIR will check synchronization for all replicas, and display a log file, as shown in the example in Figure 11.22. Examine this log file. If OK appears next to a server's name, the replicas on that server are fully synchronized.

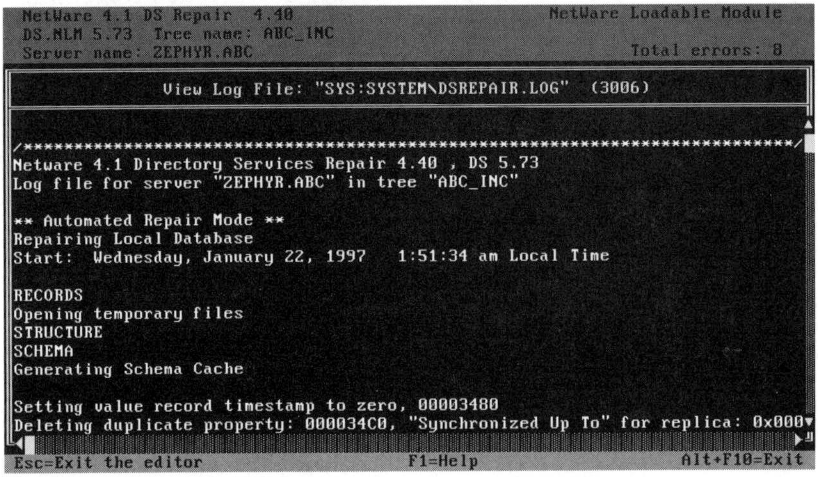

FIGURE 11.22

The DSREPAIR log file displays the synchronization status for all servers.

```
NetWare 4.1 DS Repair  4.40                          NetWare Loadable Module
DS.NLM 5.73  Tree name: ABC_INC
Server name: ZEPHYR.ABC                                   Total errors: 8

┌──────────────────────────────────────────────────────────────────────────┐
│              View Log File: "SYS:SYSTEM\DSREPAIR.LOG"   (3006)             │
├──────────────────────────────────────────────────────────────────────────┤
│                                                                           ▲│
│/*****************************************************************************/│
│Netware 4.1 Directory Services Repair 4.40 , DS 5.73                        │
│Log file for server "ZEPHYR.ABC" in tree "ABC_INC"                         │
│                                                                           │
│** Automated Repair Mode **                                                │
│Repairing Local Database                                                   │
│Start:  Wednesday, January 22, 1997    1:51:34 am Local Time               │
│                                                                           │
│RECORDS                                                                    │
│Opening temporary files                                                    │
│STRUCTURE                                                                  │
│SCHEMA                                                                     │
│Generating Schema Cache                                                    │
│                                                                           │
│Setting value record timestamp to zero, 00003480                          │
│Deleting duplicate property: 000034C0, "Synchronized Up To" for replica: 0x000▼│
├──────────────────────────────────────────────────────────────────────────┤
│Esc=Exit the editor              F1=Help                    Alt+F10=Exit    │
└──────────────────────────────────────────────────────────────────────────┘
```

Using the DSTRACE Parameter   DSTRACE is a special SET parameter that can be used to monitor the activities of NDS. Information is displayed each time NDS replicas are synchronized. This can be helpful when you are diagnosing an NDS problem.

To start tracing NDS, type this command at the server console:

```
SET DSTRACE = ON
```

The Directory Services Trace screen, shown in Figure 11.23, is now available. Press Alt+Esc at the server console to switch to this screen.

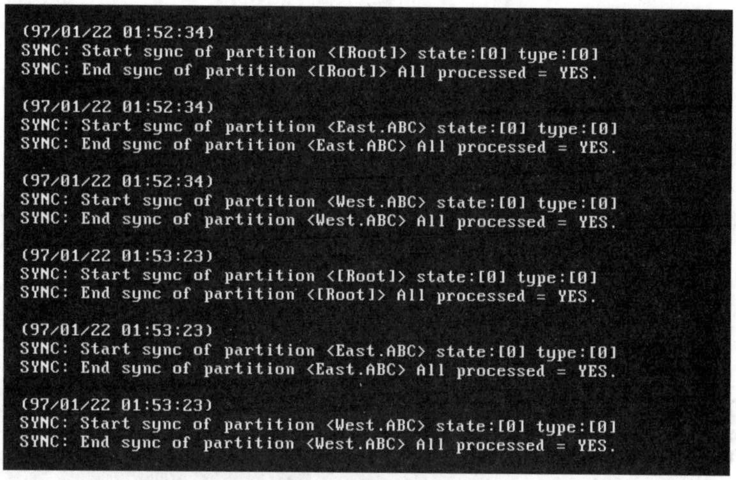

FIGURE 11.23

The DSTRACE screen displays information as NDS synchronization is performed.

```
(97/01/22 01:52:34)
SYNC: Start sync of partition <[Root]> state:[0] type:[0]
SYNC: End sync of partition <[Root]> All processed = YES.

(97/01/22 01:52:34)
SYNC: Start sync of partition <East.ABC> state:[0] type:[0]
SYNC: End sync of partition <East.ABC> All processed = YES.

(97/01/22 01:52:34)
SYNC: Start sync of partition <West.ABC> state:[0] type:[0]
SYNC: End sync of partition <West.ABC> All processed = YES.

(97/01/22 01:53:23)
SYNC: Start sync of partition <[Root]> state:[0] type:[0]
SYNC: End sync of partition <[Root]> All processed = YES.

(97/01/22 01:53:23)
SYNC: Start sync of partition <East.ABC> state:[0] type:[0]
SYNC: End sync of partition <East.ABC> All processed = YES.

(97/01/22 01:53:23)
SYNC: Start sync of partition <West.ABC> state:[0] type:[0]
SYNC: End sync of partition <West.ABC> All processed = YES.
```

You can leave DSTRACE running and check the screen periodically for problems. One of the most common problems will produce this message:

```
SYNC: End sync of partition name. All processed = NO.
```

If NO is displayed here, and the message keeps repeating after a few minutes, there is a serious problem with NDS. You should run the DSREPAIR utility, as described in the next section.

When you no longer need the DSTRACE screen, at the server console, type:

```
SET DSTRACE = OFF
```

Repairing NDS Problems

Once you have determined that there is a problem in the NDS database, you should take action to repair it. The next sections describe three ways to do this. You should try the DSREPAIR utility first. The second option, forcing replica synchronization, provides a more drastic option. As a last resort, an NDS backup can be restored.

Using the DSREPAIR Utility The DSREPAIR utility provides several options for repairing NDS problems. These are listed on the utility's Available Options menu, shown in Figure 11.24. The most useful of these is the first, Unattended Full Repair. When you select this option, NetWare scans the NDS database for errors. All errors found will be repaired if possible. The other options allow you to perform specific steps for troubleshooting, which may be useful if the Unattended Full Repair option fails, or if you are troubleshooting a specific problem.

FIGURE 11.24

The DSREPAIR utility can repair most NDS problems.

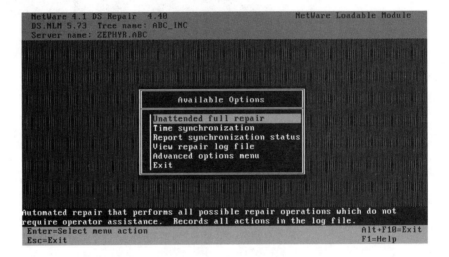

After DSREPAIR has finished scanning the database, it displays a log file. This log lists the tasks that were performed and problems that were found and corrected. Examine the log carefully and make sure that any errors were repaired.

Before you run DSREPAIR, make a backup copy of NDS using your backup software. If the NDS database becomes corrupted further, you may lose information on all replicas. Since there may be errors in the database, do not overwrite an older backup if you have one.

Although DSREPAIR can repair most NDS corruption, you may lose some of the information. After DSREPAIR has finished its work, use NetWare Administrator (NWADMIN) to look at the Directory tree and make sure that all its objects are intact. If there are still problems with NDS, you may need to force synchronization.

You can also run most of the DSREPAIR procedures remotely using the NDS Manager utility.

Forcing Synchronization   If DSREPAIR is unable to repair the problems you are having with NDS, you may want to try forcing synchronization. This option will send updates from the master replica to all other replicas. Any changes waiting on those replicas will be ignored.

If you force synchronization, you may lose changes to NDS that were made at a replica other than the master. Make a backup copy of NDS before proceeding.

Follow these steps to force synchronization using the NWADMIN utility:

1. Start the NDS Manager utility from within NWADMIN.

2. Click the Replicas button.

3. Highlight the master replica.

4. Click the Send Updates button. You will be asked to confirm the choice.

Updates will be sent to all other replicas. This process may take several minutes, and it will cause a lot of traffic on the network.

After the update process is completed, load DSREPAIR at the server and use the Unattended Full Repair option again. If there are still NDS errors that DSREPAIR cannot fix, you will need to restore a backup.

Restoring an NDS Backup   As a last resort, you can restore NDS from a backup. Assuming the backup was performed before the NDS problems began, this should permit a full recovery. Note the date of the backup. If you have made changes to NDS (such as creating users or changing rights) since that date, you must reenter them after you restore the backup.

To restore NDS, first use the Partition Manager or PARTMGR utility to delete all replicas for the partition. Then restore the partition data using your backup software. This will create a new master replica. You can then re-create the other replicas.

Be sure all users in the Directory tree are logged out of the network when you back up or restore NDS data. Do not bring down any servers, however.

Managing Server Downtime

At one time or another, your file server will go down. You might take it down to perform maintenance or reset the server, or it may go down unexpectedly due to a hardware or software problem. Because of NDS, you should be careful in these situations. The following sections discuss how to deal with planned and unplanned downtime, as well as how to remove a server permanently.

Planned Downtime   From time to time, you will need to take the server down for maintenance. This usually will not cause a problem with NDS. Once NDS notices that the server is down, other servers that need to send updates to a replica on that server will keep trying until the server comes back up. When you bring the server up, it may take several minutes to resynchronize the replicas.

If you are going to take down the server that contains the master replica for a partition, you may need to set up another master replica. If the downtime will be brief, another master should not be required.

For extended periods (several hours to a day or more), you should change another replica to master status. This will allow changes to be made to NDS objects in the partition without the use of the server that is down.

If you are bringing a server down for an extended period, you should remove any replicas that are on the server first. This will avoid the large amount of traffic resulting from other servers trying to contact the server that is down. After you bring the server back up, you can re-create the replicas.

Unplanned Downtime   A hardware or software problem can cause a server to go down unexpectedly. If this happens, diagnose the problem. If you can bring the server up within an hour or two and the hard disk containing the SYS volume is undamaged, NDS will resynchronize, and there should not be any problems.

If you have lost the SYS volume on the server, you will need to reinstall NetWare 4.11 on the server. All replicas on the server will be lost. Follow these steps to restore the server:

1. Delete the Server object and Volume objects from the NDS tree. You must use the PARTMGR or Partition Manager utility to delete a Server object.

2. If the server that crashed contained the master replica, change one of the read/write replicas to master status.

3. Fix the hardware problem and reinstall NetWare 4.11 as if it were a new server. Install the server into the same Directory tree.

4. Restore a backup of the data (not NDS) onto the server.

5. Create any replicas that are needed on the server.

6. Check the synchronization of replicas before proceeding further (use DSREPAIR, as described in this chapter).

7. If the server contained the master replica, you can reassign it as the master replica if desired. Change the status of the server that you changed in step 2 back to a read/write replica.

Removing a Server Permanently   You may wish to remove a server permanently if it is no longer needed. To do this, follow these steps:

1. Remove any replicas on the server.

2. If any master replicas were stored on the server, change another server's read/write replica to master status.

3. Bring the server down.

4. Delete the Server and Volume NDS objects. To delete the Server object, you must use the PARTMGR or Partition Manager utility.

When you remove a server, be aware that you are also removing replicas of the NDS database. Be sure you re-create the replicas on other servers to maintain fault tolerance.

Review

The advanced features of NDS include designing an effective tree organization, partitioning and replicating the NDS database, merging (combining) NDS trees, time synchronization, and troubleshooting NDS.

NDS Tree Design and Implementation

In order to take advantage of the features of NDS, you will need a well-designed Directory tree. Factors you should consider in your design include administration, network topology, Bindery Services, and tree depth.

There are several possible strategies for organizing your NDS tree:

- The *default organization* places all objects under a single Organization object, under the [Root].

- A *divisional* organization places divisions or departments of the company in branches of the tree.

- A *locational* organization divides the company into geographical locations.

- A *workgroup* organization groups users who perform the same tasks or projects.

- A *hybrid* organization combines two or more of the above strategies.

The next step in planning your network's Directory tree is to create the standards that will be used in choosing object names and properties: Choose the naming scheme for each type of object.

- Decide which properties will be defined and in what format.

- Create a *standards document* describing the plan.

Strategies for implementing NDS are related to the types of organization used:

- The *departmental* or *divisional* implementation implements NDS separately for each department, division, location, or workgroup.

- The *organizational* approach organizes and implements NDS for the entire organization at once.

- A *combined* approach combines these two options.

NDS Partitions and Replicas

The Directory can be divided into *partitions*. Each partition can be *replicated* on one or more servers. A partition consists of a container object and the objects within it. The partition is given the name of the container. The [Root] partition is the only partition in a new NDS installation.

There are four types of replicas:

- NetWare 4.11 creates a *master replica* when a partition is defined. There is only one master replica per partition.

- *Read/write replicas* contain the same data as the master replica. There can be more than one of this type of replica. Changes made to a read/write replica will be copied to the master replica.

- *Read-only replicas* allow access to NDS data but do not allow changes.

- *Subordinate references* are created automatically by NetWare. These replicas point to children of a partition that are not located on the server.

Directory Tree Merging

When you merge two Directory trees, objects in the [Root] of one tree (the *source* tree) are moved to the [Root] of the second (*target*) tree. The merge process must be performed at the server that contains the master replica of the source tree. You use the DSMERGE utility to merge Directory trees.

Before you can begin the merge process, all the servers that contain a replica of the [Root] partition for either tree must be up and accessible over the network. The schema for the trees must be the same. The trees must have different tree names. The servers containing the [Root] partitions of the trees must be running the same version of NetWare.

Troubleshooting

Most of the problems encountered in NDS deal with *synchronization*, the process of sending updates between replicas in the server. NDS can handle some loss of synchronization, but if a serious problem occurs, you must repair it. The following tools can help you determine if there is a problem:

- Check for symptoms of NDS problems, such as inconsistent behavior and unexpected changes to objects.

- Use DSREPAIR to check the synchronization of replicas.

- Use DSTRACE to display messages about NDS synchronization and detect problems as they occur.

When you have determined that there is a problem, you should act to fix it as soon as possible. You should try the following options to repair NDS corruption:

1. Use the Unattended Full Repair option of the DSREPAIR server utility to automatically fix most problems.

2. If DSREPAIR is unsuccessful, try to send updates from the master replica using the Partition Manager.

3. As a last resort, you can restore from an NDS backup.

Server downtime requires special consideration because of NDS. If you are bringing a server down for an extended period, you should remove any replicas that are on the server first. If it contains a master replica, set up another master replica on another server. If you have lost the SYS volume on a server that went down due to a hardware or software problem, you will need to reinstall NetWare 4.11 on the server.

CHAPTER

12

Advanced NetWare Management

As you have learned in the previous chapters, there is much more to networking than just accessing files and printers. In this chapter, you will learn about three NetWare 4.11 features that are especially important for complex networks:

- Internetworking, or connecting multiple servers and networks

- Internationalization, or configuring the server for use in multiple countries

- Time Synchronization, which keeps times consistent between servers

Internetworking with NetWare 4.11

Internetworking refers to building a wide-area network (WAN), metropolitan-area network (MAN), or simple multiserver system, by interconnecting multiple local networks. NetWare 4.11 provides comprehensive support for internetworking. NetWare servers on similar networks can be connected and included in the same NDS tree for central management. In addition, the *MultiProtocol Router* (MPR) software included with NetWare 4.11 allows communication between different types of networks.

The MultiProtocol Router (MPR)

A *router* receives packets from a network and sends them to another network. The networks can use different topologies and protocols. Using a router to connect different types of networks is illustrated in Figure 12.1. A router acts as a *translator*, converting data between different topologies and protocols.

FIGURE 12.1

A router receives packets from a network and sends them to another network.

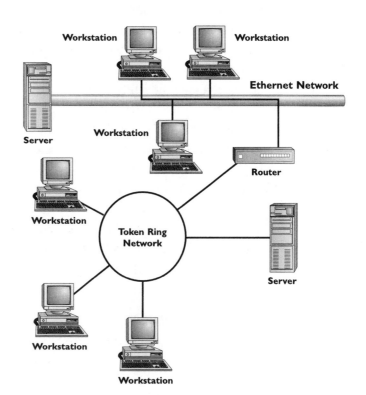

Any NetWare server that is connected to more than one network segment acts as a router, sending packets between the two. This allows you to construct a multiserver network without any additional hardware or software.

A NetWare server can act as an even better router with the MPR software. The MPR is an *intelligent router*. This means that it does not simply resend the packets, but first determines the most efficient path and then routes the packets for streamlined communication between networks. It can also filter information to avoid sending it to segments that don't need it.

Using INETCFG to Configure MPR

Once MPR is installed, you can configure it with the INETCFG utility. This utility is loaded at the server console and provides a convenient menu for setting up network boards, protocols, and bindings. It can be used to configure protocols (such as AppleTalk or TCP/IP) on the server and to manage the MPR.

When you first start INETCFG, you will be presented with the screen shown in Figure 12.2. Answer Yes to make modifications to the server's AUTOEXEC.NCF file that are required for routing and using INETCFG options.

The LOAD and BIND commands in the AUTOEXEC.NCF file are moved into a new file, INITSYS.NCF. This is the file that INETCFG makes changes to. This provides a convenient separation of commands and makes the AUTOEXEC.NCF file smaller and easier to manage.

INETCFG also adds the following commands to the AUTOEXEC.NCF file:

- LOAD CONLOG allows server console messages to be logged to a file to help in debugging.

- INITSYS.NCF executes the commands in the INITSYS.NCF file.

- UNLOAD CONLOG deactivates console logging. If this is not done, the log file can become quite large. You can control the maximum size of the log with a SET command. Unloading CONLOG also ensures that the log file is written and will not be lost if the server crashes.

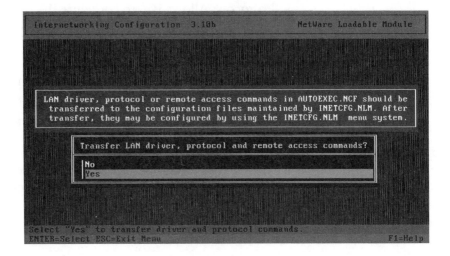

F I G U R E 12.2

INETCFG allows you to move LOAD and BIND commands out of the AUTOEXEC.NCF file.

After you have moved commands to the INITSYS.NCF file using INETCFG, you should not add LOAD or BIND commands to the AUTOEXEC.NCF file or try to modify them in this file. You should make the changes using the INETCFG utility. These changes will be written to the INITSYS.NCF file automatically.

After you have accepted INETCFG's offer to modify the configuration files, you'll see the program's main menu, as shown in Figure 12.3. This menu provides the following options for server and router configuration:

- **Boards:** Allows you to configure network boards. When you configure a network board using this option, the appropriate LOAD command for the network board's driver will be added to the server's INITSYS.NCF file automatically.

- **Network Interfaces:** Allows you to configure network boards that provide multiple ports, also called WAN boards. Each port on the board can be set up to use a different protocol.

- **WAN Call Directory:** Used to define remote servers that will communicate using PPP (Point-to-Point Protocol). This is an extension available for the MPR.

- **Protocols:** Allows you to configure the routing protocols supported by the server. Protocols include IPX, TCP/IP, AppleTalk, RIP, and NLSP.

- **Bindings:** Provides the connection between protocols and network boards. This allows you to choose the protocols that will be used for each board. The BIND commands for these protocols will be added to the INITSYS.NCF file.

- **Manage Configuration:** Allows you to configure parameters used in routing and communication, including SNMP (Simple Network Management Protocol), remote access, and the INITSYS.NCF file parameters.

- **View Configuration:** Allows you to view the LOAD and BIND commands that are currently used in the server. You can also view error messages that might have been displayed when the server was started.

FIGURE 12.3

The INETCFG utility is used to manage network connections and routers.

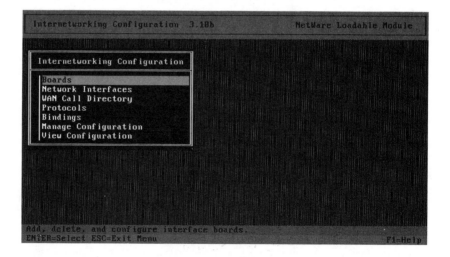

International Features

NetWare 4.11 provides many features that make it suitable for use in different countries and languages. The international features of NetWare 4.11 include the following:

- Server utilities, workstation utilities, and system status and error messages can be displayed in the chosen language.

- Numeric formats can be changed for the local country. These include the order of numbers in dates (for example, month/day/year or day/month/year) and times, and whether numbers are formatted with commas or periods as thousand separators.

- Unicode support is provided. The ASCII code used for text in computers provides only 256 characters. Many languages, such as Chinese, require many more characters. Unicode is an international standard that uses two bytes per character and allows representation of all characters in these languages.

- File names can use non-English characters, and separators (such as the backslash \) can be replaced with characters that are more appropriate for the local country.

- Support is provided for keyboards other than the standard U.S. English keyboard.

Installing an Alternate Language

When you install a NetWare 4.11 server, you are prompted to choose a language for the server. You can install more than one language.

WARNING   In order to select an alternate language, you must have a version of NetWare 4.11 that includes support for that language. Be sure that you purchase the international version, or a version specific to your language.

You can also add languages to the server at any time using the INSTALL utility, as follows:

1. Start the installation utility by typing **LOAD INSTALL** at the server console.

2. Select Product Options.

3. Select Install an Additional Language.

4. Insert the NetWare 4.11 CD-ROM, or specify a directory that contains the installation files.

5. Choose the language to install.

Changing the Server's Language

NetWare 4.11 provides complete support for alternate languages by separating messages from the programs. Any text displayed by the program (menus, error messages, status reports, and other messages) is kept in a separate *message file* instead of in the program file (EXE or NLM) itself.

Message files include all of the messages displayed by the utility or NLM. Message files are given the same name as the utility or NLM, with the MSG extension. For example, the message file for the MONITOR utility is MONITOR.MSG.

The NetWare server program itself, SERVER.EXE, has a message file (SERVER.MSG). By replacing this file with a file for the appropriate language, you can run the server in that language. To do this, first bring the server down. Then copy the MSG file for the chosen language into the directory where SERVER.EXE is located. The file is found on the NetWare 4.11 CD-ROM under the INSTALL directory, in a subdirectory with the name of each language. When you bring the server back up, the new language will be used.

Changing the Server's Keyboard Type

NetWare 4.11 includes a utility, KEYB.NLM, which is used to select the type of keyboard used on the server. At the time of this writing, NetWare 4.11 includes keyboard support for U.S. English, French, Italian, German, and Spanish.

To use KEYB, type **LOAD KEYB** followed by the keyboard type. To see a list of valid keyboard types, type **LOAD KEYB** by itself.

Changing the Language for NLMs

You could replace the MSG file for each NLM with the version for the new language. However, this would be difficult and time consuming. NetWare provides an easier way with the LANGUAGE command. You can type this command at the server console at any time to select a language. Any NLM loaded after you enter the LANGUAGE command will display its messages in that language.

The LANGUAGE command uses a *language designator* to represent each possible language. This designator is a number defined for each language. These numbers range from 0 to 15, as follows:

0	French (Canada)
1	Chinese
2	Danish
3	Dutch
4	English
5	Finnish
6	French
7	German
8	Italian
9	Japanese
10	Korean

11	Norwegian
12	Portuguese
13	Russian
14	Spanish
15	Swedish

Although many languages are listed here, Novell has not yet provided support for all of them. At the time of this writing, supported languages include English, French, Italian, German, and Spanish.

Setting a Workstation's Language

Each workstation has a NWLANGUAGE environmental variable. This variable sets the language used when the user at that workstation runs NetWare utilities. You can set the language in the following ways:

- The NetWare client software includes a SET command for the language in the STARTNET.BAT file.

- You can include a SET NWLANGUAGE = *language* command in the AUTOEXEC.BAT file, or type it manually at the DOS prompt.

- You can use the DOS SET command in the user, profile, or container login script.

The language used in the NWLANGUAGE variable is a word to define each language. This is actually the directory name that the information for that language is stored under. Typical language directory names include ENGLISH, FRENCH, ITALIAN, GERMAN, and SPANISH. For example, the following SET command sets the workstation language to English:

```
SET NWLANGUAGE=ENGLISH
```

Using Time Synchronization

Because NDS is based on a database distributed across multiple servers, all the servers must keep the same time to accurately document changes to files, to order changes made to NDS objects, and for messaging applications.

NDS uses a process called *time stamping* to assign a time to each change in the Directory tree. Changes can be made to an object in the network from any server at any time. Time stamping ensures that these changes are made in the correct order and that all replicas receive the correct information.

Every activity in NDS is documented with a time stamp. Time stamps use *UTC* time. UTC stands for Universal Coordinated Time (the acronym comes from the French). This is the international standard for accurate time. UTC is the new name for *Greenwich Mean Time*, or GMT.

The UTC system is independent of time zones. Because of this, the entire network can have a standard time even if servers are located in parts of the world with different time zones. When you install a server, NetWare 4.11 asks you for a *time zone offset*. NetWare 4.11 then uses this offset to calculate the local time from the network's UTC time. For example, the time offset for Boise, Idaho is 7:00:00 behind, or seven hours behind, UTC. If the time in Boise is 2:00 a.m., UTC time is 9:00 a.m. NetWare also takes daylight saving time into account.

Types of Time Servers

Unfortunately, clocks in computers tend to deviate slightly, so servers can end up with different times. To compensate for this problem, NDS's time synchronization feature uses *time servers* for keeping time standardized across the network. There are four types of time servers, each with a particular purpose. The next sections examine each of these types.

Single Reference Time Server

A *single reference time server* provides a single, authoritative source of time on the network. The first NetWare 4.11 server installed on a network defaults to this configuration.

If you use a single reference time server, you must configure all other servers as secondary time servers. Each of these must receive the time from the single reference server. This is the typical configuration for small networks. Figure 12.4 shows an example of a small network using a single reference time server.

F I G U R E 12.4

A single reference time server is the only source of time on its network.

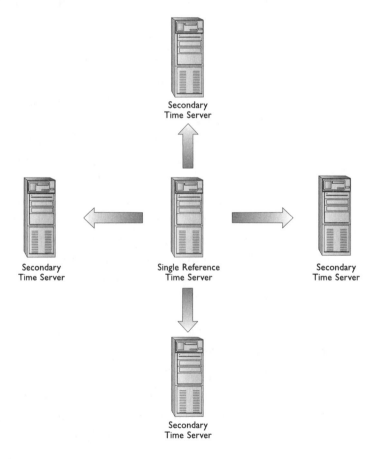

WARNING Because the single reference time server never adjusts its clock, you must be sure that its time is set correctly.

Primary Time Servers

Primary time servers negotiate, or "vote," with other primary and reference servers on the network to determine the correct time. If a primary server finds itself to be out of synchronization with the network time, it gradually speeds up or slows down until it is back in synchronization. Since primary time servers work by negotiation, there must be at least one other time source—a reference server or another primary server—on the network.

Primary time servers are frequently used on WANs, because they can provide a local time source for secondary time servers and workstations that would otherwise need to cross WAN links for a time source.

The negotiation process of primary time servers ensures that the servers agree on a time, but this time is not guaranteed to be accurate. In situations where accurate time is important, you should use a reference time server along with one or more primary servers. Figure 12.5 shows a typical primary time server arrangement.

Secondary Time Servers

A *secondary time server* provides the time to client workstations but not to any other servers. When you install a new server on a network that already has a NetWare 4.11 server, the new server will default to being a secondary time server.

Secondary time servers do not participate in the voting process to determine the correct time. They get time information from a primary or single reference time server. You must define at least one primary server, or a single reference server, before you can configure a server as a secondary time server.

FIGURE 12.5

Primary time servers
vote with other primary
and reference servers
to determine the
correct time.

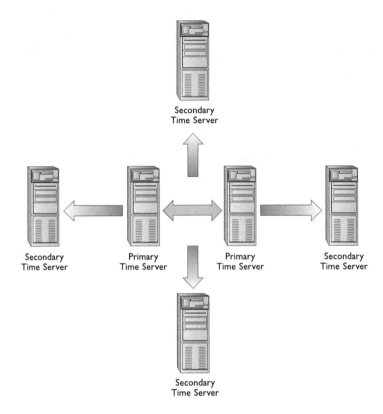

Reference Time Servers

A *reference time server* is the final piece of the puzzle. It is usually
attached to an external time source. This could be an accurate hardware clock or a modem or radio link to a reliable time source, such as
the Rugby Atomic Clock or the U.S. Naval Observatory.

Although the reference time server will adjust its time to match the
external source, it does not adjust its clock in the negotiation process.
When primary time servers negotiate the network time, the reference
server's time is considered an accurate source, and the primary servers
will eventually correct themselves to match that time. If you use a reference server, you must configure at least one primary time server.
Figure 12.6 shows a network arrangement using primary and reference
time servers.

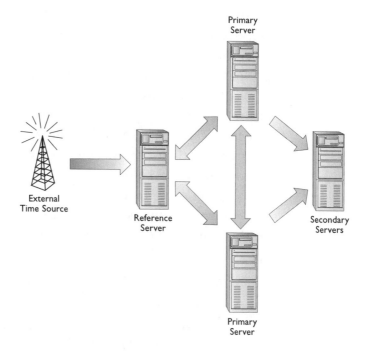

FIGURE 12.6

A reference time server is usually attached to an external time source.

Reference, single reference, and primary time servers are called *time sources* or *time providers*. Secondary time servers are called *time consumers*.

Methods of Time Synchronization

You can choose to install time synchronization in either the default configuration or a custom configuration. The default configuration will work well in most single-location networks. For larger networks and networks with multiple locations, a custom configuration will be more efficient.

Default Configuration

The default time synchronization configuration uses one single reference time server to provide the time to all servers on the network. The first server installed will be the single reference time server. All other servers on the network are configured as secondary time servers when they are installed.

In the default configuration, the single reference server broadcasts time information using the *Service Advertising Protocol* (SAP), a standard NetWare communication protocol. SAP is an effective means of communication. However, because SAP packets are broadcast to the entire network, using SAP will increase traffic on your network, particularly over WAN links.

NetWare 4.11 provides this default method to simplify installation and to enable network administrators to set up a network without necessarily understanding the complexities of the time synchronization process. This can be an effective strategy, but it has the following disadvantages:

- The single reference time server is a *single point of failure*. If this server goes down, all other servers will lose their source of synchronized time. One of the other servers can take over as the single reference server, but you must arrange this manually with a SET command at the server.

- All servers in the network will need to contact the single reference server frequently to receive the current time. This adds traffic to the network, particularly if servers are at opposite ends of a WAN link. Worse, if a server loses its connection to the single reference server, it will also lose time synchronization.

- Because each server is not given a specific list of time servers to receive time from, any server that claims to be a single reference time server will be used. This means that if a server is accidentally configured as a time provider, there will be conflicting sources of time on the network.

Custom Configuration

Using a custom configuration, you can optimize time synchronization on your network. You'll need to plan your custom configuration, using the right combination of primary, secondary, and reference time servers to minimize network traffic.

Don't use a custom configuration unless you really need to, because it requires careful planning and maintenance. The default configuration is usually sufficient for a small company or department.

Custom configurations require you to create a file, TIMESYNC.CFG, at each server to specify time sources. And, each time you add a new time source to the network, you will need to update each of those TIME-SYNC.CFG files. NetWare does not provide a centralized method for maintaining these files.

Planning a Custom Configuration   When you are creating a plan for custom time synchronization, the main factors to consider are the physical location of servers and the speed of network connections between them. Here are some general rules to follow:

- Create primary time servers (or reference time servers, if you're using them) in major locations.

- Arrange for servers near each primary time server to receive their time from that server.

- Be sure that there are strong network links between each of the primary time servers.

- If you use a reference time server, place it near the network backbone, where it can be accessed easily.

In this strategy, because you use multiple primary and reference servers, or *time sources*, there is no single point of failure. As long as network communication lines remain open, servers will have more than one available source of time. This ensures that no server will lose time synchronization.

You should avoid using more than five primary and reference time servers on a network, because the traffic generated by the voting process can slow down the network. For larger networks, you will want to use multiple time provider groups, as described in the next section.

Using Time Provider Groups

A *time provider group* usually consists of a reference time server, one or more primary time servers, and a number of secondary time servers. A simple time provider group is shown earlier, in Figure 12.6.

In a large network with many servers communicating across WAN links, single time provider groups are not practical. The voting process used by primary servers will add traffic to the WAN link, creating a bottleneck. In this situation, you should use multiple time provider groups.

If you use multiple time provider groups, it is important to use some form of external time source for synchronization. If each location's reference time server communicates with the same external source (such as a radio time signal), you can keep a consistent time across all locations without adding traffic to the WAN.

An example of a network using multiple time provider groups is shown in Figure 12.7.

Implementing and Managing Time Synchronization

In order to set up and maintain time synchronization on your network, you need to adjust settings on each server. These settings will determine what type of time server the server will act as and which server it will use as a time source.

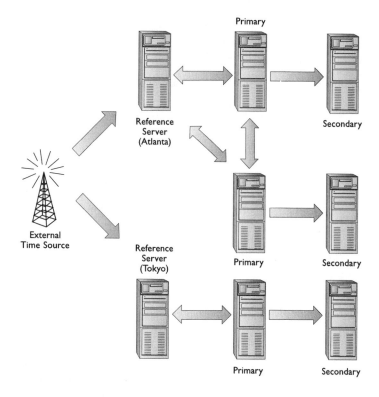

FIGURE 12.7

Multiple time provider
groups should be used on
a larger network.

Setting Time Synchronization Parameters

There are several SET parameters you can use to control your network's time synchronization. These SET commands all begin with SET TIMESYNC, and they are described in Table 12.1. Rather than using the SET command, these settings can be written to the server's TIMESYNC.CFG file. You should use this method unless the change is meant to be temporary.

	SET TIMESYNC	
TABLE 12.1 NetWare 4.11 Time Synchronization SET parameters	**Parameter**	**Description**
	Configured Sources	This controls which type of time source is used. If set to ON, you must specify a list of time sources in the TIMESYNC.CFG file. If set to OFF, the SAP protocol is used to listen for a time source.

T A B L E 12.1 *(cont.)* NetWare 4.11 Time Synchronization SET parameters	**SET TIMESYNC Parameter**	**Description**
	Directory Tree Mode	If set to ON, SAP packets are ignored unless they come from the server's own Directory tree. If multiple Directory trees are used, this prevents time servers on different trees from creating conflicts.
	Hardware Clock	Controls whether the server's hardware clock will be used for time synchronization. This should only be set to OFF if the server will use as external time source.
	Polling Count	Controls how many time packets are exchanged when servers are polled. Increasing this number can create unnecessary traffic. The default is 3.
	Polling Interval	Controls how often the server polls other servers. This number defaults to 600 seconds (10 minutes). If you change this, you must use the same setting for all servers on the network.
	Service Advertising	If this is set to ON, the SAP protocol will be used to broadcast time. If it is turned off, you must create a list of time sources in the TIMESYNC.CFG file of each server.
	Synchronization Radius	This controls the maximum amount a server's time can be adjusted and still remain in synchronization with other servers. It defaults to 2000 milliseconds. Increasing this parameter may prevent servers from losing synchronization.
	Type	This determines the type of time server that the server is currently acting as. This should be Reference, Primary, Secondary, or Single Reference.

An easy way to specify SET parameters and save them in the AUTOEXEC.NCF and TIMESYNC.CFG files is to use the SERVMAN utility. This utility is loaded at the server console with the command LOAD SERVMAN.

Creating the TIMESYNC.CFG Files

If you are using a custom configuration, you must create a TIME-SYNC.CFG file for each server. This file is located in the server's SYS:SYSTEM directory. The file consists of two parts:

- **Parameters:** These are the parameters listed in Table 12.1. When they are used in the TIMESYNC.CFG file, you do not need to include the SET TIMESYNC command.

- **Time Sources:** This is a list of time sources for a custom configuration. The first server in the list will be polled as a time source. If it is unavailable, the other servers in the list will be tried.

Here is an example of a TIMESYNC.CFG file. This file is for the server CORP1, which is a primary time server. It negotiates with the servers CORP2 and CORP3 to determine the correct time.

```
#TIMESYNC.CFG for Server CORP1

# (lines beginning with # are comments)

Configured Sources = ON

Directory Tree Mode = ON

Hardware Clock = OFF


Polling Count = 3

Polling Interval = 600


Service Advertising = OFF

Synchronization Radius = 2000
```

```
Type = PRIMARY

# Time Sources


Time Source = CORP2

Time Source = CORP3
```

Since time synchronization operates at a lower level than NDS, you can't use NDS utilities to make changes to time synchronization. These changes must be made in the individual TIMESYNC.CFG files for each server.

Starting Synchronization

If you have configured time synchronization correctly, the servers should synchronize with each other as soon as they are brought online. You can verify this by issuing the **TIME** command at each server's console. Here is the typical output of the TIME command:

```
Time zone string: "MST7MDT"

DST status: ON

DST start: Sunday, April 17, 1996 2:00 am MST

DST end: Sunday, October 29, 1996 2:00 am MDT

Time synchronization is active.

Time is synchronized to the network.

Sunday, July 2, 1995 3:35:14 am UTC

Saturday, July 1, 1995 9:35:14 pm MDT
```

Check that the message "Time is synchronized to the network" is displayed on each server. If the servers are not synchronized, check the time synchronization settings.

After time synchronization is established, you should avoid changing the time on any server. If the server is a time consumer, your change will be ignored, because time is received from the other servers on the network; if it is a time provider, it will affect the network's time, which could corrupt NDS data.

Review

In this chapter, you have learned about three important network management services available in NetWare 4.11: internetworking, internationalization, and time synchronization.

Internetworking

Internetworking refers to building a wide-area network (WAN) by interconnecting multiple local networks. A *router* receives packets from a network and sends them to another network. The router can translate between different topologies and protocols.

Any NetWare server can act as a router. The MPR (MultiProtocol Router) software allows it to act as a sophisticated, intelligent router with filtering capabilities. Once MPR is installed, you can configure it with the INETCFG utility. Load this utility at the server console and use it to configure protocols on the server and to manage the MPR.

Internationalization

The international features of NetWare 4.11 include the following:

- Server utilities, workstation utilities, and system status and error messages can be displayed in the chosen language.

- Numeric formats can be changed for the local country.

- Unicode support is provided. (Unicode is an international standard that allows representation of more characters than ASCII code supports.)

- File names can use non-English characters and different separators.

- Support for keyboards other than the standard U.S. English keyboard is provided.

NetWare 4.11 provides complete support for alternate languages by separating messages from the programs. Any text displayed by the program, such as menus and error messages, is kept in a separate *message file* instead of in the program file. The message files have an MSG extension.

Time Synchronization

NDS's time synchronization feature uses *time servers* for keeping time standardized across the network. There are four types of time servers:

- A *single reference time server*, when used, is the only source of time. All other servers must be secondary servers.

- *Primary time servers* negotiate, or "vote," with other primary servers to determine the time.

- *Secondary time servers* receive the time from a primary or single reference time server and give the time to clients.

- *Reference time servers* are used with primary time servers, and are usually attached to a hardware or remote time source.

CHAPTER

13

Setting Up and
Managing the Workstation

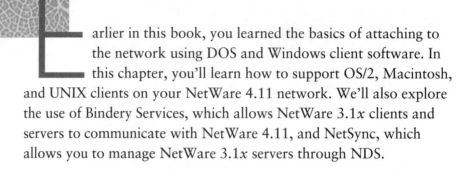

arlier in this book, you learned the basics of attaching to the network using DOS and Windows client software. In this chapter, you'll learn how to support OS/2, Macintosh, and UNIX clients on your NetWare 4.11 network. We'll also explore the use of Bindery Services, which allows NetWare 3.1*x* clients and servers to communicate with NetWare 4.11, and NetSync, which allows you to manage NetWare 3.1*x* servers through NDS.

Installing Non-DOS Clients

One of the best features of NetWare 4.11 is that it can be used with a wide variety of clients—*diverse clients*, to use Novell's term. Along with DOS and Windows clients, which we covered in Chapter 3, NetWare 4.11 supports OS/2, Macintosh, and UNIX workstations. The procedures for configuring OS/2 and Macintosh clients are described in the following sections. We'll also take a brief look at NetWare/IP, which allows support for clients using the TCP/IP protocol.

Configuring OS/2 Clients

NetWare provides support for the IBM OS/2 operating system. Users at OS/2 workstations can attach to the server or to the NDS tree.

Since OS/2 can work with the standard DOS file system, you can use OS/2 clients on your network without installing additional software on the file server. However, OS/2 includes the HPFS (High-Performance

File System). This system allows long file names (up to 255 characters, with lowercase letters) and extended attributes (other information, such as file descriptions). To take advantage of these features, you need to install the OS/2 *name space* on the server.

Installing the Long File Names Name Space

The long file names name space allows HPFS files to be stored on your server. This name space also supports Windows 95 and Windows NT long file names. You can install the name space by using the following commands at the file server console:

```
LOAD LONG.NAM
```

This loads the protocols used for the OS/2 name space. This is an NLM called LONG.NAM. After the name space is installed, this module will load automatically when you mount the volume. To install the name space on a volume, use this command:

```
ADD NAME SPACE LONG TO SYS
```

This command adds the name space to the volume and allocates space to store long file names. You can use any volume name in place of SYS. These changes are permanently written to the volume, so you execute this command only once.

After you have installed the name space, you'll be able to use the HPFS features on your server. Note the following considerations:

- Extended OS/2 naming information will be accessible from OS/2 clients only. You may be able to access the files from DOS clients, but the names will be incorrect. Since an OS/2 client can access DOS file names also, you can use an OS/2 client to copy the files to DOS names; however, the extended name information will be lost when you do this.

- The name space module (LONG.NAM) should load automatically when you mount the volume. If this module fails to load or is unloaded, files that use OS/2 naming will be inaccessible until the module is loaded.

Windows 95 can access OS/2 long file names; in fact, you may want to add the long file names space to a volume just for the use of Windows 95. Windows NT provides a similar feature.

Installing the OS/2 Requester

The NetWare Client for OS/2 is a full-featured client software package. It includes the NetWare OS/2 Requester, which is the OS/2 equivalent of the DOS Requester and provides the same functions.

To begin the installation, run the INSTALL program. There are two ways to do this:

- Place the NetWare 4.11 CD-ROM in a local or networked drive. Change to that drive and type **INSTALL** from the OS/2 command prompt.

- From the CD-ROM or the SYS:PUBLIC\CLIENT\OS2 directory on a server, run the MAKEDISK program. This program allows you to create a set of installation diskettes for the OS/2 client. You can then run INSTALL from the first diskette.

The INSTALL program includes several options, including built-in documentation. To install the client software, select Requester on Workstation from the Installation menu. You can choose from four options for different types of installations:

- **Edit CONFIG.SYS and Copy All Files:** This option is the default. It installs all of the client software, including the LAN driver, and modifies the OS/2 CONFIG.SYS file to load the network client software.

- **Only Edit CONFIG.SYS**: Makes changes to CONFIG.SYS only. This is useful if you have already installed the client software.

- **Only Copy Requester Files**: Copies the OS/2 client files to your workstation but does not modify CONFIG.SYS.

- **Only Copy ODI LAN Driver Files**: Allows you to copy optional LAN driver files from the installation directory. Drivers are provided for several common network cards. You can choose from this list, or insert a disk provided by the network card manufacturer.

Choose one of the options above (usually the first one) and click the OK button. This will begin the installation process. You are asked to choose a LAN driver, and all files are copied or modified in accordance with your selection.

After the client software has been installed, reboot the workstation. You can now log in to the network using the OS/2 version of the LOGIN program. After logging in, you can access network drives from the OS/2 desktop.

The installation program will also install a program called NetWare Tools for OS/2. This program is similar to the Windows NetWare User Tools program described in Chapter 5. It allows you to map network drives, set up printer capturing, and log in and out of servers and Directory trees.

Configuring Macintosh Clients

NetWare 4.11 includes support for Apple Macintosh clients. This support is provided by NetWare for Macintosh, which is a set of NLMs that run on your NetWare server.

NetWare for Macintosh supports the *AppleTalk* protocol. This is a proprietary protocol developed by Apple, and it is usually used on Macintosh networks. Since AppleTalk is a type of peer-to-peer networking, there is no dedicated server. In this system, each Macintosh workstation can act as a server by sharing files and printers with other stations.

NetWare for Macintosh provides the following functions:

- Files on Macintosh workstations can be shared by users on the NetWare network, as well as by other Macintosh clients.

- Macintosh users can send print jobs to printers on the NetWare network.

- NetWare users can send print jobs to printers on the AppleTalk network.

Installing NetWare for Macintosh

Unlike DOS and OS/2 clients, Macintosh workstations cannot attach to the network unless NetWare for Macintosh is loaded on the file server. NetWare for Macintosh must be installed before you can install the client software. This is offered as an option when you are installing the server.

You can also install NetWare for Macintosh on an existing server. This is an option provided by the INSTALL module. Follow these steps to start the installation:

1. Start the INSTALL utility by typing **LOAD INSTALL** at the server console.

2. Select Product Options.

3. Press ↵ to choose an item to install.

4. Select Install NetWare for Macintosh.

5. Specify a path to the installation directory. This defaults to the directory you used for your server installation, which may be a CD-ROM or a remote network directory. NetWare for Macintosh will be installed from this directory. The directory is typically \NW410\ INSTALL\ENGLISH on the NetWare 4.11 CD-ROM. If you are using a different language, substitute it for ENGLISH here.

6. Select Install NW-MAC to continue.

Final Installation Options   The files required for NetWare for Macintosh are now copied to the server. These are placed in a directory called NW-MAC under the SYS:SYSTEM directory. When this process is complete, the Final Installation Options window appears. This window offers five options, illustrated in Figure 13.1.

FIGURE 13.1

The Final Installation Options menu allows you to complete tasks needed for Macintosh connectivity.

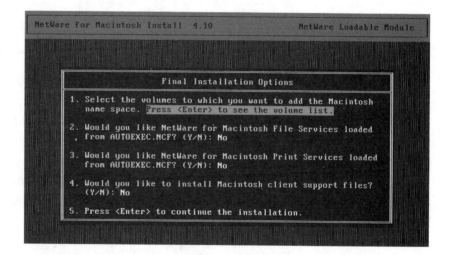

1. **Volumes for Macintosh name space**: This option allows you to select volumes to install the Macintosh name space, which provides compatibility with Macintosh file names. You must install the Macintosh name space on the SYS volume to run NetWare for Macintosh.

2. **Start file services**: This will add the command to start Macintosh file services to the server's AUTOEXEC.NCF file. This loads a module called AFP.NLM (AFP stands for AppleTalk Filing Protocol). You should choose this option if you wish to share files with Macintosh clients.

3. **Start print services:** This adds the command to start Macintosh print services to the AUTOEXEC.NCF file. The module that handles this is ATPS.NLM (ATPS stands for AppleTalk Print Services). This is needed to allow Macintosh clients to print to a network printer.

4. **Support files:** This lets you install support files for the Macintosh client. These files are installed on the server under the SYS:SYSTEM\NW-MAC directory. The next section explains how to install the software on the clients.

5. **Continue installation:** Press ↵ here to continue the installation.

When you continue the installation, you are asked to verify your choice. If you select Yes, the items you selected are installed on the server. Finally, the NetWare for Macintosh Configuration window appears. This gives you a chance to install any options you did not already choose. In addition, four options allow you to configure NetWare for Macintosh features. These options actually run individual NLMs. You can load any of these NLMs yourself if you wish to change the configuration.

- **Configure AppleTalk Stack:** Loads INETCFG.NLM, which is used to set up the AppleTalk protocol, described in the next section.

- **Configure File Services:** Loads AFPCON.NLM, which allows you to change file-sharing options.

- **Configure Print Services:** Loads ATPSCON.NLM, which allows you to control AppleTalk printing services.

- **Configure CD-ROM Services:** Loads HFSCDCON.NLM, which is used to support Macintosh CD-ROM drives.

These changes will not take effect until you bring the server down and back up. Before you do this, install the AppleTalk protocol as described in the next section. If you need to change NetWare for Macintosh options later, you can return to the Configuration window by following these steps:

1. Start the Installation utility by typing **LOAD INSTALL** at the server console.

2. Select Product Options.

3. Select View/Configure/Remove installed products.

4. Select NW-MAC from the product list. The Configuration window will be displayed, and you can make changes as necessary.

Installing the AppleTalk Protocol

To communicate with Macintosh clients, the AppleTalk protocol must be loaded on the server. Follow these steps to install AppleTalk:

1. Load the INETCFG utility by typing **LOAD INETCFG** at the server console.

2. Select Bindings and press ↵.

3. Press Insert to add a binding to the list. Select AppleTalk and press ↵.

4. A list of LAN cards is displayed. Select the one that you will be using to connect to the AppleTalk network and press ↵.

5. Press Esc to exit, and then select Yes to save your changes.

This will add the BIND statement for AppleTalk to the AUTOEXEC .NCF file. You will need to restart the server for the new binding to take effect. This will also cause the NetWare for Macintosh modules you installed (described in the previous section) to load.

Installing the Macintosh Client Software

Because the AppleTalk protocol is provided with the Macintosh operating system, you can begin using NetWare for Macintosh services right away without installing additional software on the Macintosh client. However, you need to install the client software to take advantage of NDS. The Macintosh client is called MacNDS, and it provides access to NDS, similar to the DOS Requester.

Enabling Bindery Logins   Until you install the MacNDS software, Macintosh clients will attach to the server using Bindery Services (described later in this chapter). Before you can log in with Bindery Services, you must enable bindery logins for AppleTalk using the AFPCON utility, as follows:

1. Type **LOAD AFPCON** at the server console.

2. From the Configuration Options menu, select Detailed Configuration.

3. Select User Access Information. These options control the types of logins that are allowed.

4. Press ↵ on the Allow Clear Text Password Login option and change the option to Yes. This will allow bindery attachments.

5. Press Esc to exit and save your changes.

Installing MacNDS   After you have enabled bindery logins, you can install MacNDS on the Macintosh client. Follow these steps:

1. On the Macintosh client, log in to the server. Since the client files are in the PUBLIC directory, you do not need to use the ADMIN user account.

2. Click on the NetWare volume's icon, then switch to the PUBLIC/MAC directory. Inside this directory are directories for each language available. Double-click on the appropriate language, such as ENGLISH.

3. Inside the language directory, there will be a file called MacNDS .SEA. (SEA stands for Self-Extracting Archive, and it is a Macintosh standard for compressed files.) Double-click on this file.

4. You will be asked where to install the files. Click OK to accept the default location, or browse through the folders to select another directory.

The MacNDS client is installed in a folder called MacNDS in the folder you specify. You can open this folder to run the client software.

MacNDS relies on the features of Macintosh System 7.0 or later operating system. If you are using an older operating system, you will need to access the network through Bindery Services.

Using Macintosh Utilities

NetWare 4.11 includes something new for Macintosh users: a set of utilities that allow you to work with the network. With these utilities, you can log in and out of the network, browse objects in the NDS Directory tree, select a network printer for printing, or mount a NetWare volume as a local drive. In addition to these utilities, a version of the RCONSOLE utility, which allows you to access a file server's console, is included. We'll look at each of these in the following sections.

One utility that's missing here is NWADMIN. There is currently no Macintosh version of the NetWare Administrator utility. You will need to manage the NDS tree from a DOS, Windows 3.1, Windows 95, or OS/2 workstation.

Using the NDS Tree Menu   One of the most convenient features for Macintosh users is the NDS Tree menu. After you have successfully installed NetWare Client for Macintosh, a small icon resembling a tree appears near the right end of the menu bar. Clicking this icon allows you to access the NDS Tree drop-down menu shown in Figure 13.2. This menu includes several convenient features:

F I G U R E 1 3 . 2

The NDS Tree menu allows access to NetWare features from Macintosh clients.

- **About NetWare Client:** Shows the current version and other information about the client software you have installed.

- **Login:** Allows you to enter a username and password to log in to the NetWare server or Directory tree.

- **Configure:** Allows you to configure options for the Macintosh client.

- **Connections:** Allows you to view and manage your current server and Directory tree connections.

- **Log Out Completely:** Logs you out of all current servers and Directory trees.

NetWare Directory Browser   The NetWare Directory Browser is a utility that allows a Macintosh user to browse the Directory tree, examine the objects, and change their settings relating to NetWare printers and volumes. While it's hardly NWADMIN, it is a handy utility for Macintosh users.

To activate the Directory Browser, double-click its icon; this icon is installed automatically with the NetWare client software. The Browser window includes a pull-down menu at the top from which you can select a portion of the Directory tree. Below this menu are three sections:

- The Objects section shows a list of objects in the current context.

- The Show Types section allows you to use checkboxes to determine which object types are included in the display.

- The Help section shows information about the current option or object.

Aside from browsing the Directory tree, the Directory Browser provides two more useful functions:

- To mount a volume, double-click the Volume object or select Browse ➢ Mount.

- When a Printer or Print Queue object is selected, you can use the Choose Printer or Choose Queue option from the Browse menu to select the printer for print jobs sent from the workstation.

NetWare Volume Mounter   An icon for the NetWare Volume Mounter utility is also included when you install NetWare Client. Volume Mounter allows you to quickly mount a NetWare volume, making it accessible from the Macintosh desktop.

You use the drag-and-drop method to work with the Volume Mounter icon:

- Drag a Volume object from the desktop or the Directory Browser to the Volume Mounter icon to mount the volume.

- Drag a Server object to the Volume Mounter icon to mount the volumes on that server.

When you drag one or more volumes to the Volume Mounter icon, you see the Volume Mounter window, shown in Figure 13.3. Be sure the volume or volumes you wish to mount is highlighted, then press the Mount button to complete the mount operation.

FIGURE 13.3

The NetWare Volume Mounter allows you to configure access to server volumes.

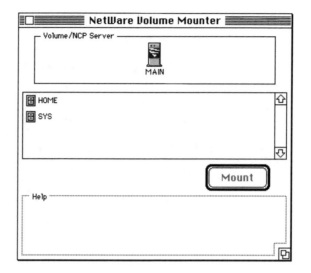

NetWare Print Chooser The NetWare Print Chooser application doesn't have an icon. Instead, you access it by double-clicking a Printer or Print Queue icon within the Directory Browser or selecting the Choose Printer or Choose Queue option. The Print Chooser window is shown in Figure 13.4.

FIGURE 13.4

The NetWare Print Chooser allows a Macintosh workstation to send files to a network printer.

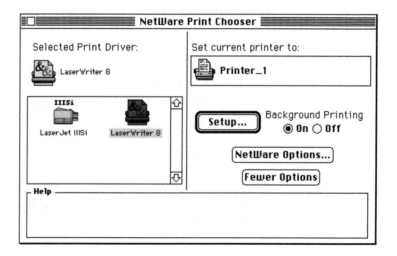

Within the Print Chooser window, you can select the Setup button to configure the default capture settings for the printer or queue. You can also drag a Printer or Print Queue object to the desktop and double-click the desktop icon when you wish to choose that printer or queue.

Remote Console   The final Macintosh utility, Remote Console, is one many administrators have wished for: it allows you to view and control a file server console remotely. It works much like the RCONSOLE utility for DOS workstations, which Chapter 10 examines in detail.

To use the remote console (on either Macintosh or DOS) you need to load the REMOTE and RSPX modules on the server, as described in Chapter 10.

The Remote Console utility is not installed by default. You can follow these steps to install it, using the same utility you used to install the NetWare client:

1. Run the NetWare Client Install utility.

2. Select Custom Install to see the Custom Installation dialog box, shown in Figure 13.5.

3. Select the Remote Console Install option.

4. Click the Install button.

After the installation process is complete, a Remote Console icon is created. Double-click this icon to open a remote console session. You can then select a server to connect to, enter the password, and view the server's screen.

The main difference in the Macintosh version of Remote Console is the keyboard configuration. Because Macintosh and PC keyboards are different, allowances were made in this version. Keystrokes also vary depending on the type of Macintosh keyboard. Table 13.1 shows the keystrokes for Macintosh Remote Console.

FIGURE 13.5

The Custom Installation dialog box allows you to install additional Macintosh client options.

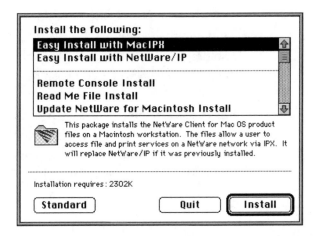

Install the following:

Easy Install with MacIPX
Easy Install with NetWare/IP

Remote Console Install
Read Me File Install
Update NetWare for Macintosh Install

This package installs the NetWare Client for Mac OS product files on a Macintosh workstation. The files allow a user to access file and print services on a NetWare network via IPX. It will replace NetWare/IP if it was previously installed.

Installation requires : 2302K

Standard   Quit   Install

TABLE 13.1

Keystrokes for Macintosh Remote Console

Key (Extended Keyboard)	Key (Standard Keyboard)	Description
Option-F2	Option-Command-2	Exits the current server and allows you to choose another
Option-F3	Option-Command-3	Switches to the previous screen
Option-F4	Option-Command-4	Switches to the next screen
Option-F5	Option-Command-5	Shows your current network address
Ins	Option-Command-I	Used when the Ins (PC) key is needed
Del	Option-Command-d	Used when the Del (PC) key is needed

If you are using a standard Macintosh keyboard, you will also notice that many NetWare utilities and NLMs expect you to use the F1 and F12 keys, which are not present on your keyboard. You can get around this by turning on the function key palette. To use it, select Edit ➢ Show Function Keys.

Choosing this option opens a window with buttons for each key, which you can access with the mouse. Other commonly needed keys, such as Ins and Del, are also included. The function key palette is shown in Figure 13.6.

FIGURE 13.6

The function key palette allows you to access keys found only on extended keyboards.

Using NetWare/IP

UNIX machines and the Internet use a protocol called TCP/IP. NetWare 4.11 includes NetWare/IP, an implementation of TCP/IP for NetWare servers and clients. This allows DOS workstations to connect to the network using TCP/IP rather than the standard NetWare IPX protocol. In addition, this allows easy connectivity with UNIX workstations and Internet gateways, and allows you to interconnect IPX and TCP/IP networks.

NetWare/IP includes two components:

- Several NLMs to support the TCP/IP protocol on the server

- The NetWare/IP client software for TCP/IP workstations

Integrating NetWare 3.1x and NetWare 4

NDS, used in NetWare 4.11 to store information about network resources, is a radical departure from the bindery used in previous versions of NetWare. In order to remain compatible with older systems—both previous versions of NetWare and older client soft-ware—NetWare 4.11 includes *Bindery Services*. Although the emphasis here is on NetWare 3.1*x*, Bindery Services also works with earlier NetWare versions.

Bindery Services uses a branch of the Directory tree to serve as a simulated bindery. All the leaf objects within a particular container object appear as a flat database to bindery-based clients. The container object that acts as a bindery is called the *bindery context*. The bindery context is set with a SET command or in the file server's AUTOEXEC.NCF file. Beginning in NetWare 4.11, you can set up to 16 different bindery contexts. All the contexts will appear as portions of the same bindery, as illustrated in Figure 13.7.

FIGURE 13.7

The contents of the bindery context container (.O=QDB_INC in this example) serve as a simulated bindery.

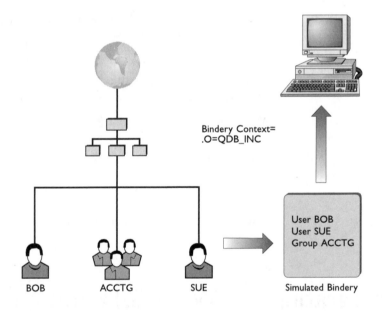

Bindery Context=
.O=QDB_INC

User BOB
User SUE
Group ACCTG

BOB   ACCTG   SUE   Simulated Bindery

When you upgrade your server from NetWare 3.1*x* to NetWare 4.11, NetWare 4.11 automatically creates a bindery context. All the users, groups, and print queues from the NetWare 3.1*x* bindery are created as objects under a single Organization object, which is defined as the bindery context. This may not be the most efficient arrangement, but it allows the network users who are still using their old NetWare setup to begin using NetWare 4.11 immediately after the upgrade.

When you install a new NetWare 4.11 server, NetWare 4.11 also creates a default bindery context. The context that contains the NetWare Server object is set up as the bindery context container.

Planning and Implementing Bindery Services

Although Bindery Services is set up automatically when you install NetWare 4.11, there are many things to be aware of when you are using Bindery Services on your server. In this section, you will learn the steps involved in planning and installing an efficient Bindery Services setup.

Planning Considerations

It is important to plan the way that Bindery Services will operate on your server. Since the bindery does not offer all the features of NDS, you must be careful to create NDS objects that will be compatible with bindery-based clients when necessary.

Object Naming   The common name of an object is used as its bindery name. Suppose a user has the following distinguished name:

> .CN=JIMS.OU=ACCT.O=ABCINC

To Bindery Services, this user is seen as simply JIMS. Since the bindery is flat, you cannot address objects in their containers. Because of this limitation, two potential problems can occur when using Bindery Services. These involve bindery-compatible naming and name conflicts.

Using Bindery-Compatible Names   Objects that will be leaf objects in the bindery context container need to use *bindery-compatible names*.

The common name of each object must follow the same rules that bindery-based objects follow in NetWare 3.1*x*.

- Spaces cannot be used in the names. If spaces are used in an object's name, they are converted to underscores for Bindery Services.

- The following *special characters* cannot be used in bindery names:

  $ (dollar sign)

  ? (question mark)

  \ (backslash)

  / (forward slash)

  " (quotation mark)

  [ ] (opening and closing square brackets)

  : (colon)

  | (vertical bar)

  <> (opening and closing angle brackets)

  + (plus sign)

  = (equal sign)

- Names are limited to 47 characters. (NDS normally allows 64-character names.)

Name Conflicts   Because NDS objects with the same common name can exist in different contexts, object names can conflict with each other when you are using Bindery Services. If you have a single bindery context set on your server, this cannot happen. However, since you can assign up to 16 contexts as bindery contexts, you must be careful that no identical names exist in those contexts.

Figure 13.8 shows an example of a Directory tree arrangement in which there could be name conflicts. If both .OU=SALES and .OU=SERVICE are set as bindery contexts, there will be a conflict because both contain a User object with the name FRED.

FIGURE 13.8

When using multiple bindery contexts, you must be careful that name conflicts do not exist between any two contexts.

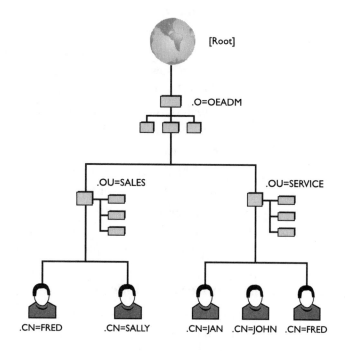

Creating Needed Objects   If you are using Bindery Services to ensure compatibility with a bindery-based application, there are several bindery objects that you may need to create manually, because they are not automatically created with Bindery Services.

When you install NetWare 3.1x, it creates the GUEST User object and the EVERYONE Group object. Bindery Services does not create these objects. If you upgraded your server from NetWare 3.1x, these objects should have been created as objects in the bindery context. If your NetWare 4.11 server is a new installation, you need to create them manually.

For example, NetWare NFS (Network File System) requires that the group EVERYONE exist in the bindery. If you are installing Bindery Services and will be using NFS, you must create the group as a leaf object in the bindery context. You will also need to add all the bindery context User objects to this group. (The current version of NFS will actually perform these steps automatically when it is installed.) If you have upgraded a NetWare 3.1x server, the EVERYONE group should have been transferred from the bindery.

Finally, NetWare creates the SUPERVISOR account when you install Bindery Services, but this is only a bindery object. Even when you upgrade a NetWare 3.1x server to NetWare 4.11, SUPERVISOR is not created in NDS and is not equivalent to the ADMIN object in NDS. The SUPERVISOR account retains Supervisor rights, but only for objects within the bindery context and for the server's file system. The SUPERVISOR password should be the same as the Admin password.

Limitations of the Bindery

Bindery-based clients will not be able to access all the information available through NDS. They will have access to only the information that would normally be provided by a bindery. Items not available to bindery clients include the following:

- E-mail name, phone number, and other extended addressing information

- Aliases and profiles

- Print job configurations

- NDS login scripts

NOTE Because bindery clients are logging into a server-centric bindery environment located on one server, the login script that they will access is the one in the MAIL directory on the server they log in to. This script must be maintained on that server, and it is not replicated to other servers. However, you can move the bindery-based login scripts to NDS using the UIMPORT utility provided with NetWare 4.11.

Planning Bindery Contexts

For most networks, one bindery context is sufficient. In fact early versions of NetWare 4 allowed only one bindery context. The ability to set up to 16 separate bindery contexts is new to NetWare 4.11. By taking advantage of this feature, you can have the benefits of Bindery Services without sacrificing the efficiency of a well-organized Directory tree.

In the Directory tree pictured in Figure 13.9, users in the ACCT and CORP Organizational Units both need access to Bindery Services. We can set the following as the bindery context:

    .ACCT.QDC;.CORP.QDC

Leaf objects in both containers will act as objects in the simulated bindery. As you can see, this is a powerful feature for combining NetWare 4.11 with earlier versions of NetWare.

Setting Up Bindery Services

You must configure Bindery Services individually for each server that will allow bindery attachments. In addition, the server must have a master or read/write replica of the partition containing the bindery context.

FIGURE 13.9

To give users in both the ACCT and CORP Organizational Units access to Bindery Services, use multiple bindery contexts.

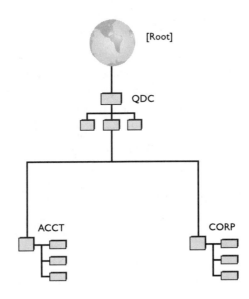

Setting the Bindery Context

The bindery context for a server is configured with the SET command. You can type this command at the server console, but it is usually more practical to add the command to the server's AUTOEXEC.NCF file. An easy way to do this is by using the SERVMAN utility, as follows:

1. At the server console, type **LOAD SERVMAN**.

2. From the Available Options menu, select Server Parameters.

3. Select Directory Services from the Parameter Category menu.

4. Select Bindery Context from the Directory Services Parameters menu.

5. Press ↵ to edit the bindery context. When you're finished, press Esc and select Yes to save your changes.

6. Press Esc twice; you will see the Update Options menu. Select the first option, Update AUTOEXEC.NCF and STARTUP.NCF

Now. Press ↵ (or change the path to your AUTOEXEC.NCF file if necessary).

7. Exit SERVMAN by pressing Esc twice, then selecting Yes.

If you need to set multiple bindery contexts, use a semicolon (;) to separate the contexts in the SET command. For example, the following command would set bindery contexts for the example in Figure 13.9 (shown earlier):

```
SET BINDERY CONTEXT = .ACCT.QDC;.CORP.QDC
```

Creating Needed Replicas

In order to use bindery emulation on a server, you must make sure the server contains a master or read/write replica of the partition containing each of the bindery context container objects. If the server does not contain such a replica, you must create it using the Partition Manager or PARTMGR utility (described in Chapter 11).

Managing NetWare 3.1x with NDS

NetWare 4.11's Bindery Services feature allows you to easily integrate NetWare 4.11 with NetWare 3.1x and older clients. A final feature of Bindery Services allows even greater integration. By using the NetSync NetWare Loadable Modules (NLMs), you can use the powerful NetWare Administrator utility to manage objects on bindery-based servers as easily as NDS objects.

How NetSync Works

NetSync allows you to *synchronize* up to 12 NetWare 3.1x servers with each NetWare 4.11 server's bindery context. The NetWare 4.11

server and associated NetWare 3.1*x* servers are referred to as a
NetSync cluster.

The NetSync NLM runs on both the NetWare 4.11 server and
the NetWare 3.1*x* servers. Its purpose is to synchronize the binderies of the NetWare 3.1*x* servers with the bindery context of the
NetWare 4.11 server. When you install NetSync, all User and
Group objects in the NetWare 3.1*x* servers are created as objects
in the NetWare 4.11 Directory's bindery context, as shown in
Figure 13.10.

FIGURE 13.10

When NetSync is
installed, NetWare 3.1*x*
objects are created as
objects in the bindery
context.

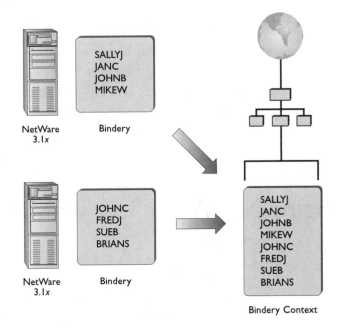

After the NetSync installation, the NetSync NLMs act continuously to
copy all objects in the NDS bindery context to each of the NetWare 3.1*x*
servers. Each server's bindery is replaced with a "super-bindery" containing all objects from all the bindery-based servers. Figure 13.11 shows
how the binderies on two NetWare 3.1*x* servers might look before and
after synchronization.

FIGURE 13.11

Each NetWare 3.1x server's bindery is replaced with a copy of the bindery context.

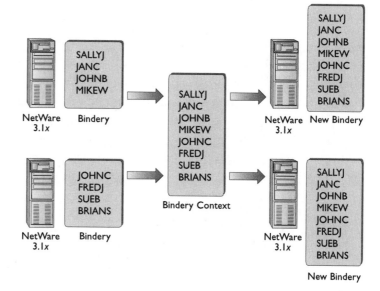

Limitations of NetSync

Before you install NetSync, you should be aware of some limitations and special considerations.

After the bindery is synchronized with NDS, you should not manage objects with the SYSCON utility on the NetWare 3.1x server because changes made in this way are not copied to the NDS bindery context. Instead, you will need to perform all user management using NDS utilities. The same warning applies to maintaining printing services with the PCONSOLE utility. For those changes to be copied to the NDS bindery context, you will need to use NDS utilities instead.

One exception to this is the accounting feature of NetWare 3.1x. Accounting information is not copied to the NDS objects, so you must use SYSCON to maintain these features. Be sure not to change any other information while using SYSCON.

Another point to consider is that trustee rights to files and directories on the NetWare 3.1*x* server are not copied to NDS. You still need to maintain these from the NetWare 3.1*x* FILER utility. You can also use the SYSCON utility, but be sure not to make other changes in SYSCON.

Similarly, you cannot use NWADMIN to maintain the NetWare 3.1*x* file system. You will need to do this using NetWare 3.1*x* utilities.

The NetWare 4.11 server's bindery context must not be changed after NetSync is installed. If it is changed, users with bindery accounts will not be able to log in. This will also cause synchronization to be lost.

User login scripts will be moved to the Login Script property of the User object in Directory Services. However, the system login script from the NetWare 3.1*x* server is not copied. If you need to execute commands from the system login script, you will need to move them to the bindery context container object's login script.

Installing NetSync

The following sections guide you through the installation of NetSync on a NetWare 4.11 server and on one or more NetWare 3.1*x* servers. To avoid any problems, follow all instructions carefully.

Before You Begin

You should perform the following tasks before installing NetSync:

1. Make sure the bindery context is valid, and this is where you want users from NetWare 3.1*x* servers to be copied.

If you have more than one bindery context set, NetSync will copy users to the first one in the list. If this is not the one you want, you will need to change the order of the contexts in the SET BINDERY CONTEXT command in the server's AUTOEXEC.NCF file.

2. Check for duplicate users and verify that no users are duplicated between the different bindery contexts of NDS and between these and any of the NetWare 3.1x servers.

The binderies of each of the NetWare 3.1x servers will be combined with any objects already in the bindery context. If any users exist in more than one of these places, only one of them will be copied. For example, if the User object FRED exists on two separate NetWare 3.1x servers, NDS will only create one FRED in the bindery context. It is best to resolve all conflicts by renaming or deleting users before beginning the synchronization process.

3. Be sure you have sufficient rights to perform the NetSync installation.

You must have full rights in the SYS:SYSTEM directory on the NetWare 4.11 server and on each of the NetWare 3.1x servers on which you wish to install NetSync. The installation program will allow you to use different login names for the NetWare 3.1x servers.

Installing NetSync on the NetWare 4.11 Server

You must perform the NetWare 4.11 portion of the NetSync installation first. The NetWare 3.1x NetSync NLM will not install properly unless it is able to communicate with NetSync on the NetWare 4.11 server. Follow these steps:

1. Load the NetSync NLM on the NetWare 4.11 server. The NetWare 4.11 version of NetSync is called NETSYNC4.NLM. Use the following command at the server console:

```
LOAD NETSYNC4
```

You will see a screen listing NetWare 3.1x servers that have been authorized for NetSync. (If this is your first installation, the list will be empty.) Press ⏎ to continue.

2. Next, authorize the NetWare 3.1*x* server. You are presented with the NetSync Options menu. Select the first option, Edit Server List.

3. Press Insert to add a new entry to the list. You will be asked for the following information:

- **3.1*x* File Server Name:** This is the name of the file server that you wish to authorize for NetSync. If you are authorizing more than one server, enter the name of the first one.

- **NetSync Password:** Enter a password to be used by the NetSync program. This is not a user or administrator password, but a temporary password. This password will be used to establish communication between the NetSync modules on the NetWare 4.11 and NetWare 3.1*x* servers during installation. Remember this password. You are not required to use the same password for each NetWare 3.1*x* server, but it is easier to remember the passwords if you do.

- **Install NetSync Files on the 3.1*x* Server:** Answer Yes to copy the files needed for NetSync to the 3.1*x* server. Under most circumstances, you will want to do this, although you would choose not to copy these files if the files were already installed or if you planned to install them manually.

- **Copy 3.1*x* Bindery to 4.*x*:** Answer Yes here to start the bindery synchronization process. Answer No only in special cases (for example, if you wish to install NetSync files but not use NetSync yet), because a negative response here would cause the servers to be out of synchronization.

4. Press Esc and then ↵. You will now be asked for a username and password for the NetWare 3.1*x* server. You need to use a username that has Read, Write, Modify, and Delete rights for the SYS:SYSTEM directory on the server. The safest way to ensure this is to use SUPERVISOR or a SUPERVISOR-equivalent user.

The password in step 4 is an actual user password and has no relation to the NetSync password that you assigned in step 3 above.

NetSync will now begin copying files to the NetWare 3.1x server. When it is finished, you should get a message stating that copying was successful. If you do not, the most likely cause is insufficient disk space on the NetWare 3.1x server. If copying was not successful, you should resolve the problem (such as deleting files to make room on the server) and then reload NETSYNC3.

5. Press ⏎ to continue. The server that you just installed should now appear in the Authorized 3.1x Servers list. You are now given the option to modify the AUTOEXEC.NCF files on the NetWare 3.1x and NetWare 4.11 servers to automatically load NetSync. (The NLM loaded on the NetWare 3.1x server is NETSYNC3.NLM.)

6. If you wish to add other NetWare 3.1x servers to the NetSync cluster, you can now repeat steps 2 through 5 for each server.

Installing NetSync on NetWare 3.1x Servers

You have now made the following changes to your NetWare 3.1x servers:

- You copied the NetSync programs to the SYS:SYSTEM\NETSYNC directory.

- You added to the AUTOEXEC.NCF file a command to load NETSYNC3.NLM.

- You installed updated versions of several system NLMs needed to run NetSync.

To finish the synchronization process, you must restart each of the NetWare 3.1x servers. Restarting them loads all the updated modules and the NETSYNC3 module. Follow these steps:

I. Make sure that all users are logged out of the NetWare 3.1x server. Type the **DOWN** command at the server console. Type **EXIT** to return to the DOS prompt, and type **SERVER** to restart the server.

You can use the MONITOR utility to display a list of users on the system and, if necessary, log them out forcefully. Also, NetWare 4.11 provides a simpler method of restarting the server: After typing the **DOWN** command, simply type **RESTART SERVER**.

2. The server will load in the usual fashion and should automatically load the NETSYNC3 module. When NetSync starts for the first time, it will present you with the following prompt:

```
4.11 Server Name:
```

3. Enter the name of the NetWare 4.11 server on which you installed NetSync. You will then be asked for the NetSync password. This is the password that you assigned in step 3 of the previous section.

After you enter the password, NetSync will begin the synchronization process. This may take several minutes. NetWare will first copy all the bindery information from the NetWare 3.1x server to the bindery context. Next, it will copy objects in the bindery context back to the NetWare 3.1x server.

You have now completed the NetSync installation. Try using NetWare Administrator to edit or create some users on the NetWare 3.1x servers to make sure that the NetWare 3.1x servers are correctly synchronized with NDS.

Now that NetSync is installed, you can no longer use SYSCON to manage users on the NetWare 3.1x server, as discussed earlier. You must now perform all administration with NDS utilities.

Using NetSync Options

The NetSync Options menu allows you to manage and fine-tune your synchronized servers. The menu becomes available in the NetWare 4.11 NETSYNC module after you have authorized at least one NetWare 3.1x server. A similar menu is available on the 3.1x server. This menu contains the following items:

- **View Active Log:** Allows you to view current events in the NetSync log file. NetSync maintains this file to keep track of operations involved in the synchronization process. This log is stored in a file called NETSYNC.LOG in the SYS:SYSTEM\NETSYNC directory. Each server maintains its own log file.

- **Log File Operations:** Allows you to maintain the log file. In the NetWare 4.11 server, an option is given to view the entire file. (In a NetWare 3.1x server, you must use a text editor to do this.) Other options allow you to control which events are shown on the log file screen, change the size of the log file, and delete the log file.

- **Edit Server List** (NETSYNC4 only): Allows you to add Net-Ware 3.1x servers to the NetSync cluster. You can also remove servers from the list. An additional option allows you to resynchronize a 3.1x server that is no longer synchronized, as explained in the next section.

- **Configuration Options:** Allows you to change some parameters that affect the synchronization process. For example, you can change the Watchdog Delay Interval, which is the amount of time a server waits before checking on the other servers in the cluster.

- **Move a Print Server** (NETSYNC3 only): Allows you to move the services of a NetWare 3.1*x* print server to a NetWare 4.11 print server.

- **Exit/Unload NetSync:** Terminates the NetSync NLM and returns to the server console. You should never unload the NETSYNC loadable modules in normal circumstances, but you may need to do this if you wish to discontinue using NetSync or to reconfigure the server. The server will unload NETSYNC automatically when you bring it down with the DOWN command.

Resynchronizing a NetWare 3.1x Server

If you make any changes to a NetWare 3.1*x* server using bindery-based utilities such as SYSCON, you must resynchronize the server's bindery with NetSync. This is done through the NetSync Options menu's Edit Server List item.

When you press ⏎ on the server name, you are given an option to recopy the server's bindery. Choose this option only if you have lost synchronization. When you do this, the information in the bindery will overwrite any changes you have made using NetWare 4.11 utilities.

Review

The subjects covered in this chapter relate to setting up NetWare workstations. You learned about using NetWare with non-DOS clients, planning and implementing Bindery Services, and using NetSync to manage NetWare 3.1*x* servers within NDS.

OS/2 Client Installation

NetWare provides support for the IBM OS/2 operating system. Users at OS/2 workstations can attach to the server or to the Directory tree.

If you wish to take advantage of OS/2's support for extended file names, you need to install the OS/2 name space on the server.

The NetWare Client for OS/2 software package includes the NetWare OS/2 Requester, which is the OS/2 equivalent of the DOS Requester. The installation program will also install a program called NetWare Tools for OS/2. This program allows you to map network drives, set up printer capturing, and log in and out of servers and Directory trees.

Macintosh Client Installation

NetWare 4.11's support for Apple Macintosh clients is provided by NetWare for Macintosh, which supports the AppleTalk protocol (a proprietary protocol used on Macintosh networks).

To take full advantage of the Macintosh client software, you need to install the AppleTalk protocol on the server. You do this with the INETCFG utility, and configure it using the AFPCON utility.

NetWare IP

NetWare/IP is software that allows you to use TCP/IP workstations in the NetWare 4.11 network, and to provide connectivity with UNIX workstations and the Internet. NetWare/IP includes two components:

- Several NLMs to support the TCP/IP protocol on the server

- The NetWare/IP client software for TCP/IP workstations

Bindery Services

Bindery Services is a set of NetWare 4.11 services that allow integration with NetWare 3.1x and older clients, servers, and applications. Bindery Services uses one or more container objects to serve as a similar object. The object that acts as a bindery is called the *bindery context*. You can set up to 16 separate bindery contexts.

Bindery Services is installed automatically when a NetWare 3.1*x* server is upgraded to NetWare 4.11. During the upgrade, a single Organization object is created and defined as the bindery context. When you install a new NetWare 4.11 server, the context that contains the server is set as the bindery context.

Since the simulated bindery does not offer all the features of NDS, you must consider several factors when installing Bindery Services:

- Bindery-compatible names must be used.

- Certain objects, such as EVERYONE and GUEST, may need to be created.

- The bindery does not provide some information that NDS would normally provide, such as e-mail names, aliases, profiles, print job configurations, or NDS login scripts.

You must configure Bindery Services for each server that will allow bindery attachments. The server must have a master or read/write replica of the partition containing the bindery context. You must set the bindery context with a SET command, usually located in the server's AUTOEXEC.NCF file. Multiple contexts are separated by semicolons.

Managing NetWare 3.1*x* through NDS

The NetSync NLMs allow you to manage bindery-based servers using NetWare 4.11 utilities. You can *synchronize* up to 12 NetWare 3.1*x* servers with each NetWare 4.11 server's bindery context. The NetWare 4.11 server and 3.1*x* servers are referred to as a *NetSync cluster*.

The NetSync NLMs are installed on the NetWare 4.11 server and the NetWare 3.1*x* servers. The names of the NLMs are NETSYNC4 and NETSYNC3. When you install NetSync, the following steps are performed:

- All user and group objects in the NetWare 3.1x server binderies are created as objects in the NDS bindery context.

- All objects in the bindery context are copied back to each NetWare 3.1x server's bindery, resulting in a "super-bindery" containing all bindery objects and equivalent to the bindery context.

Before installing NetSync, you should be aware of its limitations and some special considerations:

- NetWare 3.1x utilities such as PCONSOLE and SYSCON cannot be used to manage objects after NetSync is installed. (The exceptions are for managing features that are not supported by Bindery Services, such as accounting.) You must use NDS utilities to manage the objects.

- Trustee rights to files and directories in the NetWare 3.1x server's file system are not copied to NDS. You must continue to use NetWare 3.1x utilities to control these rights.

- You cannot use NDS utilities to manage the NetWare 3.1x file system.

- The bindery context should not be changed after NetSync is installed, because this would cause a loss of synchronization.

- User login scripts are moved to the NDS User objects, but the NetWare 3.1x system login script is not copied. You can create this as a container login script if needed.

CHAPTER

14

Advanced Security and Auditing

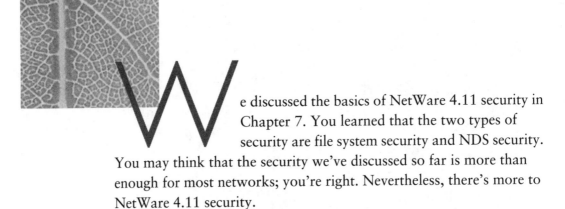

e discussed the basics of NetWare 4.11 security in Chapter 7. You learned that the two types of security are file system security and NDS security. You may think that the security we've discussed so far is more than enough for most networks; you're right. Nevertheless, there's more to NetWare 4.11 security.

In this chapter, we'll look at the issue of administration—assigning a central administrator for the entire Directory or separate administrators for certain parts. In addition, we'll take a look at the powerful auditing features of NetWare 4.11. With these auditing features, you can log just about everything you could imagine that happens on the network. After reading this chapter you should be a true NetWare 4.11 security expert.

Before we discuss administration, here's a brief overview of the basics of NDS security.

The tools that you use to control file system and NDS security (most importantly, NWADMIN) were introduced in Chapter 7. Refer to that chapter for information on how to perform the tasks described in this chapter.

NDS Security Overview

NDS security is used to control access to objects in the Directory—users, groups, printers, and entire organizations. You can control users' abilities to modify and add objects and to view or modify their properties. With an understanding of NDS security, you can assign users the rights they need in the Directory, while maintaining a secure network.

Like the file system, NDS security assigns rights through the use of trustees. The trustees of an object are called *object trustees*. An object trustee is any user (or other object) who has been given rights to the object. The list of trustees for an object is called the *Access Control List*, or *ACL*. Each object has a property containing the ACL.

NDS security provides two categories of rights: object rights and property rights. *Object rights* are the tasks that a trustee can perform on an object. There are five types of object rights:

- **Supervisor:** The trustee is granted all of the rights listed below. Unlike the Supervisor right in the file system, the NDS supervisor right can be blocked by the Inherited Rights Filter (IRF).

- **Browse:** The trustee can see the object in the Directory tree. If the Browse right is not granted, the object is not shown in the list.

- **Create:** The trustee can create child objects under the object. This right is available only for container objects.

- **Delete:** The trustee can delete the object from the Directory. In order to delete an object, you must also have the Write right for All Properties of the object.

- **Rename:** The trustee can change the name of the object.

Property rights are the tasks that a trustee can perform on the object's properties. This allows the trustee to read or modify the property values. There are five types of property rights (see list below), which are not the same as the types of object rights.

- **Supervisor:** The trustee is given all of the property rights listed below. Once again, this right can be blocked by the IRF. Trustees with the Supervisor object right are automatically given Supervisor rights to All Properties of the object.

- **Compare:** The trustee is allowed to compare the property's values to a given value. This allows the trustee to search for a certain value but not to look at the value itself.

- **Read:** The trustee can read the values of the property. The Compare right is automatically granted to a trustee who is granted the Read property right.

- **Write:** The trustee can modify, add, or remove values of the property.

- **Add Self:** The trustee is allowed to add or remove itself as a value of the property. For example, a user who is granted the Add Self right for a group can add himself or herself to the group. The Write right is automatically granted to a trustee who is granted the Add Self property.

Property rights can be granted in two ways: All Properties or Selected Properties. When All Properties is granted, the same list of rights is granted to each of the properties of the object.

NDS Inheritance

NDS uses a system of *inherited rights*. When an object trustee is given rights to a container object, the trustee also receives the same rights for all children of the object. Inheritance affects both object rights and property rights.

Object rights are inherited in the same fashion as file system rights. When a trustee is given object rights for an object, the rights are inherited by child objects—the trustee receives rights for these objects also, unless the rights are blocked by the IRF or an explicit trustee assignment.

Property rights can be inherited in the same manner as object rights, with one exception—only rights given with the All Properties option can be inherited. If a trustee is given rights to Selected Properties of an object, those rights cannot be inherited by child objects. This is because each of the different types of objects, such as Users and Organizational Units, has a different list of properties.

When a trustee is given rights to a container object, the rights flow down the Directory tree until they are blocked. You can block inherited rights in two ways: with a new trustee assignment or with the Inherited Rights Filter (IRF).

The *Inherited Rights Filter* (IRF) controls which rights can be inherited. The IRF cannot be used to grant rights; it can only block or allow rights that were given in a parent directory. The IRF is simply a list of the rights that a user or other trustee can inherit for that object from its parents. If a right is included in the IRF, it can be inherited. If you leave a right out of the IRF, that means no trustee can inherit that right for that object.

Security Equivalence

There are several situations in NDS in which a trustee automatically receives all of the rights given to another trustee. This is referred to as *security equivalence*. The two types of security equivalence are:

- **Implied security equivalence** means that an object receives rights given to its parent containers.

- **Explicit security equivalence** is given with the Security Equal To property, group membership, or Organizational Role occupancy.

Effective Rights

A user's *effective rights* are the tasks the user can actually perform on the object. If you find it necessary to calculate effective rights manually, you can do so by following these steps:

1. Start with any explicit rights given to the user for the object.

2. If no explicit rights have been given to the user, calculate the inherited rights—any rights given to the user for parent objects minus those blocked by the IRF.

3. Add any rights given to the user's security equivalents for the object. These include group memberships, Organizational Roles, or members of the user's Security Equivalent To property.

Assigning NDS Administrators

In a large network, it is important to determine who will administer—or control—the Directory tree and the objects within it. You can use two kinds of administration in NetWare 4.11: *centralized administration* and *distributed administration*. Both of these are made possible by NDS, and they are discussed in the following sections.

Centralized Administration

It is possible to use the ADMIN user account, or a group of administrators, to control the entire network. This is one of the benefits of NDS, and it may be the best solution for smaller organizations. NetWare 4.11 assigns a central administrator, the ADMIN user, by default. The ADMIN user is given the Supervisor right to the [Root] object and inherits rights to all objects unless they are blocked.

Even if you choose to use distributed administration on your network, you should keep one user (such as the ADMIN account) with full rights to the entire Directory tree. This account is required to assign other administrators, move objects in the tree, merge trees, and manage time synchronization.

A central administrator can also be used in emergencies, such as when a portion of the Directory tree is left without an administrator.

WARNING   Avoid logging in with the ADMIN account unless you require the rights to administer the entire Directory tree. If the ADMIN account is left logged in unattended, someone could cause serious damage to the network.

Distributed Administration

One of the most important advantages of NDS security is that it allows distributed administration. You can assign separate administrators to different branches of the Directory tree, as well as a separate administrator for the server's file system. The following sections describe the types of administrators that you can create.

Container Administrators

You can create an administrator who has rights to one container in the Directory tree and the objects within it. This assignment is called a *container administrator*. Since the Directory tree is divided by locations, divisions, or workgroups, this is often the best way to distribute administrative tasks. A container administrator is illustrated in Figure 14.1.

FIGURE 14.1

A container administrator has rights to NDS objects in a single container.

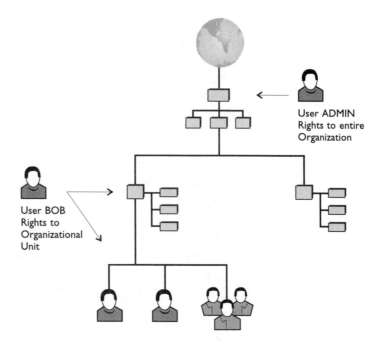

User ADMIN
Rights to entire
Organization

User BOB
Rights to
Organizational
Unit

You can assign the rights for a container directly to the user who administers it. However, the Organizational Role object is a better way to create container administrators. By using an Organizational Role as the administrator, you gain the following benefits:

- If the job of container administrator is switched to a different user, you can simply make the new user the occupant of the Organizational Role object.

- If two or more users will share the job of container administration, you can assign multiple occupants to the Organizational Role.

- If some containers are too small to have their own administrator, you can assign the same user to two or more Organizational Roles.

As you can see, the Organizational Role provides a flexible, simple method of assigning container administrators. Follow these steps to create a container administrator:

1. Create the Organizational Role object. You should create this object inside the container that it will administer. See Chapter 6 for details on creating Organizational Roles.

2. Assign the Organizational Role as a trustee of the container, and give it rights. The type of rights depends on your network security plans:

- Assign the user Supervisor or full rights [SBCDR] if the administrator will control the file system also. If you give the administrator the Supervisor right to the container, that account also inherits Supervisor rights to the file system of any servers in the container.

- Assign the Browse, Create, Delete, and Rename [BCDR] rights separately if you wish to assign a separate administrator for the file system.

3. Assign any other rights you wish to give the administrator, such as file system rights (if they were not assigned in step 2).

4. Make one or more users occupants of the Organizational Role.

Exclusive Container Administrators

In a network for which security is very important, you may want to make the container administrator the only administrator for the container. You can assign an *exclusive container administrator* by blocking the rights of central administrators (such as ADMIN) with the IRF. This allows you to maintain a highly secure network. Figure 14.2 illustrates the concept of an exclusive container administrator.

When you create an exclusive container administrator, there is no longer a central administrator. Therefore, you should take the following precautions when you set up this type of administrator:

- If the container administrator rights are assigned to an Organizational Role object, it is best to give explicit rights for the container to a second user (or Organizational Role) also. Otherwise, if the Organizational Role object is deleted, you lose control over that branch of the Directory tree. If this happens, there is no easy solution.

- Make sure that the Organizational Role object also has the Supervisor right to its own object. This allows the container administrator to add other administrators. In addition, the ADMIN user can be added to the Organizational Role temporarily if a central administrator is required.

WARNING

If you do use exclusive administrators, you should coordinate with them and re-establish a central administrator before performing operations such as moving trees. You can restore a central administrator's rights. The exclusive administrator simply needs to change the IRF to allow inheritance again.

FIGURE 14.2

An exclusive container administrator is the only user with rights to a container.

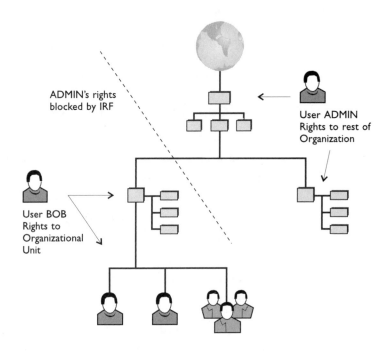

As noted earlier, if at all possible, it is best to keep a central administrator in addition to the container administrators. A central administrator will be needed when merging Directory trees or moving objects in the tree. This user provides a solution for emergencies when the container administrator is deleted or the user who occupies the role is not available.

Here are the steps required to create an exclusive container administrator:

1. Create the Organizational Role object. You should create the Organizational Role within the container that it will administer.

2. Assign one or more users as occupants of the Organizational Role. It is important to do this now, because after the following steps are performed, the ADMIN user will no longer be able to add users to the role.

3. Assign the Organizational Role as a trustee of the container object. You should assign full rights [SBCDR] to ensure that an IRF of an object or container does not prevent access.

4. Give the Organizational Role the Supervisor right to its own object. This step ensures that the occupant of the role can add other occupants. If a central administrator is needed (such as when merging trees), the ADMIN user can be added to this role.

5. Change the IRF of the container so that only the Browse object right and the Read [R] property right are granted. This allows other administrators to examine objects in this branch of the Directory tree but not to control them.

6. If ADMIN or another user has an explicit trustee assignment to the container, remove the assignment so that the container administrator will have the only control over the container.

7. If ADMIN or another user has rights to the administrator Organizational Role object, remove those rights. This prevents other administrators from restricting the exclusive container administrator's rights or giving themselves rights. (If the administrator Organizational Role object is located in the container it will administer, the IRF will prevent other administrators from accessing it.)

WARNING   The NetWare Administrator utility does not allow you to filter the Supervisor right unless you have already given this right to a container administrator. You should also assign this right to at least one other user because if the administrator Organizational Role is deleted, you lose access to that branch of the Directory tree.

File System Administrators

You can assign a separate administrator for the file system of a server. As with other types of administrators, this assignment is best accomplished with an Organizational Role object. This type of administrator is illustrated in Figure 14.3.

You can create a file system administrator by following these steps:

1. Create the Organizational Role object, and add one or more users to it.

FIGURE 14.3

A file system administrator is given rights to the file system.

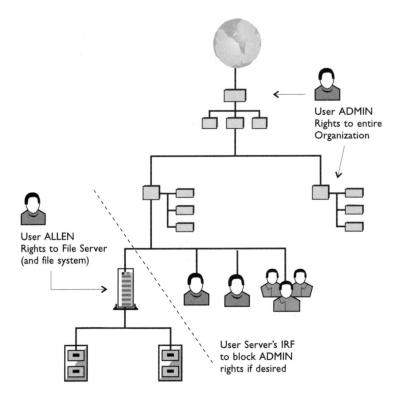

User ADMIN
Rights to entire
Organization

User ALLEN
Rights to File Server
(and file system)

User Server's IRF
to block ADMIN
rights if desired

2. Make the Organizational Role a trustee of the File Server object with the Supervisor right. The administrator will inherit the Supervisor right for all volumes on the server. As an alternative, you can assign file system rights separately for each volume (or only one volume) on a server.

3. If you wish the administrator to be an exclusive administrator of the file system, block the rights of other administrators by removing the Supervisor right from the file server's IRF.

4. ADMIN (or another administrator) was given rights to the file system when the server was installed. You need to remove this trustee assignment to create an exclusive file system administrator.

If you create an exclusive file system administrator, be sure to assign the file system rights to at least one other user so that you will not lose access to the server.

Other Types of Administrators

In NetWare 3.1*x*, you could assign a variety of managers and operators. You can use Organizational Roles to duplicate these administrators in NetWare 4.11:

- User account managers and workgroup managers: These can be replaced with container administrators in NDS. You can use Organizational Roles to create user account managers and workgroup managers, as described in the previous sections. Unlike NetWare 3.*x*, NetWare 4.11 doesn't provide an easy way to give trustee rights to all members of a group; you can use containers to give trustee rights to all members of a group.

- Print queue operator: Print Queue objects in NDS have a Print Queue Operators property. You can create a print queue operator by adding a user or Organizational Role to the list of print queue operators.

- Print server operator: The Print Server object has a Print Server Operators property. You can add users or an Organizational Role to the Operators list to assign operators.

These are not the only types of administrators you can assign. The flexibility of NDS security allows you to create highly specialized types of administrators. You can create Organizational Roles that combine the roles described above or assign specific rights to suit the needs of your network.

Auditing the Network

Another distinctive feature of NDS security is its auditing capabilities. By assigning an auditor on the network, you give a user the ability to monitor the activities of other users. Auditing is another area in which the ADMIN user (or other administrator) is not always the final authority. Although the network auditor is assigned by the administrator, the auditor is the only user with access to auditing features. The administrator cannot access this information. Even changes made to NDS or the file system by the administrator can be monitored by the auditor.

The auditor is able to monitor events (specific actions) in NDS or the file system. Events can include user actions, changes in NDS and file system security, and the usage of network resources.

Auditing provides the following benefits:

- Ensures that users and administrators are following company policies.

- Monitors unauthorized access to the file server.

- Determines if users are accessing the wrong objects or files.

- Troubleshoots network and file server problems.

Obviously, the average small company network has little use for auditing. Auditing features have the greatest benefit for large enterprise-wide networks and for highly secure networks, such as those required by government agencies and government-regulated businesses.

Creating a Network Auditor

To begin an audit on your network, follow these steps:

1. Determine who will perform the audit. You can assign an existing user on the network as an auditor or create a User object for this

purpose. This user is usually a member of management or an outside auditor rather than a network administrator.

2. Enable auditing for the container volume or object. This procedure is explained in the next sections.

3. Give the auditing password for the container or volume to the auditor. The remaining steps are performed by the auditor, as explained later in this chapter.

The password referred to here is an *auditor's password*. This password is assigned for each container or volume to be audited and has no relation to actual user passwords.

To enable and control auditing on the network, you use the AUDITCON utility. This program is located in the PUBLIC directory on the server. You can start it by typing AUDITCON at a workstation. You can use this utility to perform auditing tasks on both NDS containers and volumes. The AUDITCON main menu is shown in Figure 14.4.

FIGURE 14.4

The AUDITCON utility allows you to configure and control auditing.

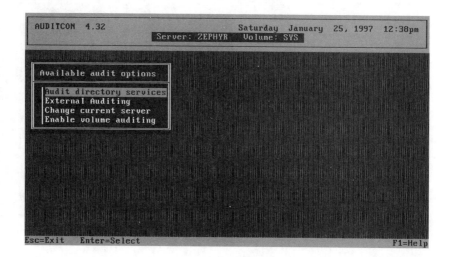

Auditing a Volume

To begin auditing a volume, follow these steps:

1. Log in as ADMIN or equivalent.

2. Type AUDITCON to start the utility.

3. From the AUDITCON main menu, select Enable Volume Auditing. If your server has more than one volume, you can choose the volume.

4. To set an audit password, choose Auditing configuration, then Set Audit Password.

5. At the prompt shown in Figure 14.5, enter the password you have chosen for the auditor. (You are asked to enter it twice for verification.)

6. Give the password to the auditor. The auditor can now perform auditing tasks, as described later in this chapter.

FIGURE 14.5

Enter a password to begin auditing the volume.

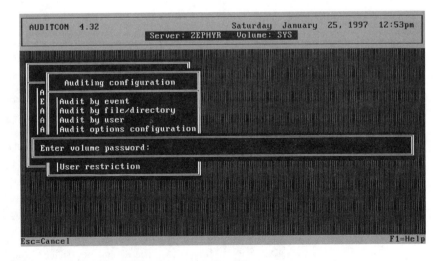

Auditing an NDS Container

You can enable auditing for any NDS container object by following these steps:

1. Log in as ADMIN or equivalent.

2. Type **AUDITCON** to start the utility.

3. From the AUDITCON main menu, select Audit Directory Services.

4. From the Audit Directory Services menu, you can use the Change Context option to select the context of the container you wish to audit.

5. Select Audit Directory Tree.

6. In the list of container objects in the Session context, shown in Figure 14.6, highlight the container object you wish to audit, and then press F10.

7. Select Enable Container Auditing.

8. At the prompt, enter the password you have chosen for the auditor. You are then asked to enter it again for verification.

9. Give the password to the auditor. The auditor can now perform auditing tasks, as described in the next section.

Performing Auditing Tasks

After you have enabled auditing and given the password to the auditor, the auditor can use the AUDITCON utility to monitor activities on the network. This section explains these tasks from the auditor's point of view.

FIGURE 14.6

Select the container object to be audited.

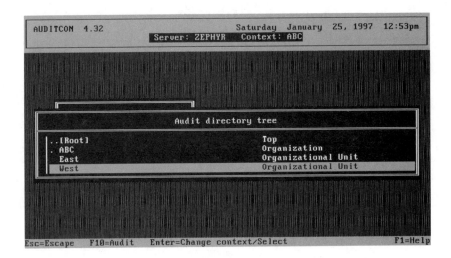

First, run the AUDITCON utility. To audit a volume, select Auditor volume login, then enter the password. To audit an NDS container, follow these steps:

1. Select Audit Directory Services.

2. Select the correct context, if necessary.

3. Select Audit Directory Tree.

4. Choose the container to audit, and press F10.

5. Select Auditor Container Login, and then enter the password.

Changing the Auditor's Password

As an auditor, the first thing you should do is change the auditor's password. This ensures that the network administrator who enabled the auditing process cannot access auditing information. After the auditor's password is changed, the user with the password (the auditor) is the only user who can use the AUDITCON utility for that container or volume. All auditing activities, including ending the audit, are performed by the auditor.

To change the password, follow these steps:

1. Run AUDITCON, and log in as the auditor.

2. From the Available Audit Options menu, shown in Figure 14.7, select Auditing Configuration.

3. Select Change Audit Password.

4. Enter the new password.

Selecting Events to Audit

When auditing is enabled, events for the container or volume are logged. As auditor, you can select which events are included in the audit. Different options are available for volumes and for NDS containers.

Selecting Volume Events   After logging in as the volume auditor, select Auditing configuration. You are given three choices:

- Audit by Event allows you to monitor certain types of events.

- Audit by File/Directory allows you to choose directories or files to monitor.

FIGURE 14.7

The Available Audit Options menu allows you to perform auditing tasks.

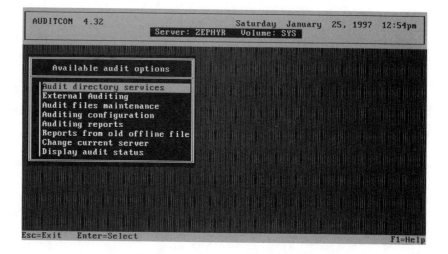

- Audit by User allows you to monitor activities of certain users on the volume.

You can use any of these types of auditors or a combination of them. This allows for versatile auditing options.

Selecting NDS Container Events   After logging in as the NDS container auditor, select Auditing Configuration. You are given two choices:

- Audit by Event allows you to choose which NDS events (create, delete, and so on) are to be audited.

- Audit by User allows you to choose one or more users whose NDS activities you wish to monitor.

You can use either one of these options or combine them—audit certain events, regardless of the user, and certain users, regardless of the event.

Managing the Audit Data File

Each time an event that has been selected for auditing occurs, an entry is added to the audit data file. A second file, the audit history file, is used for other types of events. As auditor, you can view the events in these files and control how the files are used. From the Available Audit Options menu, select Audit Files Maintenance. You are presented with the following options:

- Close Old Audit File closes the old audit file, which exists if there was a previous audit on the object or volume. This option allows all users, not just the auditor, to access the old audit file.

- Copy Old Audit File allows you to copy the old audit file to a text file in the directory you specify.

- Delete Old Audit File erases the old audit file.

- Display Audit Status displays information about the audit file, such as its size and the date it was created.

- Reset audit data file creates a new audit file. The current file becomes the old data file, which can be maintained with the options listed previously.

WARNING

Audit files can become quite large and can use up your volume's space if you are not careful. Watch the available disk space while auditing is occurring. In addition, reset the audit file (by using the Reset audit data file option on the Audit file maintenance menu) after reports have been run, and delete the old file or move it to a volume with ample space.

Creating Audit Reports

In a large network, thousands of events happen every day, and the audit data file can become quite large. Fortunately, you do not need to sort through the file yourself. The reporting features of AUDITCON allow you to create a report for very specific types of events.

To access reporting options, select Auditing reports from the Available Audit Options menu. You'll see the Auditing reports menu, shown in Figure 14.8. The reporting process involves two steps: creating a report filter and viewing or printing the report.

Creating a Report Filter   First, you must create a *report filter* for the report. This is a set of conditions that the entries must match to be included in the report. You can create multiple filters. You can save the filters and use them to run a report regularly.

To create a report filter, follow these steps:

1. From the Auditing reports menu, select Edit Report Filters. A list of the existing filters is displayed. The first time you use this feature, the list is empty.

FIGURE 14.8

The Auditing Reports menu allows you to specify reporting options and run reports.

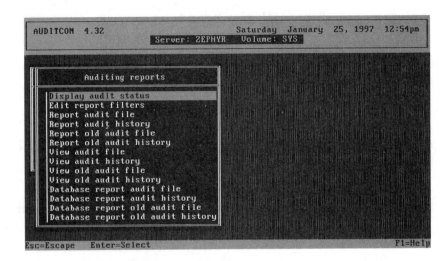

2. Press Insert to create a new filter.

3. Select the type of events to be included in the report. You can select multiple options, or just a single option. The event types are:

   ■ Report by Date/Time allows you to report events on a certain date (or list of dates and times).

   ■ Report by Event presents you with a list of events from which you can select the ones to be included in the report.

   ■ Report Exclude Paths/Files allows you to exclude certain files (in a volume) or containers (in NDS) to be excluded from the report.

   ■ Report Exclude Users allows you to list users whose actions will not be included in the report.

   ■ Report Include Paths/Files lets you report on certain files or NDS containers only.

- Report Include Users allows you to report the actions of certain users.

4. After you have made your selections, press Esc. When you are asked for a name for the filter, enter it, and press ↵.

Viewing the Report   After you create a report filter, you can view the report on the screen. This provides a simple way to browse through the report and to make sure that your report is set up correctly before printing it.

From the Auditing reports menu, select View Audit File. You are then asked to select a filter. Select the filter you have created from the list, and press ↵. The report is displayed on the screen. You can use the arrow keys to browse through the report.

Printing the Report   In order to print a report from a report filter, you must first create the report in a text file by following this procedure:

1. From the Auditing reports menu, select Report audit file.

2. Choose a filter from the list.

3. When you are asked for the name of the file, enter a file name, and press ↵.

The audit report is created in the file you specified. You can then send it to a printer using a text editor or the DOS COPY command.

By default, the report file is created in the auditor's home directory. Since this is an ordinary text file, it can be read by any user who has access to that directory. To be sure that no users or administrators on the network can access the file, you can specify a floppy disk or local hard disk. Also, be sure to delete the report file after printing it.

Ending the Audit

After the auditing process is complete, you must end the audit. This prevents the auditor from accessing any further system information and ensures that audit data files do not grow too large. The auditor should follow these steps to end the audit:

1. Select Auditing Configuration from the Available audit options menu.

2. From the Auditing Configuration menu, select Disable Container Auditing.

3. Answer Yes to Disable Auditing.

4. Exit the AUDITCON utility.

WARNING   Auditing can be disabled only if you have the auditor's password. Don't let the auditor leave without ending the audit or giving you the password. Without the password, the only way to end auditing is to delete the NDS container or reformat the volume and restore from a backup.

Review

This chapter has covered two aspects of NDS security:

■ The different types of administration that are possible.

■ The use of auditing to monitor the network.

Administration

Two types of administration are possible in NDS: *centralized administration* and *distributed administration*. You can also use a combination of both methods. You can assign three types of administrators in the Directory:

- A **container administrator** has rights for all objects within a container.

- An **exclusive container administrator** has rights for all objects in a container; in addition, the IRF is used to prevent other administrators from having rights to the container's objects.

- A **file system administrator** has rights for a server's file system. An IRF can be used to block the rights of other administrators if desired.

By using Organizational Role objects, you can also create other types of administrators to suit the needs of your network.

Auditing

NetWare 4.11 allows you to *audit* an NDS container or a volume. An *auditor* is assigned to the task. This auditor can monitor all *events* that occur, such as the creation, deletion, and modification of files.

Auditing is managed with the AUDITCON utility. As administrator, you use AUDITCON to enable auditing for a container or volume. A password, which you give to the auditor, is assigned when auditing is enabled. This *auditor's password* is not the same as user passwords.

The auditor can perform tasks such as viewing and printing reports of events, controlling the types of events that are audited, and ending the audit process. The auditor can change the auditor's password; when the auditor's password changes, no other user (including the administrator) can control auditing or access the auditing information.

CHAPTER

15

Managing Your NetWare 4.11 Server

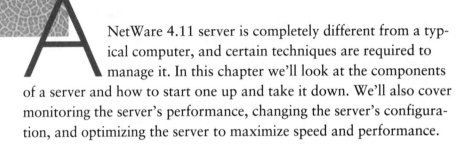

A NetWare 4.11 server is completely different from a typical computer, and certain techniques are required to manage it. In this chapter we'll look at the components of a server and how to start one up and take it down. We'll also cover monitoring the server's performance, changing the server's configuration, and optimizing the server to maximize speed and performance.

Components of a Server

In Part II of this book we looked at the basic components of a server. The following sections review that information and provide additional details. The server and network are composed of hardware—the server itself, a network card, and cabling—and software, the NetWare 4.11 server software.

Hardware Components

The hardware components of a NetWare 4.11 server include the following:

- **The processor (CPU):** NetWare 4.11 requires a PC-compatible machine with a 386 or better CPU. (To run at any kind of respectable speed, you'll need at least a 486.)

- **RAM (Random Access Memory):** NetWare 4.11 requires at least 20MB of RAM. Refer to Part IV of this book for details on calculating RAM requirements.

- **Disk storage:** NetWare 4.11 uses a DOS partition for the SERVER.EXE file and a NetWare partition to hold at least one NetWare volume (SYS).

- **Network board and cabling:** Without this, the server won't do you much good. The network board allows the server to communicate with workstations and other servers.

Software Components

The main software component of a NetWare 4.11 server is the SERVER.EXE program. This program loads from DOS but takes over the operating system completely (and can even remove DOS from memory). This is the actual NetWare server software.

Other components include disk drivers, which allow communication with disk drives in the server, and LAN drivers, which allow communication with the network board. Finally, support modules add various capabilities to the server. You usually don't need to load these NLMs, as they are loaded by other NLMs that use their services.

How Servers Are Identified

NetWare 4.11 uses unique *network addresses* to identify devices on the network. The network address combines network number and Mac address (or node id). Several types of numbers are involved:

- The **internal network number** is set for each server and uniquely identifies the server.

- The **MAC address** is wired into each network card. You cannot usually change it. (One exception is ARCnet cards, in which you *must* change it to a unique value.)

- The **network number,** or **external network number,** is used by multiple servers on the same network segment. All servers on a segment use the same external network number.

Starting the Server

To start a network server, you must perform the following steps. Usually these are all done from within batch files, which are discussed later in this chapter.

1. Boot DOS on the server computer.

2. Execute the SERVER.EXE program.

3. Load the disk driver. This is usually done in the STARTUP.NCF file.

4. Select the server's name and internal network number. This is usually done in the AUTOEXEC.NCF file.

5. Load the LAN driver. This is usually done in the AUTOEXEC.NCF file.

6. Bind the LAN driver to the network.

Configuring the Server

Luckily, you usually won't need to manually start a server. By specifying the correct information in the server's configuration files, you can make just about everything automatic. It is possible to bring the server up and load all needed software automatically—all you need to do is turn the machine on. Each of the configuration files is described in the following sections.

The AUTOEXEC.BAT File

This file is technically not a NetWare file, but you'll use it on almost every server. DOS uses this file to execute commands when it starts.

Thus, you can use it to execute the SERVER.EXE file automatically and give control to NetWare. Here's what a typical AUTOEXEC.BAT file looks like:

```
CD \NWSERVER

SERVER
```

This is usually as complicated as it gets. Since NetWare takes over completely, you cannot use any DOS drivers or other software in this file. In fact, you should be sure that the AUTOEXEC.BAT file and CONFIG.SYS—the other configuration file used by DOS—are empty aside from these commands to ensure that all of the machine's memory is available for NetWare's use.

Both AUTOEXEC.BAT and CONFIG.SYS are located in the root directory of the server's boot drive—usually drive C: if you boot from a hard disk, or A: if you boot from a floppy.

The STARTUP.NCF File

Once SERVER.EXE is run, NetWare takes over. The STARTUP.NCF file contains commands that the NetWare server processes as soon as it comes up. There are restrictions as to the types of commands that can be placed in this file. It is usually used for disk drivers and not much else. Settings for memory allocation are sometimes required in this file also.

The STARTUP.NCF file is located on the DOS side of the server configuration, in the same directory as the SERVER.EXE program. This is because NetWare cannot access the NetWare volume until it loads the disk driver. If you need to load other commands, you should use the AUTOEXEC.NCF file, described in the next section.

STARTUP.NCF usually contains just one command that loads the disk driver. Here's an example of this file, which loads the IDE disk driver:

```
LOAD IDE PORT=2f8 INT=A
```

The SYS volume will be automatically mounted when the disk driver is successfully loaded. The AUTOEXEC.NCF file, described next, is located on this volume.

The AUTOEXEC.NCF File

The AUTOEXEC.NCF file is a handy file that you can use to execute any NetWare server command when the server starts. This file is located on the NetWare SYS volume and is read and executed after the STARTUP.NCF file and disk driver are taken care of.

The most important uses for this file are to specify the file server's name and internal network number and to load and bind the network drivers. It is also used to specify the server's time zone and time synchronization information. Here's an example of a simple AUTOEXEC.NCF file:

```
SET TIME ZONE = MST7MDT

SET DAYLIGHT SAVINGS TIME OFFSET = 1:00:00

SET START OF DAYLIGHT SAVINGS TIME = (APRIL SUNDAY
FIRST 2:00 AM)

SET END OF DAYLIGHT SAVINGS TIME = (OCTOBER SUNDAY
LAST 2:00 AM)

SET DEFAULT TIME SERVER TYPE = SINGLE

SET BINDERY CONTEXT = .OU=GROUP1.O=WEST

FILE SERVER NAME WEST_23

IPX INTERNAL NET 44998

LOAD NE2000 PORT=300 INT=5 FRAME=ETHERNET_802.2

BIND IPX TO NE2000 NET=99
```

You can edit this file, along with STARTUP.NCF, using an option in the INSTALL NLM.

Server Batch Files

AUTOEXEC.NCF and STARTUP.NCF aren't the only batch files NetWare 4.11 uses. You can create your own files to execute common commands. Use the NCF (*NetWare Command File*) extension when you create server batch files. Any command you can type at the server can be used in a command file.

Optimizing the Server and Network

NetWare 4.11 is stable enough that it can run for months at a time without a problem. However, it is important to monitor network and server performance. In this way you can correct problems before they become severe. You can also use various settings to optimize and streamline your network for maximum performance.

Optimizing Memory and CPU Performance

The server's memory is used to store the NetWare 4.11 operating system, device drivers, NLMs, and buffers for disk and network communication. Because many different types of memory storage are required, NetWare 4.11 uses sophisticated *memory management* techniques. By understanding how memory is managed and how it affects network performance, you can keep your network running smoothly.

Memory Allocation

Memory allocation is the process that NetWare uses to assign memory needed by the system or applications. NetWare 4.11 assigns memory in 4KB blocks, or *pages*. The memory manager assigns, or *allocates*, pages of memory needed by the application. The pages can be located in several different areas of memory, but they appear as a single block of memory to the application.

NLMs or system programs are assigned an *allocation pool* when they start. The allocation pool is based on an estimate of the memory that the application requires. As the application requests memory pages, NetWare assigns them from this pool, and when the application frees the memory, it is returned to the pool. Memory is assigned efficiently because each application uses its own memory pool.

Memory Deallocation   When an NLM no longer needs memory, it turns the memory over to the system. This process is called *deallocation*. When memory is deallocated, it is simply marked as unused. However, the memory is not available to other applications yet.

Garbage Collection   *Garbage collection* is a process that runs periodically (every 15 minutes by default) on the server. This process finds areas of memory that have been deallocated and returns them to the main memory pool so that they can be used by other applications. You can use SET commands to control how often garbage collection is performed and improve its efficiency.

Monitoring Memory Usage

The Memory Utilization option in the MONITOR utility allows you to view the server's total allocated memory. In addition, you can press ↵ when the name of a system module is highlighted to view detailed memory information about that module. The Memory Utilization screen is shown in Figure 15.1.

SET Commands for Memory Management

You can use several SET commands to control the allocation and use of memory. Type these commands at the server console followed by the equal sign (=) and the desired value for the parameter. You can also

FIGURE 15.1

MONITOR's Memory
Utilization screen displays
information about
memory use.

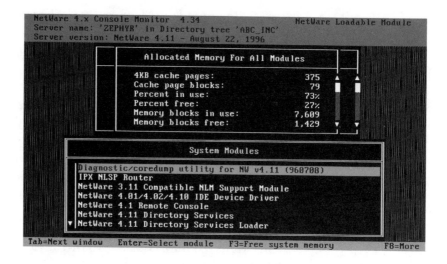

```
NetWare 4.x Console Monitor  4.34                    NetWare Loadable Module
Server name: 'ZEPHYR' in Directory tree 'ABC_INC'
Server version: NetWare 4.11 - August 22, 1996

              ┌──────── Allocated Memory For All Modules ────────┐
              │  4KB cache pages:              375    ▲           │
              │  Cache page blocks:             79                │
              │  Percent in use:               73%                │
              │  Percent free:                 27%                │
              │  Memory blocks in use:       7,609                │
              │  Memory blocks free:         1,429    ▼           │
              └──────────────────────────────────────────────────┘

              ┌──────────────── System Modules ──────────────────┐
              │ Diagnostic/coredump utility for NW v4.11 (960708) │
              │ IPX NLSP Router                                   │
              │ NetWare 3.11 Compatible NLM Support Module        │
              │ NetWare 4.01/4.02/4.10 IDE Device Driver          │
              │ NetWare 4.1 Remote Console                        │
              │ NetWare 4.11 Directory Services                   │
              │▼NetWare 4.11 Directory Services Loader            │
              └──────────────────────────────────────────────────┘
Tab=Next window    Enter=Select module    F3=Free system memory       F8=More
```

place these commands in the server's STARTUP.NCF file. Here's an example of a SET command, showing the correct syntax (capitalization is optional):

SET GARBAGE COLLECTION INTERVAL = 25

Most servers can run efficiently with no change to these parameters. Be sure that you understand what the settings mean before changing them. If a setting does not solve your problem or improve speed, change it back to the default.

- **SET Garbage Collection Interval** controls how often the garbage collection process is performed. This value is in minutes and can range from 1 to 60. The default is every 15 minutes.

- **SET Number of Frees for Garbage Collection** allows garbage collection to be automatically performed when an NLM completes a certain amount of *free* calls to deallocate memory. The default is 5,000. This value can range from 100 to 100,000.

- **SET Minimum Free Memory for Garbage Collection** sets the number of bytes that must be in the system memory pool for successful garbage collection. This value ranges from 1,000 to 1,000,000 and defaults to 8,000.

The following two SET commands cannot be typed at the console but must be in the STARTUP.NCF file.

- **SET Auto Register Memory Above 16 Megabytes** defaults to ON. This allows EISA computers to automatically use memory above 16MB if available. You may need to set this to OFF to provide compatibility with the disk controller.

- **SET Reserved Buffers Below 16 Megabytes** reserves buffer space in the lower 16MB of memory for device drivers that are limited to that area. You can set this value between 8 and 300; it defaults to 16.

Checking CPU Performance

The type and speed of the server's CPU can dramatically affect system performance. If your server is running slowly, you can use the SPEED command and the MONITOR utility to determine the cause of the problem.

First, type **SPEED** at the server console to verify that your CPU is running at its normal speed. SPEED calculates a number based on CPU performance; this should be approximately 90 for a 386/16, 900 for a 486/33, and 3,000/?? or more for a Pentium-based machine. If your server displays an unusually low number, check the Turbo or Speed switch on the server, and be sure it is set to the highest speed.

Next, you should check if an application is using a high amount of the CPU's resources. Select Scheduling Information in the MONITOR utility to display the percentage of the CPU's time used by each NLM. Figure 15.2 shows the Scheduling Information screen. Most NLMs use between 2 and 10 percent. If an NLM is using a higher percentage, unload it, or configure it differently. Of course, if you are running an intense application such as a backup or database, you can expect its utilization to be high.

FIGURE 15.2

The Scheduling
Information screen can
be used to detect NLMs
that are overworking
the CPU.

```
NetWare 4.x Console Monitor  4.34                    NetWare Loadable Module
Server name: 'ZEPHYR' in Directory tree 'ABC_INC'
Server version: NetWare 4.11 - August 22, 1996

  Process Name                   Sch Delay       Time       Count        Load

  Console Command                        0          0           0       0.00%  ▲
  Console Logger   0                     0          0           0       0.00%  ▐
  IPXRTR I/O                             0          0           0       0.00%  ▐
  IPXRTR LSP Flood                       0        115           3       0.00%  ▐
  IPXRTR Timer                           0      1,063          54       0.03%  ▐
  MakeThread                             0          0           0       0.00%  ▐
  Media Manager                          0          0           0       0.00%  ▐
  MONITOR main                           0          0           0       0.00%  ▐
  Remirror                               0          0           0       0.00%  ▐
  Remote                                 0     41,376         391       1.39%  ▐
  RIPSAPUpdateProce                      0          0           0       0.00%  ▐
  RSPX                                   0          0           0       0.00%  ▐
  SNMP Agent       0                     0          0           0       0.00%  ▐
  Sync Clock Event                       0          0           0       0.00%  ▐
  TimeSyncMain                           0        105           3       0.00%  ▼

  Interrupts                                     3,305          56       0.11%  ▼

+=Increase delay   -=Decrease delay   Esc=Previous list                F8=More
```

Optimizing Disk Performance

The speed of disk access on NetWare volumes also affects the speed
of the server and the network. NetWare 4.11 provides sophisticated
cache mechanisms that move frequently accessed information from
the disk to the server's RAM for faster access. You can optimize these
mechanisms to streamline performance. In addition, the *file compression* and *block suballocation* features allow the server to store more
information on available disk space.

Monitoring Cache Buffers

A NetWare server always sets a certain amount of RAM aside for
cache buffers. When blocks are read from the disk, they are first transferred into the cache. If the same information is needed again, it can be
read from RAM rather than accessing the disk drive. Blocks written to
the disk are also written to the cache, and blocks in the same area are
written all at once. This provides a dramatic improvement in disk
speed.

You can view cache statistics by using the Cache Utilization option
in the MONITOR utility. This screen, shown in Figure 15.3, provides
several pieces of information about the performance of the cache.

Many of these concern *cache hits*. A cache hit occurs when the information required is found in the cache, and the disk does not need to be accessed.

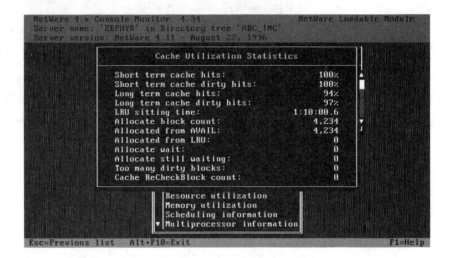

F I G U R E   15.3

The Cache Utilization
Statistics screen provides
information about the
disk cache.

If the server is running smoothly, the short-term and long-term cache hit percentages should be 90 percent or higher. When these numbers are low, the server runs slowly, and you should consider adding more memory. Applications that read many files with little repetition, such as backups, can cause a low cache hit percentage; this is nothing to worry about.

Optimizing Cache Buffers

The simplest solution to cache problems is to add more RAM to the server. You can also use the following SET commands to optimize the cache process:

- **SET Dirty Disk Cache Delay Time** specifies how long the server waits after a write request before it is written to the disk. This value can range from .1 second to 10 seconds and defaults to 3.3 seconds. You can set this to a higher value if users frequently write to the disk. This may improve access speed.

- **SET Maximum Concurrent Disk Cache Writes** specifies the amount of write requests the server waits for before beginning to write them to the disk.

- **SET Minimum File Cache Buffers** controls the minimum amount of cache buffers that are available. When NLMs are loaded, they take memory away from cache buffers. You can set this parameter to make sure some buffers are always available. This value defaults to 20 and can be set as high as 1,000.

- **SET Minimum File Cache Report Threshold** sets a threshold for warnings about low cache buffers. It can be set between 0 and 1,000 and defaults to 20. When the amount of available cache buffers decreases below the set amount, a warning is displayed on the server console.

- **SET Read Ahead Enabled** can be set to ON or OFF. This parameter controls whether the server reads ahead when reading from the disk. This means that extra blocks are read into the cache, assuming that they will be requested next. The default is ON. This improves disk access speed in most cases.

- **SET Read Ahead LRU Sitting Time Threshold** controls the read ahead process. Reading ahead writes over the least recently used (LRU) areas of the cache. These areas must be sitting, or unused, for the set amount of seconds before they are overwritten. The sitting time can range from 0 seconds to 1 hour and defaults to 10 seconds.

Block Suballocation

The *block suballocation* feature of NetWare 4.11 was introduced in Chapter 2. This feature divides the blocks used for disk storage into portions as small as 512 bytes, allowing more efficient use of disk space. This eliminates the space wasted by very small files and by files that use a fractional block.

How Suballocation Works   Block suballocation uses two types of blocks on the volume: normal blocks and suballocated blocks. A file always begins at the boundary between two blocks. Whole blocks are used for as much of the file as possible. If a partial block is left at the end of the file, the block is suballocated. The remaining suballocation units (512-byte fragments) of the block can be used for suballocated portions of other files. Normal blocks and suballocated blocks are illustrated in Figure 15.4.

FIGURE 15.4

Block suballocation uses normal blocks and suballocated blocks to optimize disk storage.

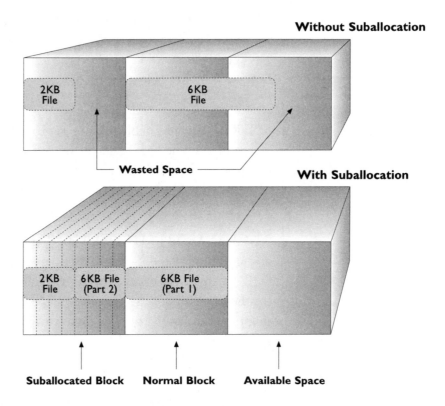

Enabling Block Suballocation   You can enable block suballocation for a volume when the volume is created. You can also enable it later with the INSTALL utility. Once enabled, you cannot disable it without reformatting the volume. Follow these steps to enable suballocation on a new volume:

1. Start the INSTALL module by typing **LOAD INSTALL** at the server console.

2. Select Volume Options.

3. Press ↵ when the volume name is highlighted. The status of the volume is shown.

4. Move the highlight to Block Suballocation, and press ↵.

5. Press ↵ to toggle the suballocation from OFF to ON.

6. Press Esc to exit, and save the changes.

Controlling Suballocation with File Attributes   To use some files efficiently, you should avoid using suballocation. Files that are added to frequently, such as database files, should not be suballocated. You can turn off suballocation for a file using the Ds (Don't Suballocate) file attribute. To set this attribute, use the FLAG command:

FLAG *filename* DS

File Compression

The NetWare 4.11 *file compression* feature, introduced in Chapter 2, allows files that are not currently in use to be compressed. This can dramatically improve the amount of disk storage available on your server and yet keeps the files available for easy access.

NetWare checks for files that have not been accessed for several days. When such a file is found, it is compressed into a temporary file. If the compression process is successful and the compressed file is significantly smaller, the original file is deleted, and the compressed file is put in its place.

You can use file attributes to disable compression for specific files or directories and to determine whether a file is compressed. Information about these attributes is given in Chapter 7.

Activating File Compression   NetWare 4.11 enables file compression by default; however, if you have upgraded to NetWare 4.11 from a previous version of NetWare, you must activate the feature manually. Once activated, you cannot disable file compression without re-creating the volume; however, you can disable compression for directories and files. You can also use a SET command to disable compression on the server. Follow these steps to enable file compression:

1. Start the INSTALL utility by typing **LOAD INSTALL** at the server console.

2. Select Volume Options.

3. Press ↵ when the desired volume is highlighted.

4. Change the File Compression option to ON.

5. Press Esc to exit, and save the changes.

Disadvantages of File Compression   Although NetWare's file compression eliminates the problems of most compressed file systems, there are some disadvantages to using compression. You should take these into account when deciding whether to activate file compression on your server.

- **Speed of access:** When a user requests a file that has been compressed, a delay occurs as the server uncompresses the file. In most networks this won't happen very often, but if your users frequently access files that no one has used for more than seven days, the network may slow to a creeping halt. Depending on the file size and the server speed, decompression can take from 30 seconds to as long as 10 minutes. You can avoid this delay by turning off compression on these files. Using a SET parameter, you can also change the time that NetWare waits before compressing the files.

- **Backups:** Files backed up from a compressed volume should be restored onto a volume that also has compression enabled, to ensure that space is available. In addition, unless the backup system supports compression, files are restored in an uncompressed state, and NetWare compresses them after seven days. Thus, restoring an entire volume could require a much greater amount of disk space than the original volume.

- **Compression is enabled permanently:** Once you enable compression on a volume, you cannot turn it off and uncompress the files without re- creating the volume (which erases all data on the volume!). You can, however, disable compression for individual files and directories. You can also disable compression with a SET command, described in the next section.

- **Server Performance:** In a heavily used server, compression and decompression can happen constantly, which can slow your server. However, this slowing is minimal and well worth the increase in available storage.

Controlling File Compression with Set Commands   You can optimize the file compression process with a variety of SET parameters. These allow you to enable or disable compression, control how often compression is performed, and fine-tune the compression process. The SET commands listed below can be typed at the server console, or you can add them to the server's STARTUP.NCF or AUTOEXEC.NCF file to permanently set the parameter.

- **SET Compression Daily Check Stop Hour** specifies an hour in military time when the server stops checking for files that are ready to compress. You can use this setting, along with the Check

Starting Hour setting described below, to ensure that the compression process happens at a time when few users are on the network. The default is 6 (6:00 a.m.).

- **SET Compression Daily Check Starting Hour** sets the time that the server begins checking for files to compress. The default is 0 (12:00 midnight).

- **SET Minimum Compression Percentage Gain** controls the level of compression that is required in order to keep the file compressed. For example, if this value is 10 percent, the file must be at least 10 percent smaller; otherwise, the original, uncompressed version of the file is kept.

- **SET Enable File Compression** can be ON or OFF and controls whether the compression process will occur. The default is ON. If you set this to OFF, there may still be compressed files on the server, but no additional files will be compressed.

- **SET Maximum Concurrent Compressions** specifies the number of volumes that can be compressing files at the same time. This defaults to 2. Larger values may slow the server considerably.

- **SET Convert Compressed to Uncompressed Option** can be set to 0, 1, or 2. This parameter controls what is done with a file after it is accessed and subsequently uncompressed. Option 0 keeps the file compressed, 1 keeps it compressed after the first access only, and option 2 leaves the file uncompressed. The default is 1.

- **SET Uncompress Percent Disk Space Free to Allow Commit** is quite possibly the longest SET command available, but understanding its purpose is simple. This specifies the percentage of the volume's space that must be available before a file is uncompressed. This parameter prevents uncompressed files from filling up the volume.

- **SET Uncompress Free Space Warning Interval** controls how often a warning is displayed when there is not enough free space to uncompress a file. This parameter can be set to a value in minutes or to 0 to disable the warnings.

- **SET Deleted File Compression Option** controls whether compression is performed on deleted files. (Files are still available for salvage using the FILER or NWADMIN utilities.) The setting can be 0, 1, or 2. Option 0 never compresses deleted files; option 1 compresses them one day after deletion; and option 2 compresses files immediately when deleted.

- **SET Days Untouched Before Compression** controls how many days a file must remain untouched before it is compressed. The default is seven days.

File Attributes for File Compression   Several of the new NetWare 4.11 file attributes are related to file compression. File attributes are explained in detail in Chapter 7.

- **Ic (Immediate Compress)** can be used to specify that a file (or directory of files) should be compressed immediately each time it is written to. This compression happens regardless of the time of day and may slow the server.

- **Dc (Don't Compress)** can be used to prevent files or directories from being compressed. This can be used on a file that needs to be accessed quickly or one that must be updated frequently.

- **Cc (Can't Compress)** is set automatically by the server. This attribute indicates that the file has been left uncompressed because the savings in disk space would be insufficient if it were compressed.

Disk Controller Considerations

The speed of disk access on the server depends heavily on the type of drive and controller used. The main types of disk drive are IDE (Integrated Drive Electronics) and SCSI (Small Computer Systems Interface). While IDE drives are most commonly used in PCs, SCSI devices are better suited for NetWare servers. SCSI is a reliable, intelligent protocol and allows a greater number of drives—up to 16 with the latest SCSI-2 devices.

High-end SCSI controllers include such features as a built-in cache, bus mastering, and PCI or VESA local bus interfaces. By taking advantage of these devices, you can streamline disk performance on your network.

Using Turbo FAT Indexing

The File Allocation Table (FAT) keeps track of each file on the volume and lists the blocks that the file occupies. Randomly accessed files that are added to frequently can be spread across many different blocks on the disk, which can slow access.

To alleviate this, NetWare includes turbo FAT indexing. When a file is randomly accessed and has more than 64 FAT entries, a turbo FAT is created for the file. This is an index of the location of blocks for that file only. With its own index, the file can be quickly accessed.

The turbo FAT is loaded into memory when the file is accessed. A single SET parameter, SET Turbo FAT Re-Use Wait Time, controls how long the turbo FAT is kept in memory, in case the file is accessed again. This value defaults to about five minutes.

Optimizing Network Communication

The final category of server performance is network communication. You can use packet and buffer settings and the new Packet Burst Protocol to streamline communication between the server and clients. NetWare 4.11 also supports Large Internet Packets, which can improve communication between multiple servers in an enterprise network.

Packets and Buffers

All communication between the server and clients is divided into *packets*, set amounts of bytes that are transmitted at the same time. Each packet includes a header that identifies the destination and source of the packet and the data itself. Figure 15.5 illustrates packet transmission. The size of packets and the buffers used to transfer them can be changed to improve performance.

FIGURE 15.5

Data sent over the network is divided into packets.

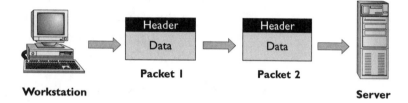

Changing Packet Size

Changing Packet Size   The size of packets depends on the software and hardware used and on the topology of the network. Default packet sizes are 1,514 bytes for Ethernet and 4,202 bytes for ARCnet and Token Ring.

You can modify the packet size used with the Maximum Physical Receive Packet Size parameter but not with the SET command at the server console. Instead, use SERVMAN, or change the STARTUP.NCF file manually. The change takes effect when the server is restarted.

You can use different packet sizes only if your network interface cards and drivers support them; consult their documentation for more information. If your network uses a router, you must consider the packet size that it supports; see the section Using Large Internet Packets (LIP) later in this chapter for more details.

Packet Receive Buffers   NetWare reserves an area of memory for *packet receive buffers*. These buffers are used as an intermediate area to hold each packet in as it is transferred between the server and other servers or clients. To ensure efficient communication, make sure that sufficient packet receive buffers are available.

The main screen of the MONITOR utility displays the current amount of available packet receive buffers. NetWare allocates additional packet receive buffers when needed. You can control the minimum and maximum amounts with SET commands. Here are the SET commands used for packet receive buffers:

- **SET Maximum Packet Receive Buffers** sets the maximum amount of buffers that can be allocated. This parameter defaults to 100. You can set this value between 50 and 4,000. If the MONITOR statistics show that the maximum amount of buffers are being used, you should increase this number.

- **SET Minimum Packet Receive Buffers** sets the minimum amount of buffers. NetWare allocates this amount when the server is started. This allows the server to run at optimal speeds immediately. The minimum amount can range from 10 to 2,000 and defaults to 50. If the server is slow after you start it, you can increase this number.

- **SET Maximum Service Processes** allows you to control the amount of communications that can be processed at the same time. This may reduce the need for additional packet receive buffers.

- **SET New Packet Receive Buffer Wait Time** is the time that NetWare waits when additional buffers are needed without allocating them. This prevents the number of buffers from being increased by a brief period of high usage. This period of time ranges from .1 second to 20 seconds and defaults to the minimum .1 second.

Monitoring Network Interface Cards

You can use MONITOR to display statistics for the Network Interface Cards (NICs) in the server. You can access this information through the LAN/WAN Information option. The type of statistics provided depends on the NIC and driver software used on the server. The statistics include packets sent and received, errors, and other information. This screen is shown in Figure 15.6.

FIGURE 15.6

Network Interface Card statistics provide details about communication through the board.

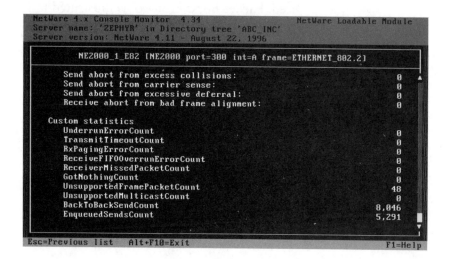

For example, the Enqueued Sends Count statistic (provided for NE2000 cards) lists the amount of times that the card was busy when a packet was ready to be sent. This can indicate that communication between the server and NIC is too slow. You can improve performance in this situation by switching to a 32-bit (VESA or PCI) NIC or a high-performance card.

Using Packet Burst Protocol

In normal communication, packets are sent one at a time, and an acknowledgment is sent after each packet. This requires two-way communication for each packet. Two-way communication can be particularly slow when a WAN link is involved because each acknowledgment must be sent across the WAN before the next packet can be sent.

Using Packet Burst Protocol, multiple packets can be sent without individual acknowledgments. This protocol allows much faster transfers of large files. Up to 64KB can be sent in a single *burst*, or group of packets. Packet burst can improve performance across the network between 10 and 300 percent, depending on the server and the way it is used. Packet Burst Protocol is illustrated in Figure 15.7.

FIGURE 15.7
Packet Burst Protocol improves the speed of network communication.

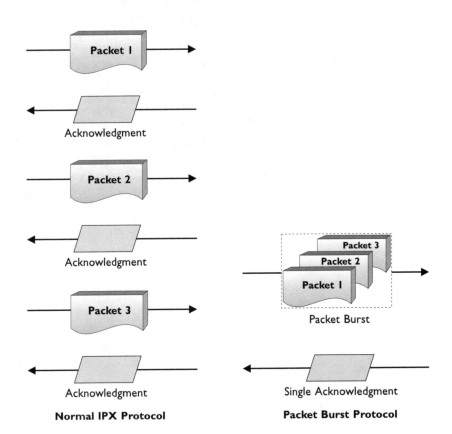

How Packet Burst Works

The client (using the NetWare DOS Requester) and the server negotiate to determine the size of the packet bursts, also called the *window size*. The server may also use a delay, called the *burst gap time*, to ensure that packets are sent slowly enough for the client to keep up. These parameters are set automatically.

Once Packet Burst Protocol is enabled, the client sends a single request and receives an entire burst of packets. After the packets are received, it sends an acknowledgment. The acknowledgment specifies which packets were received correctly. If any packets were not received, they are re-sent individually; there is no need to resend the entire packet burst. This error-correction process is illustrated in Figure 15.8.

FIGURE 15.8

Packet Burst Protocol resends packets that were received incorrectly.

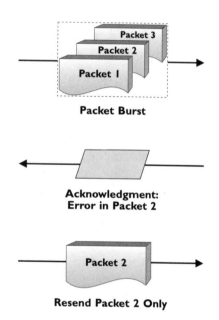

Packet Burst

Acknowledgment:
Error in Packet 2

Resend Packet 2 Only

Enabling and Optimizing Packet Burst

Packet burst is automatically enabled on the NetWare 4.11 server. It is also enabled automatically on the client by the NetWare DOS Requester provided with NetWare 4.11. If clients are still using the NetWare shell, you must upgrade them in order to take advantage of Packet Burst Protocol, which requires the NetWare DOS Requester.

When a workstation establishes a connection with a server, the client and server negotiate to determine whether packet burst can be used. If a client is used that does not support packet burst, the normal NetWare protocols are used instead. The DOS Requester also supports servers that do not use packet burst; in fact, a client connected to two servers might use packet burst with one and not the other.

To disable packet burst for individual clients, set the PB BUFFERS parameter in the DOS Requester section of the NET.CFG file. This value can range from 0 to 10. Setting this to 0 disables packet burst entirely. Higher values can be used to increase the amount of packets that can be sent from the workstation at one time.

Higher values for the PB BUFFERS parameter do not always increase performance. If this value is set too high, performance can actually decrease because more memory is required. Low numbers such as 2 or 3 provide acceptable performance.

Using Large Internet Packets (LIP)

The *Large Internet Packet* feature provides another method of improving the speed of communication on the network. As described in a previous section, packet sizes can be changed to improve communication. The client and server negotiate to determine the packet size. Ethernet and Token Ring topologies allow larger packet sizes to be used.

When a NetWare server is used as a router, however, the packet size of routed packets is limited to 512 bytes. This causes all communication through the router to be limited to smaller packets. By using the Large Internet Packet feature, you can avoid this limitation and allow full-size packets to be routed. The use of routers with and without Large Internet Packets is shown in Figure 15.9.

LIP can be used in conjunction with Packet Burst Protocol for maximum performance. This allows several large packets to be sent across the network with a single acknowledgment. Using LIP with Packet Burst Protocol eliminates the bottlenecks associated with normal network communication and offers a streamlined alternative.

F I G U R E 15.9

Large Internet Packets
allow more efficient use of
a router.

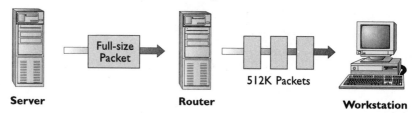

Without Large Internet Packets

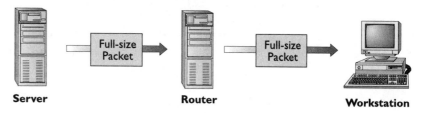

With Large Internet Packets

Enabling LIP   Large Internet Packets are enabled by default at the Net-
Ware 4.11 server and the client using the NetWare DOS Requester. You
must also ensure that the correct packet size is set for the router.

The SET Maximum Physical Receive Packet Size parameter can
change the allowable packet size on each server that acts as a router.
This parameter can range from 618 to 24,682. The default value,
4,202, is sufficient to allow LIP for Ethernet or Token Ring protocols.

Review

In this chapter, we've examined the components of a server, how
to start one up and take it down, and how to change the configuration
for maximum speed and performance.

Server Components

The hardware components of a NetWare 4.11 server include the following:

- **The processor (CPU):** NetWare 4.11 requires a PC-compatible machine with a 386 or better CPU. (To run at any kind of respectable speed, you'll need at least a 486).

- **RAM (Random Access Memory):** NetWare 4.11 requires at least 20MB of RAM. Refer to Part IV of this book for details on calculating RAM requirements.

- **Disk storage:** NetWare 4.11 uses a DOS partition for the SERVER.EXE file and a NetWare partition to hold at least one NetWare volume (SYS).

- **Network board and cabling:** Without this, the server won't do you much good. The network board allows the server to communicate with workstations and other servers.

The main software component of a NetWare 4.11 server is the SERVER.EXE program. This program loads from DOS but takes over the operating system completely (and can even remove DOS from memory). This is the actual NetWare server software.

Other components include disk drivers, which allow communication with disk drives in the server, and LAN drivers, which allow communication with the network board.

NetWare 4.11 uses *network numbers* to identify devices on the network:

- The *internal network number* is set for each server and uniquely identifies the server.

- The *network card address* is wired into each network card. You usually cannot change it.

- The *network number*, or *external network number*, is used by multiple servers on the same network. All servers use the same number.

Configuration of the Server

You can configure the server using several special files:

- AUTOEXEC.BAT runs under DOS and is a list of commands needed to execute the SERVER.EXE program.

- STARTUP.NCF is a list of NetWare commands that are executed when the server starts. It is used to load disk drivers.

- AUTOEXEC.NCF executes next and is used to set parameters and load network drivers.

- You can create your own batch file with the NCF extension to execute a set of commands.

Optimizing the Network

It is important to monitor server and network performance in order to detect problems before they become severe. You can also optimize and streamline your network using SET commands and other settings. The major areas that affect performance are memory and CPU, disk access, and network communication.

Memory and CPU Performance

NetWare 4.11 uses sophisticated *memory management* techniques. Memory is divided into 4KB blocks called *pages*. These pages are *allocated*, or made available, for each NLM or other application that requires memory. These pages may not be located in a single area of memory, but the application sees them as one block.

When an NLM or system program starts, it is given an *allocation pool* of memory based on an estimate of the memory it will require while running. When the application requests memory, it is used from this pool and returned to it when it is no longer in use. Because each application uses its own memory pool, memory can be easily managed.

When an application no longer needs an area of memory, it is returned to the system, or *deallocated*. A periodic *garbage collection* process finds these areas of memory and returns them to the main memory pool, allowing them to be used by other applications.

CPU Performance   The CPU speed and type of the server can also affect system performance. You can use the SPEED command to determine whether your server is operating at the optimum speed. In addition, the Scheduling Information screen in the MONITOR utility shows you if a particular NLM is using a large part of the CPU's resources.

Disk Performance

The speed of disk access on NetWare volumes also affects the speed of the server and the network. Areas relating to disk access include cache buffers, disk controllers, turbo FAT indexing, file compression, and block suballocation.

NetWare sets aside a certain amount of RAM as *cache buffers*, which optimize performance because they are used to hold information from the disk drive and limit use of the disk.

Suballocation and Compression   NetWare's *suballocation* feature divides the blocks used for disk storage into portions as small as 512 bytes, allowing for more efficient use of disk space. This eliminates the space wasted by very small files and by files that use a fractional block. Block suballocation is enabled individually for each volume and can be changed only when the volume is created.

The *compression* feature allows files that are not currently in use to be compressed. When a file has not been accessed for several days, it is compressed into a temporary file. If the file is significantly smaller, it replaces the original file.

Other Factors The disk controller and drive type affect disk performance. IDE drives are commonly used, but SCSI drives are more suited to a NetWare server. High-end 32-bit (PCI or VESA local bus) disk controllers should be used whenever possible for optimum performance.

The *turbo FAT indexing* feature provides an extra index for files that use more than 64 different areas of the disk. This makes access to the file more efficient. The turbo FAT is kept in the server's RAM while the file is being accessed. Only randomly accessed files can be indexed with the turbo FAT.

Network Communication

The final category of server performance is network communication. You can monitor and optimize several factors in order to improve communication:

- The *packet size* is negotiated between the client and server; larger packets can improve performance.

- The number of *packet receive buffers* is controlled by SET commands that control the amount of RAM used to hold packets. You can use MONITOR to determine the correct settings.

- MONITOR allows you to check statistics for the server's NIC (Network Interface Card). These statistics provide information about the amount of use, errors that have occurred, and performance limitations.

- The *Packet Burst Protocol* allows several packets to be sent with a single acknowledgment. This improves communication speeds, especially over WAN links. Packet burst is enabled by default.

- A NetWare server used as a router is typically limited to 512-byte packets. The Large Internet Packet (LIP) feature allows packets to be passed through the router without limiting their size. This improves speed and can be used in combination with Packet Burst Protocol for maximum efficiency. LIP is enabled by default.

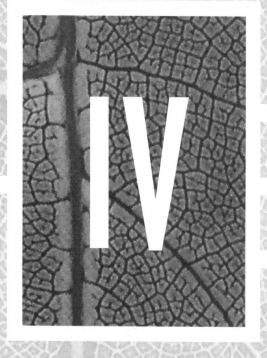

P A R T

IV

INSTALLING AND
CONFIGURING NETWARE 4.11

CHAPTER

16

Installing NetWare 4.11

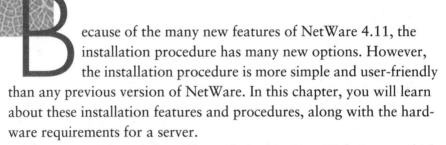

ecause of the many new features of NetWare 4.11, the installation procedure has many new options. However, the installation procedure is more simple and user-friendly than any previous version of NetWare. In this chapter, you will learn about these installation features and procedures, along with the hardware requirements for a server.

The IntranetWare package also includes NetWare Web Server, which allows you to use the NetWare 4.11 server as a World Wide Web (WWW) server. We'll also look at the process of installing and configuring the Web server in this chapter.

This chapter is devoted to the considerations you will need to make when installing a brand new NetWare 4.11 server. If you are upgrading an older version of NetWare, read Chapter 17 for the details of the upgrade process. For a detailed account of the installation process and the problems you might encounter, you may wish to refer to *The Complete Guide to NetWare 4.11/IntranetWare* by James Gaskin (Sybex, 1997).

Choosing the Server Hardware

When you choose the machine on which to run your server, think of the future. If your budget can handle it at all, buy a better machine than you currently need. You'll eventually be glad you did. NetWare 4.11 has heftier requirements than any previous version of

NetWare, and you can bet that the next version will require even more. If you plan ahead now, you can support increased user loads in the future, and perhaps even when the next version of NetWare comes around.

How Much Memory?

Novell recommends 20MB as the minimum amount of RAM (Random Access Memory) in a NetWare 4.11 server. This amount should be sufficient for typical small-company (under 20 users) networks. Larger networks will definitely need more than 20MB. More information about NetWare 4.11's memory requirements can be found in Chapter 19.

You will need more than 20MB in the following situations:

- If you plan to install the Macintosh or OS/2 name spaces, described later in this chapter.

- If you have more than 1GB of hard disk storage, or are using a high-capacity storage device such as a CD-ROM jukebox.

- If your network will have 50 or more users.

- If you will use additional services, such as NFS or TCP/IP.

Third-party applications may require additional memory. Consult their documentation for details.

Remember, memory can be the most important factor in determining your server's speed—make sure that you have more than enough. In addition, be sure that your server can be upgraded to additional amounts of RAM when needed.

NetWare 4.11 will always take advantage of additional memory if it's available. If your server is running slowly, there's a good chance that a memory upgrade will help more than a processor upgrade would.

How Much Disk Storage?

The minimum amount of disk space required for a NetWare 4.11 partition is 75MB. However, if you plan on installing all of the NetWare files (including optional files, such as client software, online documentation, and OS/2 utilities) you will need at least 100MB. An existing NetWare 3.1x server will need to have approximately 40MB free to perform the upgrade to NetWare 4.11.

Of course, in addition to disk space required for the server, you will need storage for the data and programs needed by the users on your network. This amount will depend on the types of applications used on the network. For a small company, a 540MB drive may be sufficient, but err on the side of caution. Larger companies should have at least 1GB of disk storage.

Because of the extremely low price of disk storage (at the time of this writing, about $180 for 540MB and $350 for 1GB), we recommend that you install a larger drive than you currently need, in order to give your network "room to grow." However, there is a limit to how far you should go with this, since larger disk drives will require additional RAM. For a good estimate, calculate the maximum amount of disk space you think your data will ever require—and double it.

Choosing a Processor

An ideal NetWare 4.11 server ranges from a 486 DX/2 66 MHz processor for 20–30 users to a Pentium 100 MHz for 100 users or more. Faster Pentium and Pentium Pro processors can support even more users. NetWare 4.11 takes advantage of the features of the latest processors, so a Pentium-class processor provides a definite advantage.

This is an ideal configuration; in reality, a high-end 486 can handle over 100 users without too much slowdown. However, a faster processor will help if you are running one or more complex NLMs, such as NetWare Web Server.

The processor is important, but a NetWare server is more likely to be slowed down by the speed of disk access and network connections. Be sure you have considered those—buying a 200 MHz Pentium Pro server is no guarantee that your network will be speedy.

Other Hardware Considerations

Not every PC is suitable as a NetWare server. You should buy one that matches the exact needs of your network. There are several other hardware items to consider, described in the following sections.

Novell Labs' "Tested and Approved" certification is one good indication that a machine is suitable for running NetWare. However, you should still be sure the configuration meets your needs.

CD-ROM Drive

A CD-ROM drive is required to install NetWare 4.11, and to install additional software later. Be sure the CD-ROM drive is compatible with NetWare 4.11. Currently, the only CD-ROM drives directly supported by NetWare 4.11 are those which use the SCSI or IDE interface—see the section on disk controllers below.

Most of the cheaper CD-ROMs use a proprietary interface which is not suitable for NetWare server use. These include CD-ROMs attached to a sound card. If the CD-ROM uses a separate interface from the disk drives, be sure it supports SCSI.

Disk Drives and Controllers

The disk controller used should be fast and efficient. SCSI (Small Computer Systems Interface) has been the most popular standard for NetWare servers.

The SCSI standard has gone through several revisions. Be sure your hardware supports SCSI-2, or the latest standard, SCSI-3.

IDE (Integrated Drive Electronics) drives are also used in some NetWare servers. These drives are generally cheaper, but not as fast as SCSI. A new standard, EIDE (enhanced IDE) has changed that, and IDE drives are becoming as fast as SCSI drives. However, IDE controllers usually support only 2 or 4 drives, while SCSI supports at least 6. Although IDE support is built into NetWare 4.11, EIDE is not supported. To use it, the vendor of the controller must provide a NetWare driver.

Ideally, the disk controller you use should also support the CD-ROM drive. NetWare now supports IDE CD-ROM drives. SCSI drives have been supported for a long time, and support may be more reliable. For this reason, SCSI is still the best interface to use.

LAN Card(s)

Of course, the server won't do you much good without a LAN card. You will want one that supports the high-speed bus (PCI, EISA, or VESA). Purchase the card that supports the type of network you are using. Also, be wary of "generic" LAN cards. They may not be reliable, and may not support NetWare properly. Be sure the card includes a NetWare 4.11 driver, or is at least NE-2000 (the Novell standard) compatible.

Motherboard and Bus

The computer's bus is also an important consideration. The PCI bus gives a major advantage if you use PCI LAN cards and disk controllers. The VESA Local Bus standard offers similar features, but there are few available LAN cards for this standard.

As for the motherboard, there is one factor to consider: how much memory it can support. Be sure that you can add additional memory in the future as usage on your server increases. In addition, consider the number and type of slots. You may need ISA slots for some older add-in cards. And be sure you have enough high-speed slots for the amount of cards you intend to use.

Other Hardware

If you plan on using printers attached to the NetWare server, you will need one or more printer ports. A typical machine will come with one, but you may need to specify more. Alternatively, the printers can be attached to workstations or directly to the network, if they support it. In addition, you may need serial ports to attach to a modem or other communications link.

Probably the least important pieces of server hardware are the video card and monitor. Since you'll typically leave it locked in a room alone, there's no need for a fancy video display. Get a cheap but reliable monitor—monochrome is usually fine—and a video card to match. Higher-end video cards may have compatibility problems with NetWare, so in this case cheaper is better.

Some people go a little bit further and don't use a monitor on the server at all. We advise against this, because a monitor is essential for troubleshooting the server. At the very least, keep one nearby that you can borrow when needed. If you have several servers in the same room, you can use one monitor with a hardware switching device.

Performing the Installation

When you begin the NetWare 4.11 installation process, you can choose either the Simple installation or Custom installation. The custom installation allows you to access all of the options described in *Installation Options* later in this chapter. The simplified installation, on the other hand, makes these assumptions:

- You have already created a DOS partition on the disk and installed DOS on it, and the rest of the disk is available for NetWare.

- All available disk space will be used as a NetWare partition, and a single volume, SYS, will be created.

- IPX internal and external network numbers will be randomly generated, or NetWare will use the external network number of the existing network if it detects one.

- Only the IPX protocol will be installed.

- STARTUP.NCF and AUTOEXEC.NCF will not contain any extra commands.

- The U.S. English keyboard layout will be used.

- NDS will be set up with a single Organization object; the ADMIN user will be created under this object. If a Directory tree exists already, the new server will be added to that tree instead.

If you need to choose a different option for any of the above items, you must use the Custom installation.

Using the Simple Installation

To begin the Simple installation, follow these steps:

1. Choose whether you will install the server from a CD-ROM or from a remote server.

2. Bring the new server machine up as a workstation.

3. Load the CD-ROM or network drivers to access the installation directory.

4. Switch to the CD-ROM drive or map a drive to the correct network location.

5. Type **INSTALL** to begin the installation. You will see the INSTALL program, shown in Figure 16.1.

FIGURE 16.1

The INSTALL Program allows you to choose simple or custom installation.

If this is the first NetWare 4.11 server on the network, you are asked to define the name of the Directory tree and the name of the first Organization object to be created under the [Root]. If you are installing a server on an existing NetWare 4.11 network, you'll be asked to choose the Organization or Organizational Unit to place the server in. (See Figure 16.2.)

FIGURE 16.2

Enter the NDS information for simple installation.

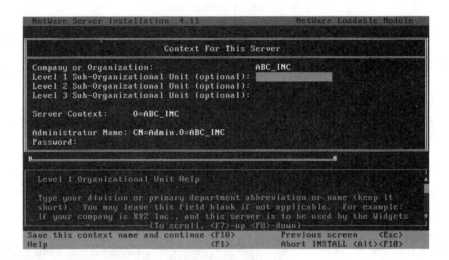

During the Simple installation process, you'll be prompted to take the following steps:

1. Provide a name for the server. The name can range from 2 to 47 characters, and should be unique. Ideally, the name should reflect the location of the server or the department that uses it.

2. Specify a disk driver. Choose the driver for your controller. It will be loaded immediately and tested.

3. Select a LAN driver. Choose the driver to match your network card.

4. Insert the license diskette. This will configure the server for the amount of users you have purchased.

5. Choose which files to install into the SYSTEM and PUBLIC directories.

6. Specify the NDS context into which to install the server. If this is the first server in the NDS tree, you can create a new context.

After answering these questions, the files are copied and the server is ready to go. It's best to bring it down and back up before attempting to log in.

Using the Custom Installation

The custom installation asks a few more questions than the simple installation, and does not assume anything. The options are listed in the next section. Because NetWare 4.11 uses a more intelligent installation program than earlier NetWare versions, it is important to have the server PC already hooked to the network when you begin the installation. The installation program will detect the existing network, and allow you to integrate the new server into the existing Directory tree.

After selecting the Custom Installation, you are asked to specify disk drivers and LAN drivers. If this is the first NetWare 4.11 server on the network, you are asked to define the name of the Directory tree and the name of the first Organization object to be created under the [Root]. If you are installing a server on an existing NetWare 4.11 network, you will be asked to choose the Organization or Organizational Unit to place the server in.

Custom Installation Options

NetWare 4.11 provides several options during the installation process. These allow you to change the settings for the server, and to determine which services will be available. To access all options, select Custom Installation when you begin the installation. The options that can be changed include:

- **International Support:** If you have an international version of NetWare 4.11, you will be given a choice of languages when you begin the installation. Besides installing support for that language, the INSTALL program itself will prompt you in the language you have chosen.

- **Protocol Support:** The IPX protocol, described in Chapter 5, is installed by default. You can choose additional protocols to install, such as AppleTalk or TCP/IP. (See Figure 16.3.)

- **Disk Partitioning:** You can specify the size of the NetWare partition to create, and specify additional volumes to be created within it.

- **NDS Options:** You can choose which container in the Directory to install the server object into, or use a separate Directory tree.

FIGURE 16.3

The Protocol Support options allow you to add protocols to the server.

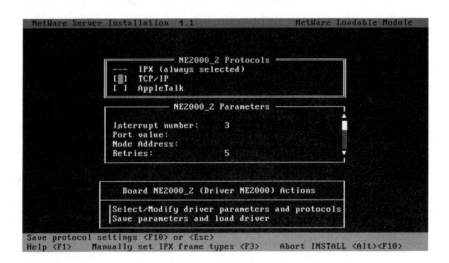

Here are the basic steps you will follow for a Custom Installation of NetWare 4.11:

1. Provide a name for the server. The name can range from 2 to 47 characters, and should be unique. Ideally, the name should reflect the location of the server or the department that uses it.

2. Choose an IPX Internal network number. This number can range from 1 to FFFFFFFE (hex). The only limitation is that

each server must have a unique number. NetWare will choose a random number as a default; this is usually fine, unless you have decided upon a system for numbering servers. Write the number down for future reference.

3. Choose a directory on the DOS partition to install files to. The default is C:\NWSERVER.

4. You are now allowed to modify the keyboard mapping, code page, and country code for your specific language needs.

5. Choose the DOS or NetWare file name format. The NetWare format allows non-standard characters to be used in names; it can cause incompatibilities, so it's best to choose the DOS format.

6. You are allowed to add extra SET commands to the AUTOEXEC.NCF file or STARTUP.NCF file if desired.

7. The INSTALL program will offer to add the SERVER command to the AUTOEXEC.BAT file, making NetWare 4.11 start automatically when the machine boots. This is very helpful if the power goes out.

8. Specify a disk driver. Choose the driver for your controller. It will be loaded immediately and tested.

9. Select a LAN driver. Choose the driver to match your network card.

10. You are asked if you wish to install optional protocols. These include TCP/IP and AppleTalk.

11. Specify the size for the DOS and NetWare partitions on the disk.

12. Specify the size for the SYS volume and any additional volumes you wish to create at this time.

13. You are then prompted to insert the license diskette. Doing so will configure the server for the amount of users you have purchased.

14. Choose which files to install into the SYSTEM and PUBLIC directories.

15. Specify the NDS context to install the server into. If this is the first server in the NDS tree, you can create a new context.

Using Online Documentation

As with previous versions of NetWare, NetWare 4.11 includes online documentation on CD-ROM. You can view the documentation directly from the CD-ROM on a workstation or install it on the server for viewing from any workstation attached to the server.

All the paper manuals for NetWare 4.11 are included in online form. DynaText uses a *hypertext* system, which means that you can click on highlighted words and instantly skip to the section to which they refer. You are probably familiar with similar hypertext systems, such as the Help system in Microsoft Windows. You can view graphics, tables, and screen shots by clicking on their icons.

To access the online documentation, you run the *DynaText Viewer*. NetWare 4.11 includes viewer programs for several operating systems, including Microsoft Windows, Macintosh, OS/2, and Novell UnixWare. An example of the Windows viewer program is shown in Figure 16.4.

Installing the DynaText Viewer

The DynaText Viewer includes an automated setup utility. You can run this utility under Windows to set up online documentation on the network, and also to install the viewer on the workstation. Follow these steps:

1. Mount the NetWare 4.11 Operating System CD-ROM on the server's CD-ROM drive. Map a drive to this volume at the workstation. If the workstation has a CD-ROM drive, you can insert the CD-ROM at the workstation instead.

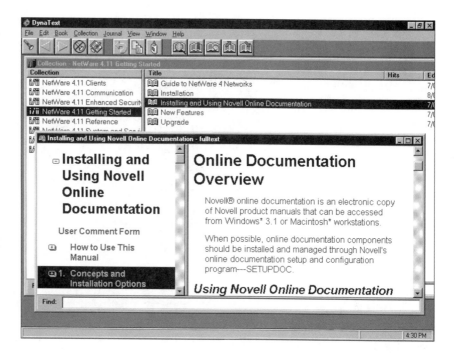

FIGURE 16.4

F I G U R E 16.4

The DynaText Viewer allows you to view online documentation.

2. Run the SETUPDOC.EXE program in the root directory of the CD-ROM drive. You will now see the initial setup dialog box, shown in Figure 16.5.

3. Click the Document Collections Install button to install the documentation in a network directory. (Optionally, you can access the documentation from the CD-ROM instead.)

4. Choose a source directory; this is usually the CD-ROM drive.

5. You are now prompted for a destination directory on the network, as shown in Figure 16.6. Traditionally, the SYS:DOC directory is used.

6. Select which documentation collections to install. Different collections may be available in different languages.

F I G U R E   16.5

The SETUPDOC
program allows you to
install online
documentation.

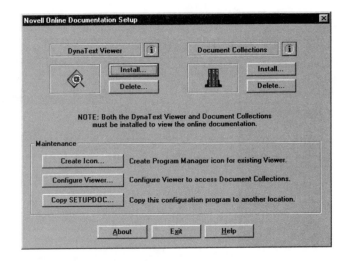

F I G U R E   16.6

Choose a destination
directory for the online
documentation.

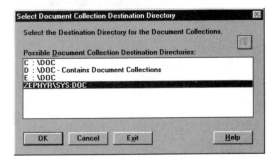

7. Confirm the installation by clicking OK.

8. After the document collections are installed, you are returned to the main SETUPDOC dialog box.

9. Click the Dynatext Viewer Install button to install the viewer on the workstation.

10. Select the source and destination directories. The viewer files are now installed.

11. You are now given the option of creating an icon for the viewer.

12. You are now returned to the main SETUPDOC dialog box. In the Maintenance section of the dialog box, choose Configure Viewer.

13. Choose the Viewer directory. You can now select the collections that will be available to the viewer on this workstation.

14. After you have selected the collections, click OK to finish the configuration.

15. Press Exit to end the SETUPDOC program.

Using NetWare Web Server

The World Wide Web is one of the most popular areas of the Internet. Internet users can use Web documents to publish hypertext information. This is accomplished through Web servers, which use the HTTP protocol. If you have an Internet connection, you can access Web documents on servers throughout the world.

The client you use to read Web documents is called a *Web browser*. The most popular Web browser, Netscape Navigator, is included as part of Novell Internet Access Server, included with the IntranetWare package. Documents on the Web are usually written in HTML, a text markup language designed for that purpose. A Web browser interprets the HTML codes and displays the document.

A Web server does not have to be a specialized machine. Currently, the majority of servers on the Web run under UNIX. Novell has made it possible to run a Web server on a NetWare 4.11 server via the NetWare Web Server software. We will look at the process of installing and configuring NetWare Web Server in the following sections.

You can use the NetWare Web Server on any server for local (intranet) Web services. If you wish to make documents available through the Internet, your network must have a continuous connection to the Internet.

Configuring the TCP/IP Protocol

The Internet and Web services use the TCP/IP protocol suite (named for its main protocols, Transport Control Protocol and Internet Protocol). Before you can install NetWare Web Server, you must configure the server to support the TCP/IP protocol.

You can easily configure TCP/IP using the INETCFG utility, which we introduced in Chapter 10. The main INETCFG menu is shown in Figure 16.7. It includes options to configure protocols, network cards, and bindings.

FIGURE 16.7

The INETCFG utility allows you to configure TCP/IP and other protocols.

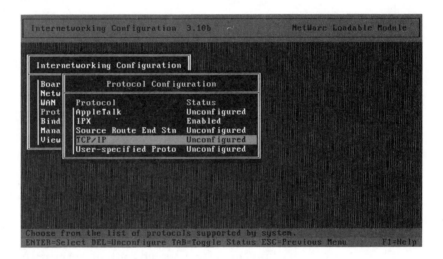

Follow these steps to configure the TCP/IP protocol:

1. Select Protocol Configuration from the INETCFG menu.

2. You are now shown a list of protocols that can be configured on the system. If TCP/IP is already configured, the word *Enabled* appears to the right of TCP/IP; if it doesn't, select the TCP/IP option and press ↵ to configure it.

3. The TCP/IP Protocol Configuration screen is now displayed, as shown in Figure 16.8. This screen allows you to enable the TCP/IP

protocol and specify various options. If you are unsure of the settings you need, the default settings will work in most cases.

FIGURE 16.8

Specify options to
configure the TCP/IP
protocol.

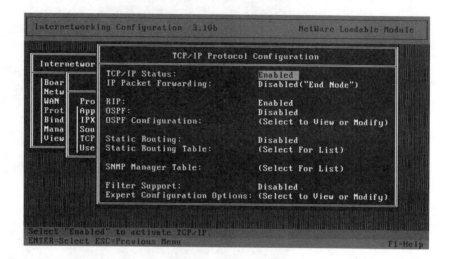

4. Press Esc to return to the main INETCFG menu.

5. Select Bindings from the main menu. You see a list of current protocol bindings for your server, as shown in Figure 16.9. Most likely, the list includes only IPX.

6. Press Ins to add a binding. You see a list of protocols that have been enabled. Select TCP/IP from this list.

7. You now see a list of options for binding the TCP/IP protocol, as shown in Figure 16.10. Specify the IP address and subnet mask for your network, and change the other options as desired. (See Part VIII for the meanings of these options.)

8. Press Esc to return to the main menu, and answer Yes to save the changes to the network card bindings.

9. Exit INETCFG.

FIGURE 16.9

Add TCP/IP to the list of network card bindings.

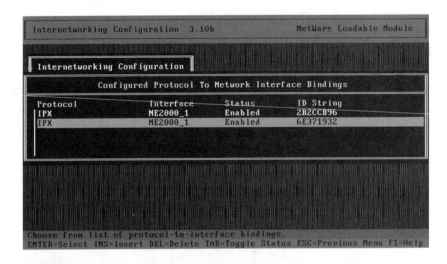

FIGURE 16.10

Enter options for binding the TCP/IP protocol.

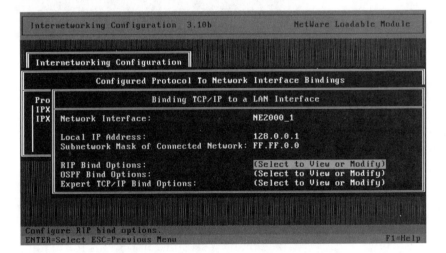

You have now completed the installation of the TCP/IP protocol. The NLMs required for the TCP/IP protocol are loaded automatically when you start the server. Restart the server before installing the NetWare Web Server.

Installing the Web Server

The NetWare Web Server software is normally included on the same CD you installed NetWare 4.11 from. Be sure you have successfully installed the TCP/IP protocol and restarted the server. You can then proceed with the following steps to install the Web server:

1. Insert the CD into the server's CD-ROM drive. Optionally, you can use a different server's drive if you mount the CD as a NetWare volume.

2. From the server console, type **LOAD INSTALL** to start the installation utility.

3. Select Product Options from the main INSTALL menu.

4. A list of products that can be installed is now displayed, as shown in Figure 16.11. Select Install NetWare Web Server to proceed with the installation.

FIGURE 16.11

Select Install NetWare Web Server from the product options.

5. Specify the drive and directory to install the Web server from. The default setting is usually correct.

6. The installation program now copies files into a temporary directory for installation. This takes between five and ten minutes. A progress display is shown while copying.

7. After the copy process completes, you are asked for a host name for the Web server. This is the local machine name that will be advertised by the Web server. By default, the server's name is used. This prompt is shown in Figure 16.12.

FIGURE 16.12

Enter a host name for the Web server.

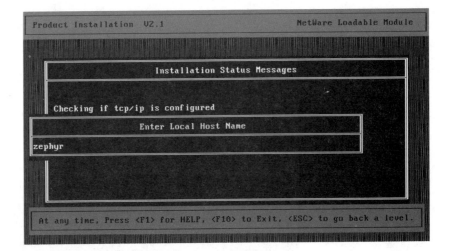

```
Product Installation  V2.1                    NetWare Loadable Module
┌──────────────────────────────────────────────────────────────────┐
│                    Installation Status Messages                    │
│                                                                    │
│  Checking if tcp/ip is configured                                  │
│  ┌──────────────────────────────────────────────────────────────┐ │
│  │                    Enter Local Host Name                       │ │
│  │ zephyr                                                         │ │
│  └──────────────────────────────────────────────────────────────┘ │
│                                                                    │
└──────────────────────────────────────────────────────────────────┘
 At any time, Press <F1> for HELP, <F10> to Exit, <ESC> to go back a level.
```

8. Next you are asked for an administration password for the Web server (see Figure 16.13). This password will be required to change the Web server's configuration.

9. The installation program now copies files into their final directories. If the Web server installation finishes properly, you will see the final status of the installation, as shown in Figure 16.14.

You have now successfully installed the NetWare Web Server. Before it can be used, you must restart the server. The NLMs the Web server uses will be loaded automatically the next time the server starts.

FIGURE 16.13

Enter an administration
password for the Web
server.

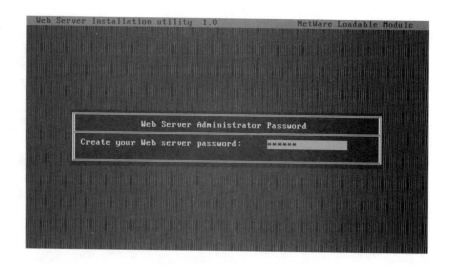

FIGURE 16.14

The Web server
installation is now
complete.

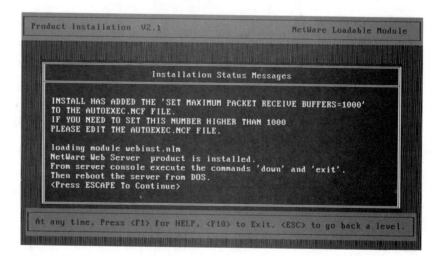

When the Web server is running, it occupies a screen on the server console. Switch to this screen to see the current status of the Web server, including the number of requests currently being handled, the Web server name, and the location of the served documents. This status screen is shown in Figure 16.15.

FIGURE 16.15

The status screen for the
NetWare Web Server
displays statistics about
· the server's usage.

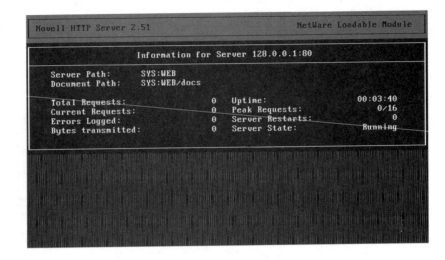

Installing Netscape Navigator

Now that you have NetWare Web Server running, you'll need to install a Web browser to view documents from the server. A popular browser, Netscape Navigator, is included with the IntranetWare package. You can install Netscape on as many workstations as you wish. Versions are included for Windows 3.1 and Windows 95. Follow these steps to install Netscape at a workstation:

1. Be sure the workstation's client is configured to support TCP/IP. Client 32, described in Chapter 5, offers this as an option. Reinstall Client 32 if necessary to add TCP/IP support.

2. Mount the NetWare 4.11 Operating System CD-ROM on the server's CD-ROM drive. Map a drive to this volume at the workstation. If the workstation has a CD-ROM drive, you can insert the CD-ROM at the workstation instead.

3. Choose Run from the Start Menu (Windows 95) or from the Program Manager's File menu (Windows 3.1).

4. Enter the path and file name for the SETUP utility. Substitute your CD-ROM drive or mapped drive for **D:**.

For Windows 95:

```
D:\PRODUCTS\WEBSERV\BROWSER\N32E201\SETUP.EXE
```

For Windows 3.11:

```
D:\PRODUCTS\WEBSERV\BROWSER\N16E201\SETUP.EXE
```

5. Follow the instructions in the installation program. For a default installation, click the Next button in each dialog box.

The installation program will automatically create an icon or Start Menu entry for Netscape Navigator.

Review

Because of the many new features of NetWare 4.11, the installation procedure has many new options. Many of the options can be chosen automatically. Depending on the installation method you choose and the speed of your hardware, the installation will take between 20 minutes and an hour.

Hardware Requirements

NetWare 4.11 requires the following hardware to run efficiently:

- **Memory:** 20MB is the official minimum. This will support a small company; for a large company, 32MB is a practical minimum.

- **Disk Storage:** 75MB is the minimum for a partition, but you may need up to 100MB for the software. Data files will require additional storage.

- **Processor:** The ideal processor ranges from a 486 DX/2 66 to a Pentium 100 or faster.

- **Other Hardware:** A CD-ROM drive is required. Fast and efficient disk controllers and LAN cards should be used.

Choosing an Installation Method

You can choose either the Simple installation or Custom installation. The simple installation makes these assumptions:

- You have already created a DOS partition on the disk and installed DOS on it, and the rest of the disk is available for NetWare.

- All available disk space will be used as a NetWare partition, and a single volume, SYS, will be created.

- IPX internal and external network numbers will be randomly generated, or NetWare will use the external network number of the existing network if it detects one.

- Only the IPX protocol will be installed.

- STARTUP.NCF and AUTOEXEC.NCF will not contain any extra commands.

- The U.S. English keyboard layout will be used.

- NDS will be set up with a single Organization object; the ADMIN user will be created under this object. If a Directory tree exists already, the new server will be added to that tree instead.

If you need to choose a different option for any of the above items, you must use the Custom installation. The Custom Installation includes these additional options:

- **International support:** If you have an international version of NetWare 4.11, you will be given a choice of languages when you begin the installation. Besides installing support for that language, the install program itself will prompt you in the language you have chosen.

- **Protocol Support:** The IPX protocol, described in Chapter 5, is installed by default. You can choose additional protocols to install, such as AppleTalk or TCP/IP.

- **Disk Partitioning:** You can specify the size of the NetWare partition to create, and specify additional volumes to be created within it.

- **NDS Options:** You can choose which container in the Directory to install the server object into, or use a separate Directory tree.

Using NetWare Web Server

The IntranetWare package includes NetWare Web Server, a server for the World Wide Web. To install and configure the server, you must complete the following steps:

- Configure the TCP/IP protocol

- Install NetWare Web Server

- Install Netscape Navigator on client workstations

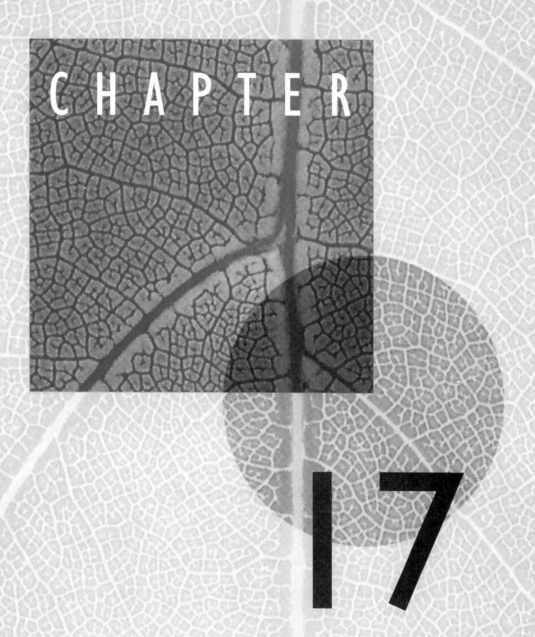

CHAPTER

17

Upgrading to NetWare 4.11

One of the greatest strengths of NetWare 4.11 is that it can benefit existing networks as well as brand new ones. Using the INSTALL and MIGRATE utilities provided with NetWare 4.11, you can easily upgrade an existing NetWare 3.1*x* server to NetWare 4.11 without losing any of the data, users, or rights that you have set up. Even NetWare 2.*x* and non-NetWare operating systems can be upgraded using these features.

Upgrading a network is a complicated process, but be glad you're learning it from the NetWare 4.11 perspective. NetWare 4.11 is the easiest version yet for upgrading. If you perform the upgrade correctly, users will come back the next day without knowing the difference.

In this chapter, you'll learn the following fine points of the upgrade process:

- **Hardware Requirements:** Find out if your server is up to the upgrade, or if you'll need a shiny new one to replace it—or simply an upgrade for the old one.

- **Planning the Upgrade:** There are actually four different ways to upgrade. We'll show you how to choose the right one.

- **Performing the Upgrade:** Step-by-step processes for all four methods.

Here's the most important tip for a successful upgrade to NetWare 4.11: Make a backup first. To be completely safe, make two of them, and restore a few files to test the backup. This may sound paranoid, but there are many steps involved in the upgrade process, and many things can go wrong. Ninety-five percent of the time, everything works fine—but it isn't easy to explain to the CEO of the company that you're in "the other five percent." Play it safe.

Hardware Requirements

You can upgrade most existing NetWare 3.1*x* servers to NetWare 4.11 without purchasing additional hardware. However, NetWare 4.11 is a more sophisticated operating system and requires more resources to run efficiently. You may need to install additional RAM or disk storage in order to achieve optimum performance. Table 17.1 summarizes the difference between NetWare 3.1*x* and NetWare 4.11 hardware requirements. Minimum requirements are given, along with suggested hardware for optimal performance in a simple network. You should determine the requirements of your own server using the methods described in the next sections.

T A B L E 17.1 NetWare 3.1*x* and NetWare 4.11 Hardware Requirements	**Operating System**	**RAM (Minimum/ Optimal)**	**Disk Storage (Minimum/ Optimal)**	**Processor (Minimum/ Optimal)**
	NetWare 3.1*x*	4MB/8MB	50MB/500MB	386/486
	NetWare 4.11	20MB/32MB	90MB/500MB–1GB	386/486, Pentium, or Pentium Pro

After considering the options in the next sections, you may discover that your machine needs quite a bit of help. If you're running NetWare 2.*x*, there is very little chance that your machine is capable of running NetWare 4.11. A 286 processor will not work with NetWare 4.11 at all. In many cases, the best idea is to buy an entirely new machine to serve as the NetWare 4.11 server. If your budget supports it, a new machine can provide you with improved speed, reliability, compatibility, and expandability.

As a final benefit, a new machine will allow you to use the *across-the-wire migration* method to upgrade the server. Across-the-wire migration transmits the data across the network to create a copy of the old server's setup on the new server. This method, described in more detail later in the chapter, doesn't make any changes to your existing server, and if something goes wrong, you can quickly bring the old server back online.

If you do have to buy a new server machine, don't write off the old server completely. If it's not too old, it will probably make a fine workstation. Be sure the upgrade is a success before you reformat that hard drive, though.

Do You Need More Memory?

NetWare 4.11 definitely requires more memory than any previous version. The minimum RAM required is officially 20MB. Your NetWare 3.1*x* server may have run just fine with 8MB, but you'll need at least 20MB for an efficient NetWare 4.11 server. If you have more than a few users on the network, 32MB is a good idea.

In general, if your NetWare 3.1*x* server was running efficiently before, you'll need 8–12MB more memory to run NetWare 4.11 at the same level of efficiency. If your server was not running efficiently, this is your chance to add even more RAM and bring it up to speed.

Be sure that you also have plenty of room for additional memory. If you add a disk drive, additional software, or additional users to the network, you'll need it.

Do You Need More Disk Storage?

Disk storage requirements haven't changed much between Net-Ware 3.12 and NetWare 4.11. You can assume that you will need about 40MB of extra space in order to perform the upgrade. If you do need additional space, you can use the *same-server migration* method, in which you transfer the data temporarily to a workstation before replacing (or upgrading) the server. This method is described in more detail later in this chapter.

The DOS partition also needs to be a bit larger for NetWare 4.11 (about 10MB as opposed to 5MB). If you need to increase the size of this partition, you'll have to reformat the drive. Once again, this is a good use for the same-server migration method.

Do You Need a Faster CPU?

NetWare 4.11 puts a higher load on the processor (CPU) than previous versions. Although any 386 or higher machine can still run NetWare 4.11, you may wish to seriously consider a processor upgrade. A 386 might suffice for NetWare 3.12 networks of up to 30 or 40 users, but for NetWare 4.11 you will definitely need a 486 or better for that many users. Considering the low price, you might even consider starting with a Pentium. You may not need the power now, but you will before long.

This is the category where you should think seriously about purchasing an entirely new machine. There are very few machines that can be upgraded to a higher processor without great expense and inconvenience. In addition, a new machine would be built with parts that were intended to work together, and are new and unlikely to fail—or if they do fail, at least they'll be under warranty.

If you're still running NetWare 2.*x* on a 286 machine, you should forget any notions of running NetWare 4.11 on it. To begin with, NetWare 4.11 requires a 386 as a minimum (a 486 is more realistic); and besides, if your machine is that old, chances are that very few of the parts, if any, are worth saving.

What about Other Hardware?

A server is only as fast as its disk access and network connectivity. You'll need the following hardware for an efficient NetWare 4.11 server:

- A high-speed bus—EISA or the more recent PCI. VESA local bus is another alternative, but is not well supported by network card manufacturers.

- Network cards that support the bus you've chosen.

- Disk controllers that support the high-speed bus, and fast disk drives.

- A CD-ROM drive. Unless you have another server with a CD-ROM drive on the same network, you'll need this to install the server and for occasional maintenance.

Planning the Upgrade

Upgrading your network to NetWare 4.11 is definitely not something that you should do spontaneously. In order to upgrade without problems, you must plan carefully. This includes choosing the method of upgrading, and preparing hardware, software, and users for the transition.

Choosing an Upgrade Strategy

The first consideration when upgrading is the type of upgrade you will use. There are actually four methods of upgrading:

- **INSTALL program:** Use this method to quickly upgrade NetWare 3.1x or 4.x servers to NetWare 4.11.

- **In-place upgrade:** Use this method to quickly upgrade a NetWare 2.x server (if it is capable of running NetWare 4.11).

- **Across-the-wire migration:** Use this method to move data and users to a new server running NetWare 4.11.

- **Same-server migration:** Use this method when you need to upgrade an existing server's hardware and upgrade to NetWare 4.11.

In practice, you'll usually use the INSTALL program for upgrading the same server, or the across-the-wire migration if you are upgrading to a new server. Let's take a closer look at all four methods.

Upgrading with the Installation Program

This is the easiest method of upgrading. It involves simply running the INSTALL program from the NetWare 4.11 installation CD-ROM. This method works for NetWare 3.1x and 4.x servers only. The NetWare 4.11 files are installed over the previous version's files. Users, trustee rights, and all other information are converted to NetWare 4.11 format.

Because no data is copied over the network, this is the fastest method of upgrading. In fact, if all goes smoothly, you could be done within half an hour. However, there are some disadvantages to consider:

- Once you've started the upgrade, there's no turning back. If something goes wrong, you'll need to either resolve the problem or re-install the old NetWare version and restore a backup. If you are upgrading from a version of NetWare 3.1x supplied on floppy diskettes, you might be busy for quite a while.

- The server must be brought completely down in order to begin the upgrade.

- This method won't work if you're replacing the NetWare 3.1*x* server with a new machine, or if you need to change the partition sizes on the hard disk. Be sure your existing machine can handle NetWare 4.11 before you try.

- If you are running NetWare 2.*x*, you can't use this method. (See the in-place upgrade, described next.)

Most importantly, keep a backup of the old server, and be sure you know where the disks or CD-ROM for the old NetWare version are, in case you have to revert to the old system.

Using the In-Place Upgrade

If you're running NetWare 2.*x* on the old server, this is the first option you should consider. This is a two-step process, illustrated in Figure 17.1:

- The NetWare 2.*x* disk partition is converted into a NetWare 3.1*x* partition. You do this using the 2XUPGRDE.NLM server utility. This utility also converts the bindery into NetWare 3.1*x* format.

- Use the INSTALL program to install NetWare 4.11, as described in the previous section.

This method is the simplest and quickest method if you are upgrading from NetWare 2.*x*. However, it shares the disadvantages of the INSTALL program, described in the previous section.

Make sure that your machine meets the minimum hardware requirements before you use this option, as you can't use the in-place upgrade method if your NetWare 2.*x* machine is a 286. Unless you had a very large budget when you first installed the server, it's very unlikely that you are running NetWare 2.*x* on a machine that is capable of running NetWare 4.11 at all—let alone running it efficiently.

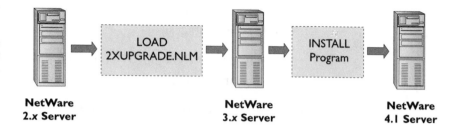

FIGURE 17.1

The in-place upgrade is
the simplest method of
upgrading NetWare 2.*x*
to NetWare 4.11.

More commonly, you'll replace the NetWare 2.*x* server with a new
machine, and use the across-the-wire migration method to transfer
the data.

The in-place upgrade method is used only for NetWare 2.*x* (and
rarely, at that).

Using Across-the-Wire Migration

If you're replacing your old NetWare 3.1*x* or 2.*x* machine with a new
NetWare 4.11 server, this is the way to go. In the across-the-wire
method, you install a brand new NetWare 4.11 server on the new
machine, then add it to the network. You then use the MIGRATE
utility to copy all data, users, and trustee assignments from the old
server to the new server. Once you're sure the new server is operational, you can bring the old server down and start using the new one.
This process is illustrated in Figure 17.2.

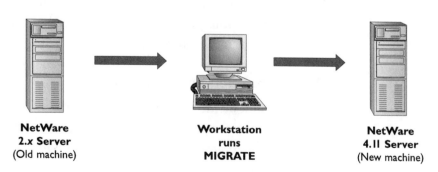

FIGURE 17.2

The across-the-wire
migration can be used to
migrate to a new server
machine.

The across-the-wire method is much safer than the in-place method. It has these advantages:

- Because you're keeping the old server intact, you can put it back online at a moment's notice.

- There are always two copies of the data, so there is less risk of data loss (but make a backup anyway).

- This is the only method that can be used if you're upgrading to a brand new machine. In fact, you can even use it to upgrade from one NetWare 4.11 server to another if you need to replace the server with a better machine.

- You can actually migrate data from multiple volumes on the old server to a single volume on the new NetWare 4.11 server. In addition, you can migrate multiple NetWare 3.1*x* or 4.*x* servers to the same NetWare 4.11 server. This allows you to easily reconfigure the network for efficiency, if the new server can handle the load.

- You can even migrate data from a server running Microsoft LAN Manager or IBM LAN Server.

The across-the-wire method has one principal disadvantage: It's *slow*. The process can take anywhere from half an hour to 4 or 5 hours. The actual time will depend on the speed of the servers (both the new one *and* the old one) and the speed of communication over the network. Be prepared to spend the better part of a day to complete this process—or a night, if the company doesn't want the users to spend a day without network access. You'll need to keep users off the old server during the migration process.

Using Same-Server Migration

The final method combines features of both the in-place method and the across-the-wire method. A single server is used, but information is migrated across the network. Confused? Figure 17.3 illustrates the process.

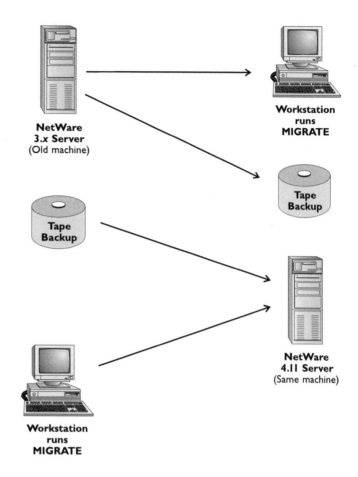

FIGURE 17.3

The same-server migration can be used if new disk partitions are needed.

Here's a play-by-play for the same-server migration method:

1. Data files are backed up to a tape.

2. The bindery is migrated from the old server to a workstation, and stored on the workstation's hard drive.

3. The bindery is converted to NetWare 4.11 (NDS) format on the workstation.

4. The server's hard disk is erased, the machine is upgraded as needed, and NetWare 4.11 is installed.

5. Data is restored from the tape backup to the upgraded server.

6. The bindery (or now, NDS data) is migrated back from the workstation to the server.

The main advantage to the same-server method is that you don't need an additional machine. The disadvantages are many, however:

- The only copy of the bindery data ends up on the workstation. There is some risk that it will be damaged in the conversion process, and that would not be a good thing.

- Because data files are migrated using a backup device, you may lose file attributes and trustee information.

- You may need quite a large hard disk on the workstation to hold the bindery files.

- This is the slowest migration process. With a slow NetWare 2.x or 3.1x server and lots of data, you could end up spending the whole day migrating.

- Some tape devices and software may not be compatible with the MIGRATE utility, and it would be better not to find this out during migration.

- As with the in-place upgrade, if you're running NetWare 2.x, there isn't much chance that your existing server will run NetWare 4.11.

Preparing for the Upgrade

Regardless of the type of upgrade you will be performing, there are certain things you should do to prepare. The better prepared you are, the less likely you are to run into a major problem. Here are the important considerations:

- Schedule a time for the upgrade. Make an estimate of the downtime, then double it. Be sure that all users are informed, and that they are logged out when you begin.

- In scheduling your upgrade, be sure you can reach Novell technical support, your Novell reseller, or a qualified consultant (unless you're *really* confident).

- Make a backup. Then hide it and make another one. Nobody has ever regretted making one too many backups.

- Delete all unneeded files from the server.

- If you are upgrading from NetWare 3.1*x*, run the BINDFIX utility twice on the NetWare 3.1*x* server. BINDFIX is similar to NetWare 4.11's DSREPAIR, and is used to repair problems in the bindery. The first time will repair any problems with the bindery; the second will ensure that you have a backup copy of the bindery files. If BINDFIX reports any errors, consult the NetWare 3.1*x* documentation.

- If you are upgrading from an earlier version of NetWare 4.*x*, run the DSREPAIR utility and be sure there are no errors in the NDS database.

Performing the Upgrade

Now you're ready to begin the actual upgrade process. Before you start, read all of the instructions given below, as well as those given in the NetWare manuals, very carefully. Be sure you have a good backup of all data and bindery information on the server. Be sure you understand the different upgrade methods, and have chosen the correct one for your particular needs.

Upgrading with the INSTALL Program

This is the simplest option. You can use it *only* for NetWare 3.1*x* or 4 servers. Also, be sure that the server meets all of the NetWare 4.11

hardware requirements. All you need is the NetWare 4.11 installation CD-ROM, or access to a server with the CD-ROM mounted. Follow these steps:

1. Bring the server down.

2. Insert the CD-ROM into the drive.

3. Load the drivers to access the CD-ROM drive from DOS. This includes a CD-ROM driver if the drive is in the server, or a network driver if the CD-ROM is mounted in another server.

4. Change to the CD-ROM drive and type **INSTALL**.

5. Follow the step-by-step instructions provided on the screen shown in Figure 17.4. See Chapter 16 for detailed instructions.

After the upgrade, test the server. Be sure all old applications work. You will also want to install the new DOS or Windows client software to take advantage of NDS. Instructions for installing this software can be found in Chapter 5.

The installation places all former bindery objects (users, groups, etc.) in a single Organization object which you specify during the installation. This object will be set as the bindery context automatically. If your network is large and complex, you will probably want to reorganize with Organizational Units after you've made sure the upgrade was a success.

Upgrading NetWare 2.x with the In-Place Upgrade

This is the simplest upgrade for NetWare 2.x, but will only work if your NetWare 2.x server is able to run NetWare 4.11. Follow these steps:

1. First, create an upgrade disk:

   ■ Create a bootable DOS disk with the DOS command SYS A:.

FIGURE 17.4

The installation program includes an option to upgrade an existing NetWare 3.1x server.

- Copy FDISK.COM and FORMAT.COM from the DOS directory onto the disk.

- Copy the files in the UPGRADE directory on the NetWare 4.11 installation CD-ROM to the disk.

2. Bring the NetWare 2.x server down, then boot the machine using the bootable upgrade disk.

3. Type **A:SERVER** to start the server. This uses the NetWare 3.12 SERVER.EXE.

4. Enter the server name and IPX internal network number at the prompts. To keep things simple, use the same information as the NetWare 2.x server. Your server is now running as a NetWare 3.1x server.

5. Load the disk driver from the upgrade disk. Use the type of driver that corresponds with your server hardware. For example, for an IDE disk:

```
LOAD A:IDE
```

6. Load the 2XUPGRDE.NLM file by typing **LOAD A:2XUPGRDE** at the server console prompt.

7. This NLM will upgrade the NetWare 2.*x* file system to Net-Ware 3.1*x*. After the upgrade to a NetWare 3.1*x* partition is complete, take the server down. You should not bring it up again until you complete the upgrade to NetWare 4.11.

8. Follow the steps in the previous section to use the Installation program to upgrade from NetWare 3.1*x* to NetWare 4.11.

Performing the Across-the-Wire Migration

The across-the wire method is a bit more complicated. You'll need a workstation running Windows or Windows 95 to perform the migration. In addition, the workstation and both servers must be accessible from the same network. Follow these steps to prepare for the migration:

1. Install a new NetWare 4.11 server on the new server machine, following the instructions in Chapter 16.

2. If you require support for the Macintosh or OS/2 name space, install it on the NetWare 4.11 server now, following the instructions in Chapter 13.

3. From the workstation, log in to the NetWare 4.11 server.

4. Map a drive to the NetWare 3.1*x* or NetWare 2.*x* server. You will need the SUPERVISOR password.

You are now ready to run the migration utilities. The two utilities you will use are called DS Migrate and File Migration. Both were introduced in NetWare 4.11, and are available from the Tools menu of NWADMIN. For previous versions of NetWare 4, you can use the MIGRATE utility described in the next section.

Migrating the Bindery

The DS Migrate utility allows you to convert bindery objects (users, printers, etc.) on a NetWare 3.1*x* server to NDS objects in the Net-Ware 4.11 Directory. To start this utility, choose Tools ➤ DS Migrate from the NWADMIN menu. The migration process consists of three main steps:

- **Discovery:** Choose a NetWare 3.1*x* server to migrate from. The bindery is discovered, or loaded into memory for use by DS Migrate. The bindery is now displayed in a format similar to an NDS tree.

- **Modeling:** Next, you are allowed to modify (model) the structure of the bindery objects, in order to make them more compatible with your Directory tree organization. You can create, rename, delete, or move objects. You can also modify trustee rights and merge sections of the Directory tree.

- **Configuration:** In the final step, the objects you have chosen are merged into the Directory tree.

Once you've finished DS Migrate, the objects are normal NDS objects, and you can modify them with NWADMIN.

Migrating Files

After you have successfully migrated the bindery objects to the Directory tree, you can migrate the files from the server to a volume on the new server. To start the File Migration utility, choose Tools ➤ File Migration from the NWADMIN menu. Figure 17.5 shows the initial File Migration dialog box. Follow these steps to migrate files:

1. Choose a source server (NetWare 2.*x* or 3.1*x*).

2. Choose a destination server, volume, and directory for the transferred files.

3. The files are copied, using the workstation as a buffer. This process may take quite a while, depending on the amount of data and the speed of the servers.

FIGURE 17.5

The File Migration utility allows you to transfer files from server to server.

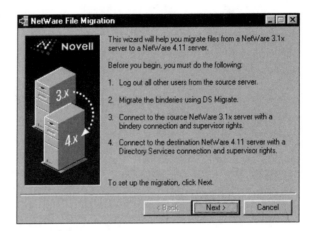

After you have successfully migrated bindery objects and files, test the new server. If everything works, you can bring down the old server.

Performing the Same-Server Migration

The same-server migration can be useful in the following circumstances:

- If you wish to upgrade NetWare 2.*x* and cannot run the in-place upgrade utility (for example, if you need to upgrade the machine along the way).

- If you need to use the same server, but wish to change disk partition sizes or upgrade the server's hardware.

The same-server migration uses the DOS-based MIGRATE utility. The DS Migrate and File Migration utilities introduced in the previous section do not support same-server migration.

In order to perform the same-server migration, you will need a workstation with a large hard drive attached to the network. Follow these steps:

1. Back up all data on the old server to a tape. (As always, two backups are better than one.)

2. On the workstation, run the MIGRATE utility. You will need to run this from the NetWare 4.11 installation CD-ROM. The main MIGRATE screen is shown in Figure 17.6.

FIGURE 17.6

The MIGRATE utility allows you to transfer data between a server and a workstation.

3. Select the source server.

4. Select the workstation as the destination.

5. Select the data to migrate (the bindery only).

6. Press F10 to view the MIGRATE menu, shown in Figure 17.7.

FIGURE 17.7

The MIGRATE main menu provides options for the migration process.

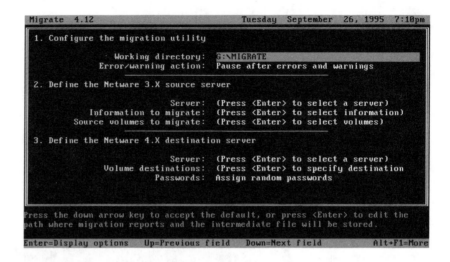

7. Press ↵ to begin the migration.

8. After migration is complete, double-check your backup of the server.

9. Repartition the server's hard disk if needed.

10. Install a new copy of NetWare 4.11 on the server, using the instructions in Chapter 16.

11. Restore the data to the new server from the backup tape you created in step 1.

12. Run MIGRATE at the workstation.

13. Select the workstation as the source, and NetWare 4.11 as the destination.

14. Press F10 to view the MIGRATE menu.

15. Press ↵ to migrate the bindery to the new server.

Review

Using the install and MIGRATE utilities provided with Net-Ware 4.11, you can easily upgrade an existing NetWare 3.1*x* server to NetWare 4.11 without losing any data, users, or rights that you have set up. Even NetWare 2.*x* and non-NetWare operating systems can be upgraded using these features.

Hardware Requirements

Depending on the hardware needed to support a new NetWare 4.11 server, you may wish to consider a new machine. If you keep the existing machine, follow these guidelines:

- **Memory:** NetWare 4.11 requires a minimum of 16MB RAM.

- **Disk storage:** You should have at least 40MB free.

- **Processor:** If your processor is a 386 or slow 486, or if it is bogged down running the current software, you may wish to consider a new machine.

- **Other hardware:** Other necessities include a high-speed bus, high-speed network and disk controller cards, and a CD-ROM drive.

Types of Upgrade

The first consideration when upgrading is the type of upgrade you will use. There are actually four methods of upgrading:

- **INSTALL program:** This is the easiest method of upgrading. It involves simply running the INSTALL program from the Net-Ware 4.11 installation CD-ROM. This method works for NetWare 3.1*x* servers only. The NetWare 4.11 files are installed over NetWare 3.1*x* files. Users, trustee rights, and all other information are converted to NetWare 4.11 format.

- **In-place upgrade:** This is the simplest method for NetWare 2.*x*. First, the NetWare 2.*x* disk partition is converted into a Net-Ware 3.1*x* partition. You do this using the 2XUPGRDE.NLM server utility. This utility also converts the bindery into Net-Ware 3.1*x* format. Second, you use the INSTALL program to install NetWare 4.11.

- **Across-the-wire migration:** With this method, you install a brand new NetWare 4.11 server on the new machine, then add it to the network. You then use the MIGRATE utility to copy all data, users, and trustee assignments from the old server to the new server. Once you're sure the new server is operational, you can bring the old server down and start using the new one.

- **Same-server migration:** This method copies the bindery to a workstation and the data to a backup device, then they are restored onto the server after NetWare 4.11 is installed.

In practice, you'll usually use the INSTALL program for upgrading the same server, or the across-the-wire migration if you are upgrading to a new server.

Configuring NetWare 4.11

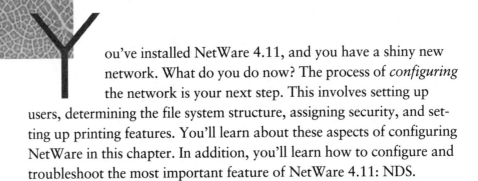

ou've installed NetWare 4.11, and you have a shiny new network. What do you do now? The process of *configuring* the network is your next step. This involves setting up users, determining the file system structure, assigning security, and setting up printing features. You'll learn about these aspects of configuring NetWare in this chapter. In addition, you'll learn how to configure and troubleshoot the most important feature of NetWare 4.11: NDS.

Configuring the Network

After you've installed most software, you can immediately begin using it. This isn't entirely true with a network operating system. After you've installed NetWare 4.11, you still have some tasks ahead of you. Nobody can log in until you set up User objects. You will also need to configure access to applications and create the objects needed for printing. As you configure your NetWare network, it changes from a new, generic network to a customized solution for your particular needs.

Creating User Objects

In most cases, your network will have one or more users—people who log into the network and use its resources. Users must log in to perform any work on the network.

In NetWare 3.1*x* and earlier versions, you would have to set up access for each user on the server—and if the same user accessed multiple servers, you would have to set up that user on each one. NDS has changed matters completely. You now create a User object—an NDS object that allows a user access to the network. The properties of the User object specify who the user is, what he or she can access, and who can control his or her rights.

When you install NetWare 4.11, a single User object is created: ADMIN. The ADMIN user is given full rights for the entire NDS tree. You can log in immediately as ADMIN. It's best to use this account just for creating User objects. Since ADMIN has full privileges, don't leave it logged in any longer than necessary. Once you're logged in, you can use the NetWare Administrator or NETADMIN utilities to create additional User objects and give them rights.

In NDS, ADMIN isn't always the only administrator. The rights of ADMIN can be limited, and administrators can be created for certain parts of the Directory tree.

Creating Groups

Group objects can be handy for giving users the same rights in the file system. Most commonly, these are used to assign rights needed for an application or data directory. For example, you can create a group called SPREADSHEETS. You would give the Group object rights to all of the directories needed for use of the spreadsheet software and data files. Groups are a good way to assign file system rights because multiple users usually need the same rights.

You can create Group objects using the NetWare Administrator utility. The Group object has a Membership property, which contains a list of users (User objects) that belong to the group. Each User object can belong to any number of groups.

When you create a new User object, you typically assign it membership in one or more of the groups. This way you can assign rights for the applications or data that the user needs to access without granting rights individually.

Another type of group is the *natural group* created when User objects are inside the same container object. Information about NDS configuration is presented later in this chapter.

The File System

You created one or more disk *volumes* during the installation of NetWare 4.11. The volume is the largest division of file storage in the NetWare 4.11 system. Volumes are further divided into directories and subdirectories. One of the most important aspects of configuring the network is the assignment of directories for data and program files.

When you install applications on the network or provide a location for data files, you should keep the following in mind:

- **Accessibility:** Keep the directory structure simple so that the users can find files easily.

- **Security:** Position the directories so that it will be easy to make security assignments. Take advantage of the fact that child directories inherit rights from parent directories. Thus, you can create a single directory for spreadsheet data, then subdivide the directory for particular projects. Giving a user access to the data directory allows him or her access to all of the projects.

- **Backups:** A useful strategy is to separate program and data files. This makes it easy to perform backups because the files that need to be backed up (the data files) are always in the same place.

Configuring Security

When you created User objects, you assigned the most fundamental aspects of network security. By ensuring that each user of the network has a User object and uses passwords, you can keep track of who is logged into the network and which user wrote a certain file or made a certain change.

As you learned in Part II of this book, there are actually several tasks involved in making the network secure:

- **Login security:** Assign User objects for each user. Be sure that passwords are required.

- **Server security:** Be sure the server console is protected. You can use a password to lock the console, but the best strategy is usually to keep the server in a locked room, if possible.

- **File system security:** Give users the rights they need to files using Groups or container objects to assign the same rights to multiple users.

- **NDS security:** Assign network administrators—users who have the right to manage, create, or delete Users or other objects in the Directory. In a small network, ADMIN might be the only user with these rights, but in a large network, you can assign multiple administrators.

If you're starting with a small NetWare 4.11 network, the most important elements of security are file system security and login security. Be sure to create the NDS structure so as to support multiple administrators in the future. (NDS configuration is discussed later in this chapter.)

Configuring Printing

As you learned in Chapter 9, several components are needed to configure printing on the network. Here's a review of the key components:

- In order to print to a printer on the network, you must first send the data to a *print queue*. The print queue stores each set of data, or *print job*, that it receives. The jobs are then sent, one at a time, to the print server (described next). Print queues serve two main purposes:

  - They allow users to continue working at their workstations while the printer prints.

  - They allow multiuser printing. Many users can add jobs to the queue, and they are printed in the order received.

- The *print server* accepts print jobs from print queues and sends them to the appropriate printer. In NetWare 3.1*x,* print servers were limited to 16 printers; in NetWare 4.11, this limit has been increased to 256. This allows you to easily use a single print server for the entire network. You create the Print Server object in NDS. The properties of the Print Server object provide identification information and define the list of printers the server can send jobs to.

- You must create a Printer object to represent each network printer. The properties of the Printer object identify the printer and list the print queues that the printer accepts jobs from. Other properties define the type of printer and how it is accessed. Printers can be attached to a server, to a workstation, or directly to the network.

- CAPTURE is a TSR (terminate and stay resident) program for DOS systems that allows you to *redirect* printing to a network printer. You specify a local printer port (usually LPT1, LPT2, or LPT3) in the CAPTURE command. After the CAPTURE command is executed, any printing that your workstation sends to this port is redirected to the network queue you specified.

■ Before data is sent to the printer, it is sent to the *port driver*. The port driver receives data from the print server and transmits it to the printer. The port driver is also called NPRINTER and is run by NPRINTER.EXE (DOS), NPRINTER Manager (Windows 95) or NPRINTER.NLM (NetWare 4.11).

To implement basic printing services, follow these steps:

1. Create a Print Server object.

2. Create a Print Queue object for each printer. You can also choose to share a queue with another printer.

3. Create a Printer object for each printer.

4. Assign the Printer object to the Print Queue object, and the Print Server to the Queue.

5. Set up the workstations to run CAPTURE. This is usually done using a login script.

NWADMIN (NetWare Administrator) and PCONSOLE, a DOS utility used to manage printing, include Quick Setup options which can perform steps 1 through 4 for you. PCONSOLE's Quick Setup screen is shown in Figure 18.1. The Quick Setup option automatically creates all of the needed objects and connects them.

This is only a summary of network printing. See Chapter 9 for more information about printing features and utilities.

FIGURE 18.1

The Quick Setup option in PCONSOLE allows you to quickly configure printing.

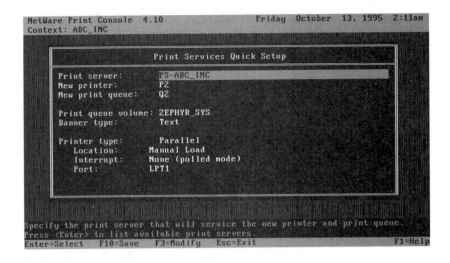

Configuring NDS

The next phase of configuring the network involves configuring NDS. This includes designing an effective directory structure, implementing NDS, troubleshooting, and merging Directory trees.

NDS Design

The process of designing an effective NDS structure is a complicated one—so complicated that one of the CNE tests is devoted to the topic. For a small network, though, you can create a simple design and begin using NDS right away.

For a small network (up to 20 users), it may be acceptable to keep all objects under a single Organization object. This is the default organization that is created when NDS is installed, and many companies never change it. However, it doesn't give you many of the benefits of NDS. For a more effective design, you should divide the tree into Organizational Unit objects for locations, divisions, or workgroups. This allows users in the same branch to receive the same rights and makes it easy to assign an administrator over a certain group of users.

Factors you should consider in your design include:

- Administration

- Network topology

- Bindery Services

- Tree depth

The most visible aspect of your NDS plan is the structure, or organization, of the Directory tree itself. There are several possible strategies for organizing your NDS tree:

- The *default organization* places all objects under a single Organization object, under the [Root].

- A *divisional* organization places divisions or departments of the company in branches of the tree.

- A *locational* organization divides the company into geographical locations.

- A *workgroup* organization groups users who perform the same tasks or projects.

- A *hybrid* organization combines the above strategies.

The next step in planning your network's Directory tree is to create the standards for choosing object names and properties:

- Choose the naming scheme for each type of object.

- Decide which properties will be defined and in what format.

- Create a *standards document* describing the plan.

Don't overdo it when designing the NDS organization. For a five- to 10-user company, the default organization is usually the most practical. Try not to divide the Directory tree unnecessarily.

Implementing NDS

Strategies for implementing NDS are related to the types of organization used:

- The *departmental* or *divisional* type of organization implements NDS separately for each department, division, location, or workgroup.

- The *organizational* approach organizes and implements NDS for the entire organization at once.

- A *combined* approach combines these two options.

Merging Directory Trees

You may have chosen to install several NetWare 4.11 servers with their own Directory trees in several different departments or divisions within your network. Eventually, you may want to merge them into a single tree. This allows all of the objects to be managed from a single Directory and gives you all of the benefits of NDS.

When you merge two Directory trees, objects in the [Root] of one tree (the *source* tree) are moved to the [Root] of the second (*target*) tree. The merge process must be performed at the server that contains the master replica of the source tree.

You use the DSMERGE utility to merge Directory trees. DSMERGE is an NLM that you can load at the server console.

You learned about merging Directory trees and NDS troubleshooting in Chapter 11. This information is included here as a review, because it is important to understand for the proper installation of a network and because it is included in the Installation and Configuration Workshop CNA test.

Merging Considerations

There are several conditions that must exist before you can begin the merge process. Check all of the following items before you merge the trees.

- All servers that contain a replica of the [Root] partition for either tree must be up and running, and they must be accessible over the network.

- The schema for the trees must be the same. If you have used a product that extends the Directory schema on one tree, you must make the same changes on the other tree.

- The [Root] object of the source tree cannot contain leaf or Alias objects.

- The trees must have different tree names.

- The servers containing the [Root] partitions of the trees must be running the same version of NetWare, and have the same NDS schema.

- You must have the password for an administrator with access to all objects in each Directory tree.

To protect your data, back up the Directory of both trees before you begin. Most NetWare backup programs include an option to back up NDS information.

The Merge Process

Follow these steps to merge Directory trees:

1. Start the DSMERGE utility by typing **LOAD DSMERGE** at the server console. You must do this on the server containing the master replica of the source tree. The main DSMERGE screen is shown in Figure 18.2.

FIGURE 18.2

The DSMERGE utility allows you to merge Directory trees.

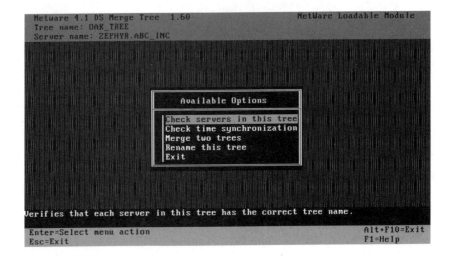

2. Select the Check Time Synchronization option to display a list of servers and their time synchronization status. The difference in times (Time Delta) must be under two seconds for all servers in both trees. You may need to change each server to use the same time source.

3. Select the Merge Two Trees option. The source tree is set to the server's tree automatically. Fill in the destination tree, and provide an administrator name and password for each tree, as shown in Figure 18.3.

FIGURE 18.3

Enter information in the Merge Trees Information screen to merge two trees.

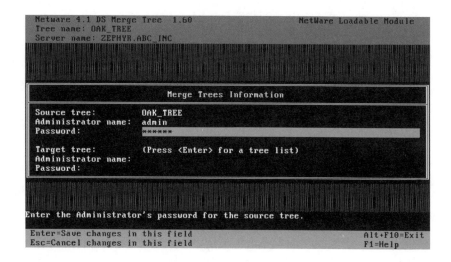

FIGURE 18.3

Enter information in the Merge Trees Information screen to merge two trees.

4. Press F10 to perform the merge. The merge process may take quite a while, depending on the existing replicas and the speed of your network.

If you wish to merge several trees into a single destination tree, you must merge them one at a time. Allow one merge process to finish before merging the next tree.

Troubleshooting NDS

NDS is the most important new feature of NetWare 4. Not surprisingly, it is also the most common source of problems with NetWare 4.11 servers. In the following sections, you will learn how to avoid some of the most common NDS problems and how to correct them when they do occur.

In a large organization in which time is critical, you may want to consult Novell technical support and avoid troubleshooting NDS problems by yourself, or you can try your local NetWare Reseller or consulting company. It may be worth the expense.

Avoiding NDS Problems

There is no way to avoid every NDS problem. In fact, if you deal with a NetWare 4.11 server for any length of time, you will undoubtedly handle several problems. However, the most common NDS problems can be avoided with a bit of planning. Here are some tips to keep NDS running smoothly:

- Always keep at least three replicas for each partition. We've mentioned this before, but it can't be stressed enough. If a replica is lost, even if it's the master replica, it can be restored if another replica is available.

- Use your backup software to make frequent backups of the NDS database. The frequency depends on how often changes are made in your network, but it should be done at least once a week. Many backup programs back up NDS data automatically while other data is being backed up.

- Use a single workstation to manage NDS partitions—when you are splitting partitions, merging partitions, or moving container objects. This will make it easy to keep track of the changes you have made and to avoid inconsistencies. Otherwise, conflicting messages can be received from different locations in the network, causing NDS corruption.

- Never let any server's SYS volume run out of space. The NDS database is kept in a hidden directory on the SYS volume. If the volume runs out of space, no changes can be made to NDS, and the server loses synchronization with other replicas. To be safe, keep at least 50MB free at all times. If possible, keep space-consuming data, such as print queues, on a volume other than SYS.

- Use DSREPAIR (described later in this chapter) to check synchronization before performing any complicated NDS operations, such as merging partitions, splitting partitions, and moving container objects. (It is also a good idea to make a backup copy of NDS immediately before performing any of these operations.)

Managing NDS Inconsistencies

NDS is a distributed database; each change you make to NDS begins at the replica where you make the change and is passed to each of the other servers that contains a replica. Depending on communication delays, network use, and the complexity of the change, it can take anywhere from ten seconds to an hour or two for all replicas to receive the change.

Fortunately, NDS was designed with this limitation in mind. The NDS database is *loosely consistent*, which means that it remains functional even if replicas do not have exactly the same information. You may notice these inconsistencies, but they do not necessarily represent a problem with NDS.

The process that NDS uses to send information between replicas is called *synchronization*. Two replicas are synchronized if they contain exactly the same information. In a busy network, the synchronization process is happening constantly to incorporate the latest changes. The process is different depending on the type of change.

Simple changes, such as adding a User object or changing a property, are synchronized quickly. All that is required is to send an update to each server that has a replica of the partition where the object is located. Creating a partition is also a relatively simple task.

Complex changes include joining partitions, moving partitions, and merging Directory trees. These changes require updates to multiple partitions, and each server with a replica of any one of the partitions must be contacted to send updates. In a network with many servers, these changes can take a long time—possibly an entire day or longer. Luckily, the only effect on users during this period is a slight slowdown.

Symptoms of NDS Problems

Although some inconsistencies between NDS replicas are a normal occurrence, severe inconsistencies may be an indication of a corrupt NDS database or another problem. Here are the symptoms you should watch for:

- Changes made to an NDS object or its rights seem to disappear.

- An object or its properties change unexpectedly. For example, a user can no longer log in because the password is incorrect, but the user has not changed the password.

- Errors may be inconsistent. For example, a user may be able to log in after several attempts.

- Unknown objects, shown with question marks, appear in the Directory tree. It is normal for these objects to show up when a server has been removed or when a partitioning operation is in progress. However, if they appear without an apparent cause, there may be a problem.

If you notice any of these symptoms, or if any part of NDS seems to behave inconsistently, follow the instructions in the following sections to narrow down and correct the problem. If a corrupt Directory is not repaired, it will probably become worse. Be sure to diagnose and correct the problem as soon as you notice any symptoms.

Checking NDS Synchronization

If the problems you are having with NDS are not severe, you should let the servers run for a few hours before attempting any repairs. NDS double-checks itself, and it may repair the problem automatically. If you take the servers down, it prevents NDS from synchronizing and correcting errors.

If the problem persists after the servers have run for a few hours, you should check the synchronization of the servers. You can use the DSREPAIR and DSTRACE utilities to check synchronization, as described in the following sections.

Using DSREPAIR DSREPAIR is a versatile utility that can be used to solve many NDS problems. You can use one of the functions of DSREPAIR to check the synchronization of replicas on the network. You should do this if you suspect a problem in NDS. In addition, you should check the synchronization before performing a major operation, such as merging trees, splitting partitions, joining partitions, or moving a container object.

To use this function of DSREPAIR, follow these steps:

1. Start the DSREPAIR utility by typing **LOAD DSREPAIR** at the server console.

2. Select Replica Synchronization.

3. Enter a full distinguished name for the administrator and password. These are used by DSREPAIR to log in to NDS.

4. DSREPAIR checks synchronization for all replicas and displays a log file, as shown in Figure 18.4. Examine this log file. If OK appears next to each server, the server is fully synchronized.

FIGURE 18.4

The DSREPAIR synchronization log displays the synchronization status for all servers.

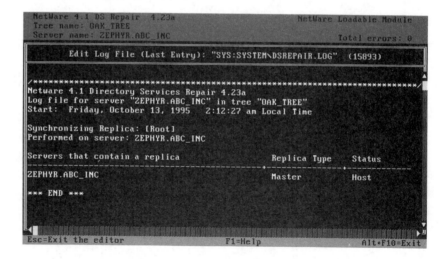

WARNING

While DSREPAIR is checking synchronization, it locks the NDS database. This may cause temporary problems with user logins, administration, and printing. You may wish to warn users or perform the repair when few users are active.

Using the DSTRACE Parameter   DSTRACE is a special SET parameter that can be used to monitor the activities of NDS. Information is displayed each time NDS replicas are synchronized. This can be helpful when you are diagnosing an NDS problem.

To start tracing NDS, type this command at the server console:

```
SET DSTRACE = ON
```

This command enables the Directory Services Trace screen, shown in Figure 18.5. Press Alt+Esc at the server console to switch to this screen.

You can leave DSTRACE running and check the screen periodically for problems. One of the most common problems produces this message:

```
SYNC: End sync of partition name. All processed = NO.
```

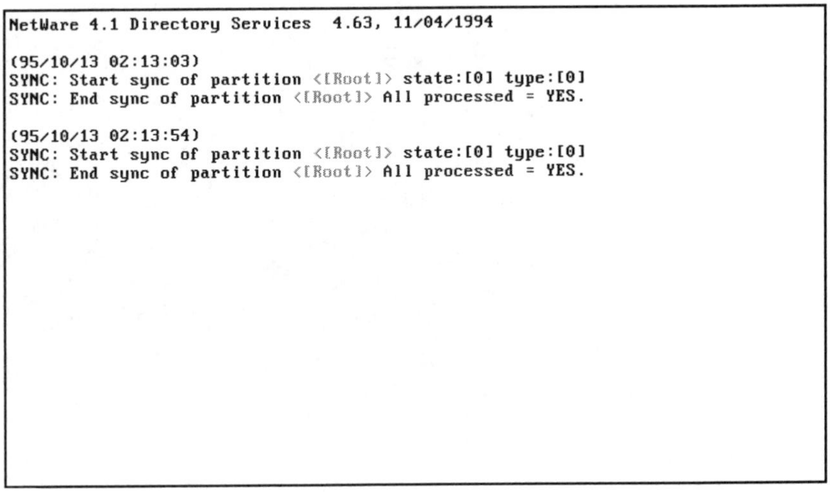

FIGURE 18.5

The DSTRACE screen displays information as NDS synchronization is performed.

```
NetWare 4.1 Directory Services  4.63, 11/04/1994

(95/10/13 02:13:03)
SYNC: Start sync of partition <[Root]> state:[0] type:[0]
SYNC: End sync of partition <[Root]> All processed = YES.

(95/10/13 02:13:54)
SYNC: Start sync of partition <[Root]> state:[0] type:[0]
SYNC: End sync of partition <[Root]> All processed = YES.
```

If NO is displayed in this message and the message keeps repeating after a few minutes, there is a serious problem with NDS. You should run the DSREPAIR utility, as described in the next section.

When you no longer need the DSTRACE screen, type the following at the server console:

```
SET DSTRACE = OFF
```

Repairing NDS Problems

Once you have determined that the NDS database has a problem, you should take action to repair it. The next sections describe three ways to do this. You should try the DSREPAIR utility first. The second option, forcing replica synchronization, provides a more drastic option. As a last resort, an NDS backup can be restored.

Using the DSREPAIR Utility   The DSREPAIR utility provides several options for repairing NDS problems. These are listed on the Available Options menu in DSREPAIR, shown in Figure 18.6. The most useful of these is the first, Unattended Full Repair. When you select this option, NetWare scans the NDS database for errors. All errors found are repaired if possible. The other options allow you to perform specific steps for troubleshooting, which may be useful if the Unattended repair fails, or if you are troubleshooting a specific problem.

WARNING   Before you run DSREPAIR, make a backup copy of NDS using your backup software. If the NDS database becomes corrupted further, you may lose information on all replicas. Since there may be errors in the database, do not overwrite an older backup if you have one.

After DSREPAIR has finished scanning the database, it displays a log file. This log lists the tasks that were performed and problems that were found and corrected. Examine the log carefully, and make sure that any errors were repaired.

Although DSREPAIR can repair most NDS corruption, you may lose some of the information. After DSREPAIR has finished its work,

FIGURE 18.6

The DSREPAIR utility can repair most NDS problems.

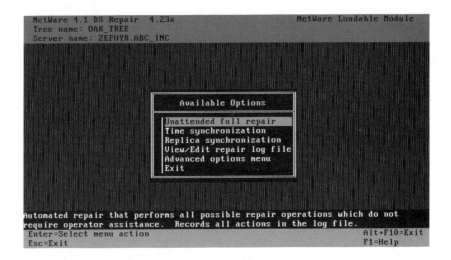

use NetWare Administrator (NWADMIN) to look at the Directory tree and make sure that all its objects are intact. If there are still problems with NDS, you may need to force synchronization.

Forcing Synchronization   If DSREPAIR is unable to repair the problems you are having with NDS, you may want to try forcing synchronization. This option sends updates from the master replica to all other replicas. Any changes waiting on those replicas are ignored.

If you force synchronization, you may lose changes to NDS that were made at a replica other than the master. Make a backup copy of NDS before proceeding.

Follow these steps to force synchronization using the NWADMIN utility:

1. Start the Partition Manager utility from within NWADMIN.

2. Click the Replicas button.

3. Highlight the master replica.

4. Click the Send Updates button. You will be asked to confirm the choice.

Updates are sent to all other replicas. This process may take several minutes, and it will cause a lot of traffic on the network.

After the update process is complete, load DSREPAIR at the server and use the Unattended Full Repair option again. If there are still NDS errors that DSREPAIR cannot fix, you will need to restore a backup.

Restoring an NDS Backup As a last resort, you can restore NDS from a backup. Assuming the backup was performed before the NDS problems began, this should permit a full recovery. Note the date of the backup. If you have made changes to NDS (such as creating users or changing rights) since that date, you must re-enter them after restoring the backup.

To restore NDS, first use the Partition Manager or PARTMGR utility to delete all replicas for the partition. Then restore the partition data using your backup software. This creates a new master replica. You can then re-create the other replicas.

Be sure all users in the Directory tree are logged out of the network when you back up or restore NDS data.

Review

After you've installed NetWare 4.11, you must configure the network before it can be used. This includes creating User objects, configuring access to applications, and creating the objects needed for printing. Completing these tasks converts the network to a customized solution for your particular needs.

Network Configuration

Before you can use the network and server, you must configure the following items:

- Create a *User object* for each user of the network.

- Create *Groups* to assign rights to users easily.

- Organize and set up the *file system*.

- Make basic *security* assignments.

- Create Objects for *printing*.

Designing the NDS Tree

For a small network (up to 20 users) it may be acceptable to keep all objects under a single Organization object. This is the default organization when NDS is installed, and many companies never change it. However, it doesn't give you many of the benefits of NDS. For a more effective design, you should divide the tree into Organizational Units for locations, divisions, or workgroups. Dividing the tree in this way allows users in the same branch to receive the same rights and makes it easy to assign an administrator over a certain group of users.

Factors you should consider in your design include:

- Administration

- Network topology

- Bindery Services

- Tree depth

There are several possible strategies for organizing your NDS tree:

- The *default organization* places all objects under a single Organization object, under the [Root].

- A *divisional* organization places divisions or departments of the company in branches of the tree.

- A *locational* organization divides the company into geographical locations.

- A *workgroup* organization groups users who perform the same tasks or projects.

- A *hybrid* organization combines the above strategies.

Merging Directory Trees and Troubleshooting NDS

If you have created multiple Directory trees for different departments or divisions within your network, you may want to merge them into a single tree. This allows all of the objects to be managed from a single Directory. When you merge two Directory trees, objects in the [Root] of one tree (the *source* tree) are moved to the [Root] of the second (*target*) tree. The merge process must be performed at the server that contains the master replica of the source tree. Use the DSMERGE utility at the file server to merge Directory trees.

Follow these guidelines to avoid NDS problems:

- Always keep at least three replicas for each partition. We've mentioned this before, but it can't be stressed enough. If a replica is lost, even if it's the master replica, it can be easily restored if another replica is available.

- Use your backup software to make frequent backups of the NDS database.

- Use a single workstation to manage NDS partitions—splitting partitions, merging partitions, and moving container objects. This makes it easy to keep track of the changes you have made and to avoid inconsistencies.

- Never let any server's SYS volume run out of space. The NDS database is kept in a hidden directory on the SYS volume. If the volume runs out of space, no changes can be made to NDS, and the server loses synchronization with other replicas. To be safe, keep at least 50MB free at all times. If possible, keep space-consuming data, such as print queues, on a volume other than SYS.

- Use DSREPAIR to check synchronization before performing any complicated NDS operations, such as merging partitions, splitting partitions, and moving a container object. (It is also a good idea to make a backup copy of NDS immediately before performing any of these operations.)

CHAPTER

19

Taking Care of the
NetWare 4.11 Server Environment

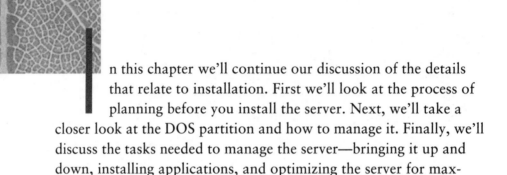

n this chapter we'll continue our discussion of the details that relate to installation. First we'll look at the process of planning before you install the server. Next, we'll take a closer look at the DOS partition and how to manage it. Finally, we'll discuss the tasks needed to manage the server—bringing it up and down, installing applications, and optimizing the server for maximum performance.

Planning the Server and Network

Before you even install a NetWare 4.11 server, you should make certain considerations. How will the server be used? How many users will access it? You should answer these and other questions and write a complete plan before you begin the process of installation. In the next sections, we'll look at the most important aspects to plan.

Keep It Simple

An effective network design doesn't have to be complicated. In fact, the simpler the better. A simple design provides efficient access to resources while facilitating network management. Here are some tips in planning the network:

- When possible, users should attach to the server where the resources they need are located.

- Locate users near the servers they attach to. Accessing resources that are on a server across a WAN link can take a long time.

- Whenever possible, use the same hardware and software for clients—network software, network cards, and the workstations themselves. Also use consistent IRQ, DMA, and other settings when possible. This makes troubleshooting a breeze.

- If a certain group of users uses high amounts of network bandwidth, keep them on their own segment of the network. CAD users are an example of users who should have their own segment of the network.

Consider Fault Tolerance

A NetWare 4.11 network can provide very effective fault tolerance. Depending on the needs of the company and the users, you may wish to improve fault tolerance in these areas:

- Use disk mirroring (SFT I), disk duplexing (SFT II), or redundant servers (SFT III). These systems provide high levels of fault tolerance but may exceed your budget.

- Use redundant network cables when possible, in case a connection is lost.

- Use UPS (uninterruptible power supplies) on the server and on any critical workstations.

- Run virus protection software on the server and workstations.

- Plan a strategy for backing up network files, and test backup hardware and software to ensure that it works: Back up a few files, and try restoring them.

Maximize Network Performance

The most important thing you can do to optimize network performance is determine a *baseline* for the network. A baseline is a measure of performance when the network is running smoothly. Establishing a baseline allows you to quickly determine if the network is running too slow. In addition, follow these tips:

- Use bridges and filters to keep data from being sent unnecessarily.

- If much routing is needed, consider using a dedicated router rather than your server.

- Try to use consistent protocols throughout as much of the network as possible.

Configuring and Managing the DOS Partition

Although the NetWare 4.11 server is not a DOS machine, it usually does need a DOS partition. This partition is used to start the server. It holds the SERVER.EXE program and other server files that are used before the NetWare volume is mounted.

If you plan to use the Simplified Installation of NetWare 4.11 option in the INSTALL program, you need to create a DOS partition before you begin installation. You can configure the DOS partition using the DOS utility, FDISK. Follow these steps to create a DOS partition for the server.

These steps should be performed before installation. Changing partitions on an existing server erases all data on the disk. If you need to repartition an existing server, consider the across-the-wire migration, described in Chapter 17.

1. Boot the server with a DOS disk. If DOS is already installed, simply boot the hard disk.

2. Type **FDISK** to start the FDISK program.

3. Select Display Partition Information to list the partitions on the disk. If a NetWare partition exists, it is listed as Unknown.

4. Delete any existing partitions on the disk.

5. Create a new DOS partition. The DOS partition for NetWare 4.11 should be at least 15MB.

6. You are now required to reboot. Since the partition has been re-created, you need to boot using a boot disk.

7. Type **FORMAT C: /S** to format the DOS partition.

8. Install DOS on the new partition, following the instructions that come with your version of DOS. Just about any version can be used, since it is unloaded when the NetWare 4.11 server starts.

9. Proceed with the NetWare installation.

Although 15MB is the required size for a DOS partition, it's usually helpful to have at least 25MB. Most disks are large enough that this size won't take much away from your total NetWare storage. If you wish to store diagnostic information when the server crashes, add the server's memory to the total size.

Managing the NetWare 4.11 Server

Next, we'll look at the tasks you need to perform to manage the server. These include the processes of taking the server down and bringing it back up, when required. We'll also look at the MONITOR utility and how you can interpret its statistics and optimize the network and server.

Bringing the Server Up

Starting a NetWare 4.11 server is a simple process. Here are the steps for starting a typical server:

1. Turn the server on. DOS will be started.

2. Change directories to the NetWare 4.11 directory (usually C:\NWSERVER).

3. Type **SERVER** to start the SERVER.EXE program. DOS is unloaded, and NetWare 4.11 starts.

You can automate this process so that the server starts automatically. This is a very good idea because you'll want the server to start up if the power goes out or the system resets for any other reason. To automate the process, simply add these commands to the AUTOEXEC.BAT file on the server:

```
C:

CD \NWSERVER

SERVER
```

Sometimes the AUTOEXEC.NCF file on the server runs commands that you don't want it to run. For example, a command in the file may be causing the server to crash. The solution? Simply type this command instead of SERVER:

```
SERVER /na
```

This command starts the server without running the AUTOEXEC.NCF file. If the SERVER command is in the AUTOEXEC.BAT file, you need to abort the boot process by pressing Ctrl+C or use a boot disk to bypass the system's AUTOEXEC.BAT file. Although less likely, commands in STARTUP.NCF can cause problems. Use this command to skip the file:

```
SERVER /ns
```

Alternately, since STARTUP.NCF is located in the DOS partition, you can edit it before you start the server.

If you are using DOS 6.0 or above, there is a simple method to stop the AUTOEXEC.BAT file from executing. As soon as you see the message "Starting MS-DOS," press F5. The commands in the AUTOEXEC.BAT file are skipped, and you go immediately to the DOS prompt. If you use the menu feature of DOS 6.0 and above, this option is easier to use.

Taking the Server Down

Taking the server down is very simple. Just type **DOWN** at the console prompt. You are asked to verify the action if any files are open. Next, you'll see another prompt. Just type **EXIT**. You return to the DOS prompt and can restart the server or safely turn off the power.

If you need to take the server down for any reason, always do it the correct way by using the DOWN command. If you turn the power off without doing this, the data on the disk could be damaged.

Monitoring and Optimizing Server Performance

In this section, we'll take a look at the things you can do to run your server at its best possible speed and to keep it running smoothly without crashes. You can use the MONITOR utility, which allows you to view operating parameters and SET commands, which can improve performance. The areas on the server that can be improved include memory, CPU, and disk access.

Much of this information was presented in Chapter 15. It is included here as a review and because it is part of the Installation and Configuration Workshop CNE test.

Optimizing Memory and CPU Performance

The server's memory is used to store the NetWare 4.11 operating system, device drivers, NLMs, and buffers for disk and network communication. Because many different types of memory storage are required, NetWare 4.11 uses sophisticated *memory management* techniques. By understanding how memory is managed and how it affects network performance, you can keep your network running smoothly.

Memory Allocation

Memory allocation is the process that NetWare uses to assign memory needed by the system or applications. NetWare 4.11 assigns memory in 4KB blocks, or *pages*. The memory manager assigns, or *allocates*, pages of memory needed by the application. The pages can be located in several different areas of memory, but they appear as a single block of memory to the application.

NLMs or system programs are assigned an *allocation pool* when they start. The allocation pool is based on an estimate of the memory that the application requires. As the application requests memory pages, NetWare assigns them from this pool, and when the application frees the memory, it is returned to the pool. Memory is assigned efficiently because each application uses its own memory pool.

Memory Deallocation   When an NLM no longer needs memory, it turns the memory over to the system. This process is called *deallocation*. When memory is deallocated, it is simply marked as unused. However, the memory is not available to other applications yet.

Garbage Collection   *Garbage collection* is a process that runs periodically (every 15 minutes by default) on the server. This process finds areas of memory that have been deallocated and returns them to the main memory pool so that they can be used by other applications. You can use SET commands to control how often garbage collection is performed and improve its efficiency.

Monitoring Memory Usage

The Memory Utilization option in the MONITOR utility allows you to view the server's total allocated memory. In addition, you can press ↵ when the name of a system module is highlighted to view detailed memory information about that module. The Memory Utilization screen is shown in Figure 19.1.

FIGURE 19.1

MONITOR's Memory Utilization screen displays information about memory use.

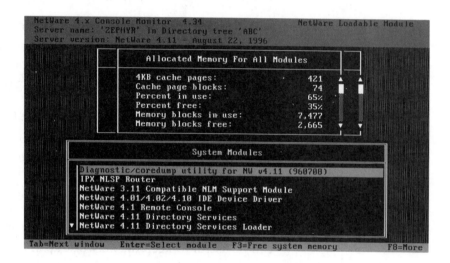

```
NetWare 4.x Console Monitor  4.34                    NetWare Loadable Module
Server name: 'ZEPHYR' in Directory tree 'ABC'
Server version: NetWare 4.11 - August 22, 1996

                    Allocated Memory For All Modules
             4KB cache pages:                    421      ▲   ▲
             Cache page blocks:                   74
             Percent in use:                     65%
             Percent free:                       35%
             Memory blocks in use:             7,477
             Memory blocks free:               2,665      ▼   ▼

                          System Modules
       Diagnostic/coredump utility for NW v4.11 (960708)
       IPX NLSP Router
       NetWare 3.11 Compatible NLM Support Module
       NetWare 4.01/4.02/4.10 IDE Device Driver
       NetWare 4.1 Remote Console
       NetWare 4.11 Directory Services
     ▼ NetWare 4.11 Directory Services Loader

 Tab=Next window    Enter=Select module    F3=Free system memory      F8=More
```

SET Commands for Memory Management

You can use several SET commands to control the allocation and use of memory. You can also control whether several types of memory protection errors display messages on the console or abend the server. Type these commands at the server console followed by the equal sign (=) and the desired value for the parameter. You can also place these commands in the server's STARTUP.NCF file. Here's an example of a SET command, showing the correct syntax (capitalization is optional):

```
SET GARBAGE COLLECTION INTERVAL = 25
```

Most servers can run efficiently with no change to these parameters. Be sure that you understand what the settings mean before changing them. If a setting does not solve your problem or improve speed, change it back to the default.

- **SET Garbage Collection Interval** controls how often the garbage collection process is performed. This value is in minutes and can range from 1 to 60. The default is every 15 minutes.

- **SET Number of Frees for Garbage Collection** allows garbage collection to be automatically performed when an NLM completes a certain amount of *free* calls to deallocate memory. The default is 5,000. This value can range from 100 to 100,000.

- **SET Minimum Free Memory for Garbage Collection** sets the number of bytes that must be in the system memory pool for successful garbage collection. This value ranges from 1,000 to 1,000,000 and defaults to 8,000.

- **SET Auto Restart After ABEND** controls whether the server will reboot automatically when an abend (server crash) occurs. This can be useful to keep the network up and running, but can prevent you from finding out when a crash occurs. This setting is OFF by default.

The following two SET commands cannot be typed at the console but must be in the STARTUP.NCF file.

- **SET Auto Register Memory Above 16 Megabytes** defaults to ON. This allows EISA computers to automatically use memory above 16MB if available. You may need to set this to OFF to provide compatibility with the disk controller.

- **SET Reserved Buffers Below 16 Megabytes** reserves buffer space in the lower 16MB of memory for device drivers that are limited to that area. You can set this value between 8 and 300; it defaults to 16.

Checking CPU Performance

The type and speed of the server's CPU can dramatically affect system performance. If your server is running slowly, you can use the SPEED command and the MONITOR utility to determine the cause of the problem.

First, type **SPEED** at the server console to verify that your CPU is running at its normal speed. SPEED calculates a number based on CPU performance; this should be approximately 90 for a 386, 900 for a 486, and 3,000 or more for a Pentium-based machine. If your server displays an unusually low number, check the Turbo or Speed switch on the server, and be sure it is set to the highest speed.

Next, you should check if an application is using a high amount of CPU resources. Select Scheduling Information in the MONITOR utility to display the percentage of CPU time being used by each NLM. Figure 19.2 shows the Scheduling Information screen. Most NLMs use between 2 and 10 percent. If an NLM is using a higher percentage, unload it, or configure it differently. Of course, if you are running an intense application such as a backup or database, you can expect its utilization to be high.

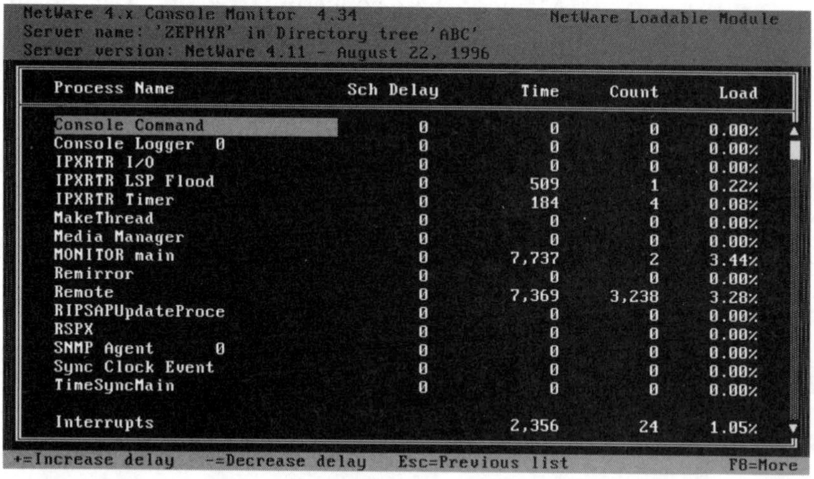

FIGURE 19.2

The Scheduling Information screen can be used to detect NLMs that are overworking the CPU.

```
NetWare 4.x Console Monitor  4.34              NetWare Loadable Module
Server name: 'ZEPHYR' in Directory tree 'ABC'
Server version: NetWare 4.11 - August 22, 1996

   Process Name           Sch Delay      Time     Count     Load

  Console Command              0            0         0     0.00%  ▲
  Console Logger  0             0            0         0     0.00%
  IPXRTR I/O                    0            0         0     0.00%
  IPXRTR LSP Flood              0          509         1     0.22%
  IPXRTR Timer                  0          184         4     0.00%
  MakeThread                    0            0         0     0.00%
  Media Manager                 0            0         0     0.00%
  MONITOR main                  0        7,737         2     3.44%
  Remirror                      0            0         0     0.00%
  Remote                        0        7,369     3,238     3.28%
  RIPSAPUpdateProce             0            0         0     0.00%
  RSPX                          0            0         0     0.00%
  SNMP Agent      0             0            0         0     0.00%
  Sync Clock Event              0            0         0     0.00%
  TimeSyncMain                  0            0         0     0.00%

  Interrupts                             2,356        24     1.05%  ▼

+=Increase delay    -=Decrease delay    Esc=Previous list         F8=More
```

Optimizing Disk Performance

The speed of disk access on NetWare volumes also affects the speed of the server and the network. NetWare 4.11 provides sophisticated *cache* mechanisms that move frequently accessed information from the disk to the server's RAM for faster access. You can optimize these mechanisms to streamline performance. In addition, the *file compression* and *block suballocation* features allow the server to store more information on available disk space.

Monitoring Cache Buffers

A NetWare server always sets a certain amount of RAM aside for *cache buffers*. When blocks are read from the disk, they are first transferred into the cache. If the same information is needed again, it can be read from RAM rather than accessing the disk drive. Blocks written to the disk are also written to the cache, and blocks in the same area are written all at once. This provides a dramatic improvement in disk speed.

You can view cache statistics by using the Cache Utilization option in the MONITOR utility. This screen, shown in Figure 19.3, provides several pieces of information about the performance of the cache. Many of these concern *cache hits*. A cache hit occurs when the information required is found in the cache, and the disk does not need to be accessed.

If the network is running smoothly, the short-term and long-term cache hit percentages should be 90 percent or higher. When these numbers are low, the server runs slowly. Applications that read many files with little repetition, such as backups, will cause a low cache hit percentage; this is nothing to worry about.

FIGURE 19.3

The Cache Utilization
Statistics screen provides
information about the disk
cache.

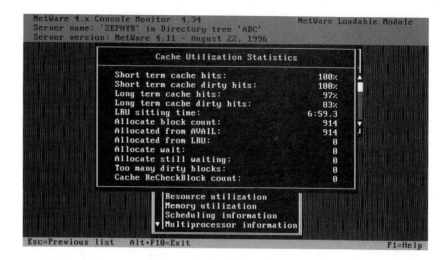

```
NetWare 4.x Console Monitor  4.34              NetWare Loadable Module
Server name: 'ZEPHYR' in Directory tree 'ABC'
Server version: NetWare 4.11 - August 22, 1996

                      Cache Utilization Statistics

              Short term cache hits:              100%
              Short term cache dirty hits:        100%
              Long term cache hits:                97%
              Long term cache dirty hits:          83%
              LRU sitting time:                 6:59.3
              Allocate block count:                914
              Allocated from AVAIL:                914
              Allocated from LRU:                    0
              Allocate wait:                         0
              Allocate still waiting:                0
              Too many dirty blocks:                 0
              Cache ReCheckBlock count:              0

                  Resource utilization
                  Memory utilization
                  Scheduling information
                  Multiprocessor information

Esc=Previous list    Alt+F10=Exit                            F1=Help
```

Optimizing Cache Buffers

The simplest solution to cache problems is to add more RAM to the
server. You can also use the following SET commands to optimize the
cache process:

- **SET Dirty Disk Cache Delay Time** specifies how long the server
  waits after a write request before it is written to the disk. This
  value can range from .1 second to 10 seconds and defaults to 3.3
  seconds. You can set this to a higher value if users frequently
  write to the disk. This may improve access speed.

- **SET Maximum Concurrent Disk Cache Writes** specifies the
  amount of write requests the server waits for before beginning
  to write them to the disk.

- **SET Minimum File Cache Buffers** controls the minimum amount
  of cache buffers that are available. When NLMs are loaded, they
  take memory away from cache buffers. You can set this parameter to make sure some buffers are always available. This value
  defaults to 20 and can be set as high as 1,000.

- **SET Minimum File Cache Report Threshold** sets a threshold for warnings about low cache buffers. It can be set between 0 and 1,000 and defaults to 20. When the amount of available cache buffers decreases below the set amount, a warning is displayed on the server console.

- **SET Read Ahead Enabled** can be set to ON or OFF. This parameter controls whether the server reads ahead when reading from the disk. This means that extra blocks are read into the cache, assuming that they will be requested next. The default is ON. This improves disk access speed in most cases.

- **SET Read Ahead LRU Sitting Time Threshold** controls the read ahead process. Reading ahead writes over the least recently used (LRU) areas of the cache. These areas must be sitting, or unused, for the set amount of seconds before they are overwritten. The sitting time can range from 0 seconds to 1 hour and defaults to 10 seconds.

Block Suballocation

The *suballocation* feature of NetWare 4.11 was introduced in Chapter 2. This feature divides the blocks used for disk storage into portions as small as 512 bytes, allowing more efficient use of disk space. This eliminates the space wasted by very small files and by files that use a fractional block.

How Suballocation Works   Block suballocation uses two types of blocks on the volume: normal blocks and suballocated blocks. A file always begins at the boundary between two blocks. Whole blocks are used for as much of the file as possible. If a partial block is left at the end of the file, the block is suballocated. The remaining suballocation units (512-byte fragments) of the block can be used for suballocated portions of other files. Normal blocks and suballocated blocks are illustrated in Figure 19.4.

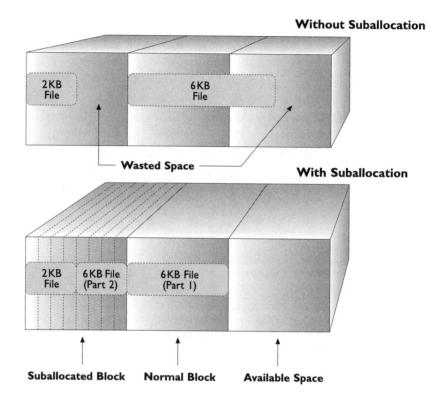

FIGURE 19.4

Block suballocation uses
normal blocks and
suballocated blocks to
optimize disk storage.

Enabling Block Suballocation You can enable block suballocation for a volume when the volume is created. You can also enable it later with the INSTALL utility. Once enabled, you cannot disable it without reformatting the volume. Follow these steps to enable suballocation on a new volume:

1. Start the INSTALL module by typing **LOAD INSTALL** at the server console.

2. Select Volume Options.

3. Press ↵ when the volume name is highlighted. The status of the volume is shown.

4. Move the highlight to Block Suballocation, and press ↵.

5. Press ↵ to toggle the suballocation from OFF to ON.

6. Press Esc to exit, and save the changes.

Controlling Suballocation with File Attributes   To use some files efficiently, you should avoid using suballocation. Files that are added to frequently, such as database files, should not be suballocated. You can turn off suballocation for a file using the DS (Don't Suballocate) file attribute. To set this attribute, use the FLAG command:

    FLAG *filename* DS

File Compression

The NetWare 4.11 *file compression* feature, introduced in Chapter 2, allows files that are not currently in use to be compressed. This can dramatically improve the amount of disk storage available on your server and yet keeps the files available for easy access.

NetWare checks for files that have not been accessed for several days. When such a file is found, it is compressed into a temporary file. If the compression process is successful and the compressed file is significantly smaller, the original file is deleted, and the compressed file is put in its place.

You can use file attributes to disable compression for specific files or directories and to determine whether a file is compressed. Information about these attributes is given in Chapter 7.

Activating File Compression   NetWare 4.11 enables file compression by default; however, if you have upgraded to NetWare 4.11 from a previous version of NetWare, you must activate the feature manually. Once activated, you cannot disable file compression without re-creating the volume; however, you can disable compression for directories and files. You can also use a SET command to disable compression on the server. Follow these steps to enable file compression:

1. Start the INSTALL utility by typing **LOAD INSTALL** at the server console.

2. Select Volume Options.

3. Press ↵ when the desired volume is highlighted.

4. Change the File Compression option to ON.

5. Press Esc to exit, and save the changes.

Disadvantages of File Compression   Although NetWare's file compression eliminates the problems of most compressed file systems, there are some disadvantages to using compression. You should take these into account when deciding whether to activate file compression on your server.

- **Speed of access:** When a user requests a file that has been compressed, a delay occurs as the server uncompresses the file. In most networks this won't happen very often, but if your users frequently access files that no one has used for more than seven days, the network may slow to a creeping halt. Depending on the file size and the server speed, decompression can take from 30 seconds to as long as 10 minutes. You can avoid this delay by turning off compression on these files. Using a SET parameter, you can also change the time that NetWare waits before compressing the files.

- **Backups:** Files backed up from a compressed volume should be restored onto a volume that also has compression enabled, to ensure that space is available. In addition, unless the backup system supports compression, files are restored in an uncompressed state, and NetWare compresses them after seven days. Thus, restoring an entire volume could require a much greater amount of disk space than the original volume.

■ **Compression is enabled permanently:** Once you enable compression on a volume, you cannot turn it off and uncompress the files without re-creating the volume (which erases all data on the volume!). You can, however, disable compression for individual files and directories. You can also disable compression with a SET command, described in the next section.

■ **Server performance:** In a heavily used server, compression and decompression can happen constantly, which can slow your server. However, this slowing is minimal and well worth the increase in available storage.

Controlling File Compression with SET Commands   You can optimize the file compression process with a variety of SET parameters. These allow you to enable or disable compression, control how often compression is performed, and fine-tune the compression process.

The SET commands listed below can be typed at the server console, or you can add them to the server's STARTUP.NCF or AUTOEXEC.NCF file to permanently set the parameter.

■ **SET Compression Daily Check Stop Hour** specifies an hour in military time when the server stops checking for files that are ready to compress. You can use this setting, along with the Check Starting Hour setting described below, to ensure that the compression process happens at a time when few users are on the network. The default is 6 (6:00 a.m.).

■ **SET Compression Daily Check Starting Hour** sets the time that the server begins checking for files to compress. The default is 0 (12:00 midnight).

■ **SET Minimum Compression Percentage Gain** controls the level of compression that is required in order to keep the file compressed. For example, if this value is 10 percent, the file must be at least 10 percent smaller; otherwise, the original, uncompressed version of the file is kept.

- **SET Enable File Compression** can be ON or OFF and controls whether the compression process will occur. The default is ON. If you set this to OFF, there may still be compressed files on the server, but no additional files will be compressed.

- **SET Maximum Concurrent Compressions** specifies the number of volumes that can be compressing files at the same time. This defaults to 2. Larger values may slow the server considerably.

- **SET Convert Compressed to Uncompressed Option** can be set to 0, 1, or 2. This parameter controls what is done with a file after it is accessed and subsequently uncompressed. Option 0 keeps the file compressed, 1 keeps it compressed after the first access only, and option 2 leaves the file uncompressed. The default is 1.

- **SET Uncompress Percent Disk Space Free to Allow Commit** is quite possibly the longest SET command available, but understanding its purpose is simple. This specifies the percentage of the volume's space that must be available before a file is uncompressed. This parameter prevents uncompressed files from filling up the volume.

- **SET Uncompress Free Space Warning Interval** controls how often a warning is displayed when there is not enough free space to uncompress a file. This parameter can be set to a value in minutes or to 0 to disable the warnings.

- **SET Deleted File Compression Option** controls whether compression is performed on deleted files. (The files are still available for salvage using the FILER or NWADMIN utilities.) The setting can be 0, 1, or 2. Option 0 never compresses deleted files; option 1 compresses them one day after deletion; and option 2 compresses files immediately when deleted.

- **SET Days Untouched Before Compression** controls how many days a file must remain untouched before it is compressed. The default is seven days.

File Attributes for File Compression   Several of the new Net-Ware 4.11 file attributes are related to file compression. File attributes are explained in detail in Chapter 7.

- **Ic (Immediate Compress)** can be used to specify that a file (or directory of files) should be compressed immediately each time it is written to. This compression happens regardless of the time of day and may slow the server.

- **Dc (Don't Compress)** can be used to prevent files or directories from being compressed. This can be used on a file that needs to be accessed quickly or one that must be updated frequently.

- **Cc (Can't Compress)** is set automatically by the server. This attribute indicates that the file has been left uncompressed because the savings in disk space would be insufficient if it were compressed.

Disk Controller Considerations

The speed of disk access on the server depends heavily on the type of drive and controller used. The main types of disk drive are IDE (Integrated Drive Electronics) and SCSI (Small Computer Systems Interface). While IDE drives are most commonly used in PCs, SCSI devices are better suited for NetWare servers. SCSI is a reliable, intelligent protocol and allows multiple drives—up to 16 with the latest SCSI-2 devices.

High-end SCSI controllers include such features as a built-in cache, bus mastering, and PCI or VESA local bus interfaces. By taking advantage of these devices, you can streamline disk performance on your network.

Using Turbo FAT Indexing

The File Allocation Table (FAT) keeps track of each file on the volume and lists the blocks that the file occupies. Randomly accessed files that are added to frequently can be spread across many different blocks on the disk, which can slow access.

To alleviate this, NetWare includes turbo FAT indexing. When a file is randomly accessed and has more than 64 FAT entries, a turbo FAT is created for the file. This is an index of the location of blocks for that file only. Because the file has its own index, it can be quickly accessed.

The turbo FAT is loaded into memory when the file is accessed. A single SET parameter, SET Turbo FAT Re-Use Wait Time, controls how long the turbo FAT is kept in memory, in case the file is accessed again. This value defaults to about five minutes.

Review

Several details of the installation process were introduced in this chapter. These include planning the server, managing the DOS partition, and managing and optimizing the server.

Planning the Server

Before you even install a NetWare 4.11 server, you should make certain design considerations, including the following, which simplify the network design:

- Users should log into the server that contains the resources they need.

- If users use other servers, locate them near the servers they log into. Accessing resources that are on a server several hops away can take a long time.

- Whenever possible, use the same hardware and software for clients—network software, network cards, and the workstations themselves. This makes troubleshooting a breeze.

- If a certain group of users, such as CAD users, uses high amounts of network bandwidth, keep them on their own segment of the network.

Depending on the needs of the company and the users, you may wish to improve fault tolerance in these areas:

■ Use disk mirroring (SFT I), disk duplexing (SFT II), or redundant servers (SFT-III). These systems provide high levels of fault tolerance but may exceed your budget.

■ Use redundant network cables when possible, in case a connection is lost.

■ Use UPS (uninterruptible power supplies) on the server and on any critical workstations.

■ Run virus protection software on the server and workstations.

■ Plan a strategy for backing up network files, and test backup hardware and software to ensure that it works.

Maximize performance of the network by following these tips:

■ Determine a baseline, or typical performance, for the network.

■ Use bridges and filters to keep data from being sent unnecessarily.

■ If much routing is needed, consider using a dedicated router rather than your server.

■ Use standard protocols, such as IPX and TCP/IP.

Optimizing the Server

It is important to monitor server and network performance in order to detect problems before they become severe. You can also optimize and streamline your network using SET commands and other settings. The major areas that affect performance are memory and CPU, disk access, and network communication.

Memory and CPU Performance

NetWare 4.11 uses sophisticated *memory management* techniques. Memory is divided into 4KB blocks called *pages*. These pages are *allocated*, or made available, for each NLM or other application that requires memory. These pages may not be in a single area of memory, but the application sees them as one block.

When an NLM or system program starts, it is given an *allocation pool* of memory based on an estimate of the memory it will require while running. When the application requests memory, it is used from this pool and returned to it when it is no longer in use. Because each application uses its own memory pool, memory can be easily managed.

When an application no longer needs an area of memory, it is returned to the system, or *deallocated*. A periodic *garbage collection* process finds these areas of memory and returns them to the main memory pool, allowing them to be used by other applications.

CPU Performance   The CPU speed and type of the server can also affect system performance. You can use the SPEED command to determine whether your server is operating at the optimum speed. In addition, the Scheduling Information screen in the MONITOR utility shows you if a particular NLM is using a large part of the CPU's resources.

Disk Performance

The speed of disk access on NetWare volumes also affects the speed of the server and the network. Areas relating to disk access include cache buffers, disk controllers, turbo FAT indexing, file compression, and block suballocation.

NetWare sets aside a certain amount of RAM as *cache buffers*, which are used to hold information from the disk drive and to avoid using the disk quite as much. You can view statistics relating to cache buffers in MONITOR; several SET commands allow you to optimize their use.

Suballocation and Compression   The *block suballocation* feature of NetWare 4.11 divides the blocks used for disk storage into portions as small as 512 bytes, allowing for more efficient use of disk space. This eliminates the space wasted by very small files and by files that use a fractional block. Block suballocation is enabled individually for each volume and can be changed only when the volume is created. It can also be controlled for individual files and directories using file attributes.

The *file compression* feature allows files that are not currently in use to be compressed. When a file has not been accessed for several days, it is compressed into a temporary file. If the file is significantly smaller, it replaces the original file.

File compression is enabled by default for each volume. You cannot change the setting without re-creating the volume. You can use file attributes to disable compression for individual files and directories or to specify files or directories to be compressed each time they are written to. You can also use a SET command to prevent any files from being compressed.

Other Factors   The disk controller and drive type used affect disk performance. IDE drives are commonly used, but SCSI drives are more suited to a NetWare server. High-end 32-bit (PCI or VESA local bus) disk controllers should be used whenever possible for optimum performance.

The *turbo FAT indexing* feature provides an extra index for files that use more than 64 different areas of the disk. This makes access to the file more efficient. The turbo FAT is kept in the server's RAM while the file is being accessed. Only randomly accessed files can be indexed with the turbo FAT.

PART

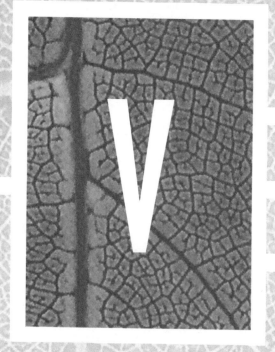

V

CONCLUSION

CHAPTER

20

The Current State of Networking

Congratulations! If you've been reading this book in order, you have covered a lot of territory. There's quite a bit of information to learn and remember, so before going in for the tests, review the appropriate chapters again, and complete the practice questions at the end of each chapter and on the CD-ROM that comes with this book. Be sure to read the information about the CNA programs in the introduction to this book, and check out the learning tools, also on the CD-ROM that comes with this book.

To conclude this book, we're going to take a closer look at network use in the real world. How many networks are out there? How many CNAs are currently in the workforce? What does the job market look like for aspiring CNAs? This chapter should give you a good idea of what to expect in your travels as a CNA. In the next chapter, we'll look at trends and technologies that will shape the future of networking.

NOTE

All of the information in this chapter is current as of the date of this writing. Computer and networking technology changes very quickly. Because of this, we highly recommend that you subscribe to a few PC and network magazines to keep yourself knowledgeable about current conditions, and about what the future may hold. *InfoWorld*, *Network World*, and *LAN Times* are a few good ones. You may be a network expert now, but if you ignore the changes in technology and industry, you'll quickly find yourself out of date (and, possibly, out of a job).

Network Statistics

We've been talking about networks throughout this book. Networks range from LANs to MANs to WANs, and use a vast array of technologies, topologies, and network operating systems. It would be simple if all the networks used NetWare 4.11, but there are actually a wide variety of network operating systems in use. The information we've gathered here should give you some idea of what to expect if you're hired to work on a network.

An important point to keep in mind is that not everyone is using the latest technology. Many corporations have tight budgets, and both users and administrators often avoid change—if it works, why fix it? You will still find many networks using NetWare 3.1x, and even earlier versions of NetWare. In some cases, your job will be to upgrade these to NetWare 4.11. Many companies, however, would prefer to keep that old network running as long as it will last.

How Many Networks Are There?

In the past several years, networks have grown from a budding innovation to a multimillion-dollar industry. There are an estimated 1.5 million networks in use in the United States, and this number is constantly rising. It is becoming cheaper and easier to set up a network, and most companies with five or more PCs now have a network of some sort connecting them.

Network Topologies

As for the type of network topologies used (the wiring and protocols used for network communication), Ethernet is the clear winner. Other topologies used include ARCnet Token Ring, and FDDI. These topologies are explained in detail in the following sections.

Ethernet

The Ethernet standard was developed by Xerox, Intel, and Digital Equipment Corporation. The first version was produced in the 1960s, and the current standard, Ethernet 2.0, was developed in 1982. It is the most common network topology used. Estimates of Ethernet use range from 60 to 90 percent of all networks in the world. There are believed to be at least 1 million Ethernet nodes around the world. (They're not all hooked together, of course.)

Ethernet uses either coaxial cable or unshielded twisted pair cable (thinnet). Ethernet can be used with thick coax cable (thicknet) and fiber optic cable. Older networks typically use thin coax, or 10base2. This can be fun to troubleshoot because coaxial cabling works like old-fashioned Christmas tree lights: If one node is disconnected, the entire network goes down. The newer standard, 10baseT, uses independent connections between each workstation and a hub. If a workstation is disconnected, it has no effect on the other stations.

The maximum speed for Ethernet is 10Mbps. In the real world, speed will usually be slower than that, due to network cards, PC processing power, and delay as data is transmitted through the hub. Nevertheless, it provides a definite advantage over ARCnet, which is typically limited to 2.5Mbps. A standard for *Fast Ethernet* is emerging; it allows speeds of up to 100Mbps using Category 5 twisted pair cable. You'll learn more about that in the next chapter.

In terms of usability and reliability, there's a big difference between the topologies used with Ethernet. 10base2 (thinnet) can be unreliable and difficult to troubleshoot. In contrast, the 10baseT standard is probably the easiest network type to troubleshoot. Unfortunately, a majority of Ethernet networks use the older thinnet wiring. If you get to make a choice, stick to 10baseT.

ARCnet

ARCnet (Attached Resources Computer Network) was developed by Datapoint Corporation in the late 1970s. It was a very popular standard for some time, but has recently been eclipsed by Ethernet.

Although ARCnet has few advantages for new networks, it is used by a large number of older networks that are still in use. ARCnet, like Ethernet, can use a variety of cabling standards. It typically uses coaxial cable but can use twisted pair if the equipment supports it. Since most of the existing ARCnet networks are old, coax cable is very common.

ARCnet operates at a maximum speed of 2.5Mbps, and in practical terms 50–60 percent of that is typical. Thus, it pales by comparison to Ethernet. However, the speed is largely dependent on the number of nodes; for smaller networks, it runs reasonably fast. Also, there are high-speed alternatives to ARCnet: ARCnet Plus, which operates at 20Mbps, and TCNS, a proprietary standard from Thomas Conrad Corp. which allows speeds up to 100Mbps over standard ARCnet coaxial cable, fiber-optic cable, or twisted pair.

ARCnet networks are a bit more difficult to configure and troubleshoot than Ethernet 10baseT, chiefly because each workstation must be given a unique node number, usually set by a DIP switch in the network card. However, they're still much easier than 10base2.

ARCnet is not very practical for new networks, largely because of its high cost and lack of support. But for the next few years at least, you shouldn't be surprised to find yourself supporting an ARCnet network.

Token Ring

The Token Ring standard was developed by the IEEE, but didn't become popular until IBM made a revised version of the standard. It works well for high-traffic networks, and it is widely used in systems that need to link NetWare networks with IBM mainframes. It is not as common as Ethernet, but it is used in many companies.

The original Token Ring specification allowed speeds of 1 to 4Mbps. IBM's version allows speeds up to 16Mbps. The cable types are defined by IBM standards, and include shielded twisted pair (STP), unshielded twisted pair (UTP), and fiber optic cable. Multi-station access units (MAUs) are used as hubs to connect nodes to the Token Ring network.

Token Ring networks are highly reliable, because nodes are constantly checking on each other. When a node goes down, you should be able to easily tell which one it is. Also, although the name is "Ring," Token Ring uses a star topology; this means one node's problems can't affect any others. There are some considerations specific to Token Ring, but in general it's easy to work with.

FDDI

FDDI, or Fiber Distributed Data Interface, is a standard designed around fiber-optic cable and high-speed connections. It has some amazing capabilities: the network can operate at speeds of up to 100Mbps; up to 1,000 nodes can be included in the network; and network connections can be as far as 62 miles (100 kilometers) apart.

These capabilities don't come without a price. FDDI network cards and hubs are expensive, and fiber optic cable costs as much as 10 times the price of good quality twisted pair cable. Thus, FDDI is only used when it's required—in networks that require high speeds, large amounts of nodes, or long distances between nodes.

Because of these high costs, and the fact that FDDI is a relatively new standard, this is not a common network configuration. You will usually only see it in large corporations and in high-tech areas such as CAD and data acquisition. In addition, FDDI is often used as a network backbone, connecting multiple networks and multiple buildings.

FDDI is extremely reliable and can survive in situations where other networks would easily fail. However, you may find it hard to work with because of the difficulty of wiring (and purchasing) the fiber optic cable.

NetWare Versions

With all of the advantages of NetWare 4.11 you've been reading about, you would expect everyone to use it—but at the moment, that's not the case. NetWare 3.1*x* is still more widely used. Here are the versions of NetWare you can expect to see in the real world.

NetWare 3.1*x*

NetWare gained its current popularity as a result of NetWare version 3.11. This version introduced several enhancements to the NetWare operating system, including optimization for the 386 (or better) processor, and support for many more users, more memory, and more disk storage. NetWare 3.12, introduced to correct some of the deficiencies and bugs in NetWare 3.11, includes several features created for NetWare 4, including the DOS requester and the new menu system.

While NetWare 4.1 has grown to comprise over 10 percent of existing networks, NetWare 3.1*x* is still much more common, with between 50 and 60 percent of all networks worldwide.

Although Novell is still selling NetWare 3.12, they are now encouraging the use of NetWare 4.11, as it costs less than NetWare 3.1*x*, and includes all the features you've read about in this book—NDS, auditing, and so on. Although it has not been officially announced, Novell will most likely stop selling and supporting NetWare 3.1*x* some time in the next year or two.

NetWare 2.*x* and Earlier Versions

NetWare 2.*x* was, at one time, the most popular network operating system worldwide. There are still quite a few companies that haven't upgraded, so don't be surprised if you run into a NetWare 2.*x* server here and there. Although much of the functionality is the same, NetWare 2.*x* does not include all of the features of 3.11—not to mention 4.11. It does not include MHS, ODI support, or disk mirroring, among other things. It also has much lower limits on the amount of users, the amount of disk storage, and the amount of memory.

For some companies, the cost of upgrading from NetWare 2.*x* may be too high for their budgets. NetWare 2.*x* was capable of running on a 286 machine, so a new machine must often be purchased to run Net-Ware 3 or 4. However, the number of 2.*x* users is decreasing steadily. There is one very compelling reason to upgrade—Novell no longer sells or supports NetWare 2.*x*. Many companies find themselves forced to upgrade when they experience a major network problem.

NetWare 4.0, 4.01, and 4.02

Before NetWare 4.1, Novell presented NetWare 4 as an enterprise networking system—specifically designed for large, multi-location networks, with features such as NDS. NetWare 4.0 was the first version of this system and was not trusted by many administrators—and for good reason. It had many bugs and was difficult to work with. These problems were gradually corrected in NetWare 4.01 and Net-Ware 4.02, which Novell provided as free upgrades to those who had bought NetWare 4.0.

With NetWare 4.1, Novell resolved the remaining problems associated with NetWare 4.02. For example, NetWare 4.02 had no way to move or delete an entire container object and its contents; this can now be done from PARTMAN or the Partition Manager utility in NetWare Administrator as discussed in Chapter 11. NetWare 4.1 is now practical (and affordable) for all networks, large and small.

If you run into a NetWare 4.0, 4.01, or 4.02 network, recommend an upgrade to NetWare 4.11 as soon as possible. There are still many bugs that can cause serious problems for your network. Also, running NetWare 4.11 in the same Directory tree as earlier versions can cause corruption of NDS data.

NetWare 4.1

This brings us to NetWare 4.1, considered by Novell to be a multi-purpose network environment for practically everybody. Although the earlier versions of NetWare 4 were not very popular, NetWare 4.1 is now used in over 10 percent of the networks in the world. With the release of the latest version, 4.11, this is expected to increase.

NetWare 4.11 and IntranetWare

The latest version, NetWare 4.11—formerly known by the code name Green River—was released in mid-1996. This version added some important new features. Although originally available by itself, Net-Ware 4.11 is now sold as part of IntranetWare, Novell's solution for Internet servers and company-wide intranets. The IntranetWare package includes several Internet-related utilities that integrate with NetWare.

Other Network Operating Systems

Other popular Network Operating Systems were introduced in Chapter 1. You might run into any number of them in your career. One to watch out for in particular is Windows NT 4.0—it includes many of the features of NetWare 4.11, and is gaining in the market. There have even been predictions that it will overtake NetWare 4.1 in the next five years. Of course, in this industry, almost anything can happen in five years.

The State of Computers

Let's take a look now at the workstations that are found on networks. These range from 8088 systems that boot from floppies (honestly!) to top-of-the-line Pentium Pro multimedia workstations. As you might have guessed, not all companies have moved to the latest and greatest workstations. The next sections should give you an idea of what to expect.

An Overview of PC Technologies

The old NetWare 3.1*x* CNA program included a test called DOS/Microcomputer Concepts. Since basic knowledge of computers is now being taught as early as elementary school, Novell no longer requires this test. It is a good idea to have an understanding of PC concepts and history, though, so here's a quick overview of the concepts.

Basic PC Components

A PC includes the following basic components:

- **A motherboard,** which includes:

  - The CPU (Central Processing Unit)—also called the processor—is the heart of the PC. The CPUs used in PC-compatible machines are usually manufactured by Intel Corp. These range from the early 8086 and 8088 to the latest Pentium and Pentium Pro.

  - The memory (RAM, or Random Access Memory)

  - The BIOS (Basic Input/Output Services)

- **Controller cards,** which may include the following:

  - A disk controller, which allows the PC to communicate with disk drives.

  - An I/O (Input/Output) controller, which provides one or more serial ports, used for communications, and parallel ports, usually used for printers.

  - A NIC (Network Interface Card), which allows the PC to communicate with servers on the network.

- **Storage devices,** including hard disk drives, floppy disk drives, and tape backup drives.

- **A case** and **power supply** to hold the PC together and power the components.

- **A monitor** to send output to the user.

- **A keyboard** to receive input from the user.

Microprocessors (CPUs)

Although Pentium processors and their successor, the new Pentium Pro or P6, are the latest processors, not everyone uses them—or needs them. Practically speaking, a 486/33 or higher processor can be used for just about any application, and even a 386 is usable for DOS-based applications. Nevertheless, you'll find many companies trying the nearly impossible—running Windows applications from the network using a 386, or even a 286. It may work, but it will be very slow.

Statistically, 486 machines are the most common workstations in corporate use, but there are still a great many 386 (and lower) machines out there. Some applications don't need anything better, and some companies aren't willing to spend the money to upgrade.

Remember that the latest client software requires a 386 or better processor—so although a 286 can access the network, you won't be able to access NDS from that workstation.

Don't forget Macintosh machines, which are also popular in many companies, particularly those involved with graphic design or art. The Macintosh architecture uses a 68000-series CPU, developed by Motorola. They use a proprietary OS released by Apple. The latest Mac OS is System 7.5. The newest Macintosh machines, called Power Macs, use the Power PC processor, a new processor line from Motorola and IBM. The PowerPC is as fast as a Pentium, and in some cases faster. At this writing, Apple has purchased NeXT, and has plans to create a new Mac OS based on NextStep.

The Data Bus

The PC uses a data bus to communicate with the controller cards. All information that is sent to a disk drive, displayed on the screen, or transmitted over a network has to travel through this bus. The memory and CPU also communicate using the data bus. The standard bus, developed with the advent of the PC, is the ISA bus. Newer standards allow faster communication. These include the following:

- EISA is an enhanced version of ISA, and is often used for network servers.

- VESA local bus is a popular high-performance bus standard. It became very popular as the first high-speed bus available at a reasonable price. Inexplicably, it is not well supported by NetWare or by network cards.

- PCI is the latest bus innovation, and is well-supported by NetWare and by network cards. The PCI bus is much faster than VESA, and allows full 32-bit communication between I/O cards and the motherboard.

- PCMCIA, or PC Card, is a standard for credit-card sized adapters. These are traditionally used to connect network cards and other peripherals to portable notebook computers. In addition, some new desktop PC models include slots for PC cards.

Operating System Choices

In many ways, the operating system (OS) used on a workstation or stand-alone PC is more important than the hardware. After all, users interact with the OS constantly; they usually don't have to deal with hardware. In fact, in recent years the most common reason for hardware upgrades has been to support the latest and greatest OS.

Selecting an operating system used to be a simple matter of choosing between different versions of DOS. With the advent of Windows and other graphical environments, everything has changed.

We'll now look at the most common operating systems used on network workstations and stand-alone PCs in the corporate world.

MS-DOS

MS-DOS (Microsoft Disk Operating System) was the first operating system provided on IBM PCs. At the time of this writing, the current version is 6.22. This is the last version, as Microsoft is focusing development on graphical systems that do not require DOS. (Technically, there's a version of DOS hidden inside Windows 95, which identifies itself as DOS 7.0. However, it's not currently available by itself.)

You will still see DOS 5.0 on many network workstations, and DOS 3.3 is not uncommon. There are even a few machines here and there, still running DOS 1.0. Most of these machines could benefit from a DOS upgrade. The latest versions are more versatile, include more commands, and can support higher levels of hardware—DOS versions below 4.0, for example, can't access more than 32MB per disk partition.

Other DOS Versions

Other companies have produced Disk Operating Systems as well:

- Digital Research produced DR-DOS. Novell bought DR-DOS 6.0 from them, and later upgraded it and marketed it as Novell DOS 7.0. Novell is no longer in the DOS market.

- IBM has maintained PC-DOS as long as MS-DOS. It was originally a licensed version of MS-DOS, so there are many similarities. The latest version, PC-DOS 7, is more recent than any version of MS-DOS and includes a variety of new features.

Microsoft Windows 3.x

The last great computer revolution came when Microsoft introduced Windows 3.0, and the world became interested in GUI (Graphical User Interface) computing. (Of course, the Macintosh had been available with a powerful GUI—comparable to Windows 95—for years, but Apple simply didn't have the marketing budget of Microsoft.) Microsoft quickly followed up with Windows 3.1, which fixed the bugs in 3.0 and became a fixture in most workplaces. At least half of the computers in use in businesses today are running Windows.

Alternate versions of Windows include Windows for Workgroups, which includes peer-to-peer networking features, and Windows 3.11, a minor upgrade which fixed a few bugs.

Technically, Windows isn't an operating system. It actually runs on top of DOS. The latest version of Windows, known as Windows 95, is an entirely self-contained OS. (Although it does include a DOS command-line interpreter, which identifies itself as DOS 7.0.)

Don't underestimate DOS, as its users still form a significant percentage of corporate computer users, and many of the most popular accounting packages and specialized software run only under DOS. DOS applications usually run much faster than their Windows equivalents will run on much cheaper computers, and seldom crash.

Microsoft Windows 95

At the time of this writing, Microsoft's latest consumer OS, Windows 95, is still going strong. Windows 95 has overtaken Windows 3.1x and is quickly becoming the most popular desktop operating system.

Windows 95 is a true 32-bit, multitasking OS that includes many features not found in Windows 3.1. (Although DOS is still hidden inside it, it's now integrated as a single system.) To take full advantage of Windows 95, you'll need to run 32-bit applications whenever possible.

Microsoft plans to release an updated version of Windows, possibly under the name Windows 97. At the time of this writing, it is expected to be available in early 1998.

Windows NT Workstation

Microsoft's Windows NT Workstation is a client workstation operating system similar to Microsoft Windows—it uses the same user interface as Windows 3.*x*, and can run most Windows applications. The latest version of NT, 4.0, provides user interface elements similar to Windows 95, and can run most Windows 95 applications. Unlike Windows 3.1*x* (or even Windows 95), Windows NT Workstation is a 32-bit, pre-emptive multitasking operating system. Thus, it can run quickly, and communicate with hardware at optimum speeds over high-speed buses such as PCI, and can run just about any application in the background.

Windows NT doesn't offer much of an advantage as a NetWare client. However, Microsoft is working on NetWare support for future versions, which would allow a tight integration between Windows NT (workstation or server) and NetWare 4.1. Novell has already released a Windows NT requester, which allows full client access to NDS.

OS/2 Warp and Warp Connect

IBM's OS/2 was originally Microsoft's attempt to create a new, 32-bit OS in the late '80s. Microsoft decided to abandon the project, and IBM took over. OS/2 is a very robust system. The latest version, OS/2 Warp 3.0, runs Windows applications almost as quickly as Windows itself, and performs extremely well with OS/2 applications. It includes many of the features found in Windows 95, and was available a full year earlier. Unfortunately, due to the stranglehold Microsoft has on the market, there aren't very many OS/2 applications. Nevertheless, it's worth a try.

OS/2 Warp Connect is the latest package from IBM. Although it is more expensive, it includes a full array of network support. It can easily connect with NetWare, Windows NT, and even Windows 95, and also includes tools for Internet support.

Most companies with five or more computers are using a network of some sort. Nevertheless, there are many companies using PCs in stand-alone configurations. In some cases this is a good idea; if each user has a unique set of applications to run, and a unique set of data to work with, it may be practical. However, even the simplest peer-to-peer network, such as those built into Windows for Workgroups or Windows 95, can save a lot of time over inserting and removing disks when users need to share or swap data.

The Job Market for Networking Experts

As a final consideration, let's take a look at the network job situation. As a CNA, you have a wide variety of jobs available—Network Administrator, Network Consultant, LAN Technician. Many jobs require a CNA or CNE, and do not require even a college degree. If you have a degree and a CNA, you can get an even better job. Of course, a CNA won't help you unless you really understand the information and can apply the knowledge in real life. Make sure you practice and understand all of the information covered in this book, rather than simply memorizing it. It's helpful to set up your own network to practice on, or use the one at work. Don't do anything that can take the network down, of course.

Novell's current estimate is that there are over 75,000 CNEs. Although the job market varies widely depending on your local area and other factors, a network administrator job which requires a CNE will typically pay between $25,000 and $65,000 annual salary, with an average near $40,000.

With about 40 million NetWare networks, the number of CNEs and CNAs is surprisingly low. As a result, there is a high demand for knowledgeable network administrators.

NetWare Resellers and Education Centers

There are approximately 30,000 authorized Novell resellers throughout the US and the world. These companies often employ CNEs and CNAs (in fact, the NetWare Gold Authorized Reseller program requires that a company employ a certain amount of CNEs), and a job with one will give you a wide variety of experience with many different networks, and will also be an excellent introduction to the "real world" of networking.

There are currently about 1,700 Novell Authorized Education Centers (NAECs). These centers provide authorized Novell education and can provide you with the testing you will need to complete your CNA and CNE certification. NAEC's employ Certified Novell Instructors (CNIs). The CNI is a higher level of certification than CNE, and requires additional tests. In addition, prospective CNI's must take the official Novell CNE courses and teach classes for evaluation.

Review

This chapter has gone over some of the real world considerations about networking.

In the past several years, networks have grown from a novelty to a multimillion-dollar industry. There are an estimated 1.5 million networks in use in the United States, and this number is constantly growing. It is becoming cheaper and more simple to set up a network, and most companies with five or more PCs now have a network of some sort connecting them.

There are many different network topologies:

- Ethernet, used by about 60 percent of networks

- ARCnet, an older standard which is still widely used

- Token Ring, a reliable but more expensive alternative

- FDDI, an extremely high-speed system using fiber-optic cable

PCs on the network can be set in a variety of configurations, and use a variety of processors, motherboards, and other components. The components of a PC include:

- Motherboard

- Controller cards

- Storage devices

- Case and power supply

- Monitor

- Keyboard

Finally, we've looked at the job market for CNAs and other Net-Ware experts. The market outlook for CNAs seems very bright, as the networking industry continues to grow and embrace NetWare 4 as a premier network operating system. In the next chapter, we'll take all of these considerations one step further and look at what's in store for the future.

CHAPTER

21

What's in the Future for Networking?

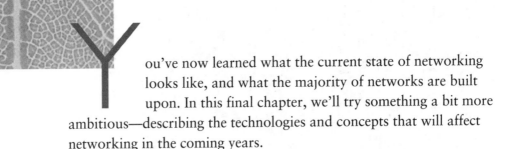

ou've now learned what the current state of networking looks like, and what the majority of networks are built upon. In this final chapter, we'll try something a bit more ambitious—describing the technologies and concepts that will affect networking in the coming years.

We will now take a look into the crystal ball of networking. Like all crystal balls, it's a bit hazy—and sometimes downright misleading. The future isn't easy to predict in an industry that turns itself upside down every five years or so.

Some of the technologies introduced in this chapter are already in use—or will be, by the time you read this book. However, we'll still consider them the future, since they are not in widespread use yet.

New Networking Hardware and Topologies

Although some companies are happy (or at least stubborn) with their vintage 1982 ARCnet networks, there continue to be new innovations in network standards, connections, hardware, and protocols. Here we'll look at the new Fast Ethernet standards, and two revolutionary standards—ISDN and ATM.

Fast Ethernet

The popular Ethernet standard, with a maximum transmission speed of 10 Mbps, is showing its age. One alternative is Fast Ethernet, also known as 100baseT. Fast Ethernet allows speeds up to 100MBPS. This standard was approved by the IEEE in 1995, and is becoming popular for high-speed networks.

There are additional costs to consider when talking about Fast Ethernet. Although Fast Ethernet uses the same type of cabling as Ethernet 10baseT (unshielded twisted pair, category 5) it requires six pairs of wires, rather than the two pairs required by normal Ethernet. Thus, cabling may be more expensive. In addition, hubs and NICs that support Fast Ethernet are currently more expensive when compared with standard Ethernet.

ISDN (Integrated Services Digital Network)

ISDN is a replacement for the conventional phone system. It uses digital lines in place of ordinary analog phone lines. In its basic form, it can support speeds of up to 2Mbps—nothing amazing for a network, but revolutionary for a phone-system link.

Although ISDN is over 10 years old, it hasn't quite caught on in the United States because of the lack of support from local phone companies. (It is used heavily in some parts of Europe.) However, it is gradually growing in popularity and is supported by many phone companies already. Some major U.S. cities already provide ISDN service as an alternative for phone connections in homes and businesses.

The advantage of ISDN over conventional phone systems is that it is digital, and can *multiplex*—several conversations can be carried at once, or a combination of voice, computer data, fax, and even video can be sent at once.

Once ISDN becomes an accepted standard, you can expect it to revolutionize the world of wide-area networking. Branches throughout the world could be connected using inexpensive ISDN service provided by phone companies.

The latest ISDN rage is *broadband ISDN*, which transmits multiple digital signals at once, and can achieve speeds of up to 300Mbps. Although you won't see that speed in your local phone system anytime soon, you may see it in your company's network.

ATM (Asynchronous Transfer Mode)

ATM is a high-speed network architecture based on broadband ISDN and is expected to revolutionize network communications and become a standard in the next few years. It is already in use in some cutting-edge corporate networks.

The current ATM standard offers an effective throughput of 155.52Mbps—over 15 times the speed of Ethernet. Future versions are expected to increase this to 622Mbps, and even further. Speeds up to 2.4Gbps (Gigabits per second) have been tested, and will undoubtedly become available in the next few years.

ATM currently requires fiber-optic cabling, but even that may change. The ATM Working Group, an organization of companies that are working to develop standards, is investigating methods of using the ATM standard on ordinary Category 3 or Category 5 unshielded twisted pair wire.

In addition to the expense of fiber-optic or category 5 cabling, the devices needed to implement ATM on a network—switches and hubs—are currently quite expensive. Over the next few years it should become affordable even for small companies, however.

New Network Operating Systems

NetWare 4.11 is a fine NOS, but there are alternatives, as you learned in Chapter 1 of this book. In this section we'll look at alternatives which are planned for the future, both from Novell and from other companies. The good news is that NetWare 4.11 will probably continue to be the latest version of NetWare for at least the coming year.

Novell: 32 Bits and Beyond

Of course, NetWare plans to continue to upgrade NetWare 4.11. Here are a few of the improvements in store:

- Upgrades to the NetWare 4 file system will allow files and directories to be managed as part of NDS; in other words, there will no longer be a distinction between NDS security and file-system security.

- Novell has announced that it will not release any future versions of NetWare separately. Instead, new versions will be included with the IntranetWare package, as is NetWare 4.11.

- The next releases of NetWare—code named "Moab" and "Park City" (the names of small cities in Utah) may include such features as 64-bit communication with peripherals (assuming hardware supports it) and distributed parallel processing—the ability to run a NetWare server on several machines, each handling part of the load.

Of course, you shouldn't necessarily expect these predictions to come true. Novell has changed strategies before, and you can expect them to continue to adapt to market conditions.

Microsoft: Destination Cairo

As you've probably heard, the big news from Microsoft is code-named Cairo. This is the next major release of Windows NT Server, which is scheduled for release in 1998. It is expected to include the following:

- More compatibility with Windows 95; in fact, Cairo may replace Windows 95 as well as NT.

- Features to integrate NDS with Windows NT

- A directory service, similar to NDS

Microsoft has already released Windows NT 4.0, which has a user interface similar to Windows 95. Their most recent announcements involve the integration of NetWare—the ability to manage a NetWare 4.11 network from within Windows NT, and for the Windows NT server to emulate a NetWare server in some ways. Considering the money Microsoft spends on marketing, expect these products to receive a lot of attention in the months and years ahead. Use of Windows NT Server is expected to increase dramatically over the next few years, with the possibility of eventually eclipsing use of NetWare 4.11.

New PC Hardware

Next, we'll take a look at the future of hardware. Many of these improvements won't help much with a server, but will greatly improve workstation performance. Let's look at the latest innovations in PC systems, Macintosh clients, and the peripherals they use.

Microprocessors

The biggest news in microprocessors at the moment is Intel's sequel to the Pentium—the P6, or as Intel calls it, the Pentium Pro. (Never mind the fact that the "Pent" prefix means 5.) Economical Pentium Pro systems are already available at this writing, although few users really need that kind of speed.

The Pentium Pro performs roughly twice as fast as a Pentium processor of the same clock speed. However, it is optimized for 32-bit applications. This means that you'll need to run a 32-bit operating system, such as Windows 95, and 32-bit applications to see the most improvement. In fact, since portions of Windows 95 are still 16-bit, a Pentium may be faster in some cases (Windows NT Workstation does not have this problem.) Since NetWare is also a 32-bit OS, the P6 also runs well as a NetWare server, although it may be overkill for most networks.

For Macintosh and compatible computers, the latest version of Motorola's PowerPC chip gives new machines a processor that compares to the P6.

Motherboards

Intel has recently begun manufacturing the ATX motherboard, which is now available. These motherboards use a completely different layout than current motherboards. They run cooler, and will fit into a smaller case, while still including a full complement of ISA and PCI slots. These boards also cost less to manufacture and provide easier access to slots, cables, and other connections.

Although not quite so new, the Plug and Play standard is also revolutionizing motherboards. This standard allows you to install drive controllers, LAN cards, and other peripherals, without messing with jumpers, DIP switches, memory addresses, or IRQ settings.

Don't forget everything you learned about setting up network cards yet, though—although most of the new motherboards support the Plug and Play standard, very few network cards and other controllers do at present. In addition, the operating system needs to support the standard. Currently, only Windows 95 supports the standard. Hopefully, a future version of NetWare will include Plug and Play support (it would sure make the Network Technologies CNE test easier to pass).

Disk Storage

Hard drive technology hasn't changed much recently, and no major changes have been announced at this time. However, one change is always occurring: the price decreases. The price for 1GB IDE drives has already dropped below $250, and will probably be under $150 in 1998. SCSI drives are typically a bit more expensive, but not too far behind.

Optical storage devices are also decreasing in price. Writable CD-ROM drives (CD-R) are now available for under $500, and are rapidly becoming less expensive. Other devices are less standard, but allow even more storage.

Finally, you may see floppy disks as we know them disappear—although it won't happen overnight. Economical, high-capacity alternatives are emerging. These include the very popular ZIP drive, from Iomega, which stores 100MB on a disk slightly larger than a 3.5" floppy. The disks cost about $10 apiece. Syquest is marketing the EZDrive as an alternative, with a slightly larger capacity and higher speed. Both Syquest and Iomega are now producing drives, as upper-end alternatives, that store 1GB or more per disk.

Monitors

Although they won't do your server much good, innovations continue in the area of monitors. Monitors as large as 21" are becoming available at a reasonable cost. In addition, desktop LCD monitors are emerging into the market. These are nearly flat devices that display sharp, flicker-free images, similar to the better notebook computer displays. The catch? They're a bit expensive at the moment. The minimum price for such a device is currently about $900. The price will undoubtedly decrease, and these monitors may eventually replace conventional CRT monitors.

New Network Concepts

Not only are there constant improvements in every area of networking technology, there are also entirely new technologies emerging. Sometimes it's hard to keep up with all of the new ideas and proposals, but here are a few hot topics that are making the rounds. One or more of them may be a concern on your network in the future.

Computer Telephony

One of the latest trends, both for network and single-PC applications, is the integration of telephone functions into the computer, otherwise know as *computer telephony*. Imagine answering the phone by clicking a button on your workstation, or receiving voice-mail messages in the same inbox as e-mail messages. This is made possible by a *voice card*, which interfaces between a PC (either a server or workstation) and the phone system. Using these systems, a PC can act as a telephone, a voice-mail system, a fax-on-demand system, or even a multi-line phone system.

There are two standards competing for the telephony market right now. Not surprisingly, these systems are produced by Novell and Microsoft. Novell's standard, TSAPI, provides a standard interface for NetWare NLMs and client software to access voice functions. Microsoft's entry is called TAPI, and provides the same function for Windows 95 and Windows NT. Which one becomes a standard in the future will depend on the application software that becomes available. Several telephony applications are currently available, but none have yet become popular.

While TAPI focuses on workstation operating systems, TSAPI is based on a NetWare server and telephone switch. This means that TSAPI may be more practical for large-scale corporate use, but a TAPI application may find its way to your home PC (in fact, Microsoft has included one with Windows 95).

Application Servers

While a file server allows for printer and file sharing, another type of server is being used more and more frequently in modern networks: the application server. This is a type of server that is used to run a "back end" for applications, such as accounting software. This greatly reduces the processing power required at the client workstation.

Popular application servers at this time include NetWare 4.11, UNIX, and Windows NT. Many networks are beginning to use Windows NT as an application server on NetWare 4.11 networks. Novell's preferred application server solution was UnixWare, but Novell is now discontinuing that product. Instead, Novell will focus on enhancing NetWare 4.11's features as an application server.

Internet Connectivity

You've probably heard a lot about the Internet recently. Although it's been around for over 10 years, the Internet has gained enormous popularity in the last few years. As the popularity and importance of the Internet increases, the process of providing a connection between your network and the Internet will become more and more important.

Right now, the most widely used feature of the Internet is e-mail. Using MHS, Groupwise, or almost any other e-mail system and a piece of software and hardware called a *gateway*, you can send messages to, and receive messages from, other people connected to the Internet. Because UNIX is still the most common operating system for Internet nodes, gateways typically operate using TCP/IP.

The World Wide Web (WWW) is the most popular Internet area, as well as the fastest growing. WWW servers can make hypertext information—similar to the Windows help system or Novell's Dyna-Text documentation—available to people in every corner of the world. Anyone with an Internet connection and a Web browser—software that allows Web access—can view your documents, called *Web pages*.

Speaking of the similarity between the Web's hypertext system and that of DynaText, a good example is the fact that Novell has made the DynaText online documentation for NetWare 4.11 available as a Web document. It provides searching, linking, and graphics, similar to the DynaText viewer. If you have a Web browser, try this address: http://www.netware.com/.

Traditionally, Web pages are provided by placing them on a UNIX machine that has an Internet connection and acts as a web server (technically, an HTTP, or HyperText Transfer Protocol, server). However, NetWare 4.11's simplified TCP/IP support makes it easy to attach a NetWare server directly to the Internet, and the NetWare Web Server, part of the IntranetWare package, allows it to act as a web server. Over the next several years, a good portion of the UNIX Web servers will be gradually replaced by NetWare and Windows NT (which also has a number of web servers available, as do Windows 3.*x*, Windows 95, and Macintosh systems).

Video Conferencing

If you've dreamed of the day when you could look at your bosses on your computer screen and have a conversation with them in real time, you're in luck—video conferencing isn't science fiction anymore. You may never have to leave your desk again...unless you're the one who has to maintain the video conferencing system.

AT&T actually introduced a video conferencing system in the 1970s that would work over ordinary phone lines, but it was clumsy and produced pictures of extremely poor-quality. The video conferencing systems of today are getting close to the reality of a picture that looks as good as your TV. Connections can be made over normal phone lines. In addition, new network standards like ATM make it possible to send digital video over the LAN, and ISDN may eventually improve the quality of pictures going over phone lines.

Recently, AT&T and other vendors, such as Intel, established a standard for video conferencing systems. This means that systems from different vendors will actually be able to communicate with one another. Thanks to this, and the increasing quality of PC processing and video, video conferencing is starting to become downright practical. Just wait—you'll see the day when the CEO can appear in a window on your computer, look at your desk, and criticize you for not working hard enough.

CNA Certification and the Job Market

Innovations in the world of networking are not limited to strictly technological aspects of the field. Novell continues to update the CNA program to reflect the newest versions of NetWare, as well as the current state of technology. Of course, just being a CNA won't qualify you for most jobs anymore—you'll need to be experienced with NetWare, and possibly with other NOSs.

One additional certification you may consider is the MCSE certification for Microsoft's Windows NT. With the growing popularity of Windows NT, this will soon be as useful as a CNA for the job market. Regardless of the certifications that you have, one thing is certain: The network market is growing steadily. New networks are being installed daily, and there will always be a need for professionals to maintain them.

To keep yourself ready to enter the job market, be sure to keep up with the latest network developments. Network administration is one area where you can't finish learning and then just work comfortably for 10 years.

Review

This chapter has explained some of the latest innovations in networking—both those that are available now, and those that have been announced for the near future. We've done our best to be accurate, but the future is never completely predictable; be sure to read magazines to keep up with current developments.

Here's a quick recap of what we've covered in this chapter:

- **Improvements to network topologies** include several competing standards for Fast Ethernet, ISDN (Integrated Services Digital Network), and ATM (Asynchronous Transfer Mode).

- **New network operating systems** from Novell and Microsoft will include more features, and provide increased compatibility with competing products.

- **New concepts in networking** include embedded systems, computer telephony, application servers, Internet connectivity, and video conferencing.

- **CNA and CNE certification**—and certification for other systems—will continue to be an important part of qualifying for a job in the network industry.

Well, you've reached the end of this book. But as you've read in this chapter, we are nowhere near the end of computing or networking. Things change almost daily, and it may be hard to keep up—but it's worth the effort. Networks will become more and more important to companies in the future, and with this knowledge you can be a part of that future.

APPENDIX

A

Answers to
CNA Practice Test Questions

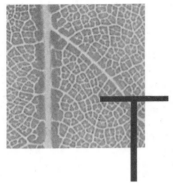

his appendix contains the answers to the CNA practice test questions that appear in Chapters 5 through 10.

Chapter 5

1. NetWare Directory Services (NDS):

   A. Stores information for each network resource

   B. Uses a tree-like structure

   C. Refers to each resource as an object

   D. All of the above

   Answer: D

2. Which of the following is *not* a benefit of NDS?

   A. Better organization of resources

   B. Fault tolerance

   C. An efficient file system

   D. Increased security

   Answer: C

3. The type of organization NDS uses is:

   A. Server-centric

B. Network-centric

C. Noncentralized

D. Resource-centric

Answer: B

4. The three basic types of NDS objects are:

A. Container, Leaf, [Root]

B. Properties, Values, Objects

C. Organization, Organizational Unit, Country

D. Typeless, typeful, distinguished

Answer: A

5. The [Root] object:

A. Can be located anywhere in the Directory

B. Contains all objects in the Directory

C. Can be deleted when it is no longer needed

D. All of the above

Answer: B

6. Container objects include:

A. Country, Group, Organization

B. Organization, [Root], Group

C. Country, Organization, Organizational Unit

D. Organization and Group

Answer: C

7. Leaf objects include:

   A. User, Group, Organization

   B. User, Printer, Resource

   C. User, Group, Printer

   D. All container objects, plus User

   Answer: C

8. NDS properties:

   A. Are the same for all objects

   B. Are used by container objects only

   C. Are all optional

   D. Can be assigned values

   Answer: C

9. An object's name in its context is:

   A. Its distinguished name

   B. The relative distinguished name

   C. Its common name

   D. Its context name

   Answer: A

10. An object's context is:

   A. Any object in the same container

   B. The container object it resides in

C. Its common name

D. The name of the Directory tree

Answer: B

11. A relative distinguished name (RDN)

    A. Begins at the [Root] object

    B. Begins at the current context

    C. Begins with the first Organization object

    D. Uses the default system context (DSC)

    Answer: B

12. Which is an example of a *typeless* name?

    A. CN=FRED.OU=ACCT.O=ORION

    B. CN=FRED

    C. FRED.ACCT.ORION

    D. CN=FRED.ACCT.O=ORION

    Answer: C

13. The protocol usually used with NetWare is:

    A. VLM

    B. IPXODI

    C. IPX

    D. TCP/IP

    Answer: C

14. In which order does data flow through Client 32 components?

   A. CLIENT32, LSL, IPX, LAN driver

   B. LSL, IPX, LAN driver, CLIENT32

   C. IPX, LSL, CLIENT32, LAN driver

   D. LAN driver, LSL, IPX, CLIENT32

   Answer: D

15. Which program represents the main NetWare Client?

   A. IPX.NLM

   B. CLIENT32.NLM

   C. LSLC32.NLM

   D. CNE2000.NLM

   Answer: B

16. Until you log in, the only files you can access are:

   A. LOGIN.EXE and client software

   B. All files in the PUBLIC directory

   C. All files in the LOGIN directory

   D. All files on the SYS: volume

   Answer: C

17. Which is the correct order of NetWare file system organization?

   A. Directory, file, volume

   B. Volume, directory, file

C. File, volume, directory

D. File, directory, NDS

Answer: B

18. The NDIR utility:

   A. Must be used in place of the DOS DIR command

   B. Lists files in the current directory

   C. Lists information about NDS objects

   D. All of the above

   Answer: B

19. The NLIST utility:

   A. Can be used to list volumes or other NDS objects

   B. Displays a list of files in the current directory

   C. Is another name for NDIR

   D. Was used in NetWare $3.1x$

   Answer: A

20. Which is the correct syntax to map drive F: to the SYS:PUBLIC directory:

   A. MAP F: SYS\PUBLIC

   B. MAP SYS:PUBLIC /D=F

   C. MAP SYS:PUBLIC=F:

   D. MAP F:=SYS:PUBLIC

   Answer: D

21. Which backup strategy takes the longest time to back up data?

   A. Incremental

   B. Differential

   C. Full

   D. Partial

   Answer: C

22. Which backup strategy takes the longest time to restore data?

   A. Incremental

   B. Differential

   C. Full

   D. Partial

   Answer: A

Chapter 6

1. The two utilities used to manage NDS objects are:

   A. NetWare Administrator and NWADMIN

   B. NETADMIN and NetWare Administrator

   C. SYSCON and NETADMIN

   D. NDSADMIN and NWMANAGE

   Answer: B

2. The Create function in NWADMIN is found under:

   A. The File menu

B. The Function menu

C. The Actions menu

D. The Object menu

Answer: D

3. The required properties when creating a User object are:

A. Login name and address

B. First name and last name

C. Login name and last name

D. Network address and first name

Answer: C

4. A user template:

A. Is created for each user

B. Specifies defaults for new User objects

C. Lets you change all User objects at once

D. Lets you control access rights

Answer: B

5. The menu item used to display property values is:

A. Properties

B. Values

C. Attributes

D. Details

Answer: D

6. The Move option can move which types of objects?

A. User, Server, and Printer

B. Container objects only

C. Leaf objects only

D. User objects only

Answer: C

7. NETADMIN can be used to manage:

A. User objects only

B. Only the basic NDS objects

C. All NDS objects

D. Bindery objects

Answer: C

8. The Group object can group users:

A. In the same container only

B. In different containers only

C. In the same or different containers

D. In the [Root] container only

Answer: C

9. To assign a user to an Organizational Role, you use the:

A. User's Role property

B. Organizational Role's Member property

C. User's Profile property

D. Organizational Role's Occupant property

Answer: D

10. The NetWare Server object:

    A. Can be created when you wish to install a new server

    B. Is created automatically when the server is installed

    C. Is deleted automatically when the server is removed

    D. Can be used to add logins to the server

    Answer: B

11. The Alias object:

    A. Represents, or points to, another object

    B. Is created whenever an object is deleted

    C. Can be used instead of the User object

    D. All of the above

    Answer: A

12. Which is the correct MAP command for the Directory Map DATA?

    A. MAP F:=DATA:

    B. MAP F:=DATA.MAP

    C. MAP F:=DATA

    D. MAP F: DATA /DM

    Answer: C

Chapter 7

1. The two types of NetWare 4.11 trustee rights are:

   A. File system security and NDS security

   B. File system security and object rights

   C. Trustee rights and object rights

   D. All properties and selected properties

   Answer: A

2. Which of the following can NOT be a trustee:

   A. Organization

   B. User

   C. Organizational Role

   D. File

   Answer: D

3. The File Scan right:

   A. Allows you to copy files

   B. Allows you to list files in a directory

   C. Allows you to read the contents of files

   D. Allows you to search for a file

   Answer: B

4. The IRF affects:

   A. Security equivalence

B. Inherited rights

C. Explicit assignments

D. All of the above

Answer: B

5. File attributes:

A. Are always set by NetWare itself

B. Are always set by the user

C. Cannot be changed

D. Give a file certain behaviors

Answer: D

6. You can manage file system security with:

A. NetWare Administrator

B. NETADMIN

C. SYSCON

D. SECURE

Answer: A

7. The IRF lists:

A. Rights to be blocked

B. Rights to be granted

C. Rights allowed to be inherited

D. Rights that cannot be inherited

Answer: C

8. The list of trustees for an object is stored in:

A. The Trustees property

B. The ACL

C. The Trustee database

D. The Trustee file

Answer: B

9. The two types of rights in NDS are:

A. Object rights and file rights

B. Object rights and property rights

C. All Properties and Selected Properties

D. Object rights and the IRF

Answer: B

10. Inherited rights can be blocked with:

A. The IRF

B. An explicit assignment

C. Both A and B

D. None of the above

Answer: C

11. Explicit security equivalences can be granted with:

A. Container occupancy

B. Group, Organizational Role, Security Equal

C. Group, container occupancy

D. All of the above

Answer: B

12. Which of the following does NOT affect effective NDS rights:

   A. Explicit rights

   B. Inherited rights

   C. Rights given to child objects

   D. Rights given to parent objects

   Answer: C

13. The [Public] Trustee:

   A. Assigns rights to all users when logged in

   B. Assigns rights to anyone attached to the network

   C. Assigns rights to ADMIN only

   D. Assigns rights to the file system only

   Answer: B

Chapter 8

1. Which is the correct order for login script execution:

   A. User, container, default, profile

   B. Container, user, profile, or default

   C. Container, profile, user, or default

   D. Container, default, user, or profile

   Answer: C

2. The container login script is executed:

   A. For each container the user is in

   B. For the user's parent container

   C. For the profile container only

   D. For the [Root] container only

   Answer: B

3. Which is a correct MAP command in a login script?

   A. MAP F:=SYS:APPS

   B. #MAP F:=SYS:APPS

   C. MAP NEXT SYS:APPS

   D. MAP F:=SYS

   Answer: A

4. The INCLUDE command:

   A. Exits the login script and starts another

   B. Executes another script, then returns

   C. Adds commands to a login script

   D. Adds a login script to the Profile object

   Answer: B

5. Which of the following is NOT a valid comment:

   A. REM Do not change this script

   B. ***Do not change this script***

c. # Do not change this script

d. ;Do not change this script

Answer: C

6. To use a DOS program in a login script:

A. Include the name of the program only

B. Include # and the name of the program

c. Include ; and the name of the program

D. Place the program in an INCLUDE file

Answer: B

7. The two components of NAM are:

A. NAL and NAM

B. NAL and NMENU

c. NAL and Application Objects

D. NAL and Windows 95

Answer: C

8. NAL runs under which operating systems?

A. Windows 95 only

B. Windows 3.1 or Windows 95

c. DOS or Windows 3.1

D. DOS, Windows 3.1, or Windows 95

Answer: B

9. Application objects are created using:

   A. NAM

   B. NWADMIN

   C. APCONFIG

   D. NAL

   Answer: B

10. To configure NAL as the Windows shell, which of these files is modified?

    A. SYSTEM.INI

    B. WIN.INI

    C. SHELL.INI

    D. SHELL.INF

    Answer: A

11. Which operating system does not have a corresponding Application object?

    A. Windows 95

    B. Windows 3.*x*

    C. OS/2

    D. Windows NT

    Answer: C

12. To give a user access to an application, modify the:

   A. User Object's Application property

   B. Application Object's Association property

   C. Both A and B

   D. None of the above

Answer: C

Chapter 9

1. The NDS objects used for printing are:

   A. Print server, print queue, port driver

   B. Print server, print queue, printer

   C. Printer, print server, port driver

   D. CAPTURE, printer, print server

Answer: B

2. The number of printers controlled by a NetWare 4.11 print server:

   A. Is limited only by the server's memory

   B. Is limited to 16 printers

   C. Is limited to 256 printers

   D. Is limited to 3 parallel printers and 2 serial printers

Answer: C

3. There are three basic types of network printers:

   A. Workstation, server, queue

   B. Workstation, server, directly connected

   C. NDS, bindery, workstation

   D. Dot matrix, laser, daisy wheel

   Answer: B

4. Which is the correct CAPTURE command to capture the LPT2 port to the CHECKS queue?

   A. CAPTURE J=2 P=CHECKS

   B. CAPTURE L=1 B=2 Q=CHECKS

   C. CAPTURE LPT2 P=CHECK_PRINTER

   D. CAPTURE LPT2 Q=CHECKS

   Answer: D

5. The Print Server object:

   A. Is not used in NetWare 4.11

   B. Moves jobs from the print queue to the printer

   C. Moves jobs from the print queue to the port driver

   D. Stores a list of jobs to be printed

   Answer: C

6. To start a workstation printer, you use the _____ program.

   A. RPRINTER

   B. REMOTE

c. WPRINTER

d. NPRINTER

Answer: D

7. Which is the correct order of components when a print job is processed?

   A. CAPTURE, print queue, printer

   B. CAPTURE, print queue, print server, port driver, printer

   C. CAPTURE, port driver, print server, print queue, printer

   D. Port driver, CAPTURE, print queue, print server, printer

   Answer: B

8. CAPTURE can use which LPT ports?

   A. LPT1-3

   B. LPT1-5

   C. Only those you have the hardware for

   D. LPT1-9

   Answer: D

9. The Print Server object:

   A. Is created automatically when the printer is installed

   B. Needs to be created for each printer

   C. Can handle up to 256 printers

   D. Is not needed for most printers

   Answer: C

10. You can stop and continue a print job with which NWADMIN functions?

    A. Pause and play

    B. Pause and resume

    C. Hold and resume

    D. Hold and unhold

    Answer: C

11. The number of printers on the network is limited by:

    A. The print server

    B. The number of ports on the server

    C. The number of queues

    D. Disk storage available

    Answer: A

12. You can CAPTURE to:

    A. A printer or a print server

    B. A printer only

    C. A printer or a queue

    D. A printer or NPRINTER

    Answer: C

Chapter 10

1. Commands that you can use at the server console include:

   A. DOS commands

   B. NLMs and console commands

   C. NLMs only

   D. DOS or NLM commands

   Answer: B

2. The NetWare core operating system does *not* include:

   A. File sharing

   B. NDS

   C. Network Management

   D. Printer sharing

   Answer: C

3. NLMs come from:

   A. Novell

   B. Third parties

   C. Both of the above

   D. None of the above

   Answer: C

4. The two parts of a NPA disk driver are:

   A. NPA and CDA

   B. HAM and CAM

   C. HAM and CDM

   D. NPA and HDM

   Answer: C

5. LAN Driver modules have the extension:

   A. NLM

   B. DRV

   C. LAN

   D. MOD

   Answer: C

6. The command to display configuration information is:

   A. DISPLAY CONFIG

   B. MODULES

   C. CONFIG

   D. VERSION

   Answer: C

7. The command used to prevent logins is:

   A. SET LOGIN = NO

   B. DISABLE LOGIN

c. LOGIN OFF

D. SECURE CONSOLE

Answer: B

8. The two commands needed to bring down the server are:

A. DOWN and QUIT

B. DOWN and RESET

c. DOWN and CLS

D. DOWN and EXIT

Answer: D

9. The key used to switch screens in RCONSOLE is:

A. F3 or F4

B. Alt+Esc

c. Ctrl+Esc

D. Alt+F3 and Alt+F4

Answer: D

10. The two modules you must load to enable remote access are:

A. REMOTE and MONITOR

B. REMOTE and ACCESS

c. RSPX and REMOTE

D. RSPX and RCONSOLE

Answer: C

APPENDIX

B

NetWare Commands Quick Reference

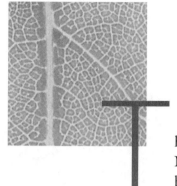

his appendix is intended as a handy reference to the various NetWare 4.11 commands. It is organized into four sections based on the types of commands used in NetWare:

- **Workstation commands** are executed from a DOS workstation and accept parameters on the command line.

- **Menu and Windows utilities** provide a full user interface in DOS or Windows to allow access to available functions.

- **Console commands** can be typed directly at the file server console.

- **Console utilities** (NLMs) can be loaded at the file server with the LOAD command.

This appendix lists only the most common commands that you are likely to use or encounter frequently when managing a NetWare 4.11 network. For a complete reference, see the Novell *Utilities* manual.

Workstation Commands

CAPTURE

Redirects a printer port on the workstation to a print queue or printer on the NetWare 4.11 server. The following example redirects the LPT1 port to the CHECKS print queue:

```
CAPTURE L=1 Q=CHECKS
```

CX

Use this command to change your current NDS context—the NDS container object that will be used by default when searching for objects. For example, this command sets the current context to .O=ADMIN:

```
CX .O=ADMIN
```

FLAG

Allows you to manage file attributes or to display the attributes for an existing file. The FLAG command is followed by a path or filename as well as options to specify attributes to be added or removed. FLAG, by itself, displays the attributes of all files in the current directory. Here are some examples of the FLAG command:

```
FLAG SYS:ETC\DATA +H
```

adds the Hidden attribute to the SYS:ETC\DATA directory.

```
FLAG *.* N
```

sets all files in the current directory to Normal (read/write).

```
FLAG SYS:PUBLIC\FILER.EXE +RO
```

gives the FILER.EXE file the Read Only attribute.

LOGIN

Logs you in to a NetWare 4.11 server or NDS tree. If not specified, LOGIN uses the default server or tree in the workstation's NET.CFG file. The /NS switch can be added to attach to a server without logging out of the current server or tree. The following command logs in the user TED on the tree OAK_TREE:

```
LOGIN OAK_TREE/TED
```

LOGOUT

Ends your current login session and allows another user to log in. By default, you are logged out of all servers. However, you can also log out of just one server, keeping your connection to the others, by specifying the server name:

```
LOGOUT SERVER1
```

MAP

Use this command to map a drive letter, or network drive, to a volume and directory on the server. This command can also be used with Directory Map objects.

```
MAP J:=SYS:APPS\PROGRAM
```

maps the network drive J: to the APPS\PROGRAM directory on the SYS volume.

```
MAP S3:=SYS:PUBLIC
```

maps the third search drive to the PUBLIC directory.

```
MAP K:=WP
```

maps network drive K: to the volume and directory specified by the Directory Map object WP.

NCOPY

Copies files from one directory to another. This command can be used with both local and network directories and can copy entire directory structures.

```
NCOPY C:\DOS\*.* F:\PUBLIC\DOS
```

copies all files in the DOS directory on local drive C: to the PUBLIC\DOS directory on network drive F:.

```
NCOPY C:\*.* /S
```

copies all files on drive C:, including subdirectories, to the current directory.

```
NCOPY F:\BACKUP\*.* C:\ /S/E/V
```

copies all of the files from the BACKUP directory, including subdirectories and empty directories, to drive C: and verifies each file.

NDIR

Lists the files in a directory. This command is similar to the DIR command in DOS but also displays NetWare file attributes and ownership information. NDIR has a wide variety of options that enable you to search for files or list specific types of information. Here are some examples:

```
NDIR
```

lists all files in the current directory, using the default format.

```
NDIR *.* /R
```

displays a list of rights for each file in the current directory.

```
NDIR F:\*.TMP /SUB
```

lists all files with a TMP extension on drive F:, including those in subdirectories.

```
NDIR F:\*.* /SUB /OW EQ SUE.ACCT.STECH
```

lists all files owned by the user SUE on the network drive F:. If the user is in the current context, the full distinguished name is not necessary.

```
NDIR F:\PUBLIC\*.* /CR BEF 03-22-97
```

lists all files in the PUBLIC directory created before March 22, 1997.

NLIST

A general-purpose utility for listing NDS objects. Can be used to list users, servers, or any other type of NDS object or to look for objects with a certain property. Here are several examples:

```
NLIST USER /A
```

lists all users in the current context.

```
NLIST SERVER /B
```

lists all bindery servers.

```
NLIST USER WHERE "GROUP MEMBERSHIP" = ACCTG
```

lists all users who are members of the ACCTG group.

```
NLIST USER SHOW "TELEPHONE NUMBER"
```

lists all user names and their telephone numbers (if defined).

```
NLIST GROUP /S
```

lists all groups defined in the Directory tree.

```
NLIST *
```

lists all objects in the current context.

NPRINT

Allows you to send a text file to a network print queue. For example, the following command sends all files with the TXT extension in the current directory to the LASER1 print queue:

```
NPRINT *.TXT Q=LASER1
```

NPRINTER

Starts the driver for a workstation printer or a remote printer. This program remains in memory to drive the printer until you unload the driver. The following command sets up the LASER1 printer attached to the current workstation:

```
NPRINTER LASER1
```

NVER

Displays NetWare version information, such as the server you are attached to and the revision of client software.

PURGE

Purges deleted files from the current directory, preventing them from being salvaged with the FILER or NWADMIN utilities. The /A switch can be added to purge all files on the server.

```
PURGE *.*
```

purges all deleted files in the current directory.

```
PURGE \*.* /A
```

purges all deleted files on the volume.

RENDIR

Renames a directory. This command can be used on local directories or on the NetWare server. The following command renames the BACKUP directory on the SYS volume and gives it the new name TEMP:

```
RENDIR SYS:BACKUP TEMP
```

RIGHTS

Displays your current rights in a directory of the file system. This command also allows you to grant or revoke rights to a user or to maintain the IRF. Here are a few examples of the RIGHTS command:

RIGHTS VOL1:USERS R W C F /NAME=KRISTEN

gives the user KRISTEN the Read, Write, Create, and File scan rights for the VOL1:USERS directory.

RIGHTS SYS:DATA REM /NAME=JohnS

removes all rights that user JohnS had in the SYS:DATA directory.

RIGHTS SYS:APPS\WP /T

lists all trustees of the SYS:APPS\WP directory.

RIGHTS . R F /F

sets the IRF for the current directory (referred to with a single period) to Read and File scan only.

SEND

Sends a message to a user or group. This is similar to the BROAD-CAST console command.

SEND "Please log out immediately" BOB, SVEN

asks users BOB and SVEN to log out.

SEND "System going down at 3:00" EVERYONE

sends a message to the EVERYONE group.

SEND /A=C

sets your workstation to receive messages only from the console or the system.

WHOAMI

Displays information about your current login session and the server or servers you are attached to.

Menu and Windows Utilities

FILER

A general-purpose utility for managing files and directories in the NetWare file system. Can be used to copy, rename, or delete files; to manage rights to files and directories; to control file attributes; and to salvage deleted files.

NAL (NetWare Application Launcher)

Provides the user with a friendly interface to launch applications. You can manage these applications by creating Application objects in the NWADMIN utility.

NDSMGR (NDS Manager)

A Windows-based utility that allows you to manage partitions and replicas in the NDS database and perform NDS troubleshooting functions. This utility is examined in detail in Chapter 11.

NETADMIN

A DOS utility for managing users and other NDS objects on the network. Can be used to create, rename, or delete objects; grant trustee rights; and manage property values.

NETUSER

Allows you to map drives, capture printers, and send messages to users on the network from a simple menu-based interface.

NWADMIN (NetWare Administrator)

A Windows utility for managing NDS objects. Can be used to create, rename, or delete objects; manage rights to other objects; and control property values. This utility can also manage files and directories in the file system and control NDS partitioning and replication. Chapter 6 is a guide to using the NWADMIN utility.

NMENU

Allows you to create user-friendly menus with specific commands for a user or department. This menu system works only under DOS, and is now rarely used. Chapter 8 explains the new Windows-based menu system, NAM (NetWare Application Manager).

PARTMGR

A DOS utility that allows you to manage partitions and replicas in NDS. This utility is explained fully in Chapter 11.

PCONSOLE

This utility provides a Print Console from which you can control all aspects of printing, including creating printers, print queues, and other NDS printing objects. It also includes a quick setup feature for setting up printers and queues.

PRINTCON

Allows you to manage print job configurations—specific sets of parameters that can be referenced with a quick CAPTURE command.

PRINTDEF

Allows you to define printer commands and forms, which can be used to send special codes to the printer to control print modes.

RCONSOLE

Allows you to establish a connection to the server and access the server console from a DOS workstation. While RCONSOLE is attached to a server, you can use the following key commands:

- **Alt+F1** activates the RCONSOLE Available Options menu. This menu allows you to navigate between screens, view files, and directories on the server, and transfer files to the server.

- **Alt+F2** exits the RCONSOLE utility. You will be asked to confirm your selection.

- **ALT+F3** moves to the next server screen, similar to ALT+ESC at the server console.

- **ALT+F4** moves to the previous server screen.

- **ALT+F5** shows the network address of your workstation.

Console Commands

BIND

Connects a network protocol, such as IPX, to a network adapter driver that you have loaded. For example, to bind the IPX protocol to the NE2000 driver:

```
BIND IPX TO NE2000 NET=1
```

BROADCAST

Sends a message to all users on the system or to a specific user or group. Similar to the SEND workstation utility.

DISABLE LOGIN

Prevents users from logging in to the network. Does not affect those who are already logged in.

DISMOUNT

Dismounts a NetWare volume. This command is necessary if you are removing the volume, changing its parameters, or maintaining it with the VREPAIR utility. For example, to dismount the SYS volume:

```
DISMOUNT SYS
```

DOWN

Brings the server down. This can be followed by the EXIT command to return to DOS or by the RESTART SERVER command to restart the server.

ENABLE LOGIN

Allows login to the server after the DISABLE LOGIN command has been used. Also resets accounts that have been locked by the intruder detection feature.

EXIT

Exits the server and returns to DOS. This can be used only after the DOWN command.

LOAD

Loads a NetWare Loadable Module (NLM) into the server's memory. NLMs serve as device drivers, add additional functions to the system, or allow you to manage the server. For example, this command starts the MONITOR utility:

```
LOAD MONITOR
```

MODULES

Displays a list of the currently loaded modules (NLMs).

MOUNT

Mounts a volume so that it can be used. For example, this command mounts the VOL1 volume:

```
MOUNT VOL1
```

SET

Sets a parameter for server performance. Typing SET by itself lists the available commands. The SERVMAN and MONITOR utilities allow you to manage these parameters in a more user-friendly way.

UNLOAD

Removes an NLM from memory. For example, to unload the MONITOR utility:

```
UNLOAD MONITOR
```

VERSION

Displays information about the version of NetWare that is running and about the network drivers that are loaded.

Console Utilities (NLMs)

CDROM

Allows a CD-ROM disk in the server to be mounted as a NetWare volume.

DSMERGE

A utility to merge NDS Directory trees. Can also be used to check synchronization.

DSREPAIR

A general-purpose utility for repairing problems with the NDS Directory. DSREPAIR will diagnose and advise you of problems—and fix them if possible.

EDIT

Allows you to edit a file on a NetWare volume. Useful for editing AUTOEXEC.NCF, TIMESYNC.CFG, and other server configuration files. For example, to edit the AUTOEXEC.NCF file:

```
LOAD EDIT AUTOEXEC.NCF
```

INSTALL

Allows you to install additional Netware features, manage the server's configuration, and manage licensing for NetWare and other applications.

MONITOR

Displays information about the server's memory, processor, disks, and many other components, and allows you to set server parameters. Useful for fine-tuning the server's performance.

NETSYNC

Allows you to manage a NetWare 3.1*x* server from NetWare 4's NDS utilities. NETSYNC is actually two NLMs: NETSYNC4, loaded on the NetWare 4 server, and NETSYNC3, which you can load on up to 12 NetWare 3.1*x* servers.

NPRINTER

Loads the port driver for a server-attached printer. PSERVER will usually load NPRINTER automatically.

PSERVER

Starts a print server, corresponding to a Print Server object in NDS. Can be used to control printing in progress and change settings. The following command starts the PS1 print server:

```
LOAD PSERVER PS1
```

REMOTE

Allows users to attach to the server using RCONSOLE. The RSPX NLM must also be loaded for this function.

SERVMAN

Provides a user-friendly system for changing server parameters. The SET command can be used to change these settings manually. The functions of SERVMAN are also available in the Server Parameters option of the MONITOR utility.

SBACKUP

Provides a basic backup system for files in NetWare volumes and for the NDS database. This utility is examined in Chapter 5.

VREPAIR

Analyzes and repairs problems in a disk volume. The volume must be dismounted before VREPAIR is used. If only one volume is currently dismounted, VREPAIR will automatically repair that volume; otherwise, you will be asked which volume to repair. Because this NLM will be unavailable when the SYS: volume is dismounted, it is helpful to keep a copy of it in the server's DOS partition.

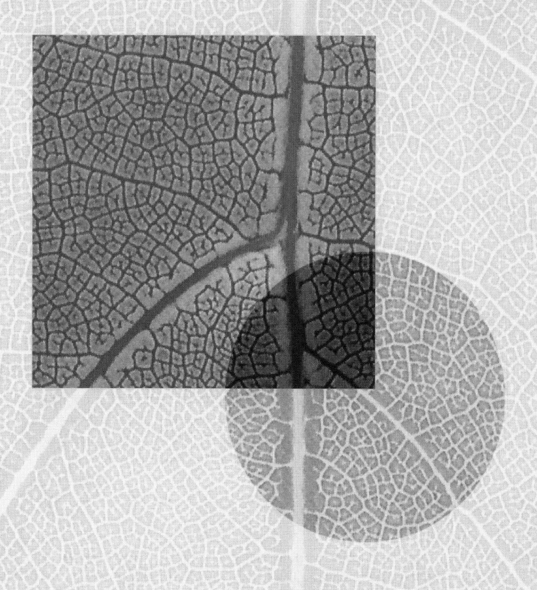

Glossary

Abend   Short for abnormal end. This is NetWare's term for a server crash. An abend is usually caused by an application (NLM) writing to an area of memory that belongs to the operating system.

Access Control List (ACL)   The property of an NDS object that contains the list of *trustees* or other objects that have rights to the object.

Across-the-Wire Migration   One of the two possible migration strategies from NetWare 3.1*x* to NetWare 4.11. In the across-the-wire strategy, a new NetWare 4.11 server is connected to the same network as the NetWare 3.1*x* server, and data is copied over the network.

Additive Licensing   NetWare 4.11's licensing system, which allows you to add licenses when your network needs to allow more user logins. For example, you can add a 5-user license to a 25-user license for a total of 30 possible users.

Alias Object   An object used to represent, or point to, another object in the NDS tree. Alias objects can be created to make a resource in a different context available in the local context. Netware can create Aliases automatically when an object or container is moved.

Aliased Object   The object that an Alias object refers to. Also called the *source* object.

AppleTalk   A networking system developed by Apple for use with Macintosh computers. The software for AppleTalk connectivity is built into the Macintosh operating system (MacOS or System 7). NetWare for Macintosh allows connectivity between AppleTalk and NetWare networks.

Attributes   File attributes are stored for each file and directory on a server's file system. Attributes are used for security and for status information for the file. For example, the Read-Only attribute prevents a file from being written to or erased, and the Can't Compress attribute indicates that NetWare was unable to compress the file.

Auditing   A NetWare 4.11 service that allows a user, or auditor, to monitor activities on the network. The auditor can monitor the file system or an NDS container. Auditing is done through the AUDITCON menu utility.

Auditor's Password   A password that is set when you begin an audit on a volume or NDS container. The auditor should change this password when the audit begins. The password is required for all auditing activities, including ending the audit.

Authentication   Part of the login process, in which NDS verifies that the user's password, access rights, and other settings are correct. Authentication is handled by the nearest read/write or master replica.

Backup Engine   Part of the NetWare Storage Management System (SMS). The backup engine is the front end, or user interface, to the backup software. Novell's SBACKUP is a backup engine that can be run on the server or on a DOS or Microsoft Windows workstation.

Base Schema   The NDS base schema defines the structure of NDS—which objects are possible, which properties an object can have, and so forth. The NDS base schema is written to the server when NDS is installed. Third-party applications can extend, or add to, this schema using the NetWare API (Application Program Interface).

Batch File   A file containing a list of commands to be executed. DOS batch files have the extension BAT. Examples include AUTOEXEC.BAT, which executes when the workstation is booted, and STARTNET.BAT, which is used to attach to the network. NetWare also provides batch file capability for the server in the form of NCF (NetWare Command Files).

Bindery   The database used to store information about users, printers, and other network objects in NetWare 3.1*x* and earlier versions. The bindery is a simple, flat database, which is stored separately on each server. NetWare 4.11 replaces the bindery with NetWare Directory Services (NDS).

Bindery Context   The context that will be provided as a simulated bindery by Bindery Services. You can set up to 16 separate contexts to serve as bindery contexts. These will be combined into a "bindery" that bindery-based clients can access.

Bindery Services   NetWare 4.11's service that allows the simulation of a bindery. By using the Bindery Services feature, clients using older client software, such as the NetWare DOS shell, can access the network. A branch of the NDS tree, the bindery context, is used as a simulated bindery.

Block   One of the divisions of a hard disk. NetWare stores files on the volume in terms of blocks. In NetWare 3.1*x* and earlier, entire blocks are always used. Block sizes are typically 4K for NetWare 3.1*x* and variable for NetWare 4.11.

Block Suballocation   A NetWare 4.11 feature that allows smaller portions of disk blocks to be used. Each block is divided into 512-byte units, which can be used instead of entire blocks. This feature allows more efficient use of disk space.

Caching   A technique used by NetWare servers to increase disk performance. Data read from the disk drive is stored in a block of memory, or *cache*. When clients request this data, it can be read directly from the cache, avoiding the use of the disk. NetWare provides both read and write caching.

Cache Buffer   NetWare sets aside a portion of the server's memory as cache buffers. These buffers hold information for the file system. The number of cache buffers depends on the amount of available memory.

Cache Hit   A statistical term used when data was successfully read from the disk cache. A high percentage of cache hits indicates that the number of cache buffers is sufficient for the application and that the server is running smoothly.

Centralized Administration   One of the two types of administration in NetWare 4.11. In centralized administration, a single (central) administrator has rights to manage the entire NDS tree. The other type of administration is *distributed* administration.

Child Object   In NDS, an object that is under a container object. The container object is referred to as the *parent object*.

Client   Any device that attaches to the network server. A workstation is the most common type of client. Clients run *client software* to provide network access.

Common Name   In NDS, a name associated with a leaf object. This is the name given to the object when it is created. The common name designator is abbreviated CN in typeful naming.

Compile   In the menu system, the process of converting a *menu source file* into a *menu data file* that can be used by the NMENU program. The MENUMAKE program is used to compile menus.

Container Administrator   An administrator that is given rights to a container object and all of the objects under it. A container administrator can be *exclusive,* meaning that no other administrator has access to the container.

Container Object   In NDS, an object that contains other objects. Container objects include Organization, Organizational Unit, and Country objects. The [Root] object is also a specialized kind of container object. Objects within a container can be other container objects or *leaf objects*, which represent network resources.

Container Security Equivalence   See *Implied Security Equivalence.*

Context   In NDS, an object's position within the Directory tree. The context is the full path to the container object in which the object resides.

Current Context   The current position in the Directory tree, maintained for a workstation connection. By default, objects are assumed to be in this context, unless you specify the full *distinguished name*. The current context is also called the *default context.*

Custom Device Module (CDM)   Part of the NPA (NetWare Peripheral Architecture) system of device drivers. The CDM provides an interface between the device and the Host Adapter Module (HAM).

Custom Installation   One of the two installation options for NetWare 4.11. The Custom installation option allows you to specify all parameters for the server during the installation process.

Data Migration   A system where less-used data is moved to a high-capacity storage device, such as a *jukebox*. The HCSS (High-Capacity Storage System) is the NetWare 4.11 service that handles data migration.

Dedicated Server   A server that serves no other purpose; it cannot be used as a workstation. All NetWare 3.1*x* servers and most NetWare 4.11 servers are dedicated. NetWare 4.11 provides a nondedicated server option through NetWare Server for OS/2.

Default Context   See *Current Context.*

De-Migrate   The process of moving data back from a high-capacity storage system that it was migrated to. This is done when a user attempts to access the file that was migrated.

Departmental Implementation   One of the methods of implementing NDS. In this method, departments or other divisions of the company are moved to NDS one at a time, each with its own Directory tree. The trees can be merged later.

Device Driver   Software that allows a workstation or server to communicate with a hardware device. For example, disk drivers are used to control disk drives, and network drivers are used to communicate with network boards.

Directly Connected Network Printer   One of the types of network printer allowed by NetWare 4.11. This type of printer is attached to the network rather than to a workstation or server. Directly connected printers can operate in either *remote mode* or *queue server mode.*

Directory   In NDS, the database that contains information about each of the objects on the network. The Directory is organized into a treelike structure, the *Directory tree*, with a *[Root] object* on top and *leaf objects* at the bottom. To distinguish it from disk directories, the NDS Directory is written with a capital *D.*

Directory Map   A special NDS object that is used to map directories in the file system. The MAP command can specify the name of the Directory Map object rather than the exact directory name. The directory name is contained in a property of the Directory Map object.

Directory Tree   See *Directory*.

Distinguished Name   In NDS, the full name of an NDS object. This includes the object's *common name* and its *context*, or location in the Directory tree. Also referred to as the *full distinguished name*.

Distributed Administration   One type of administration allowed by NetWare 4.11. (The other option is *centralized administration*.) In distributed administration, separate administrators are assigned for different portions of the Directory tree and file system.

Distributed Database   A database that is contained in multiple locations. NDS is a distributed database that is contained on multiple NetWare 4.11 servers.

Distribution List   A special NDS object that is used to send e-mail messages to multiple users. This object is part of the Message Handling Service (MHS) in NetWare 4.11.

Divisional Implementation   One of the methods of implementing NDS in a network. Each division is moved to NDS separately, with its own Directory tree. This method is similar to the *departmental* implementation.

Divisional Organization   A type of NDS organization that divides the Directory tree into branches for each division or department within an organization. This is often a practical way to organize, since members of a department or division often require access to the same set of resources.

DOS Shell   The client software used for DOS workstations in Net-Ware 3.1*x* and earlier versions. The executable program for the DOS Shell is NETX.COM. The DOS Shell does not provide access to NDS, but can be used with NetWare 4.11 via Bindery Services.

DynaText   The online documentation system included with NetWare 4.11. This is provided on CD-ROM, and it can be used from the CD-ROM or installed on the network or on a workstation. You use the DynaText viewer to read and search the documentation. DynaText replaces *ElectroText* used by NetWare 3.1*x* and earlier versions.

Effective Rights   The rights that a user (or other trustee) has in a file system directory or NDS object after all factors are considered. Factors include explicit rights, inherited rights, the IRF (Inherited Rights Filter), and security equivalences.

ElectroText   An online documentation system provided with earlier versions of NetWare. This has been replaced by *DynaText* in Net-Ware 4.11.

Enterprise Networking   The type of networking required to connect an entire enterprise, or a large corporation. This usually means a WAN (wide-area network). NetWare 4.0 was intended as an enterprise net-working system, but NetWare 4.11 is suitable for networks of any size.

Events   In NetWare 4.11 auditing, the types of activities that can be monitored by the auditor for a volume or NDS object.

Exclusive Container Administrator   A special type of *container administrator* that is given rights to a container and the objects within it. The IRF (Inherited Rights Filter) is used to prevent other administra-tors from having rights in the container.

Explicit Rights   In NDS or the file system, any rights that are given directly to a user for a directory or NDS object. Explicit rights override inherited rights.

Explicit Security Equivalence   In NDS, a method of giving a trustee the same rights as another trustee. Explicit security equivalence can be assigned with Group object membership, an Organizational Role, or the trustee's Security Equal To property.

File Attributes   See *Attributes*.

File Compression   A NetWare 4.11 feature that automatically compresses files that are not in use. A compressed file can take as little as 33 percent of the space of the original file. Compressed files are uncompressed automatically when a user accesses them.

Full Distinguished Name   See *Distinguished Name*.

Garbage Collection   In NetWare 4.11 memory management, the process of returning memory that has been deallocated to the main memory pool so that it can be used by other applications.

Greenwich Mean Time (GMT)   See *Universal Coordinated Time (UTC)*.

Group Rights   NDS or file system rights that a user receives because of membership in a Group object. This is an example of *explicit security equivalence*.

Handshaking   In network communication, a process used to verify that data is sent correctly. After each packet is sent, an acknowledgment is sent back to indicate that the packet was received properly. Acknowledgments or error reports are sent according to the protocol in use.

High-Capacity Storage System (HCSS) The NetWare 4.11 service that allows data to be migrated to high-capacity storage. See *Data Migration*.

Host Adapter A hardware device that allows communication with a peripheral, such as a disk drive or tape drive. The host adapter, also called a *controller*, is usually a card that is inserted into a slot on the server's motherboard.

Host Adapter Module (HAM) One of the components of the NPA (NetWare Peripheral Architecture) device driver standard. The HAM provides communication with the *host adapter*.

Hybrid Organization An NDS organization strategy that combines two or more of the other methods: locational, divisional, or workgroup. Hybrid organizations are the most useful for larger companies.

Implementation Strategy The method used for implementing, or moving to, NDS on a network. Strategies include the departmental (or divisional) implementation and the organizational implementation.

Implied Security Equivalence In NDS, an object is security equivalent to (receives the rights of) the object's parent object and its parents, leading up to the [Root] object. This is also called *container security equivalence*. The IRF (Inherited Rights Filter) does not affect this process.

In-Place Migration One of the methods for migrating (upgrading) a server from NetWare 3.1*x* to NetWare 4.11. In this method, the server is upgraded directly to the new NOS (network operating system), leaving data files on the server intact. The alternative method is *across-the-wire migration*.

Inherited Rights In NDS or the file system, inherited rights are rights that a trustee receives for an object because of rights to the object's parent (a directory in the file system or a parent object in NDS). Inherited rights can be blocked by an explicit assignment or by the IRF (Inherited Rights Filter).

Inherited Rights Filter (IRF) In the file system, the IRF is the list of rights that a user can inherit for a directory from directories above it. An IRF also exists for each NDS object, and it lists the rights that a trustee can inherit from the object's parents. In NetWare 3.1*x*, the IRF was called the IRM (Inherited Rights Mask) and applied only to the file system.

Internetworking The process of connecting multiple local-area networks (LANs) to form a wide-area network (WAN). Internetworking between different types of networks is handled by a *router*.

IPX External Network Number A number that is used to represent an entire network. All servers on the network must use the same external network number.

IPX Internal Network Number A number that uniquely identifies a server to the network. Each server must have a different internal network number.

Jukebox A device that provides high-capacity storage to optical media. Jukeboxes are supported by NetWare 4.11's High-Capacity Storage System (HCSS).

Large Internet Packet (LIP) A system that NetWare 4.11 provides to increase the speed of network communications. Packets sent through a router are kept at their maximum possible size, rather than reducing them to 512K as in older versions of NetWare.

Leaf Object An object that cannot contain other objects and represents a network resource. Leaf objects include User, Group, Printer, Server, Volume, and many others.

License Diskette A diskette that contains licensing information and is included in the NetWare 4.11 package. This diskette controls the number of users that can log in to the network at one time. Multiple licenses can be used thanks to the *additive licensing* feature.

Local-Area Network (LAN) A network that is restricted to a local area, such as a single building, a group of buildings, or even a single room. Usually, LANs have only one server, but they can have more.

Locational Organization A method of organizing the Directory tree that divides it into Organizational Units for each geographical location of the organization. This strategy is often the best for network communication.

Logical Ports Ports used by the CAPTURE command to redirect a workstation printer port to a network print queue. The logical port has no relation to the port the printer is actually attached to, or the *physical port*.

Login Script A set of commands that are automatically executed when a user logs in. NetWare 4.11 includes Container, Profile, User, and Default login scripts. Up to three of these can be executed for each user. The login script consists of a special type of commands, called *login script commands*.

Login Security The most basic form of network security. A user name and password are required in order to log in to the network and access resources.

Master Replica   The main replica for a partition. The master replica must be available when major changes, such as partition merging and splitting, are performed. Another replica can be assigned as master if the master replica is lost.

Memory Allocation   The system NetWare 4.11 uses to provide memory for use by applications (NLMs) on the server. Memory is allocated from an *allocation pool*.

Menu Data File   A file used to run a menu, using the NMENU program. The data file is the result of *compiling* the menu source file using the MENUMAKE utility. Menu data files have the DAT extension.

Menu Source File   The file that you write, using *menu commands*, to create a user menu. This file must be compiled into a *menu data file* using the MENUMAKE utility before it can be used. Source files typically have an SRC extension.

Menu Utilities   A type of NetWare utility that presents a menu of options when it executes. Menu utilities have a consistent interface. FILER and NETADMIN are two examples.

Merging Directory Trees   The process of combining two Directory trees into a single tree. The objects in the *source* tree are combined into the *destination*, or *target*, tree. The DSMERGE utility is used to merge trees.

Merging Partitions   The process of combining an NDS partition with its parent partition, resulting in a single partition. The master replica of the partition must be available for this process.

Message File   A file used to store prompts and messages for a NetWare workstation or server utility. Message files are provided for each supported language (English, French, Italian, German, and Spanish).

Multivalued Property   In NDS, a property that can have multiple values. For example, a User object's Telephone Number property can store multiple telephone numbers.

MultiProtocol Router (MPR)   The software that provides *routing* capabilities for a NetWare 4.11 server. MPR enables communication between different types of networks.

Name Conflict   A situation where names conflict with each other. This typically happens in Bindery Services or when using NetSync. All users in the bindery context must have unique common names.

Name Space   A service that you can install on a NetWare 4.11 server volume to allow different types of file names to be used. Name spaces are available for OS/2 and Macintosh naming.

NetSync   The software that allows NetWare 3.1*x* servers to be managed through NDS utilities. This is accomplished using the NETSYNC3 NLM at the NetWare 3.1*x* servers and the NETSYNC4 NLM at the NetWare 4.11 server.

NetSync Cluster   A NetWare 4.11 server and a group of NetWare 3.1*x* servers that it can manage using NetSync. Each NetWare 4.11 server can manage up to 16 NetWare 3.1*x* servers.

NetWare Application Manager (NAM)   The system, new to NetWare 4.11, that allows you to create Application objects and control their access by users. Users can use the NAL (NetWare Application Launcher) utility to launch applications. Extensions are also available that allow you to use NAM with NetWare 4.10 networks.

NetWare Client 32   The latest software for connecting DOS, Windows, and Windows 95 workstations to a NetWare network. NetWare 4.11 includes Client 32. Client 32 consists of several NLMs; the main client software is CLIENT32.NLM.

NetWare Directory Services (NDS)   The system NetWare 4.11 uses to catalog objects, such as users, printers, and volumes, on the network. NDS uses a *Directory tree* to store this information. All of the NetWare 4.11 network's resources can be managed through NDS.

NetWare DOS Requester   One type of client software that can be used on a DOS workstation to access the NetWare 4.11 network and NDS. The VLM.EXE program is used to load the DOS Requester. In NetWare 4.11, this software is replaced by NetWare Client 32 for DOS and Windows.

NetWare Loadable Module (NLM)   An application or program that executes on the NetWare server. NLMs are used for device drivers, LAN drivers, and applications such as backup software. NetWare 4.11 includes a variety of utility NLMs, and others are available from third parties.

NetWare OS/2 Requester   The client software used to access a NetWare 4.11 server and NDS from an OS/2 workstation. The OS/2 Requester provides the same benefits as the DOS Requester.

NetWare Peripheral Architecture (NPA)   A new system that NetWare 4.11 allows for *device drivers*. The driver is divided into two modules: a Host Adapter Module (HAM) and a Custom Device Module (CDM) for each device attached to the host adapter. Older device drivers use a single program with a DSK extension. These can still be used in NetWare 4.11.

Network Address   A unique address that identifies each node, or device, on the network. The network address is generally hard coded into the network card on both the workstation and server. Some network cards allow you to change this address, but there is seldom a reason to do so.

Network-Centric   The architecture used in a NetWare 4.11 network. Objects are created for the entire network, rather than for a single server. This feature is one of the benefits of NDS.

Network Operating System (NOS)   The software that runs on a file server. NetWare 4.11 is an NOS. Other examples include NetWare 3.1*x*, OS/2 Warp, Banyan VINES, and Windows NT Server.

Nondedicated Server   A server that can also act as a workstation. NetWare 2.2 provided this capability, and NetWare 4.11 provides it through NetWare Server for OS/2. NetWare 3.1*x* does not permit nondedicated servers.

Object   In NDS, any resource on the network. Users, printers, and groups are examples of *leaf objects*. *Container objects*, such as Organizations and Organizational Units, are used to organize other objects.

Object Trustee   See *Trustee*.

Occupant   A user who has been assigned to an Organizational Role object. Each Organizational Role can have multiple occupants, stored in the Occupants property of the object.

Organization Object   Usually the highest-level container object used. Organizations are created under the [Root] object (or Country object if it is used). This object usually represents an entire organization or company. Multiple Organization objects can be used in the same Directory tree.

Organizational Implementation   One of the methods of implementing NDS. (The *divisional* and *departmental* implementations are the alternatives.) In this method, the entire Organization is moved at once. This is also called the *top-down* approach. This method is rarely practical.

Organizational Role Object An object that is used to represent a role—an administrator or other specialized user who requires access to certain NDS objects or files. This type of object is often used for container administrators. The user assigned to the Organizational Role is called the *occupant* of the role.

Organizational Unit Object The lowest-level container object. Organizational Units can be used to divide locations, divisions, workgroups, or smaller portions of the Directory tree. Organizational Units can be subdivided further with additional Organizational Units.

Packet The basic division of data sent over a network. Each packet contains a set amount of data along with a header, containing information about the type of packet and the network address it is being sent to. The size and format of packets depends on the *protocol* used.

Packet Burst Protocol A streamlined protocol available in NetWare 4.11. In this protocol, several packets (a *burst*) are sent, and a single acknowledgment is sent back. If there is an error, only the packets that were not received correctly need to be re-sent. This protocol eliminates most of the *handshaking* process.

Packet Receive Buffers Areas of memory that NetWare sets aside for receiving packets over the network. Packets are stored in the buffers until the server is able to process them.

Paging A technique possible on Pentium-class processors, and to a lesser extent on 386 and 486 processors, that allows memory to be handled in 4K blocks, or *pages*. NetWare 4.11 supports this feature for increased speed.

Parent Object In NDS, an object that *contains* another object—a container object. This is a relative term; a parent object also has parent objects of its own and is considered a child object from that perspective.

Partition (Disk)　NetWare uses disk partitions to divide a hard disk. A disk typically contains a single NetWare partition, which is used to hold one or more NetWare volumes. In addition, it can have a DOS partition to boot the server and to hold the SERVER.EXE program.

Partition (NDS)　A branch of the NDS tree that can be replicated onto multiple servers. The partition includes a container object and the objects under it, and it is named according to the name of that object. By default, a single partition—the [Root] partition—exists.

Physical Port　In NetWare 4.11 printing, the port a printer is actually attached to. This differs from the *logical ports* used in the CAPTURE command for printer redirection.

Port Driver　A component of NetWare 4.11 printing. The port driver accepts data from the print server and sends it to the printer. The port driver can be NPRINTER.EXE on a workstation, NPRINTER.NLM on a server, or a hardware device.

Primary Time Server　One of the four types of time servers. A primary server communicates with other primary servers and reference servers and negotiates, or "votes," to determine the correct time.

Print Job　A file that has been sent by a client for printing. Print jobs are stored in a *print queue* until they can be serviced by the print server.

Print Job Configuration　A set of parameters for network printing. These are similar to the parameters in the CAPTURE command. Print job configurations can be set for user and container objects.

Print Queue　The area used to hold the list of print jobs that are waiting to print. The print queue is managed through the Print Queue object in NDS. Print jobs are sent from the print queue to the print server one at a time.

Print Server   A device that is used to manage printing. The NDS Print Server object is used to manage printing. The print server itself can run on a NetWare 4.11 server (PSERVER.NLM) or in a hardware device. NetWare 3.1*x* includes PSERVER.EXE, which can run on a DOS workstation; NetWare 4.11 does not support PSERVER.EXE.

Printer Redirection   The process of mapping a logical printer port in the workstation to a network printer. The user can then print to the port as if it were an actual printer, and the print job will be sent to the print queue. The CAPTURE utility is used to start redirection.

Profile Object   A special NDS object that is used to assign the same login script to a group of users. The Profile login script is executed after the Container login script and before the User login script.

Properties   In NDS, all of the possible information that can be entered for an object. The properties of a User object include Login Name, Full Name, and Telephone Number. The information in a property is the *value* of the property.

Protocol   A method of communicating between NetWare servers and clients. The protocol is the "language" used for sending data. Data is divided into packets specified by the protocol. IPX is the typical protocol for NetWare networks.

[Public] Trustee   A special NDS trustee that can be used to assign rights to all users in the network, including those that are not logged in. This trustee is used to allow users to browse the Directory tree before logging in. You should avoid assigning rights to this trustee.

Reference Time Server   One of the four types of time servers. The reference server provides an authoritative source of time. It is often attached to an external clock, a modem, or a radio link to a time source. One or more primary time servers must be used.

Relative Distinguished Name (RDN)   A shortened version of an object's full distinguished name that specifies the path to the object from the current context. RDNs do not begin with a period. Periods can be used at the end of the RDN to move up the Directory tree.

Remote Printer   See *Workstation Printer.*

Replica Ring   A group of replicas that are synchronized. This includes a master replica and one or more other replicas.

Replication   The process of keeping copies of the NDS information on separate servers. Each *partition* in NDS has a set of replicas. These include the master replica—the original partition—and optional read/write and read-only replicas.

[Root] Object   The ultimate NDS container object. The [Root] object is created when NDS is installed, and this object contains all other objects. [Root] cannot be deleted, renamed, or moved.

Router   See *Internetworking.*

Scalability   A feature of NetWare 4.11 services, including NPA (NetWare Peripheral Architecture) and the DOS Requester. This means that features can be used as they are needed, providing benefits for both small-scale and large-scale systems.

Secondary Time Server   One of the four types of time servers. Secondary time servers are strictly time consumers; they do not provide time to any servers. They receive time from a primary or single reference server and provide the time to clients.

Security Equivalence   In NDS, any situation where an object, or *trustee*, receives the same rights given to another object. There are two types of security equivalence: *implied* and *explicit.*

Server-Centric   The type of network organization used on Net-Ware 3.1x networks. In this organization, each server keeps its own catalog of users and other resources (the *bindery*). A user who requires access to more than one server must be added to the bindery of each one. NetWare 4.11 provides a *network-centric* alternative.

Server Printer   A common method of attaching a printer to the network. The printer is attached to a printer port on the NetWare server. The port driver, NPRINTER.NLM, is used to drive the printer.

Service Advertising Protocol (SAP)   The protocol used for various NetWare 4.11 services. Single reference time servers use this protocol to broadcast time information to the entire network at once.

Simple Installation   One of the two options in the NetWare 4.11 installation. The Simple installation assumes default answers to installation questions. To specify information for all of the questions, use the Custom installation option.

Single Reference Time Server   One of the four types of time servers. If it's used, the single reference server is the only time provider on the network. All other servers must be configured as secondary time servers. This is the default configuration when NetWare 4.11 servers are installed.

Splitting Partitions   The process of creating a new partition. A container object within a current partition is specified, and that object and all objects under it are moved (split) to a new partition.

Standards Document   A document that describes the naming standards, properties, and values to be used for a network. A standards document is a vital part of NDS planning.

Storage Management Services (SMS)   The NetWare 4.11 service that allows for backup services. SMS consists of several components, ranging from the device driver that communicates with the backup device to the front end, or *backup engine*. SBACKUP is a simple backup application included with NetWare 4.11.

Synchronization   The process used by NDS to ensure that all replicas of a partition contain the same data. Synchronization is handled through *replica rings*.

Target Service Agent (TSA)   One of the components of the NetWare 4.11 Storage Management System (SMS). The TSA provides an interface to the device that will be backed up. Devices include servers, workstations, and the NDS database. A separate TSA is used for each one.

Time Consumer   A machine that receives time information but does not send time information to any other server. Secondary time servers are time consumers, as are network workstations.

Time Provider   A type of time server that provides the time to other time servers. These include single reference, reference, and primary time servers.

Time Provider Group   A group of time servers, usually including a reference server and one or more primary servers. In a wide-area network (WAN), separate time provider groups can be used for each location.

Time Server   A server that is used for time synchronization. All NetWare 4.11 servers are time servers of one type or another. The types of time servers include primary, reference, single reference, and secondary.

Time Source   See *Time Provider*.

Time Synchronization   The process by which NetWare 4.11 ensures that all servers are provided with the correct time. Time synchronization is managed through *time servers*.

Trustee   Any object that has been given rights to an NDS object or file. Trustee rights can include explicit, inherited, and effective rights.

Turbo FAT Indexing   A NetWare 4.11 service that increases disk access for large files by keeping an index, or turbo FAT (file allocation table), of the disk blocks in use by the file. NetWare uses this system automatically for larger files.

Typeful Naming   The formal method of naming NDS objects, including name types for each portion of the name. For example, .CN=Terry.OU=Mktg.O=QAZ_CO.

Typeless Naming   The more common method of NDS object naming, which does not include name types. For example, .Terry.Mktg.QAZ.CO. Typeless naming is adequate for most uses within NDS utilities.

Universal Coordinated Time (UTC)   The standard time system supported by NetWare 4.11. The abbreviation is from the French. UTC was formerly known as GMT (Greenwich Mean Time). The time zone for a NetWare server is defined in terms of difference from UTC; for example, the Mountain time zone is UTC plus seven hours.

User Template   In NDS, a special User object that is used to assign defaults when a new user is created. A user template can be created for each NDS container, and you can change the property values of this object to provide defaults for new users in the container. The user template does not affect existing users.

Values   The data that is stored in the *properties* of an NDS object. Properties can have one or more values. Some are required, and others are optional.

Virtual Loadable Module (VLM)   One of the components of the *DOS Requester*. The VLM.EXE program loads various VLMs, each for a certain purpose. For example, PRINT.VLM allows redirection of printers. VLMs that are not needed can be unloaded to increase available memory.

Wide-Area Network (WAN)   A network that extends across multiple locations. Each location typically has a local-area network (LAN), and the LANs are connected together in a WAN. WANs can be used for *enterprise networking*.

Workgroup Organization   One of the methods of organizing the NDS tree. In this method, users who perform similar functions or are participating in the same project or workgroup are grouped together in the Directory tree. This method is best used in a hybrid, or combined, organization.

Workstation Printer   A printer that is attached to a workstation on the network. NetWare 3.1*x* referred to these printers as *remote printers* and controlled them with the RPRINTER.EXE program. In NetWare 4.11, the NPRINTER.EXE program handles workstation printers.

Index

Note to the Reader: First level entries are in **bold**. Page numbers in **bold** indicate the principal discussion of a topic or the definition of a term. Page numbers in *italic* indicate illustrations.

V

SYBEX BOOKS ON THE WEB!

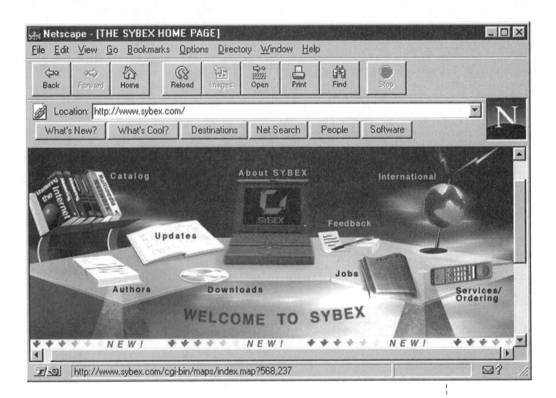

Presenting a truly dynamic environment that is both fun and informative.

- download useful code
- e-mail your favorite Sybex author
- preview a book you might want to own
- find out about job opportunities at Sybex
- order books
- learn about Sybex
- discover what's new in the computer industry

http://www.sybex.com

SYBEX®

SYBEX Inc. • 1151 Marina Village Parkway • Alameda, CA 94501 • 510-523-8233